Outcast Europe

Outcast Europe

THE BALKANS, 1789–1989
FROM THE OTTOMANS TO MILOŠEVIĆ

Tom Gallagher

London and New York

DR
43
.B35
2001

First published 2001
by Routledge
11 New Fetter Lane, London EC4P 4EE

Simultaneously published in the USA and Canada
by Routledge
29 West 35th Street, New York, NY 10001

© 2001 Routledge

Routledge is an imprint of the Taylor & Francis Group

Typeset by Expo Holdings, Malaysia
Printed and bound in Great Britain by MPG Books Ltd, Bodmin

All rights reserved. No part of this book may be reprinted or reproduced or utilised in any
form or by any electronic, mechanical, or other means, now known or hereafter invented,
including photocopying and recording, or in any information storage or retrieval system,
without permission in writing from the publishers.

British Library Cataloguing in Publication Data
A catalogue record for this book is available from the British Library

ISBN: 0–415–27089–8

476238876

CONTENTS

PREFACE

The idea for a book of this kind first occurred to me at the end of November 1992. I was in the audience at a rally of Britain's European movement in Edinburgh. It coincided with the summit of the European Union's Council of Ministers being held in the city during the fateful second half of that year when Britain held the EU Presidency.

With the USA absorbed in its year-long presidential election, Russia grappling with its retreat from communism, Germany fast retreating from Balkan involvements, and France and Italy disinclined to adopt a high profile as war raged in parts of Yugoslavia, Britain had been shaping international policy towards the region. John Major's government had adopted a minimalist policy towards the war in Bosnia-Herzegovina, emphasising humanitarian relief but refusing to promote active peace-making measures which could end the tidal flow of refugees. The siege of its capital, Sarajevo, was well into its second year and mixed communities across Bosnia were being broken up by systematic violence as Serbian and then Croatian nationalists tried to create an ethnic monopoly in order to divide the territory between the nationalist regimes installed in Belgrade and Zagreb.

Statements from British government figures, briefed by Foreign Office officials, made it clear that the conflict was seen as based on the 'normal' Balkan pattern of life in which 'ancient ethnic hatreds' predominated. What I did not expect to hear at the Edinburgh rally was this view being endorsed by one of its keynote speakers, Edward Heath, who secured Britain's entry into the European Union in 1973 when he was Prime Minister. Ted Heath, as he is known by voters and fellow politicians alike, has remained true to the idea of creating a politically unified Western Europe. At the age of 85, he retired from parliament where he had long criticised his party, the Conservatives, for moving in an increasingly nationalist and 'Eurosceptic' direction. He began his long political career in the late 1930s as an undergraduate student at Oxford University, where he vigorously opposed the policies of appeasement of Neville Chamberlain towards Hitler in Central Europe.

But it was clear from listening to Ted Heath on that cold and bright Scottish winter afternoon, as he reaffirmed the need for European unity, that there was little place in his vision for the Yugoslav lands and that he did not even regard them as part of the Europe whose unification had become his lifelong ambition. When I protested from the floor about the injustice and narrowness of such a view, he was unmoved. I would have been ejected from the meeting, but for the intervention of another speaker on the platform.

Shirley Williams, Professor of Government at Harvard University, had been the most enthusiastic pro-European member of the British Labour government of 1974–76. She gently pointed out to Ted Heath that his definition of Europe was too restrictive and that in order to succeed, the post-nationalist project in Europe had to encompass all its parts. She has since shown her commitment to integrating the Balkans with the rest of Europe by promoting various projects, especially in the area of civil society.

The argument about whether to 'ring-fence' the Balkans by containing its problems through minimal engagement or whether to recognise that problems with minorities and conflicting borders are ones that western Europe and even the USA had in abundance until recently, and that those who have overcome them should help the Balkans to do the same, flared periodically in the West during the 1990s.

With NATO's military action in Kosovo in 1999, victory appeared to go to the interventionists. But the dismal performance of organizations like the United Nations (UN) and the Organization for Security and Cooperation in Europe (OSCE) in Kosovo suggests that Western policy-makers are still reluctant to act as organizers, leaders and peace-makers in the region, empowering civic-minded forces and isolating intransigent ones. International officials are still imbued with a deep sense of fatalism about the ability of local elites and their populations to aspire to good government and modern forms of conduct. There is still plenty of evidence that the problems of the Balkans are seen as culturally determined and historically recurring and therefore beyond capable solution.

This book explores the origins of such negative attitudes towards the Balkan region. It argues that an appropriate and relatively neglected paradigm in which to explore the problems of the region is the international one. It argues that the politics of ethnicity and the economics of dependence which are the paradigms through which the contemporary Balkans are normally viewed, have acquired their intensity from unfavourable international pressures consistently applied to the region.

A shifting cast of international powers have sought to exercise hegemony, or else exercise long-term influence over the region since it became recognised as a distinctive zone of Europe in the early 19th century. An unfavourable geographical position means that the peoples of the Balkans have been poorly placed to resist such intrusions. For millennia the region has been a transitional zone where rising civilizations and competing social systems met and often collided. The powers have usually not behaved in a measured or consistent way towards the region. The durability of stereotypical attitudes held in metropolitan capitals about its inhabitants means that policies have been erratic and subject to great fluctuations. Both Western Europe and Russia have behaved in a predatory or neglectful way towards the region at different times, which has increased the local sense of insecurity.

Thus new and aspiring states in the region often acquired a sense of profound insecurity because of the unstable international environment in which the Balkans existed. It is not surprising that competing ethnic movements and national states behaved in an aggressive and vindictive way towards each other during the long era extending for a century and a half after 1789, when nationalism was the excuse for frequent wars in Western Europe as well as imperial expansion across the whole of the non-European world.

This book examines the interaction of internal and external events in the Balkans, particularly the rise of the nation-state based on a single ethnic identity, rivalry among the great powers, and the emergence of fascism and communism in shaping the politics and the economic development of the region. It looks in turn at how local crises, often having their origins beyond the region, sometimes spilled over into the rest of Europe, destabilising continental politics, most notably before the First World War. Political analysis predominates but economic, social, cultural and intellectual developments figure prominently in the narrative where they contribute to an understanding of several of the major questions which the book is exploring.

Much of the book has been written during the 1999 Kosovo crisis and its aftermath when the territory's main ethnic grouping, the Albanians, have been widely viewed first as helpless victims of state violence then as revenge-seeking aggressors, driving the Serbs, the Roma gypsies, and Muslim Slavs from their homes.

The sudden and drastic change in the respective fortunes of the groups competing for Kosovo is a familiar occurrence in the modern history of the region. Regimes have fallen, the size of states has shrunk or expanded, and populations have been moved or resettled more often, and with less warning, than elsewhere in Europe. Periodic upheavals have retarded economic development and weakened the growth of local institutions capable of ensuring the progress that has been registered in other parts of Europe.

It is easy to forget that Western Europe's history has been extremely violent. But, despite periodic wars, strong states had guaranteed a century of relative stability and material progress by the time Balkan conflicts erupted in 1912 over the fate of territory previously occupied by the Ottoman Empire as its retreat from Europe gathered pace. Early newsreels and foreign correspondents for the mass circulation press portrayed scenes of cruelty visited upon often defenceless civilians. The Balkans was on its way to acquiring one of the most negative images in world politics. Today, whenever a country, usually with a variety of ethnic groups, trembles on the brink of collapse as Indonesia seemed to do in 1999, ominous headlines warning that 'Balkanization' appears to be its unenviable fate, are hard to avoid.

This study acknowledges that much Balkan unrest has both external and local origins. The French revolution began the process of sweeping away the multicultural traditions of a region in which religion and attachment to a locality where the main badges of identity, gradually replacing them with the belief that a group feeling itself to be a nation deserved a territory of its own. Enormous suffering ensued as recurring efforts were made to establish a national monopoly on territory shared with other groups.

But foreign powers were rarely idle bystanders. The main claim which is investigated here is that continuous external interference in the affairs of the region exacerbated local disputes over territory, giving them a value which they might not otherwise have had. The unavoidably painful process of nation-building might have been less destructive if the Balkans had not become a playground for the powers to pursue their rivalries, and more compact and better-governed states might well have emerged. Thus the Balkan peoples have paid a heavy price for being located in one of the world's most sensitive geopolitical areas.

European powers have risen and fallen in the century or more since Balkan crises started making headlines. In the last fifty years, the United States has become an increasingly important force in the region. But there is remarkable consistency in the way that empires concerned to defend their global interests, competing European dynasties, Nazi and communist dictatorships, American Cold War warriors, and even European social democrats have shaped their Balkan policies.

One explanation is that rulers and their diplomatic advisers have often become prisoners of the unfortunate stereotypes which the region has acquired. The hold of such stereotypes explains why mediocre and short-term policies have been retained for a lengthy historical period. Much evidence to back up such a claim is presented in the succeeding pages.

It was originally intended to include the period 1989–99 in the narrative. The four wars fought in the former Yugoslavia, as well as increasing contact with Balkan states hoping to join the community of Euro-Atlantic democracies, have resulted in an unprecedented degree of interest in, and engagement with, the politics of the region. Many familiar mistakes were committed by statesmen and diplomats. But a few promising new approaches were adopted that offer the possibility of the Balkan peoples finding their rightful place in a united and peaceful Europe. This will only happen, I believe, if the best citizens of the region, in parties committed to inter-ethnic cooperation, in a range of local civic groups, and in everyday occupations are assisted to devise a new policy-making framework in which economic cooperation across ethnic and territorial boundaries becomes the priority for development. The performance of the Stability Pact for Southeast Europe nearly one year after it was founded in June 1999, suggests that this lesson is only very slowly being learned.

Anyway, examination of the Balkan crises of the 1990s and the role of external and local actors will have to await a planned second volume. This second volume will examine how unresolved conflicts of nationality continue to impede the modernisation of Balkan societies and estimate how damaging or constructive has been the impact of external forces, not just global or regional powers, but transnational organisations, influential opinion-formers, and even émigré groups.

This is essentially a study of the interplay between nationalism and foreign intervention in the Balkans over a two-hundred-year period. Some readers may detect an undue emphasis on particular countries at specific periods. Romania, for example, figures prominently in the second half of the book. This is so because a number of key episodes in the country's turbulent 120 years of statehood illustrate particularly well the manner of external intervention in the politics of the region and domestic responses to it.

Aspects of Yugoslav history, particularly certain Second World War events, may appear to have been lightly dealt with. This is because, in the second volume, some of the historical roots of the post-1991 conflicts will be explored in detail and limitations of space rule out duplication.

Countries like Croatia and Slovenia, part of a larger mainly South Slav state entity until 1991, receive far less attention than Greece or Albania. More attention is paid to Greece between 1945 and 1974 than in later or earlier periods. Greece's inclusion is necessary because, except for the period of non-communist rule after 1945, it faced many of the challenges of its northern neighbours and many Greeks believed themselves to be part of a common Balkan space. Indeed Greek public opinion and politicians are more at ease with a Balkan identity than are many citizens in northern parts of Romania and what was Yugoslavia, who are drawn to a Central European orientation.

Perhaps one of the most contentious aspects of the book is the inclusion of Cyprus. This disputed territory is not part of the Balkan peninsula but it is definitely part of Southeast Europe and remains a key bone of contention between two of the main players in Balkan politics: Greece and Turkey. The intensity of the Cyprus question between 1950 and 1974 highlights several of the themes of the book, particularly regarding foreign intervention, and this was sufficient reason for me to include it; indeed, it was uncanny to see the way that at key moments of the post-1991 Yugoslav crisis, Britain and the USA would repeat basic errors which helped to make the Cyprus question such an intractable one in the third quarter of the last century.

The book also shows that there was considerable continuity between Russian tsarist policies towards much of the region and those of their Soviet communist successors.

Chapter one begins with the pre-nationalist Balkan world which endured in many strata of society even as new states were formed after 1800. It examines: the historic events which shaped the ethnic composition of the region; the multicultural traditions whose roots were strengthened in Ottoman times when in Western Europe the emphasis was on religious and cultural uniformity; the growing appeal of nationalism for small but well-placed groups alienated from decaying Ottoman rule and sometimes inspired by modernising Western states; and the intervention of external powers, Britain and Russia, later France, Austria and Germany, in the affairs of the region.

Foreign intervention, it is argued, though occasionally enlightened because of the influence of liberal public opinion, had profoundly negative results. Suspicious and narrow-minded powers carved up the region in to spheres of influence. The 1878 Congress of Berlin rejected the creation of a small number of states, frustrating national movements and states which then resorted to terrorism and arms races.

Representative government brought disappointing results and was often limited in scope for countries whose borders had been arbitrarily carved out by the powers. Urban development was usually pursued at the expense of peasant welfare by insecure elites. Nationalism shaped the policies and priorities of the Balkan states but, usually, it was unable to inspire them to material endeavour. Great power meddling and the growing assertiveness of new states would result in escalating regional confrontations whose outcome was the First World War.

Chapter two examines the post-imperial era of Balkan national states which began in 1918 and had ended by 1940. It proved to be a shortlived experiment before a fresh European war and the totalitarian ideologies of fascism and communism combined to sweep away the region's fragile political institutions.

Criticism of the governing style of the Balkan monarchies and their priorities is provided by focusing on their treatment of minorities and the peasantry, as well as their policies towards neighbouring states. But the failure of Britain and France to use their primacy after 1918 to reshape the European order along lines that would make it far less easy for conflicts of nationality to burst to the surface, contributed far more to the failure of the inter-war order baptised at Versailles in 1919–20. The Allied states failed to promote a policy of collective security to promote economic cooperation and safeguard minorities, even though they were warned in 1919 that a Europe based on the self-determination of nation-states would not prove stable or long-lasting otherwise.

Despite the origins of the 1914–18 war in the Balkans, Britain and France continued to neglect the politics of the region. Britain's policy towards the region increasingly reverted to defence of her strategic and economic interests further east. Aggressively revisionist states profited from the confusion of the major democracies. In the 1930s Britain and France were prepared to deal directly with the dictators at a time when the Balkan states were making energetic efforts to step up their cooperation and stay out of a new European war. This chapter shows how stereotypical attitudes towards the Balkan region and its peoples hardened in Western capitals. An unfavourable geographical position, Western miscalculations and cynicism, and failures of governance made it impossible for the Balkans to stay out of a conflict which crystallised around a struggle for power between Germany and the Soviet Union. National independence was based on shallow roots and the adherence of elites and educated public opinion to narrow nationalism simply increased the vulnerability of Southeast Europe to major upsets in international relations.

Chapter three covers only the years from 1941 to 1948, but this was a turning point in modern European history in which nearly all the Balkan states fell under Soviet Russian control. Britain and the USA (after 1941) were required to pay more attention to Eastern Europe than ever before. Churchill and Roosevelt's alliance with Stalin meant that momentous decisions were made about the future size and status of countries occupied by Hitler, from Poland to Greece.

The chapter contends that in a war fought by the Atlantic democracies to restore freedom, Western leaders in the end were prepared to allow a new tyranny to descend on Eastern Europe. They lacked an empathy with the peoples of the region, especially the Balkans, which would have been necessary to check a new wave of aggression. They failed to devise a political strategy for Eastern Europe beyond a brief flirtation in Britain with federal solutions and frittered away the advantages which they still possessed there. Stalin, who most probably lacked a plan for gaining control of the region in the early 1940s, took full advantage of the irresolution of his Western Allies. Britain, in particular, was prepared to trade territory and allocate spheres of influence in the Balkans in order to shore up its important interests in the Middle East. The Cold War over how far into Europe Soviet domination could extend had broken out by 1948. In the end, it was rebellious communists in Yugoslavia who placed a decisive check on Soviet power. But the partition of Europe which lasted for nearly fifty years took place along a boundary which was already a deep psychological one in the minds of powerful Western politicians and diplomats, above all where Europe's Southeast was concerned.

Chapter four examines the impact of Soviet domination on the Balkans between 1949 and 1974. It shows how communist rule had a more destructive impact on Balkan economies and political standards than was the case in East-Central Europe. It examines the phenomenon of national communism which emerged in the 1960s and how, in many ways, it worsened the predicament of Balkan states. It also monitors the unique Yugoslav experiment in decentralized communism, indicating the tensions and incoherence which prevented it sinking effective roots in a still-fragmented land.

This chapter shows how attempts to move out of the Kremlin's orbit engendered much wishful thinking among the Western powers which periodically behaved with stunning lack of foresight in their own Southeast European bailiwicks: Greece and Cyprus.

Chapter Five explains why interests hostile to pluralist reform became increasingly influential in most of the communist Balkan states as the end of the Cold War approached. Xenophobic nationalism was promoted through the state media and educational system. Rigid controls on free speech and personal liberties prevented any effective challenges to communist rule except on a nationalist basis. However, the Balkans continued to be seen as peripheral to the interests of the Atlantic democracies and Western indifference played a major indirect role in strengthening the position of nationalist hardliners in Yugoslavia. The scene was set for nationalist agendas to dominate the post-communist era, which witnessed a fresh cycle of miscalculations by the major powers that dwarfed those seen in earlier periods.

I thank all the people who contributed to the making of this book.

Over many years John Horton, the Social Science Librarian at Bradford University has built up a large collection on Southeast Europe which made it an ideal research base. He always responded to requests for locating material on a wide range of subjects. Thanks are also due to the inter-library loan staff at Bradford for obtaining dozens of items while research and writing was in progress; and to Stewart Davidson for arranging the maps at the beginning of the book.

The Department of Peace Studies at Bradford University provided a good environment for finishing the book and I am grateful for the period of sabbatical leave which I obtained during five months in 1999–2000 when most of it was written.

I would also like to thank those staff of the Library of the Central European University in Budapest who assisted me during a research visit.

I am grateful to British or British-based scholars and investigators for inviting me to speak about my research, for providing materials to further it, and for allowing me to examine postgraduate theses in the general area. Special thanks are due to Professor Dennis Deletant of University College London and Dr John Allcock of Bradford University; also Dr Chris Binns, Kyril Drezov of Keele University's Department of International Relations, Ivan Fişer of Amnesty International, Dr Mark Percival who allowed me to make extensive use of his Ph.D., and Professor Bogdan Szajkowski whose insights on the southern Balkans I benefited from; and Professor Geoffrey Pridham of Bristol University whose suggestion that we edit a book on democratisation in the Balkans helped this one to come to life.

I found it useful to place the Balkans in a wider geographical framework. Accordingly, I benefited from my conversations with Professor Brian Hamnett, Dr Francisco Veiga, Júlio Garcia Erigoyen, and, not least, Patricia Lança whose welcoming Portuguese home with its book-lined shelves, tranquil garden, and exuberant hounds, was the place where some of the ideas for the book first germinated.

Jim Brooker, for his forbearance and solidarity in recent years, as always, deserves special thanks.

Romania is the part of the Balkan world I know best and visit most frequently. For friendship, hospitality, stimulating conversations, and invitations to worthwhile events not all strictly academic, I would like to thank the following: Elena and Iosif Ilieş, Viorel Andrievici, Dan Necşa, Gheorghe Cipăianu, Gheorghe Iancu, Liviu Ţirau, Simona Ceauşu and Constantin Vlad, Tibor Szatmari, Valentin Stan, Adrian Coman, Alin Giurgiu, Anton Niculescu, Aurelian Crăiuţu, and Carolyn and Ed Litchfield.

Ion Iacoş, Gabriel Andreescu, Renate Weber, and Manuela Stefanescu, past and present members of the Romanian Helsinki Committee, were among those who educated me out of stereotypical attitudes I must once have had towards the Balkans; I will always be grateful to Ion for providing me with a base in Bucharest in past years and for his friendship. Their work in challenging societal prejudice and institutional injustice has helped to revive the prospects of Romania becoming a normal and free society.

I would like to mention the hospitality I received on two occasions as the guest of Ljubomir Cucić and his colleagues at Europe House in Zagreb, an NGO which has shone a beacon in difficult times to enable Croatia to regain its rightful place in a democratising Southeastern Europe.

As the guest of Smaranda Enache and Elok Szokoly on several occasions at events organized by the Liga Pro Europa in Tirgu Mures, I was able to admire their work in combating ethnic prejudice, especially among the young. I will always recall a marvellous week spent as their guest at the Transylvanian Intercultural Academy in Sovata during July 1998.

Lastly, warm thanks are due to the reader of this book, Robert Bideleux, who, in the midst of pressing tasks, including the completion of a new history of the Balkans, made many constructive suggestions and saved me from not a few elementary errors.

ACKNOWLEDGEMENT

The author would like to thank Curtis Brown Ltd, on behalf of the Estate of Sir Winston S. Churchill, for kindly allowing permission to quote from Sir Winston Churchill's *History of the Second World War, Vol. 6: Triumph and Tragedy.*

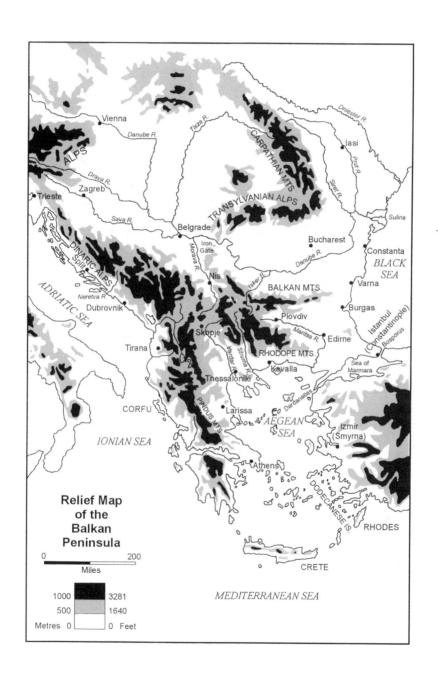

**Relief Map
of the
Balkan
Peninsula**

0   200
Miles

1000	3281
500	1640
Metres 0	0 Feet

Vienna

ALPS

Danube R.

Tisza R.

Drava R.

Zagreb

Trieste

Sava R.

DINARIC ALPS

Split

Neretva R.

Dubrovnik

ADRIATIC SEA

Belgrade

Iron
Gate

Morava R.

Nis

Isker R.

Skopje

Tirana

Vardar R.

Struma R.

Thessaloniki

CORFU

PINDUS MTS.

Larissa

IONIAN SEA

Athens

CARPATHIAN MTS.

TRANSYLVANIAN ALPS

Dniester R.

Iasi

Prut R.

Siret R.

Sulina

Bucharest

Danube R.

Constanta

BLACK
SEA

Varna

BALKAN MTS.

Burgas

Plovdiv

Maritsa R.

Edirne

RHODOPE MTS.

Kavalla

Istanbul
(Constantinople)

Bosporus

Sea of
Marmara

Dardanelles

AEGEAN
SEA

Izmir
(Smyrna)

DODECANESE IS.

RHODES

CRETE

MEDITERRANEAN SEA

CZECHOSLOVAKIA

U.S.S.R.

Vienna

AUSTRIA

Danube R.

Budapest

HUNGARY

Zagreb

Trieste

SLOVENIA

CROATIA

Drava R.

SLAVONIA

SYRMIA

BANAT

Belgrade

Sava R.

Zara
to Italy

BOSNIA

Sarajevo

HERZEGOVINA

YUGOSLAVIA

Morava R.

Nis

MONTE-
NEGRO

Lagosta I.
to Italy

ITALY

ALBANIA

Tirana

Ohrid

Skopje

Vlona

MACEDONIA

Kavalla

Thessaloniki

Larissa

Ioannina

GREECE

Athens

BUKOVINA

TRANSYLVAMIA

MOLDAVIA

BESSARABIA

ROMANIA

Ploesti

WALLACHIA

Bucharest

Danube R.

DOBRUJA

BLACK
SEA

BULGARIA

Sofia

Plovdiv

Edirne

WESTERN
THRACE

EASTERN
THRACE

Istanbul
(Constantinople)

Bosporus

Sea of
Marmara

Gallipoli

Dardanelles

Izmir
(Smyrna)

TURKEY

DODECANESE
to Italy

CRETE

0   200

Miles

Greek acquisitions from Bulgaria

Greek acquisitions from Turkey by Sevres Treaty
(restored to Turkey by Lausanne Treaty)

Yugoslav acquisitions from Austria-Hungary

Yugoslav acquisitions from Bulgaria

Romanian acquisitions from Austria-Hungary

Romanian acquisitions from Russia

**Balkans after
World War I**

CZECHOSLOVAKIA

U.S.S.R.

Vienna

AUSTRIA

Danube R.

Budapest

HUNGARY

TRANSYLVANIA
• Cluj

MOLDAVIA

BESSARABIA

Iasi

SLOVENIA

Zagreb

Drava R.

Trieste

CROATIA

SLAVONIA

VOIVODINA

BANAT

• Timisoara

R O M A N I A

• Brasov

Galati

• Ploesti

Zadar

BOSNIA

Y U G O S L A V I A

Sava R.

Belgrade

WALLACHIA

Bucharest •

• Craiova

Danube R.

DOBRUJA

Sarajevo

HERZEGOVINA

Morava R.

• Nis

BLACK
SEA

MONTE-
NEGRO

B U L G A R I A

• Sofia

ITALY

Shkoder

ALBANIA

Skopje

• Plovdiv

Tirana

Ohrid

Edirne

EASTERN
THRACE

Istanbul
(Constantinople)

Vlore

Kavalla •

Bosporus

M A C E D O N I A

Thessaloniki •

Sea of
Marmara

Gallipoli

Dardanelles

G

• Larissa

T U R K E Y

Ioannina

Izmir
(Smyrna)

R

E

E

C

E

• Athens

DODECANESE IS.

CRETE

0   200

Miles

Greek acquisitions from Italy

Bulgarian acquisitions from Romania

Russian acquisitions from Romania

Yugoslav acquisitions from Italy

**Balkans after
World War II**

Austria

Italy

Slovenia

Ljubljana

Zagreb

Croatia

Hungary

Vojvodina

Novi Sad

Romania

Bosnia and Hercegovina

Belgrade

Y u g o s l a v i a

Sarajevo

Serbia

Adriatic Sea

Montenegro

Titograd

Pristina

Kosovo

Italy

Skopje

Macedonia

International Borders
Republican Borders
Provincial Borders
Yugoslavia
1945–1991

Albania

Greece

Bulgaria

Introduction

Analysis of the Balkan wars of this decade has for too long been characterized by simplistic generalisations and sweeping judgments about the character and mentality of entire peoples, generalisations that would hardly be accepted anywhere else in the world.

Sérgio Vieira de Mello, United Nations chief spokesman on Kosovo 1998–99, *International Herald Tribune*, 25 August 1998

THE BALKANS: A ZONE OF TROUBLES

The Balkans is seen as a permanently disturbed region on the margins of Europe. Real doubt exists about whether it belongs to Europe at all. During the war in Bosnia from 1992 to 1995, British leaders were often heard to say that 'Europe' was doing its best to solve a perennial problem; such language betrayed an unconscious feeling that the region and perhaps most of its inhabitants were alien intrusions on the European landmass.

In the 1990s there has been no shortage of violent and dramatic happenings to suggest that the chaotic and unruly image long ago acquired by the countries of the Balkan peninsula is a deserved one: four separate wars have been waged in different parts of what was once the Federal Republic of Yugoslavia during the 1990s; mass unrest has threatened public order in Albania with collapse on different occasions; of all the East European countries, it was Romania, straddling the cultural divide between Central and Eastern Europe, which saw the collapse of communism assume its bloodiest form; Greece, the one country fully in the Balkans to escape communist rule, was widely seen during the ascendancy of its left nationalist Premier Andreas Papandreou as representing Balkan intransigence in some of its most troublesome forms; only Bulgaria has avoided headline grabbing upheavals, which is ironic given the country's proverbial turbulence before 1945 and the fact that the mountain range which has given the name to the entire peninsula of Southeastern Europe is to be found within its borders.

In the 1990s the power of satellite television to transmit across the planet distressing images of conflict and suffering from the Balkans has implanted a negative stereotype in perhaps a majority of the world's inhabitants who have a glancing knowledge of international affairs. 'Balkanization' is now one of the most negative paradigms in international relations. Since the First World War the term has been in use to describe the fragmentation arising from arbitrary and unpredictable behaviour involving the division of states and conflict between them.

Maria Todorova has pointed out that the pre-1914 turmoil in the Balkans was enormously important in popularising its negative image (Todorova 1997: 118–19). But, as she reminds us, the attempt to create ethnically homogeneous states which was at the root of much of the organized violence, fitted in well with developments in Western Europe over a much longer historical time-frame. Western Europe was no stranger to the organized violence, which had led to the creation of relatively compact states and which was far from exhausted as the Holocaust of the Jews would make clear. It was Bulgaria which, more than any other country in the 1940–44 years, took determined steps to shelter its Jewish population, a fact which is barely known beyond that country's borders.

Periods of calm in the region don't make headlines or else are characterised by roving reporters as harbingers of storms ahead. It is forgotten that Balkan states cooperated in the 1930s when the rest of Europe was plunging headlong towards war; indeed for the 1938 tourist season, the Balkans was promoted as Europe's 'Peace Peninsula' (Bruce Lockhart 1938: 134). In our own day, it is easily overlooked that all of war-torn Yugoslavia's neighbours made tenacious and successful efforts in the 1990s to prevent the Yugoslav wars spilling across their borders; and that Yugoslavia had enjoyed forty years of peace in the middle of the last century, and that the mix of religions and nationalities suggested older traditions of mutual co-existence.

This study does not deny the fact that much Balkan strife is local in origin, arising from attempts to build nation-states on ethnically mixed territory. But it will seek to show that continuous external interference in the affairs of the region exacerbated local disputes over citizenship and statehood, giving them a value and intensity which they might otherwise not have had. It will survey the negative impact of long periods of direct rule by imperial powers on the region, the last phase of external overlordship, promoted by the Soviet Union between 1945 and 1989, perhaps having the most destructive effect of all on interstate relations as well as human relations between citizens sharing different ethnic identities belonging to the same state. It will also examine the often calamitous impact that competition between rival powers, active in the region, has had on the capacity of Balkan peoples striving to modernise their societies and create representative forms of government.

Indeed I suggest that if there is one principal explanation for the negative image suffered by the states comprising the Balkan peninsula, it arises from the difficult relations which the West and Russia have had with the region for a century or more. More than once the interests of the major powers collided in a strategically placed region which the expanding empires of Russia and Great Britain, as well as lesser powers like Austria-Hungary and France, regarded as vital for their security.

It is not surprising that intransigent expressions of political nationalism periodically flared up as a response to outside interference. The appeal of local nationalism made it difficult for the powers to subjugate the Balkans in the way that they managed to do in the larger expanses of Central Asia and Africa. Ambitious British, German and Russian leaders from David Lloyd-George to Hitler, Stalin and Khruschev were often frustrated by stubborn local leaders like Kemal Atatürk, Josip Tito, and Enver Hoxha who mobilised nationalist sentiment to repel external power-grabs.

The Crimean War and the First World War were two international conflicts which had their formal origins in the Balkans. Lesser conflicts of terrible intensity such as the 1912–13 Balkan wars and the wars of the Yugoslav succession in the 1990s gave the region an unenviable reputation for pursuing internecine differences with peculiar ferocity. But I argue that at several key moments the behaviour of powerful external states, whether through creating unjust or unviable political solutions or else by supporting authoritarian leaders with a deeply conflictual approach to politics, made violence on this scale hard to avoid.

Contending European powers often managed to preserve a shaky balance of power by creating hastily arranged compromises that ignored the aspirations of the Balkans and intensified old disputes or else laid the basis for new ones. When foiled ambitions and ruined careers resulted from mishandling the Balkans, the region and its peoples were often damned in the metropoli of the West and later in the Kremlin. In describing the Balkan peoples and their leaders, the language used by Hitler in *Mein Kampf* and by the head of the British Foreign Office in the diary he kept in the 1940s was not dissimilar.

The Balkans did provide undeniable challenges for European politics and continue to do so. How to create political arrangements that will reconcile the desire for self-rule among peoples who often do not live in contiguous neighbourhoods and can be at loggerheads with others over the same territory is a challenge for Europe in the 21st century as it was in the 19th.

The behaviour of local leaders could be exasperating. But the primacy of nationalism can be too easily exaggerated by superficial commentators searching for a convenient label to explain a region whose politics do not fit into the patterns familiar to Middle America or Middle England. One of the main arguments of this book is that extreme forms of nationalism flared up more often in response to gross interference by external powers and that the same pressures might well have produced similar reactions in countries whose geography has bequeathed them a more settled history.

When the powers intervened in the Balkans, either individually or in concert, the needs of local inhabitants were rarely at the top of their list of priorities. They were usually pursuing policies that would advance their own imperial or national interests or prevent their rivalries spinning out of control. Often these goals were achieved at the expense of the inhabitants, even in places where there was a local consensus about what their political destiny should be.

Balkan territory was often divided up to satisfy the balance of power between large states which felt they had a legitimate stake in the region. The most notable example was the 1878 Treaty of Berlin which helped to create the Macedonian and Bosnian questions that had ominous consequences for the peace of Europe. This and other Western- and Russian-sponsored map changes left unsatisfied state nationalisms and rebellious minorities. There was little enthusiasm for creating large states which could fill the vacuum left by retreating empires or promoting a Balkan confederation. In the late 19th century such arrangements could have marginalised nationalism at a time when it was a belief system with relatively little influence on the masses who retained a local identity.

Flimsy knowledge often lay behind decisions taken in the Balkans by influential outsiders, which could have momentous consequences later. It is not unusual for statesmen and their advisers to make hasty decisions about the inhabitants of what are seen as peripheral regions which may return to haunt them later on. The place of remote peoples in the geopolitical hierarchy of nations is often assigned on the basis of patchy knowledge. The quality of advice given to ministers by diplomats based in the Balkans has often been unreliable. The Balkan capitals have usually not been a top-rank posting; that remains the case today even when Southeast European issues ranging from Cyprus to the future of disputed territories like Kosovo and Bosnia are among the biggest security challenges for Western leaders.

Obsolete policies towards the region have often been retained when perhaps it should have been clear that political conditions justifying them had altered. A limited attention span and the the unwillingness to devote energy, imagination and, if necessary, resources to overcome a problem are other long-term features of the European powers' engagement with a 'problem' region.

When policies fail, sometimes in a spectacular fashion, there has been a tendency to blame local factors rather than trace the cause to defects in the behaviour of the metropolitan powers. There is no shortage of excuses deriving from the failings of the Balkans and its peoples.

The most influential explanation for Balkan instability in the 20th century is that it rests on 'ancient ethnic hatreds' that burst to the surface periodically and with terrifying force. These bouts of tribal warfare are seen as culturally determined and historically recurring and therefore beyond capable solution. Many are the journalists, diplomats and policymakers who subscribe to such a view of the Balkans. Other once troublesome people, whose behaviour was supposedly shaped by ending cultural characteristics, have been categorised in not dissimilar ways by metropolitan commentators. In the past, the Spanish, the Irish, the Argentinians, and the Iranians have been among the peoples whose culture and history apparently rendered them incapable of modernising their societies and developing effective political institutions. It is perhaps no coincidence that unflattering and bleak accounts of their potentiality to advance have coincided with periods when leaders in these countries have confronted powerful states like Britain and the USA whose ability to shape news values gives them an important lever on the world stage.

Before the 1999 Kosovo War, Western governments were averse to acting as organizers or peacemakers in the Balkans, perhaps because they were imbued with a sense of fatalism about the willingness of local elites and their populations to benefit from such assistance.

Instead a policy of containment, preventing Balkan quarrels from destabilising adjacent regions, has been preferred. Such a minimalist approach has often resulted in deeply repressive forces prevailing, as happened in Bosnia during the 1992–95 war. But Balkan exceptionalism still permits statesmen to impose hurried settlements which violate basic tenets of democracy, ones which they would usually hesitate to impose on their own countries.

A consistently held feature of international intervention in Southeast Europe has been the belief that if state building is to be successful, the ethnic mosaic of the Balkans needs to be tidied up. No shortage of statesmen have been ready to advocate the compulsory transfer of populations in order to bring peace to Asia Minor in the 1920s, Cyprus in the 1960s, and Yugoslavia in the 1990s.

If Balkan peoples are often viewed as expendable, it may be because influential outsiders have viewed their basic political standards as being little different from the tyrannical rulers who have often ruled over them. The fact that such leaders were often helped to power by one or other of the great powers is not felt to be significant.

This book looks at the dangerous effects of such stereotypes and tries to explain why they and the often short-term and neglectful policies underlying them have been retained for a long historical period.

THE IMPACT OF GEOGRAPHY ON BALKAN HISTORY

The Balkan peninsula is the largest of the three European peninsulas that extend into the Mediterranean sea. It is bounded on the west by the Adriatic and Ionian Seas, on the east by the Black Sea, and on the southeast by the Aegean Sea (Hupchick 1994: 47). There is less agreement about its northern limits, but the Carpathian Mountains which cut across Romania before extending into Slovakia are seen as an approximate northern boundary.

From a geographical point of view, the defining feature of the region is its mountainous character. *Balkan* derives from the Turkish word for mountain and nearly 70% of the land area is comprised of mountains, hills, or upland plateaux. Indeed the peninsula is crisscrossed by mountain ranges running in all directions. They act as a barrier to communication, as is also the case in the Iberian peninsula where intensely local outlooks have bred implacable regional and subnational outlooks.

A number of rivers cross the Balkans in a southeastern direction. The most important is the Danube. It rises in south Germany and flows across the Hungarian and north Yugoslav plains before breaking through the Transylvanian Alps at the famous Iron Gate. It then broadens with the plains of Wallachia on the left and the Bulgarian uplands on the right before draining into the Black Sea. The other notable rivers are the Sava which rises in Slovenia and joins the Danube at Belgrade as well as the Maritsa, Struma and Vardar rivers which flow into the

Aegean. The valleys bordering these waterways provide arable land and the only easy overland communications.

The geography of Southeast Europe lacks any obvious centre of gravity (Hoesch 1972: 15). The long Adriatic coastline extending from the Istrian peninsula to Albania is separated from its natural hinterland by high mountains. Indeed these mountains run parallel to the coast and a Mediterranean-type climate quickly gives way to a continental one. This division between coast and mountains is a fundamental one. It forced the coastal inhabitants to look towards the open seas. Their cities were the gateways for foreign cultural influences and were often controlled by states at odds with those that existed in the highland interior (Hupchick 1994: 48, Hoesch 1972: 15).

In the eastern parts of the Balkans communications were easier. The Danube is surrounded by fertile plains as it flows eastwards between the Dinaric Alps and the Carpathians. Fertile river valleys in the Thracian plain south of the Danube make communications easier across lower lying mountains than those in the northwest. These river corridors and mountain passes opened up the peninsula to external control and were routes that invading forces could easily traverse (Jelavich 1983a: 3).

The mountainous terrain and the lack of a natural centre around which a great state might evolve retarded the development of the Balkan peninsula (Sowell 1998: 175). The region's considerable mineral wealth was usually exploited by outsiders from the Romans to the Nazi and Soviet overlords of our own times. Kingdoms like that of 4th-century BC Macedonia or medieval Serbia or Tito's Yugoslavia (effectively a communist monarchy) had relatively short life spans. Most scholars emphasise the isolation of human settlements among self-contained river valleys and upland plateaux (Hupchick 1994: 48; Hoesch 1972: 17). The local isolation in 'a jumble of mountainous valleys and cul-de-sacs' contributed to the region's striking ethnic diversity (Kostanick in Jelavich & Jelavich 1963: 2). The Montenegrin and Albanian mountain peoples remained a law unto themselves until modern times and only nominally submitted to Ottoman rule (Hoesch 1972: 16). To one local writer, unyielding geography succeeded in creating a culture of 'secrecy and distrust that are part of the stereotypical Balkan character' (Bookman 1994: 15). Competition for the peninsula's limited agricultural resources bred highly territorial microcultures, from the classical Greek city states to the modern Balkan states, unable to easily agree over frontiers (Hupchick 1994: 48).

But history written from a nationalist standpoint has often over-looked the degree to which a wide range of peoples settled and mixed with each other. Surprisingly similar traditions of music, cuisine, agricultural practice, architecture and folk culture do not suggest that the Balkan peoples, even ones who today are sharply at odds, continuously stood apart from one another.

THE BALKANS THROUGH OUTSIDE EYES

Today viewed as peripheral lands, the Balkans historically have found themselves at a crossroads where competing political systems and imperial ambitions have met and collided (Jelavich & Jelavich 1963: 131 note 12; Gallagher 1999). Parts of the region have always acted as a gateway or a bridge offering many opportunities of peaceful contact between not dissimilar peoples. Paddy Ashdown, leader of the British Liberal Democrat Party from 1987 to 1999 and a Western politician who has shown unusual empathy with the region's problems, has argued that '[T]he Balkan states have enjoyed peace chiefly where there has been an overarching power structure to bring stability', the Ottoman and Hapsburg Empires, along with the communists being seen as providing that equilibrium for longer or shorter periods (Ashdown 1999).

Better known outsiders like Henry Kissinger who characterize the Balkans as a zone of unremitting ethnic strife and deep-seated backwardness often fail to appreciate how varied levels of political development could be. Montenegro, where the severing of enemy heads was 'the poetry of warfare' and exhibiting the heads a sign of public acclaim to be remembered and marked on gravestones, was one feature of Balkan reality that endured into the 19th century (Goldsworthy 1998: 232). Another was the city of Dubrovnik, virtually within sight of Montenegro, which for hundreds of years enjoyed a republican system of government advanced for its day until Napoleon extinguished its freedom in 1806 (Jelavich 1983a: 98–9).

Transylvania, a transitional territory straddling the Balkans and Central Europe, has been notable for the mingling of religions, cultures, and languages. In the Middle Ages, when much of Western Europe was awash in the blood of religious heretics, it was a beacon of religious toleration where Hungarian Catholics and Protestants respected each other's faiths and tolerated that of the Orthodox Romanians. 'Transylvania had its high Middle Ages, cathedrals, Cistercians, a whiff of the Renaissance, its Baroque, its Enlightenment', wrote a Hungarian American perhaps tired of its new-found fame as the location of the Dracula horror movies (Lukacs 1982).

Bosnia is another meeting place where different cultures managed to coexist, if often uneasily, for centuries. But its multinational traditions finally succumbed to the furies of nationalism after the Cold War when the prospects of a common European home emerging from the embers of superpower rivalry proved a cruel deception. A Bosnia shared by Muslims and Eastern and Western Christians was always bound to be vulnerable to seismic political eruptions as long as Southeast Europe was one of the key faultlines between conflicting political systems.

Dazzling reversals of fortune have periodically occurred for empires, nations, and political systems that have created deep frustration and insecurity. Nowhere else in Europe has been accustomed to such upheavals, at least on the scale and frequency with which they have occurred in the Balkans. The latest one encompasses not just the wars in ex-Yugoslavia but the collapse of a communist social system which has brought poverty for millions of people even in countries that had remained at peace. It is perhaps no wonder that in the face of such calamities, fatalism has emerged as one of the defining characteristics of many of the Balkans' inhabitants.

Barbara Jelavich, the most accomplished historian of the region, has described the Balkans as 'a testing ground for alternative systems' and for 'the past two centuries ... a laboratory in which some of the most elusive aspects of national and liberal forms of political organization and economic development could be observed' (Jelavich 1983a: x). The collision between its multinational traditions and the new force of nationalism turned the region into Europe's principal danger zone as powers with conflicting interests and ambitions increasingly meddled in its affairs.

The Eastern Question resulting from 19th-century Anglo-Russian rivalry in the Balkans, but drawing in other states, concerned how to manage and divide the Balkan territories of the crumbling Ottoman Empire. It produced in the 1854–56 Crimean War, the only general European conflict between 1815 and 1914. The First World War, 'a conflict whose immediate origins were deeply rooted in Balkan problems', provided the region and its people with a profoundly negative image (Jelavich 1983a: x). It was one destined to endure as the Balkans was periodically convulsed by the whirlwind of war and revolution which made the period from 1914 to 1999 one of endemic conflict and repression in much of Europe's eastern half. Two Balkan wars fought in 1912 and 1913 between local claimants for the remains of the Ottoman Empire in Europe, and then the assassination in Sarajevo of the heir to the Austrian throne on 28 June 1914, bequeathed the term 'Balkanization' to the world as one denoting conflict arising from the fragmentation of political power. The Balkan states usually had conflicting territorial claims as well as ethnic minorities that had to be assimilated or driven out. They formed unstable local alliances, sought backing from outside powers in order to guarantee security or satisfy national ambitions and, in turn, were used by those powers for their own tactical advantage.

WHO IS TO BLAME?

In some eyes, it is primarily because of its adverse geographical location that the Balkans is fated to be a zone of troubles. The eastern part of Europe to which it belongs is at a disadvantage by being blocked off from the world's oceans. Coastal mountains along the Adriatic act as a barrier against the spread of cultural influences from the Mediterranean. Winter temperatures in Sarajevo may be 25 degrees colder than on the coast, little more than one hundred miles away (Sowell 1998: 175). Such rugged terrain causes high transportation costs which impede trade. Such adverse geographical conditions have inevitably frustrated efforts at political unification. On the other hand, the peninsula is separated from Asia Minor only by the narrow waters of the Turkish straits and from Italy only by the Straits of Otranto with the Danube basin being a vital passageway for a succession of foreign invaders. The Balkans has therefore lacked the physical good fortune of the northern peninsula of Scandinavia, whose geography has shielded it from the storms that have made Europe one of the world's most violent continents.

More highly charged is the viewpoint that 'people in the Balkans are fated, by history or genetics, to kill one another' (Sells 1996: xiv). It received powerful endorsement during the 1992–95 Bosnian War. David Owen, the key international mediator in that conflict wrote that '[H]istory points to a tradition in the Balkans of a readiness to solve disputes by taking up arms and acceptance of the forceful or even negotiated movement of people as a consequence of war' (Owen 1996: 3). In 1994 the President of the USA, Bill Clinton, described a 'conflict which had been there for hundreds of years ... the truth is people there keep killing each other' (Cohen 1968: 244).

Sometimes there is local endorsement for explanations of Balkan problems centred around the prevalence of 'ancient ethnic hatreds'. Adil Zulfikarpasić, a Swiss-based businessman born into a prominent Bosnian Muslim family, wrote in 1991:

> I told you that the casualties that occurred in the Lebanon in the course of a whole year would occur in Bosnia in one week. We are different, we have a different temperament, the Balkans is a dangerous region. Some nationalities faint when they see blood, but we in the Balkans go delirious. We become intoxicated. (Zulfikarpasić 1998: 151)

It is hardly surprising that parts of Southeast Europe deny a Balkan identity because of its association with unpredictability, lawlessness, and cruelty. Romania's first king, Carol I, stated in 1910 that 'we belong to the Balkans neither ethnographically, nor geographically, nor any other way' (Seton-Watson 1934: 436). The Croatian leader Franjo Tudjman (whose surname suggests that an ancestor may have been an interpreter in the Ottoman Empire) vowed in 1997 that Croatia would reject any future multilateral cooperation with Balkan states and threatened to alter the Constitution to prevent what he saw as a slide back towards old Yugoslav arrangements.

In Romania, the *Academia Romania* dictionary states that 'Balcanic' 'means *inapoiat* (backward), *primitiv*, *necivilizat*' (Goldsworthy 1998: 4). It is hardly surprising that successive foreign ministers, Teodor Melescanu and Adrian Severin, tried to advance Romania's case for NATO membership by arguing that Romania understood the problems of the Balkan region, but did not actually belong to it (Gallagher, 1998). Geographically a good case can be made that Romania lies outside the Balkans but historically, southern Romania, the seat of power, has been part of the Balkan social system as one of Romania's best contemporary historians Neagu Djuvara has admitted (Gallagher 1997: 70).

Another local view asserts that people are 'good' or 'bad' according to their social origins. Ed Vulliamy, one of the finest chroniclers of the Bosnian war, contrasted the implacable, suspicious and traditionally-minded peasants living in isolation from other ethnic groups with the cosmopolitan inhabitants of Bosnia's cities (Vulliamy 1994: 40). Prominent ethnographers and anthropologists in Yugoslavia have some-times claimed that 'there is something inherently anarchic or violent in the character of the Dinaric Alpine people, among whom Serbs and Croats are to be found'. These are the words of Cvijeto Job, a former Yugoslav ambassador who went on to say that 'much has been made of the recurrent subordination of the mercantile, more urban and Europeanized settlements along the Drava, Sava ... and other rivers by the more backward populations coming in from the hinterland' (Job 1993: 55).

Occasionally, foreign statesmen will endorse such racial stereotypes. William Gladstone, the great British Liberal of the Victorian era, advocated the mass expulsion of Turks from Bulgaria in 1876, giving dangerous currency to the belief that in the Balkans mixed populations could simply not live together (*The Economist* 1999: 28 May). His successor, David Lloyd-George, took the incompatibility of Christians and Muslims living in western Asia Minor for granted while Hitler regarded ethnic separation as an article of faith in the 1940s.

As the protracted nature of Balkan wars in the 1990s required more concentrated attention to be given to the region, foreign policymakers were struck by the ease with which tyrannical government prevailed in Serbia and Croatia, the two largest units of the former Yugoslavia. David Owen professed disgust at having to deal with 'leaders who ... displayed a callousness of mind in which the people's view never seemed to come near the conference table, despite much consulting of assemblies and the holding of referenda in circumstances of dubious democratic validity' (Owen 1996: 3). He was shocked by the propensity of politicians to lie openly and repeatedly: '[N]ever before in over thirty years of public life have I had to operate in such a climate of dishonour, propaganda, and dissembling. Many of the people with whom I had to deal in the former Yugoslavia were literally strangers to the truth' (Owen 1996: 1). But another prominent Western figure, Warren Zimmermann, the USA's last ambassador to Yugoslavia, has preferred to pay tribute to the politicians he knew from the different Yugoslav regions who tried desperately to avert the disaster of interethnic strife that brought down Yugoslavia in the 1990s (Zimmermann 1999: 124, 125–6).

Hugh Seton-Watson, a distinguished British Scholar of Eastern Europe, was always fascinated by the broad moral spectrum into which Balkan figures could be placed. He wrote in 1960 that '[O]f all my travels, I think the most enlightening were in the Balkans, whose combination of intellectual subtlety and crudity, of tortuous intrigue and honest courage revealed more truths about the political animal man than are to be found in most textbooks of political science' (Seton-Watson 1960: 15).

While perhaps denying the 'ancient ethnic hatreds' metaphor, some commentators are ready to ascribe the post-1989 Balkan crises to 'the crippling dependence of *all* [my emphasis] Balkan peoples on the ideology and psychology of expansionist nationalism' (Hagen 1999: 52). The Balkan expert, William V. Hagen, sees the Balkan states as 'all born in the 19th and early 20th century as irredentist nations—that is nations committed to the recovery of their "unredeemed" national territories' (Hagen 1999: 53). The Balkans seems to invite such sweeping generalizations from outsiders. The fact that countries like Romania, Bulgaria and Hungary have, in the 1990s, formally renounced claims to neighbouring territories which had previously been part of their national 'imagined community' is unacknowledged by Hagen. However, it remains true that nationalists are often readier to bend or flout the truth than other political practitioners because they see their cause as a sacred one. In the words of the Romanian philosopher, Emil Cioran, writing in 1935:

> The myths of a nation are its vital truths. they might not coincide with the truth; this is of no importance. The supreme sincerity of a nation towards itself manifests itself in the rejection of self-criticism, in vitalization through its own illusions. And, does a nation seek the truth? A nation seeks power. (Volovici 1991: 187)

WHAT IS TO BE DONE?

Outside forces have pursued different strategies in the Balkans since the region emerged as a major problem in international relations. Initially, the powers pursued their own interests, carrying out map changes to suit the shifting balance of power and sometimes clashing directly when compromise was beyond their reach. The diplomatic carve-up agreed at the Congress of Berlin in 1878 ruled out the creation of a viable pattern of states. The negative image of the region, its politicians, citizens, political institutions and its potential to overcome its problems handicapped the Western powers and Russia. The placing of the Balkans at the bottom of the geopolitical hierarchy of states and peoples meant that the quality of diplomacy and resultant policymaking were often poor. In 1920 E. H. Carr, a prominent British diplomatic mandarin, cautioned a group of Western ambassadors 'not to take the new nations of Europe too seriously' because their affairs 'belong to the sphere of farce' (Gati 1992: 111).

Examples from the 1850s to the 1990s show that key actors, from foreign minister to ambassador, can commit serious mistakes, some-times resulting in tragic consequences, and not risk official censure or damage to their careers. Benign neglect, avoidable errors, and an abandonment of standards usually upheld elsewhere in Europe litter the West's problematic engagement with the Balkans. The durability of mediocre statecraft based on stereotypical attitudes suggests that the Balkans and its inhabitants are usually not taken very seriously by Western policy makers.

The First World War showed the horrific cost to be paid for great-power rivalry in the Balkans. Subsequently, international competitors have often shown a preference for containing Balkan disputes, preventing European security being undermined even at the cost of allowing the triumph of local tyrannies. Containment prolonged the 1992–95 Bosnian War when the city of Sarajevo was subject to a siege that would have been viewed as barbaric even in medieval times, and various apartheid-style policies, known euphemistically as ethnic cleansing, were permitted by the West. The prestige of the major democracies, newly victorious in the Cold War, was damaged by the reluctance to enforce basic standards of civilized conduct in Europe's 'wild neighbourhood'. President Clinton justified non-intervention by recalling that 'Hitler sent tens of thousands of soldiers to that area and was never successful in subduing it' (Sells 1996: 126). He was powerfully influenced by writers such as Rebecca West and Robert Kaplan who portrayed the nationalist tensions of the region as a permanent condition (West 1941; Kaplan 1993). Richard Holbrooke, the US diplomat who eventually negotiated a diplomatic solution for Bosnia in 1995, argued that the influence on the President of writers who insisted that 'nothing could be done by outsiders in a region so steeped in ancient hatreds was profoundly negative' (Weisman 1999: *International Herald Tribune*, Paris: 18 June).

If the peace of Europe can be secured by allowing a local strongman or a particular ethnic group to dominate a mixed territory, it is a strategy that one or more powers have been ready to try out. Britain was prepared to prop up the decaying Ottoman Empire in the Balkans in order to prevent Russian control of the strategic Bosporus straits and adjacent slavic Balkan lands. In 1944, Winston Churchill, the British wartime leader, turned to Fitzroy Maclean, the Conservative MP who was the chief British liaison officer with Tito's Partisan forces in Yugoslavia, and asked: 'Do you intend to make Yugoslavia your home after the war?' Maclean said he did not. To which Churchill replied, 'Neither do I. And, that being so, the less you and I worry about the form of government they set up, the better' (Cohen 1998: 77). Later, Britain and its Cold War allies showed far less concern about the fate of

Balkan peoples under communism than they did for Central European states on the wrong side of the Iron Curtain; while countries like Poland and Czechoslovakia were viewed as belonging to mainstream European Christian civilization, those placed south and east of the Danube were regarded as marginal to it.

The Kosovo crisis of 1998–9, which resulted in an armed confrontation between NATO states and Serbia when the regime of Slobodan Milošević evicted much of the Albanian population of Kosovo from their homes, produced a forceful response from the West. It suggested that the rule book for dealing with Balkan troubles was at last being updated. The minimalist agenda of many diplomats and security chiefs, based on containing a perennial problem irrespective of the human consequences, was replaced by an effort (however clumsy in execution) of confronting Balkan tyranny and offering the region's ill-used peoples the prospect of integration with the rest of Europe.

A crafty dictator like Milošević, who for a decade had shown an ability to anticipate Western moves on the Balkan chessboard, was surprised by the toughness of the response to the fourth war he engineered in the region. Different factors whose importance increased in the 1990s may help to explain why the option of intervening with the full panoply of NATO aerial force in a Balkan conflict was taken. The cumulative impact of refugees suffering from political intolerance had, thanks to the power of television, created a climate of opinion ready to see something being done. Journalists like Martin Bell, in 1997 the first person elected to parliament as an independent in Britain for over fifty years after coming to prominence through his Bosnia coverage for the BBC, had made many British viewers uneasy about the non-interventionist stance of John Major's 1990–97 government. Aid workers who raised money in small communities around Western Europe and dispatched volunteers to carry out relief work, narrowed the gulf of perception and empathy between the safe and prosperous Europe and the Balkans. Paddy Ashdown MP, who paid over ten visits to Balkan trouble spots in the 1990s, challenged the view of the 19th-century German statesman Bismarck that 'the Balkans are not worth the bones of a single Pomeranian grenadier'. 'We know', he wrote in 1999, 'that this extraordinary region has often presented the trigger for wider conflict and ... it demands our attention' (Ashdown 1999). This view even reached into the White House where President Clinton, having acquainted himself with the writings of serious historians of the region like Noel Malcolm, wrote in May 1999:

The Former Yugoslav peoples have lived together for centuries with greater and lesser degrees of conflict but not constant 'cleansing' of peoples from their land. Had they experienced nothing but that, their nations would be homogeneous today, not endlessly diverse.

... The Balkans are not fated to be the heart of European darkness, a region of bombed mosques, men and boys shot in the back, young women raped, all trace of group and individual history rewritten or erased. (Clinton 1999, *International Herald Tribune*, Paris: 24 May)

The President's article was entitled 'On Track in Kosovo Towards Balkan Renaissance', but such a scenario is unlikely to dawn soon unless powerful states committed to open politics and free and just economic systems engage purposefully with the region, and not just from 15,000 feet in the sky as bombs are dropped on the forces and installations of a nationalist dictator. A Romanian journalist wrote in 1999:

The Balkans are not going to be pacified by airplanes with bombs, but with dollars and prosperity, which at last are going to bring more democracy and ethnic and religious tolerance. (Bogdan Chirieac 1999, *Adevârul*, Bucharest: 20 March)

Jacques Rupnik advised in 1994 that 'we must "Europeanize" the Balkans if we want to avoid "the Balkanization" of Europe' (Rupnik 1994: 111).

Until now it is negative features like ethnic rivalries, underdevelopment, foreign occupation and the imposition of collective projects from communism to nationalism which have made the Balkans a recognisable concept to the rest of the world. Perhaps now there is a chance of fulfilling the region's potential to create political systems and societies based on open, cooperative relations of the kind that have transformed the character and reputation of Western Europe since it largely abandoned its own deadly nationalist quarrels after 1945. But such a chance is unlikely to be realised as long as Serbia, strategically positioned in the heart of the peninsula, remains alienated from Western democratic states under a cunning and resilient dictator. In the aftermath of the Kosovo conflict, the reluctance of NATO to take steps to conciliate the Serbs and detach more of them from the authoritarian regime may well undermine external bids to stabilise the region. Writing in the first days of a new century, it is already apparent that the commitment and energy to reconcile the Balkans with the rest of Europe is showing signs of faltering among leaders who in 1999 briefly appeared to throw aside the lethargy and cynicism that characterised the behaviour of their predecessors to the region.

In Kosovo, certain international bureaucrats have shown little willingness to empower local people (especially women) with plenty of decision making experience, and a great deal of concern with acquiring lifestyles and salaries that insulate them as far as possible from the populations they are supposed to be helping. It remains to be seen how strong will be the local backlash against international civil servants engaged in post-conflict work whose own attitudes sometimes suggest that professing liberals can be almost as duplicitous as the Soviets once were in the Balkans when they were preaching communist internationalism.

The Greek political thinker Adamantos Korais argued in the early 1800s that the Balkans were an integral part of the European world, just lagging behind (Kitromilides 1995: 7). This is a view shared by me and which animates this book. Unless the Atlantic democracies decide no longer to treat much of the region as a political backwater where tyrants and sham democrats are allowed to hold sway, the Balkan peninsula is likely to periodically undermine the peace of Europe as it did in the 19th and 20th centuries.

Chapter 1

PATTERNS OF EXTERNAL INVOLVEMENT IN THE
BALKANS BEFORE 1914

Nearly a century ago, the British writer Saki (H.H. Munro) observed that '[T]hose Balkan peoples ... unfortunately make more history than they can consume locally' (Goldsworthy 1998: 77). But history retains a significance for the insecure states that have emerged in the Balkans in the last two hundred years. It shaped national consciousness and helped to legitimise the nation-state. Modern Balkan states not infrequently see the empires that rose and fell in medieval times as their precursors. Nationalist intellectuals have always looked for an illustrious pedigree for the country whose role in history they see it as their duty to define and explain to the world.

The first inhabitants of the Balkans about whom definite information exists are the Illyrians, who inhabited the region west of the Morava valley towards the Adriatic. They are believed by some to be the ancestors of the modern Albanians. To the east in lands stretching from the Aegean to the north of the Danube were the Thracians who had established an organized state in the 5th century BC (Jelavich 1983a: 4). A branch of the Thracians, the Dacians, who established a powerful state north of the Danube around the time of Christ are seen as a vital element in creating the Romanian nation. The Romanian national catechism asserts that modern-day Romanians are the descendants of two noble races, the Dacians and the Roman legionaries who defeated them in 101 AD after an epic struggle.

In the pre-modern period, Macedonia was the largest territorial entity to have emerged in the Balkans. During the reign of Philip II and his son Alexander the Great (334–323 BC), the kingdom of Macedonia stretched to the Persian Gulf and the Mediterranean (Bookman 1994: 45). But by medieval times, the region of Macedonia was confined to the Vardar valley, which comprises the extent of the Macedonian state which emerged after the collapse of Yugoslavia in 1991.

During its fleeting golden age, Macedonia had helped disseminate Greek culture in the Balkan peninsula. The original home of the Greeks was probably in the lower Danube region and they probably spread into the Greek peninsula from about 2000 BC on (Trevel 1936: 146). The territory of most other peoples of the region has shifted over time, despite the rhetoric of modern nationalists.

Despite the endemic factionalism familiar to observers of contemporary Greek politics, the ancient Greeks 'were conscious of their
cultural unity and shared a strong feeling of superiority to the
"barbarian" world outside' (Jelavich 1983a: 5–6). The rich culture of
the ancient Greeks would endure as the Roman empire subdued the
Balkan peninsula, starting with the annexation of the kingdom of Illyria
in 168 BC. Great cities were built connected by roads like the Via
Egnatia extending from Durres in what is now Albania to Thessaloniki
and further east (a lifeline which it is planned to revive in order to
integrate the southern Balkans into the modern European transport
system). Illyria became a prime recruiting ground for the Roman legion.
The southern Balkans provided three of the greatest Roman emperors,
Diocletian, Constantine and Justinian. But due to barbarian pressure,
the Romans were forced to relinquish part of their Balkan possessions
long before the dissolution of the empire. In 275 AD the Roman legions
withdrew from the province of Dacia north of the Danube. Many
Roman provincials stayed, retreating to the Carpathian Mountains and
uplands of Transylvania with their flocks, and their Latin language, to
re-enter history centuries later as the ancestors of the modern
Romanians (Stillman 1966: 26).

The Balkans were affected by a rapid movement of peoples in the
millennium following the eclipse of Rome; in the 4th and 5th centuries
marauders like the Goths, Huns and Avars swept across the area but did
not put down roots. They were followed by migrants like the Slavs,
Magyars and Danubian Bulgars who entered between the 6th and 10th
centuries and created powerful settlements that were to be the basis of
independent states (Stillman 1966: 27).

The Balkans were emerging as the classic transit area, 'a meeting
place for peoples and cultures where the western, oriental and Asiatic
worlds, and central European and Mediterranean peoples have all
intermingled' (Hoesch 1972: 22–3). Instead of original settlers being
displaced or killed by newcomers, a continuous assimilation of local and
foreign elements combined to produce a distinctive Balkan synthesis of
characteristics. It is shown by the number of words held in common
today by the main Balkan languages.

For over a thousand years, the imperial traditions of Rome were
carried on by the Byzantine Empire. It was the main power in the Balkans
despite its authority being frequently disputed. In 330 AD Emperor
Constantine founded the city of Constantinople on the narrow neck of
water at the Bosporus separating Europe and Asia. The best natural

harbour in the Balkans and the Mediterranean area, the city, surrounded on three sides by water, could be easily defended and was captured only twice, in 1204 and 1453 (Jelavich 1983a: 11). Constantinople became the capital of the Eastern Roman Empire and it survived the fall of Rome. As Western Europe fell into the Dark Ages, the classical world endured in Byzantium which was the most advanced state in the known world (Woodhouse 1998: 41–2). The Greek or Hellenic heritage which had to be laboriously revived in Western Europe during the medieval Renaissance survived intact in Byzantium. Modern Greeks are taught to be immensely proud of their cultural heritage and, at moments of tension between Greece and the rest of the EU in the early 1990s, Greek politicians have sometimes used it to deny the right of countries like Germany to take a stand on sensitive Balkan issues.

The Byzantine Empire was based on centralised and highly autocratic political authority which continued to influence Balkan political culture long after the empire's demise. But the Greek cultural leadership of the empire was sufficiently self-confident to allow non-Greek societies an important degree of cultural autonomy (Hupchick 1994: 100). Ethnic diversity was permitted as long as peoples like the Bulgarians accepted the view that the empire in Constantinople was the one and only protector of the one Christian empire on earth (Hupchick 1994: 90–1). Societies espousing Orthodox Christianity were free to do so in their various languages so long as they did not stray from Orthodox tenets. Dennis Hupchick has written that 'Christianity was expressed in the highly mystical, ritualised and symbolical universality of the Greek Hellenic culture of the eastern Mediterranean' (Hupchick 1994: 81). A contrast can be drawn with the Latin-based Christianity which emerged in Europe after the 5th century. It allowed no deviation from its Latin culture and emphasised the legality, practicality and militancy of Roman civilization.

The restoration of a Greek-inspired Orthodox Byzantine Empire became a powerful goal of some of the leaders of 19th-century independent Greece (Clogg 1992: 48). The Great Idea (*Megale Idaia*) was one that modern Greece was unable to accomplish. But a sense that the Byzantine Empire 'was the final perfection of human achievement, the immutable embodiment of God's will on earth', has endured among traditionally-minded Greeks (Woodhouse 1998: 89). Doctrinally, the Orthodox Church asserts that it is unsusceptible to change or improvement, thus reflecting Byzantine cultural superiority. Contemporary political autocrats without a trace of religious belief have sought to exploit these Byzantine traditions in order to acquire popular legitimacy. Tito, Yugoslavia's postwar leader, the nearest equivalent to a communist monarch, was an 'embodiment of the autocratic universal political ideology' (Hupchick 1994: 110). Romania's despotic Ceauşescu also plundered the Byzantine past for symbols and rituals to make his vile personal dictatorship palatable, at least for sections of the population (Brezianu *et al.* 1989: 9).

In the Orthodox tradition, the Church rarely challenged the state's influence. The political and religious leadership usually worked together against common internal and external enemies. Orthodox Church compliance before the power of the secular ruler was exploited ruthlessly by Balkan communist chiefs and meant that the task of building free institutions was slower than in non-Orthodox communist states shaped by Western Christian influence.

The prospects for Christian political unity were probably doomed following the decision of Pope Leo III in 800 to create a new Christian world state—the Holy Roman Empire, by crowning Charlemagne (800–814) as its emperor. The symbolism of the coronation inserted the office of Roman pope between God and emperor. The very act of the pope anointing the emperor seemed to proclaim the ultimate power of the Church over the state (Hupchick 1994: 98).

Prior to 800, Christianity had largely been an East European and North African religion but its centre of gravity now shifted from the east to the west (Khan 1995: 404). However, Orthodoxy displayed cultural effervescence in one important respect. Cyril and Methodius, two brothers from Thessaloniki developed a Slavonic literary language and an alphabet—the Cyrillic—and made the Orthodox Church far more accessible to the Slavs of Eastern Europe (Hupchick 1994: 100–1). Russia and many of the South Slav peoples had passed into the Orthodox cultural and religious orbit by the time of the formal split dividing Western and Eastern Christianity. With South Slavs in different religious camps, the prospects for political unity were reduced, making it easier for political nationalism to locate them in different adversarial camps after 1800 (Wachtel 1998: 11).

Long before, this religious enmity had sharpened into an East–West European cultural fault. Byzantium, menaced by the rise of Islam, could not count on Western solidarity to restore the Holy Lands to Christian control. The Crusaders, initially campaigning under papal sponsorship, were less concerned about freeing the holy places than about carving out new kingdoms in the East controlled by unruly and power-hungry knights (Jelavich 1983a: 22). In 1204, the Christian warriors of the 4th Crusade, rather than assail the Muslim Turks, sacked and dismantled Constantinople instead. Venice, a rising empire based on trade and sea power, wished to eliminate the Byzantine Empire as a competitor. Although the Byzantine Empire re-emerged some sixty years later, Eastern Christian civilization had been dealt a near fatal blow by its fellow Christians from the West. Lasting hatred among Orthodox believers for the 'Franks', as West Europeans were to be designated, was kept alive by memories of the way that the Crusaders looted and massacred, desecrating churches, during their orgy of destruction in Constantinople (Hupchick 1994: 20–1). Today in Greece these images of Western treachery and barbarism are retold by the monks of Mount Athos and by populist politicians keen to make xenophobia a vote winner. In no small measure, they help explain why opinion formers appealed, often with success, for solidarity with fellow Orthodox Serbs and roundly condemned what is seen as NATO aggression first in Bosnia and later in Kosovo (Gallagher 1999: 46). In 1965 there was brief hope that West–East Christian enmity might erode when the Pope and the Patriarch of Constantinople solemnly annulled the anathemas their predecessors had hurled at one another 900 years previously (Rinvolvori 1966: 167). But recent political events in the Balkans make it clear that much intricate ecumenical work is required before an inter-Church quarrel, eclipsing the Catholic–Protestant one in its intensity, can be healed.

When the Islamic Ottoman tribe invaded the European mainland in 1354 Byzantium would be confronted with an adversary which stretched its resources to breaking point. Ottoman successes were made easier by the propensity of Christian powers to fight each other and sometimes seek help from the new Islamic presence (Woodhouse 1998: 85). The rapacity of Western Crusaders and traders meant that a lot of Greeks accepted the Turkish conquest as a release (Woodhouse 1998: 98). It was only ordinary West Europeans, a motley collection of soldiers and sailors, who rallied to defend Constantinople before it was conquered in 1453, a sad reflection of today when it was only insignificant Western citizens, not their governments, who showed any practical concern about doing something to end the war in Bosnia mainly directed against blameless civilians (Woodhouse 1998: 93–4). Before the end of the 16th century, the West mounted no resistance to the Ottomans. Protestant rulers calculated that any attack on the Muslim world would help the papacy. France not only failed to resist the Turks but urged Suleiman I to attack its rival, the Hapsburg Empire (Udovicki 1997b: 36).

OTTOMAN RULE

Balkan nationalist historiography has usually painted a bleak picture of Ottoman rule and exaggerated the importance of the medieval Balkan states. What were usually 'unstable and loose-knit medieval kingdoms were prone to internal disintegration even before they succumbed to external conquerors' (Bideleux and Jeffries 1998: 60). None of these early states—the Serbian, Croatian, and Bosnian kingdoms, Wallachia and Moldovia—were national states in the modern sense (Jelavich 1983a: 26). Nobles coalesced around a strong leader. A noble could easily shift his allegiance and ally with an enemy power if it suited his personal fortunes. Territorial boundaries bore little relation to ethnic boundaries (Bideleux and Jeffries 1998: 60). There was no ethnically pure people. Barbara Jelavich has written:

> On the eve of the Ottoman invasion, a band of Slavic-speaking people separated the Romanians and Hungarians in the north from the Albanian and Greek language areas in the south. In each region, the population represented a fusion of original inhabitants with subsequent invaders, an amalgamation achieved by military conquest by the stronger group, the absorption of one people by another owing to the weight of numbers, or the acceptance of another language because of the cultural attraction offered by a more advanced civilization. (Jelavich 1983a: 27)

The medieval states have been described less as close forerunners of the modern Bulgarian and Serbian nation-states and more attempts by Bulgarian and Serbian 'upstarts' to create Orthodox Balkan empires modelled on Byzantium (Bideleux and Jeffries 1998: 60). The shared Christian faith of medieval warlords did not prevent them from allying opportunistically with the Muslim power. The peasantry, oppressed by the burden of feudalism, often welcomed new rulers who had another land system (Jelavich 1983a: 30). The less burdensome tax and labour regulations of the Ottoman Empire proved a magnetic draw for Serbs from Central Europe who fled to the Ottoman lands during the 15th and 16th centuries (Hupchick 1994: 145–6). Where torture and mutilation were concerned, the Ottoman law codes drawn up by Suleiman I ('the Magnificent'), were far more humane than the ones they superseded (Malcolm 1998: 94). The Jews fleeing persecution in Catholic Europe found no restrictions upon their faith, or their ability to engage in trade or commerce, when they arrived in Ottoman domains.

Significantly, the actions of Sultan Mehmed II, the conqueror of Constantinople, indicated that he saw himself as the heir of the

Byzantine Empire (Arnakis 1963: 126 n.18). In 1454 he installed the new head of the Orthodox Church with full Byzantine ritual and enhanced powers (Woodhouse 1998: 95). Mehmed (who had a Serb mother) was personally extremely interested in Greek thought and theological doctrine (Cohen 1998: 210). He respected the civilization he had subdued and wished to ensure a contented Christian population (Jelavich 1983a: 49). The old imperial political ideology allowed the Sultan and the Orthodox patriarch to settle into 'a situation of mutual self-interest in which the actual religious differences between them grew blurred' (Hupchick 1994: 108).

The Orthodox and Muslim elites had a common enemy, a Catholicism that was increasingly expansionary and contemptuous of other faiths. The historian Arnold Toynbee compares the record of the Ottoman Empire towards religious diversity favourably with that of West European states after 1500, which were usually ready to apply drastic measures if the religion of the people did not match that of the sovereign (Toynbee 1923: 268–9). The Ottoman record shows a willingness to work with any monotheistic religion whose leaders submitted to their authority (Jelavich 1983a: 49). Particular respect was offered to the Christians and the Jews, the 'people of the book', that is with a revealed scripture. Each religious community was regarded as an autonomous *millet* (nation) under a religious leader invested with civil powers (Woodhouse 1998: 102). As well as the Orthodox millet, there were, by the 18th century, Gregorian Armenian, Catholic, Jewish and also Muslim millets (Jelavich 1983a: 49). The millet system, in the words of C.M. Woodhouse, 'implied no connotation of national identity, though in the later age of nationalism it was to be invested with that idea ... It was simply a convenient administrative device which in fact worked extremely well' (Woodhouse 1998: 102–3). He goes on to write that '[P]rovided taxes were paid, the Turks did not care what their subjects did with themselves. Local administration, trade and education were entirely their own affair' (Woodhouse 1998: 103–4).

The Orthodox Patriarch was able to levy dues on laity and clergy alike. He could set up tribunals to decide matters of marriage, divorce and inheritance. These tribunals 'essentially took over most civil cases because Christian litigants ... preferred the verdict of their bishops to those of Turkish judges' (Woodhouse 1998: 103). But it would be wrong to imply that the Christians did not face real disadvantages in the Empire. Non-Muslims paid extra taxes and they were treated as definitely inferior in status (Jelavich 1983a: 49). The tribute of children, by which the elite Janissary regiments were recruited after 1575, was resented especially by the Albanians who rose up against it (Woodhouse 1998: 113). But many Christian families accepted it because it offered the prospect of upward social mobility for their children (Malcolm 1998: 96). (It was abolished in the late 18th century because the reduction of the Christian population in some areas was depriving the state of too much tax revenue (Woodhouse 1998: 113)).

The Romanian principalities of Moldavia and Wallachia, which fell to the Turks by the end of the 15th century, were not directly swallowed up in the Ottoman Empire. They were retained as captive but self-governing satellite states for two more centuries under a native Romanian aristocracy (Hupchick 1994: 21; Djuvara 1995: 23–32). Mass colonization by Turkish settlers was generally rare, confined to a few areas of Bulgaria, Thrace and Macedonia (Malcolm 1998: 94). There was no equivalent of the Catholic Inquisition and one Bulgarian expert asserts that, for the first two centuries of Ottoman rule, 'the lot of Balkan Christians within the empire was better than that enjoyed by most of the general population of west European states' (Hupchick 1994: 149).

The Ottoman Empire allowed talented Balkan figures, irrespective of their religious origins, to walk on a world stage, something which the totalitarian constraints of communism or the visa restrictions of the 1990s have effectively prevented in our own day.

Jason Goodwin has written:

> In an empire that stretched from the Danube to the Nile, the people of the Balkans burst on to a wider world. Ottoman bureaucrats and soldiers, drawn from the villages of Southeastern Europe, walked on an enormous stage. Forty-two grand viziers, the highest office in the empire, were Albanian by birth, and the greatest of all, Mehmet Sokulla, was a Serb. Under the Ottomans, Slavs, Greeks and Albanians ruled over Egypt, terrorised Austria, staffed the Orthodox Church...

> The Ottomans harvested Balkan talent and discouraged provincial naivete in favour of a dry, metropolitan understanding of the world's ways. They fostered ethnic and religious pluralism cemented by constant negotiations, facesaving gestures, threats and backroom deals. Disputes were settled in the imperial capital ... not in bloody mountain battles. Provincial delegates from all over the empire regularly descended on the capital, bribing and begging their way to the fount of power like modern-day lobbyists. (Goodwin 1999)

When Venice tried to re-establish itself in the Greek Peloponnese in the 17th century, their punitive taxation and proselytising efforts made

Greek peasants welcome back the Turks (McNeill 1978: 43). One Turkish historian, Samiha Ayverdi, has claimed that 'there would be no Serbs, no Bulgarians, Romanians and Greeks, had not the Ottoman Empire conquered the Balkans. If the ever present and intimidating Catholic appetite had not been able to devour them, it has been so because of the Turkish invasion and conquest' (Bora n.d. [1994]: 106). Such interpretations of the Ottoman era have been airbrushed out of much of the Balkan Christian consciousness by nationalist historiography. General Ratko Mladić, the Serbian commander who waged war against unarmed Muslim civilians in Bosnia after April 1992, justified his actions by invoking a past of Ottoman cruelty: 'Serbian mothers watched children taken away by Muslims to become Sultan's slaves, to be sold as slaves' (*The Guardian* 1993: 18 April).

Serbian racial propaganda encouraged similar actions in Kosovo during 1989–9. It was conveniently forgotten that during the Ottoman era, Albanian clans helped preserve and protect treasured Orthodox churches and monasteries dotting the Albanian landscape (Udovicki 1997b: 28–9). According to Serbian accounts, 'the Albanians protected Orthodox cemeteries from desecration because they knew that the remains of their own ancestors might lie there' (Vickers 1998: 27). What also partly explains their behaviour is the influence of syncretism (mixing together) of religious and folk beliefs in this part of Europe. Christian baptism was popular among the Muslims: it was thought to guarantee them a longer life as well as protection against mental illness or being eaten by wolves (Malcolm 1998: 129). Syncretism's hold may explain the lack of religious animosity at an interpersonal level in the Albanian lands over long periods. In Albania the diversity of faiths has traditionally been accepted without demur. Especially during the early phase of a bureaucratic Ottoman state ruling over diverse populations, 'Christian and Muslim societies lived together in relative peace and understanding, although with considerable mutual exclusivism' (Jelavich 1983a: 45).

ORTHODOXY

The Orthodox Church enjoyed more authority in the Ottoman Empire than it would in the Empire's avowedly Christian successor states. Under the Sultan it was more than a religious institution. It formed a substitute for secular leadership and preserved the language and imperial memories of some of the Balkan peoples (Kitromilides 1994:

178). The monasteries were important in preserving cultural values later to be politicised by nationalism (Hoesch 1972: 108). In mid-18th-century Bulgaria, they were responsible for the first stirrings of national awareness (Pundeff 1971: 99). Religious art conveyed the symbols and portraits of former rulers and reminded the viewer of the great Byzantine Empire of the past (Jelavich 1983a: 174–5). Among an almost wholly illiterate population, '[D]ecasyllabic epics chanted by bards and easily memorised by generations of listeners' were instrumental in preserving national identity (Vickers 1998: 16). Although the Patriarchate collaborated closely with the Ottoman government, the Orthodox Church as a whole 'kept alive the idea that its members were distinct and superior and that the Muslims were transgressors on Christian territory' (Jelavich 1983a: 174). In much of the Ottoman Balkans, Muslim, Serb, Bulgarian and Greek villages might exist side by side without much of the mixing that could diffuse their identities (Vickers 1995: 11).

As late as 1610 there were ten times more Catholics than Muslims in Kosovo (Vickers 1998: 22). But a great many Albanians thereafter converted to Islam. The lure of government service and the incentive of paying lower taxes counted much for a people often felt to have an instrumental attitude to religion. Forcible conversions were not unknown in parts of the Ottoman Empire subject to an external threat. In parts of Bulgaria, there was pressure to convert owing to its strategic location (Crampton 1997: 34). Around 1690 large numbers of Serbian families, led by the Patriarch of Pécs Arsenije IV, left Kosovo and fled across the Danube to escape Turkish revenge for supporting the Austrians in their Balkan incursion (Vickers 1998: 27). Leopold I offered asylum to them in return for many enlisting as guards on the contested frontier with Turkey in what is now Croatia. The departure of many Slavs altered the ethnic composition of Kosovo but such population movements were still relatively untypical of the Balkans. It was more commonly associated with Western Europe where, also in 1690, after the defeat of a rebellion in Ireland, the Catholic majority were oppressed by laws which for several generations prevented them worshipping their faith openly, forty years after many had been banished to the less fertile west of the island.

As an institution of the Ottoman Empire, the Orthodox Church was supranationalist in form. The Greek Church organization in Constantinople consistently resisted the spread of anti-Ottoman national movements among its multiethnic membership (Hupchick 1994: 109).

The attempt of Patriarch Cyril Loukaris to establish a bridge between Orthodoxy and the Protestant Reformation was undone by Catholic intrigues and the Cretan-born patriarch was executed in 1638 (Arnakis 1963: 132). This Orthodox churchman showed rare interest in Enlightenment thought, but Greek horizons expanded in the 18th century as international commerce fell increasingly into the hands of Greeks, Armenians, Jews, as well as other Orthodox Christians (Jelavich 1983a: 72). The relatively low standing of commerce in Ottoman Muslim society gave the Christians an important opening. Recruitment to Islam declined as Greek fortunes rose (McNeill 1978: 40–1). The most privileged of the Greeks were the Phanariot oligarchs, their names deriving from the Phanar or lighthouse district of Constantinople where most of the Orthodox Christians lived and where the Patriarchate was located (Jelavich 1983a: 54). In the 18th century, the princely thrones of Wallachia and Moldavia were sold by the Ottoman sultans to ambitious and grasping Phanariots. They energetically fleeced the local inhabitants, gathering as much revenue as they could before being recalled by the Sultan (Chirot 1976; Roberts 1951). They ruled their domains in Byzantine style, surrounded by hollow ritual and sycophantic landowners and desperate peasants (Hupchick 1994: 111). Late in the 18th century, as the Greek position in the imperial bureaucracy strengthened, some minds dreamt that it might only be a matter of time before they took over the Ottoman Empire in its entirety (Woodhouse 1998: 127; Wolff 1974: 162).

RUSSIA CHALLENGES OTTOMAN POWER

The seeds of nationalism grew out of the accelerating decline of the Ottoman Empire in the 18th century. Local chieftains, such as the notorious Ali Pasha of Ioannina who defied Ottoman control from his redoubt in Epirus for over three decades, carved out their own statelets (Fleming 1999). The decline of agriculture and commerce which resulted from the collapse of central authority, hampered the merchant community dominated by Balkan Orthodox peoples. Conditions in the Hapsburg Empire and Russia were improving as the Ottoman realms were increasingly sunk in anarchy and corruption. Merchants, due to their opportunities to travel, were 'in a good position to compare systems of government' (Jelavich 1983a: 185). Greeks, in particular, were often well educated, and they became acquainted with the doctrines of the European Enlightenment.

Ottoman troubles partly stemmed from the pressures being exerted by Russia. In the second half of the 18th century, all of the Ottomans' north Black Sea coastal possessions were lost to the reinvigorated northern empire. In 1710, under Peter the Great, Russian armies had entered the Balkan lands for the first time and advanced as far as Iaşi. When Peter called upon Balkan Christians to rise in aid of his army, the call went largely unheeded. In the Danubian provinces, the popular saying that 'a change of sovereign is a luxury of fools' may have encouraged peasants to remain bystanders in imperial power struggles. Moldavia and Wallachia were then ruled by enlightened *hospodars* (governors). Dimitrie Cantemir, a gifted writer, joined Peter in 1710 on being promised that Moldavia would become an independent state under the protection of the Tsar (Jelavich 1983a: 101). He fled to Russia on the failure of the Tsar's military campaign. In Wallachia Constantin Brancoveanu adopted a policy of balance between competing imperial forces. His 26-year-long rule saw a flowering of the arts in Wallachia. A distinctive Brancovan style was evident in the religious architecture and sculpture of the period. Elementary schooling developed along with literature and printing. Brancoveanu was one of the most enlightened rulers seen in the Balkans in modern times.[1] He remained in office until 1714 when he and his four sons were beheaded by the Ottoman authorities on suspicion of treason because of their links with Austria. Their refusal to disavow the Christian faith and so be spared the executioner's axe has given them an honoured place in Romanian history. Indeed their sacrifice is seen as testimony of the Romanian ability to remain true to the Christian faith even while submerged in the Ottoman Empire (Djuvara 1995: 156).

In the 18th century, Russia started to advance the claim that it was the legitimate successor to the empire of Byzantium. The marriage in 1472 of the then-Russian tsar to the niece of the last Byzantine emperor provided the basis for this claim (Woodhouse 1998: 109). In 1774 Tsarina Catherine the Great extracted from the Sultan the right to appoint consuls in the Ottoman Empire who could make representations on behalf of its Christian subjects (Woodhouse 1998: 120; Jelavich 1983a: 69–70). There were already significant religious, educational and trading links between Russia and Greece, Bulgaria, and tiny Montenegro, the last an impoverished principality which could not have existed without foreign assistance, especially from Russia (Hoesch 1972: 123–4; Crampton 1997: 55; Doder 1979: 233). Between 1787 and 1792 Russia fought a war with Turkey whose aim was to partition the Ottoman Empire and establish Russian control of Constantinople and the Bosporus straits. Dreaming of restoring Byzantium with a Russian prince on the throne, Catherine christened one of her grandchildren Constantine and Greek nurses were hired to teach him their language. Catherine also proposed to set up an independent kingdom of Dacia, including Moldavia, Wallachia and Bessarabia, proposing for the throne her lover and general, Potemkin (Wolff 1974: 71). In these grandiose plans the Austrians were to be awarded the western Balkans right down to Greece, the first of several partitions of the region envisaged by the great powers.

Military failure aborted Russian hopes but for the first time Britain, the dominant maritime power, became aware of potentially conflicting British and Russian interests in the Near East. The realisation gave birth to longstanding international tensions as these two European powers, and eventually others, sought to fill the vacuum left by the retreating Ottoman Empire on their own terms. Britain, fearful of too great an increase in Russian power, would soon become the chief supporter of the Ottoman Empire against Russian encroachments.

NATIONALISM DISRUPTS THE EASTERN WORLD

The ideology of nationalism would eventually overwhelm the sprawling bureaucratic empire in Constantinople which had compartmentalised its subjects into separate religious and ethnic units (L. Carl Brown 1984: 78). The rise of commercial elites and the first stirrings of a secular intelligentsia saw a gradual shift away from religion to language as a bond of unity in the Christian millets (Vickers 1998: 28). But the national idea was slow to take root and flower. It encountered stubborn resistance from traditional elements in the Christian population, not least from the Orthodox Church. The isolation of self-contained communities, exacerbated by Balkan geography and the decline of commerce in the lawless times of the 18th century, would hamper the diffusion of revolutionary ideas emanating from Western Europe.

Barbara Jelavich has written that the immediate causes of the first revolts, which history has described as nationalist uprisings, lay in the internal condition of the peninsula (Jelavich 1983a: 92). The failure of the Ottoman government to maintain law and order, especially in the countryside, required peaceful Christian as well as Muslim populations to organize their own protection. When the Serbs rose in revolt in 1804, they were reacting against local atrocities perpetrated on the Christians of the Belgrade region by that city's undisciplined janissary garrison (Hupchick 1994: 150). The Serbs claimed to be acting in the interests of the Sultan when their forces defeated a rebellious governor who had terrorised members of the Orthodox millet. Only when the central government proved unable to defend its Serb subjects from lawless officials, did the Serbs (increasingly influenced by nationalist ideas brought by fellow Serbs from north of the Danube) turn their struggle into one for autonomy and eventually independence.

Tudor Vladimirescu's 1820 revolution in Wallachia, ever since hailed as a landmark in the drive for Romanian independence, was similar to the Serbian one in origins and aims (Georgescu 1992: 111–14). It was not directed against the Sultan, who was asked to restore old conditions. Vladimirescu's proclamation partly read:

> Brothers living in Wallachia, whatever your nationality, no law prevents a man to meet evil with evil ... How long shall we suffer the dragons that swallow us alive, above us, both clergy and politicians, to suck our blood? How long shall we be enslaved? ... Neither God nor the Sultan approves of such treatment of their faithful. Therefore brothers, come all of you and deal out evil to bring evil to an end, that we might fare well. (Jelavich 1983a: 210)

Peasants eagerly supported such a manifesto promising the end of local tyranny. But their goals were social rather than national ones. The majority of peasants had local attachments based around their families, their land, and possibly local churches. The time was far in the future before there would be widespread attachment to the idea that the nation-state should command the primary allegiance of the citizen. New Balkan states would have to strive mightily through the school system and the army to create a concept of patriotic citizenship which would appeal to Balkan peasants, many of whom remained illiterate in the century and a half after the 1789 French Revolution.

Even on the eve of the Greek struggle against Ottoman rule, which has often appeared the most pristine of Balkan national uprisings, national goals seemed unfocused and uncertain. In his history of Greece, at the end of the chapter called 'The Dark Age of Greece (1453–1800)' C.M. Woodhouse has written: '... the question was whether Greece should become an annexe of Russia or even conceivably of Austria; a colony of Britain or France; a private empire of Ali Pasha of Ioannina; or whether it should remain, by virtue of the mutual cancellation of contending forces, a province of a salvaged Ottoman Empire. The last thing anybody contemplated was an independent nation-state' (Woodhouse 1998: 124).

Each of the Balkan national movements went through a long gestation phase that involved the creation of a literary language and a revival of interest in the pre-Ottoman history of the people. The Romanian grammar written by Gheorghe Sincai and Samuil Micu in 1780 was the first attempt to depict Romanian as a Latin tongue, with Latin roots and inflection (Berend 1987: 31). As Uniate theological students in Rome they had been inspired by the monuments of the Roman Empire, especially the famous column of Trajan and its scenes depicting ancient Dacia, once the name of their homeland. Their Bulgarian contemporary, a monk on Mount Athos called Paiisi, wrote books recalling 'the last great days of the medieval Bulgarian church and state' (Crampton 1997: 47). Past greatness was invoked in order to guard against the danger of Bulgaria surrendering to Greek cultural influences. Indeed, it would be Greek pretensions to revive a Byzantine empire under their auspices, more than Ottoman religious or cultural threats that, at different times, would galvanise the Romanian, Bulgarian, and eventually Albanian national movements.

In order to move from a Europe of kings and emperors to a Europe of nations, disparate groups of people had to be convinced that, despite their obvious differences, they shared an identity that could be the basis of collective action (Thiesse 1999: 12). History had to be radically reinterpreted and made highly selective. For the sense of a nation enjoying a continuous past to be invoked, the intermingling of people, their constant migratory movements, and major changes of political culture or religious allegiance had to be ignored or concealed (Bringe 1995: 13). The importance of medieval Balkan kingdoms had to be grossly inflated, their maximum size seen as being the natural and proper boundaries for new nations-in-waiting (Jelavich 1983a: 27). Prior occupation of a territory needed to be insisted upon and the claims of rivals devalued. Thus, the Romanians usually insisted upon the Daco-Romanian continuity of a people of mixed Latin and Thracian origins occupying what is post-1918 Romania. Meanwhile, many Hungarians used to insist that Romanians originated south of the Danube as pastoral Latin speakers who only crossed into present-day Romania after the arrival in the Danubian basin of the Hungarians (Hupchick 1994: 66).

The breakdown of the old Ottoman order, economic crises, the rumbles of distant revolutions, and the machinations of local powers, produced upheaval and acute uncertainty in the Balkan lands at the beginning of the 19th century. The climate of insecurity proved conducive for the spread of the belief among educated people that they were part of a national group which had a mission to establish its role in the forefront of history. The appeal of visionary nationalism was greatly strengthened by Johann Gottfried Herder, a late 18th-century German philosopher. He 'saw individuals in society only as part of the *Volk*, which can be roughly translated as the people, better, the national group. Herder believed that art, music, literature, local customs, laws—in fact most forms of cultural and political life—were manifestations of the unique spirit, or *Volksgeist*, of each people' (Jelavich 1983a: 172).

The influence of the school of German Romantic thought associated with Herder stimulated an interest in rediscovering the history of the Balkan peoples. When Herder said that the Slavs possessed superior moral and spiritual qualities which would make them 'the coming leaders of Europe', his ideas were bound to be taken very seriously in Eastern Europe (Pfaff 1995). Ethnography—a completely new field of intellectual enquiry created by the Romantics—placed 'emphasis on the importance of peasant folk song and legends as the primary vehicles for expressing a given people's native culture in its purest, most emotional form' (Hupchick 1994: 131). The emphasis often placed by Romantics on distinctive folk cultures undiluted by literary conventions or by languages spoken by neighbouring but different ethnic groups, had obvious application for promoters of political nationalism. It was only a small leap from emphasising the unique value of every ethnic group based on its shared history and language to insisting that the very same ethnic group enjoyed the 'natural right' to possess a political organization—a nation-state—of its own (Hupchick 1994: 133).

The backing that 19th century foreign scholars gave to cultural nationalists in Southeast Europe was sometimes important in assisting the rise of a fully-fledged political nationalism. Austrian and German scholars assisted Vuk Karadžić in promoting a commonly accepted and unified Serbo-Croatian language (Wilson 1970: 388–94). The distinguished philologist Jacob Grimm had no hesitation in ranking Serb poetry alongside that of Homer (Gallagher 1999: 47). In the 1820s, the French scholar Claude Furiel took it upon himself to prove that the national identity and cultural heritage of the modern Greeks sprang directly from their ancient forebears (Thiesse 1999: 12). Later, the Scottish scholar R.W. Seton-Watson, following in a long line of middle-class Scots who had assisted the Greek struggle for independence, championed the cultural rights of nationalities being subjected to assimilation in the Hungarian domains of the Hapsburg empire.

The story of the 19th century would in large measure be bound up with the rise of the nationality principle as a means of politically organizing humanity. But parallel processes of nation building and national integration involving claims to the same territory and the same populations would create violent collisions across Europe, not least in the Balkans. Here Ottoman multiculturalism had allowed distinct religious and ethnic groups to coexist in multinational territories. These populations were now lured into mutually hostile 'imagined communities' as the decline of the Empire gathered pace (Kitromilides 1994: 185). Any hope that the Enlightenment could spread its liberal and critical spirit into Balkan lands shaped by autocratic rule was dashed by the rise of nationalism, itself hopefully viewed in the beginning as one of the liberal expressions of 18th-century progressive thought (Kitromilides 1994: 65). Individual liberty was stifled by the rise of a new conformist and collective doctrine which insisted that the nation-state was the normal political division for mankind and that citizens should not possess any higher allegiance (Jelavich 1983a: 237).

Political nationalism opened up an era of escalating Christian–Muslim conflict. But it also involved 'the rejection of the shared Christian identity of the Orthodox peoples of the Balkans which had been preserved under Ottoman rule' (Kitromilides 1994: 59). Rejecting a common Christian past, intellectuals shaped by Romantic ideas produced narratives based on the distinctive history of each Balkan people. Mazzini's formula for the rights of nations, 'every nation a state and only one state for the entire nation', would be eagerly embraced by East European ideologues, many of whom possessed not a shred of the liberalism that motivated this enlightened if often naive Italian patriot (Rusinow 1995: 354; Jászi 1964: 248).

THE SPARK: THE GREEK WAR OF INDEPENDENCE

The Greek national struggle involved very few of the ordinary people who would make up the citizens of the Greek state upon its establishment in 1830. The Phanariots of the Danubian principalities played a prominent role in the national movement. Here they exercised political authority as agents of the Sultan, and dreams of empire undoubtedly inspired some of them. Alexander Ypsilantis, the son of a former governor of Wallachia, was the standard bearer of the Greek revolt in Moldavia, seen as the catalyst for the ensuing independence struggle. From a membership list of over a thousand, merchants, many of whose businesses had failed or were in difficulties, comprised over half the revolutionaries (Jelavich 1983a: 206). Military men, clergy and Greek notables also joined, but peasants were wary, unenthused perhaps by the visibility of the Phanariots, who had shown an uncommon skill for exploiting them when in the service of the Sultan. Many ordinary Greeks served with the Turkish forces until late in the Greek revolt. When the Ottoman fleet was destroyed at the Battle of Navarino in 1827, with the loss of 8,000 men, the majority of these sailors were Greeks (Jelavich 1983a: 226). Two of the leading Ottoman commanders in the war, Khurshad Pasha and Mohammed Reshid Pasha were by birth Orthodox Christians who had converted to Islam for the sake of a career in the Sultan's service (Woodhouse 1998: 140). The Orthodox Church was suspicious or hostile to the claims of revolutionary nationalism. The classic statement of the Church's position came in the work known as 'Paternal Instruction' (1798), probably written by the future Patriarch, Gregory VI, 'which counselled the pious to submit to Ottoman rule and warned against the pernicious consequences of revolutionary action for the souls of the faithful' (Kitromilides 1994: 179–80). Much later the Serbian hierarchy displayed its hostility to nationalism by vehemently opposing cultural and linguistic reforms meant to solidify Serbian identity in the new state that emerged after 1830 (Kitromilides 1994: 180).

Non-Greeks emerged as the leading defenders of Greek liberty, a not untypical element in future European nationality movements where it was gifted or restless individuals, unsure of their own identity, who proved most receptive to the nationalist ideology. George Koundouriotis was descended from the Albanian invaders of Greece in the 14th century 'and spoke Greek only with difficulty' (Woodhouse 1998: 139). His principal colleague, John Kolettis, was a Vlach who had been Ali Pasha's court doctor at Ioannina (Woodhouse 1998: 139). Few of the Greek fighters for independence were aware of their putative country's great classical heritage. According to Hupchick, '[T]hey only learnt of it later from West European classicists, who had sponsored pro-Greek Western assistance for the rebels in the first place in the mistaken notion that the Ottoman Greeks were the living embodiment of their classical ancestors' (Hupchick 1994: 110).

It was not just that paragon of intellectual romanticism, Lord Byron, but Shelley, Goethe and Schiller who unleashed a storm of enthusiasm for Philhellenism which cautious governments in London and Paris eventually had to bow before. Acts of cruelty were committed by both sides but it was the Ottoman atrocities against the Greeks that moved the liberal European conscience. The Ottoman massacre of Greeks on the island of Chios in 1823, immortalised in Delacroix's painting, enabled West European public opinion to overrule governments that might have wished to limit Greek ambitions (Woodhouse 1969: 73–4). In 1824, a series of privately financed loans which, in effect, made the City of London the financier of the revolution, proved critical in ensuring Greek success.

Greeks learned to promote a mythical heritage in their relations with the great powers. It usually proved unavailing but sometimes earned success. Thus in 1981 a British Foreign Office minister said, according to one British historian of Greece, that Greece's joining of the European Union was 'fitting repayment by Europe of the cultural and political debt that we all owe to a Greek heritage almost 3,000 years old' (Torode 1993).

The idealistic and broad-minded strand of British public opinion which, spurred on by humanistic or romantic impulses, wanted to see justice done in the Balkans would often collide with a cautious and calculating Foreign Office. The 19th-century British policy of propping up the illiberal Ottoman Empire was matched in the 1990s by a preference for dealing with tyrannical Yugoslav ethnic politicians and ignoring the minorities and mixed populations that found themselves the victims of 'ethnic cleansing' or enforced segregation.

Initially, stateless Balkan Christians expected far more from imperial Russia. Large Greek and Bulgarian communities were established in Odessa by the early 1800s. The first leader of a liberated Greece, Ioannis Capodistrias had risen in the Russian service to hold the post of foreign minister under Tsar Alexander I. But Russia had grown increasingly cautious in its Balkan policies after it had nearly fallen victim to the force of revolutionary nationalism when France's Napoleon I invaded the sprawling empire in 1812. By the 1820s the Russian preference was to try and dominate the Ottoman Empire from within. Russian–Ottoman cooperation precluded any major Russian effort to support the Serbian rebellion of Milos Obrenović. In 1821, Ypsilantis and the Greek rebels in the Danubian principalities were similarly discouraged by the Tsar (Jelavich 1983a: 211). Future events would show that Balkan national movements could only receive Russian backing provided that they subordinated themselves to Russian state interests. The ruler of Montenegro, Prince Bishop Peter II (1813–1851), whose west Balkan statelet had the longest engagement with Russia, told a Serb diplomat during his reign: 'I like Russia, but I do not like to bear the price of its aid on every occasion. I am tired of it and wish to throw off that yoke' (Doder 1979: 233). Similar frustrations were expressed in April 1999 by Zeljko Raznjatović, the Serb nationalist warlord better known as 'Arkan', who complained bitterly of Russia's refusal to 'open its nuclear hangars and target them on America' during NATO's military action against Serbia.[2]

Shifting great-power disagreements frustrated nationalist aspirations but brought a reprieve for Muslim populations in the Balkans. They faced an uncertain future if national movements, increasingly inspired by anti-Islamic sentiments, were to triumph across the peninsula. The nature of their relationship with Constantinople meant that there was no incentive to promote their own Balkan Islamic nationalism. In Bosnia, where the largest concentration of Muslims in the Balkans was to be found, the Ottoman authorities allowed the Muslim Slav majority which was most numerous in the cities and controlled most of the land, to be effectively self-ruling. Indeed the Bosnian Muslim nobility was the only 'native' and Slavic aristocracy in the Ottoman Balkans (Rusinow 1995: 367). One source claims that 'indigenous regulations' that were not characteristic of Ottoman rule elsewhere, such as the *ajans* (town councils), were left untouched until the 19th century (Zulfikarpasić 1998: 86). The Bosnian Muslims enjoyed a contractual relationship with the Sultan not unlike that which Ulster Protestants had with the British crown or Saxon settlers in Eastern Europe enjoyed with various dynastic rulers. They would be loyal subjects as long as the religious and landholding customs which defined their communities were respected by the distant emperors (Miller 1978: 214–21). Bosnian Muslims defended Ottoman frontiers, provided soldiers for the Sultan's wars, and it was Bosnians and Albanians who went to Egypt in 1798 to fight the French under Napoleon (McCarthy 1996: 72). Mehmet Ali, the Albanian born in the Macedonian port city of Kavalla, came to rule Egypt like a pharaoh in the first third of the 19th century (L. Carl Brown 1984: 43). After 1880 Sultan Abdul Hamid II's palace guard and 1st army corps consisted of Albanians whom he trusted above his other subjects (Stavrianos 1958: 501). Like the Ulster Protestants who provided a disproportionate number of military commanders in the British Empire, the Balkan Muslims were prepared to turn into rebels if their local customs and rights were encroached upon. Bosnian notables, opposed to modernising reforms from Constantinople, revolted in 1849 and 1850 (Malcolm 1994: 124–5). Like the Ulster Protestants, who took a similar step to resist Irish Home Rule, their privileged position in a sprawling empire defined by religion as much as anything else, meant that down to the 21st century, they would remain rare Europeans who remained partly stuck in the age of pre-nationalism.

GREECE AFTER LIBERATION

The new Greek state, which was internationally recognised in 1832, did not leave a gaping hole in the Ottoman Empire despite the fierceness of the struggle to create it. It was composed of only 800,000 people, one quarter of the Greek inhabitants of the empire. Endemic factionalism among powerful families seeking to grab the levers of power would dim its prestige and disappoint many of its former backers. Ironically, the Greek world role, strong under the Ottomans, shrunk after independence (McNeill 1978: 53). In the 1830s there was more migration of Greeks from Greece to Turkey than vice versa (Woodhouse 1998: 161). Perhaps only if the dream possessed by one of the more far-seeing Greek leaders, Rhigos Pheraios, of a multi-national Balkan state in which Greek was the language of administration, had become a reality, could such a parochial anticlimax have been avoided (Woodhouse 1998: 167). Most of the Greek kingdom's new subjects retained a firmly localist world view. An abortive attempt in 1854 to take Thessaly and Epirus from the Ottomans gained almost no support from the Greek population (Woodhouse 1998: 167).

The strategic location of the Greek state meant that the great powers interfered regularly in local politics. The different powers promoted their own factions which undermined effective government (McNeill 1978: 52). The British ambassador to Athens, Sir Edmund Lyons, wrote in 1841: 'A Greece truly independent is an absurdity. Greece is Russian or she is English; and since she must not be Russian, it is necessary that she be English' (Goldsworthy 1998: 27). During the Cold War, a similar domineering stance by the USA undermined liberal government and was enormously resented in Greece.

C. M. Woodhouse has written that even the British Philhellenes usually loved the land, the language, the antiquities, but not the people. 'If only, they thought, the people could be more like the British scholars and gentlemen; or failing that ... if only they were more like their own ancestors; or better still, if only they were not there at all' (Woodhouse 1969: 10, 38–9). In 1832 Greece was not even a party to the international treaty which settled the terms under which a German prince ascended the throne (Clogg 1992: 47). The appointment of Otho, a German Catholic prince, over Greek heads made it difficult for him to acquire legitimacy and his deposition in 1862 was followed by a long series of fruitless attempts to experiment with rulers who remained more attached to European royal circles than to Greece. In 1850 the Don Pacifico incident occurred in which Britain's nationalistic Foreign Secretary, Lord Palmerston, treated Greece in the way that American Presidents would bully Latin American 'banana republics' (Ridley 1972: 512–20). Don Pacifico was a British subject born in Gibraltar whose home had been plundered in an anti-Jewish demonstration in Athens in the late 1840s. He submitted exorbitant claims for damages and Palmerston sent the Mediterranean squadron to blockade Piraeus in enforcement of a whole series of demands (Woodhouse 1998: 164). In 1854 British and French forces actually occupied Piraeus to compel King Otho to renounce his alliance with Russia (Woodhouse 1998: 167).

The mid-1850s were a period of acute anxiety when the cluster of issues surrounding the decline of the Ottoman Empire, and known as the Eastern Question, boiled over into the Crimean War (Jelavich 1983a: 186). Britain, fearing that Russia would seize Constantinople and be in a position to disrupt its communications with India, fought a war lasting from 1853 to 1855 in the north Black Sea area, the only area where the two competitors could meet in direct conflict (Jelavich 1983a: 190). It ended in a technical Anglo-French-Ottoman victory but would be followed by future tremors in the next sixty years before a European conflagration erupted in 1914.

THE POWERS SPONSOR AND FRUSTRATE NATIONALITY MOVEMENTS

Balkan statelets would be frustrated at being dispensable pawns on the great-power chessboard. But the powerless have always had some weapons in the Balkans and Balkan national movements and states were able to exploit competition among the powers. The Greeks learnt that to advance their national aims, they 'must associate at a moment of crisis with a victorious great power' (Woodhouse 1998: 168). Similarly, Serbian fortunes were 'closely tied to the ebb and flow of European politics and repeated attempts to obtain Hapsburg and Russian support' (Jelavich 1983a: 203).

Skilful local politicians could occasionally appeal to the desire of a Western leader for glory. Probably no better illustration of this is provided than in the relationship between France's Emperor Napoleon III (1852–70) and Romanian nationalists seeking to achieve statehood. In 1851 Napoleon proclaimed himself the protector of the Catholics under Ottoman rule. Emerging as a sincere believer in the principle of nationalism, this impulsive ruler who preferred to view his illustrious ancestor the first Napoleon as a liberator of captive peoples, was keen to encourage nationalist sentiment among Latin peoples (Anderson 1966: 155). Upper-class Romanians had for some time identified with the Latinity of French culture (Kellogg 1995: 6). Romania was variously characterized by politicians lobbying for support in Paris as an outpost of Latin culture or as an island of Latinity in a sea of Slavic and Turkish barbarianism (Campbell 1970: 22–3). Napoleon III saw a way of enhancing his country's prestige by preserving the balance of power in Eastern Europe. He supported the union of the Danubian principalities of Wallachia and Moldavia which was realised in 1859 in order to prevent Russia controlling the mouth of the Danube and linking up with its South Slav brethren (Anderson 1966: 150–1). Lord Clarendon, the British Foreign Secretary did not regard the fate of Moldavia, 'a little barbarous province at the end of Europe', as worth justifying a break with France, so he agreed (Anderson 1966: 152). Not surprisingly, the Romanians saw France as a truly reliable friend ready to back their quest for statehood.

Romanian independence was acquired largely peacefully in stages between 1856 and 1881, thanks to the negotiating skills displayed by the first generation of nationalist leaders. The unification of Wallachia and Moldavia in 1859, like that of the Romanian kingdom with Transylvania and Bessarabia in 1918, was forced through by 'a group of men intent on "taking a chance" offered by local and international circumstances at that moment in time' (Alexandrescu 1998: 70). In an audacious move they substituted the Cyrillic alphabet with a Latin one, making Romania the only predominantly Orthodox country where Cyrillic was not in use. Eventually, the shortcomings of the Romanian social structure would dim this initial achievement. Romania lacked an indigenous middle class and professional elite, Greeks, Jews, Germans and even Armenians predominating here (Anderson 1966: 154 n.2). Much of the peasantry was landless and would remain so despite the land reform of Prince Alexandru Cuza, the first ruler of a self-governing Romania. The predominance of the small peasant holding as the basic unit of production was far more marked in Bulgaria and other Ottoman lands than it was in Romania (Todorova 1994: 61). In European terms, these Danubian provinces were exceptional for allowing the enslavement of a large population of gypsies. Slavery was abolished between 1843 and 1855, liberal nationalists viewing it as necessary in order to hasten the modernisation of society (Achim 1998: 95–7). The legacy of rural poverty and oppression, stemming in particular from Phanariot rule, is one that hampered Romanian development and may have directly contributed to extreme bouts of misrule characterising the country in the 1930s and later during the second half of the communist era.

Despite the often flimsy internal basis for creating national states, Balkan nationalism drew encouragement from the effective collapse during the 1848 revolutions of the efforts of reactionary dynastic empires like Russia and Austria-Hungary to roll back the rising tide of nationalism. The amalgamation of the patchwork of dukedoms, Church lands, and minor kingdoms in Central Europe and the Italian peninsula into unified German and Italian states, soon capable of making their mark in European affairs, gave them even greater encouragement. The ability of Cavour, the Prime Minister of Piedmont, to gain control of much of the Italian peninsula, was admired in the Balkans. There was no shortage of leaders who saw themselves as capable of uniting dispersed peoples like the Serbs, Greeks and Romanians after a Piedmontese-style national liberation struggle.

The mid-19th-century intellectual mood legitimised expansionary nationalism of this kind. Charles Darwin's theory of natural selection based on 'the survival of the fittest' was applied to nation-state politics by Napoleon III and the German Chancellor Otto von Bismarck (1862–1890) (Hupchick 1994: 131–2). Certain Greek politicians, dwelling on historic memories of their ancestors role in forging a great East Mediterranean civilization, promoted the goal of a Greater Greece based on the Byzantine Empire. In 1844, John Kolettis, a Hellenised Vlach launched this 'Great Idea' in a widely quoted speech to the Greek constituent assembly:

> The Greek kingdom is not the whole of Greece, but only a part, the smallest and poorest part. A native is not only someone who lives within this Kingdom, but also one who lives in Ioannina, in Thessaly, in Serres, in Adrianople, in Constantinople, in Trebizond, in Crete, in Samos and in any land associated with Greek history or the Greek race. (Clogg 1992: 48)

The Greek populations, numbering several millions, scattered through Asia Minor, were often foremost in the minds of Greek irredentists. In the large seaport cities of the eastern Aegean, many were prosperous, educated, and westernised (Clogg 1992: 54). But in the interior, their lifestyles were often 'little different from that of their Turkish peasant neighbours'. While they clung tenaciously to the Orthodox religion, many, particularly the womenfolk, spoke only Turkish (Clogg 1992: 55). At least in the early 19th century, 'few of these Turkish-speaking Greeks, the Karamanlides, had much consciousness of being Greek and strenuous efforts by the Greek kingdom were made to instil in them a sense of Greek ancestry' (Clogg 1992: 55). Similarly, the Romanian government before 1914 set aside large sums of money for the education of Romanian speakers living in the southern Balkans and known as the Âromanii, the Macedo-Romanians, or the Vlachs. The motive was to prevent their absorption by the Slav peoples or the Greeks in whose states they lived (Seton-Watson 1934: 383–4).

Far more momentous would be the efforts of Serb intellectuals to reach out to Serbs in Kosovo, which was seen as the cradle of Serbian consciousness and historic valour even though it remained under Ottoman rule until 1912. In 1844, the same year as the idea of creating a Greater Greece was publicly launched, Ilija Garašanin, who did much to build up Serbian institutions in the middle years of the 19th century, drew up the 'Načertanije', or draft plan for the lands to be contained in an expanded Serbian state. He believed that the imperial mission, interrupted in the middle ages by the Ottoman invasion, had to be resumed again. But unlike Kolettis's scheme, his plans were in fact kept secret until 1906 (Judah 1997: 56–8).

PAN-SLAVISM AND BULGARIAN REVOLTS

Bold *national* schemes were briefly overshadowed by the Pan-Slavic movements sponsored by Russia. The Pan-Slavs were influential in the 1860s and 1870s and they stood for the removal of all Slavic peoples from foreign rule and their organization 'into a federation of states in which Russia would take the leading role' (Jelavich 1983a: 353). Pan-Slav efforts brought hundreds of Bulgarian and other Slav students to study in Russia in this period. In 1877, when Ottoman forces were menacing Serbia, the Pan-Slavists were able to generate a powerful wave of solidarity with their South Slav brothers. In Leo Tolstoy's *Anna Karenina*, hundreds of young Russian volunteers singing patriotic songs pack into railroad cars bound for Serbia. But Pan-Slav unity was to be on Russia's terms. Slavs, like the Catholic Poles who did not appreciate the benefits of tsarist rule, were viewed as traitors to the general Slav cause. The Balkan national movements were expected 'to contribute to Russian prestige and power and to accept direction from St Petersburg' (Jelavich 1983a: 343). This was the doleful conclusion of Liuben Karavelov (1834–1879), the chief ideologue of Bulgarian revolutionary nationalism. Nearly ten years spent in Moscow enabled him to get to know official Russia well. Approaching the end of his life, he became convinced that 'the well-being of the Bulgarians will not come from the North' and that to rely on Russia was 'to suffer for another century' (Pundeff 1971: 112).

In a warning that would be applicable for our own century, he foretold that:

> If Russia comes to the Balkan peninsula as a liberator and saviour, Slavic brotherhood will be an accomplished fact; however, if she comes as a conqueror and a brutally despotic power, requiring all to fall on their knees, then her successes will crumble at once. If the Slavic nations in Austria and Turkey are struggling with such energy to take the foreign yoke off their necks, they will never voluntarily put their backs under the brotherly saddles of the Russian Slavs. (Pundeff 1971: 112)

The nature of Russian motives only really became clear in 1876–7 when the Eastern Question reached one of its critical stages. In July 1876 Russia and Austria put aside their rivalries in the Balkans to agree a partition of the Ottoman Empire. An uprising had erupted in Bosnia in 1874 and, in April 1876, taking advantage of Ottoman difficulties, Christian Bulgarians had risen in revolt. Russia declared war on Turkey in April 1877, having obtained the promise of Austrian neutrality in exchange for promising that Bosnia-Herzegovina would be ceded to Vienna (Castellan 1992: 316–17).

Russia initially shunned the assistance of the Balkan states then in existence, looking upon it as a hindrance (Jelavich 1983a: 357). But when the Turks succeeded in halting the Russians at Plevna in Bulgaria until the end of 1877, matters changed. Romanian assistance was required and proved instrumental in weakening Turkish resistance (Kellogg 1995: 173–5). Romanian leaders hoped that not only full independence but the acquisition of overwhelmingly Romanian-inhabited territory in Bessarabia, under tsarist control, would be their reward; but Prince Carol, the Romanian ruler, was to be disappointed.

Ottoman forces were driven from Bulgaria early in 1878 and a peace was signed at San Stefano in March. Under it a large Bulgarian state was created, including all of present-day Macedonia and much of northern

Greece. Britain feared that an enlarged Bulgaria would become an extension of Russia and thus shatter the balance of power in the Balkans. With Queen Victoria sending letters to her Prime Minister, Benjamin Disraeli, verging on the hysterical, a British fleet was sent to the Black Sea and a second Anglo-Russian war in the Balkans seemed imminent (Castellan 1992: 318).

But the British government faced hostile public opinion unwilling to see the Ottoman Empire propped up by a country which supposedly was meant to uphold civilized values against oriental despotism. Ottoman atrocities in Bulgaria had been fully reported in all their gruesome detail while Christian excesses tended to be ignored. The most serious international crisis to date in the Balkans coincided with the emergence of the mass circulation press as a potent force able to shape public opinion. Its impact is comparable to, but did not exceed, that of satellite television which brought atrocities in Bosnia and Kosovo into homes across the world in the 1990s, turning events in distant Balkan backwaters into the concern of millions of people only dimly aware of the political issues at stake.

In Britain, William Gladstone, the leader of the Liberal Party, revived a flagging political career by mounting an electrifying campaign denouncing the massacre of Bulgaria's Christians by the Turks. He published his pamphlet, 'The Bulgarian Horrors and the Question of the East' in September 1876 and by the end of that month it had sold 200,000 copies. Gladstone had earlier earned the gratitude of the Greeks when, after serving as governor of the Ionian Islands, he had persuaded the House of Commons to place them under Greek rule. He wished British policy in the Balkans to be guided by moral criteria, challenging the doctrine set down by Palmerston in 1848 when he argued that 'the furtherance of British interests should be the only object of a British Foreign Secretary ... [and] that it is in Britain's interest to preserve the balance of power in international affairs' (Ridley 1972: 171).

In 1994, when addressing the House of Commons for the first time as Foreign Secretary, Malcolm Rifkind repeated the words of Palmerston and said that they would be his motto. Britain was then under fire for pursuing a policy of minimal engagement in the war in Bosnia. Its refusal to support the lifting of the arms embargo, which would have enabled the Muslim-led government to defend itself in a war that its Serb adversaries were mainly directing against civilians, was widely criticised. The government's most eloquent critic was Gladstone's eventual successor as Liberal leader, Paddy Ashdown, who visited the Bosnian war zone on numerous occasions and argued that Britain was lowering standards of behaviour in the region by refusing to countenance forceful action against Serbs who had subjected the city of Sarajevo to a three-year siege and 'ethnically-cleansed' many other areas populated by Muslims.

Gladstone's 'Midlothian campaign' of public speaking on the Bulgarian crisis contained the polarised identification of underdogs and aggressors which later became a strong feature of Balkan crises in the 1990s. Intellectuals, churchmen and ordinary citizens, moved or repelled by Gladstone's rhetoric, entered the fray. The poet Swinburne who wrote in 1877 that 'the Turks are no worse than other oppressors around the world' had his counterparts among philosophers, playwrights and television personalities in the late 1990s who argued that there were many Kosovos for whom NATO refused to act.

In 1877 Tennyson's sonnet hailing tiny Montenegro which had repulsed the Ottomans centuries earlier as 'a rough rock-throne of freedom' got far more attention (Doder 1979: 182). It was accompanied by a long article about Montenegrin history written by Gladstone, no other British leader identifying himself as completely with a Balkan cause until Prime Minister Tony Blair's emotional tours of Albanian refugee camps in May 1999 (Gallagher 1999: 49). In that month, while on a visit to Bulgaria to stiffen the support of its reformist government for NATO's action in Kosovo, Blair invoked the memory of Gladstone while delivering a speech in Sofia:

> Today we face the same questions that confronted Gladstone over 120 years ago. Does one nation or people have the right to impose its will on another? Is there ever a justification for a policy based on the supremacy of one ethnic group? Can the outside world simply stand by when a rogue state brutally abuses the basic rights of those it governs? Gladstone's answer in 1876 was clear. And so is mine today.[3]

But Gladstone had been prepared to advocate what Blair was determined to resist by armed force—the deportation or expulsion of an entire community because of its ethnic background. In one of his most famous speeches on the subject, Gladstone advocated the mass expulsion of Turks from Bulgaria: 'Let the Turks carry away their abuses in the only possible manner, namely by carrying themselves out ... one and all, bag and baggage, they shall I hope clear out of a province they have desolated and profaned'.[4]

A mass expulsion of Muslims occurred in 1877–8 from lands taken not just by Bulgaria but by Serbia and Montenegro. In Belgrade and other cities, mosques and other buildings associated with Turkish rule were comprehensively demolished irrespective of their aesthetic merit. This re-writing of history was applauded by Serb militants in Bosnia during the 1990s when they were engaged in similar attacks on a rival culture. The readiness of contemporary players in Balkan conflicts to see the actions of their predecessors in rosy terms is not just a predisposition of nationalists but, on occasion, is displayed by Western leaders convinced of the rectitude of their Balkan policies.

THE CONGRESS OF BERLIN

The establishment, under Russian patronage, of a Greater Bulgaria as the leading national state in the Balkans aroused opposition from other Balkan countries. It reinforced the demands of Britain and Austria that the Eastern Question should be resolved by international arbitration (Hoesch 1972: 133). From 13 June to 13 July 1878, representatives of the signatories of the Paris peace treaty of 1856 which had ended the Crimean War assembled in Berlin under the chairmanship of Bismarck. There was no participation of the Balkan states, although their governments were allowed to send representatives to present their views at the sessions that concerned their interests (Jelavich 1983a: 360).

What ensued, under the cynical guidance of Bismarck, was a diplomatic carve-up of the region that ruled out the creation of a viable pattern of states. Decisions were made about Macedonia, Bulgaria and Bosnia which would return to haunt the peace of Europe in subsequent decades. Bulgaria was reduced to the territory between the Balkan mountains and the Danube in an autonomous principality under nominal Turkish rule, while Eastern Rumelia (which became a Turkish province with administrative autonomy) and Macedonia and Thrace were restored to the Ottomans. Where an overarching identity existed among Slavs in Macedonia, it was a Bulgarian one until at least the 1860s. The cultural impetus for a separate Macedonian identity would only emerge later and perhaps much bloodshed would have been avoided if no impediments had been put in the way of a large Slavic state. Events would consistently show that fears of any South Slav state becoming a pawn of the Russians were wildly overblown. Bulgaria had economic and cultural features that even with territorial insecurity enabled it to make greater progress in state-building than its neighbours. A large Bulgaria enjoying material progress could have become a magnet for Serbia and a South Slav state might have emerged gradually in the last decades of the 19ᵗʰ century. But the approval of the powers was vital and instead Balkan union met with implacable hostility, not least from Vienna. The reactionary Hapsburg emperor Franz Josef I was determined to crush national claims not only in his own realms but in adjacent Balkan lands, which he was persuaded by even more reactionary courtiers might be ripe for Hapsburg expansion or domination (Jászi 1964: 92).

Romanian, Serbian and Montenegrin independence were internationally recognised but Romania lost southern Bessarabia to Russia and was compensated with an outlet to the Danube and control of part of Dobruja, coveted by Bulgaria. Bosnia technically remained part of the Ottoman Empire but Austria-Hungary was allowed to establish a protectorate over it. In addition, a portion of southeastern Bosnia, the Sandžak of Novi Pazar, was simply sliced off and left in Ottoman hands (Udovicki 1997b: 26). Moreover, Serbia and Montenegro were forbidden from building a communication link between their two states, Austria seeing it as a threat to its interests (Doder 1979: 230).

The Balkanization of the Balkans was the price Europe paid for preserving several decades of peace between suspicious and narrow-minded European powers. A Balkan confederation of large ethnically mixed states where minority rights were protected by international guarantee never had a chance of getting off the ground in such a cynical atmosphere of *realpolitik*. Revolutionary solidarity and cooperation between the Balkan secular Christian elites in the drive to force back the Ottomans evaporated. The thwarted nationalism of the Serbs in Bosnia and the Bulgarians in Macedonia soon acquired an outlet in the terrorism of irredentist movements (Hoesch 1972: 135). Bulgaria and Serbia, two South Slav states with unsatisfied national programmes, would clash in wars over the next sixty-five years. Russian acquisition of mainly Romanian-populated Bessarabia would create almost permanent Romanian distrust of Russia, whether in its imperial or communist guise, down to the present.

After 1878 Turkey was, in large measure, pushed out of Europe and Russia, frustrated in its Balkan ambitions, turned eastwards (Vickers 1995: 33). Austria-Hungary seemed the winner in the latest diplomatic standoff over the Balkans. Vienna had been successful in preventing the creation of a large South Slav state. In the 1880s Austrian control over the foreign policy of Serbia, Romania and even Greece was established (Hoesch 1972: 135). But to be clients of the Hapsburgs was an unnatural position for Balkan states shaped by a nationalist outlook. Dangerous frustrations built up which, long before the outbreak of the First World War, would show more perceptive observers that, under the patronage of Bismarck, Austria's victory at the Congress of Berlin was a distinctly hollow one.

When Disraeli returned to London in July 1878 he boasted that he had brought with him 'peace with honour'. But many at the time bitterly criticised 'the peace that passeth all understanding and the honour that is common among thieves' (Stavrianos 1958: 411). However, among practitioners and advocates of diplomatic *realpolitik*, the Congress of Berlin continues to enjoy a spurious reputation. In the first days of the 1999 Kosovo conflict, the convening of a European summit to divide up the disputed province was advocated by William G. Hyland, a former editor of the influential US journal *Foreign Affairs* with the Congress invoked as a precedent which 'provided for several decades of peace' (Hyland 1999).

The international machinations associated with the Eastern Question deepened mistrust between Serbs and Albanians in Kosovo during the last quarter of the 19th century. Hitherto 'strong social similarities expressed in numerous common customs and traditions' had been apparent between two peoples who would become the most implacably opposed of any in the peninsula (Vickers 1998: 41). But mistrust between Serb and Albanian increased as nationalist tensions began to pulsate across the region. When it became clear that the Ottomans could not protect their interests, the Albanians began to assert their own national claims so as not to be overwhelmed by competitors. The exploits of Skanderberg, the Albanian chief who held out against the Turks in the 15th century, were rediscovered and popularised (Vickers 1995: 46). Prominent Albanians established the League of Prizren in 1878 to make the powers aware of the existence and separate national interests of the Albanian people. Both Montenegro and Greece received significantly less Albanian territory than they would have gained without this organized protest.

Pressure of events required the Turks, the largest Near Eastern and Balkan people without a clearcut national identity, to acquire one. In Constantinople, Western-style nationalism was gradually adopted by modernizing sections of the Turkish elite to stave off the complete dissolution of their state. In 1878 the loss of two-fifths of its entire territory and one-fifth of its population, about 5.5 million people, of whom almost half were Muslims, had been a sobering experience for the Ottoman elite (L. Carl Brown 1984: 34). The Circassians, expelled from the Caucasus in the wake of Russian conquests, were followed by other expelled Muslims from Serbia and Bulgaria. One Ottoman response was to try and divide the Christian populations. The *millet-i-Rum* which had included all Christians was divided up into national components. A separate Bulgarian Orthodox Church was sponsored in 1870 and variants of the same policy were tried with the Albanians, the Serbs, and the Vlachs (Woodhouse 1998: 183). But soon minorities were actively persecuted, especially if they were seen as acting on behalf of Russian interests. The first of a series of Ottoman massacres against the Armenians was perpetrated in 1896. Sultan Abdul Hamid II declared privately that '[T]he only way to get rid of the Armenian Question is to get rid of the Armenians' (Mount 1999). Eventually, under the cover of the First World War, as many as a million Armenians were massacred or died in forced evacuations from their homes in what is now eastern Turkey. The historian Arnold Toynbee argued that Ottoman atrocities were worse during the last dozen years of the empire than during the whole of the 19th century, and worse again during that century than between the years 1461 and 1821. He believed that

> they were not endemic, and that the revolutionary process of Westernisation was one of their causes ... the true diagnosis of the atrocities might be that they were a prolonged epidemic, to which the Near and Middle Eastern societies were subject from the time when they lost their indigenous civilizations until they became acclimatised to the intrusive influences of the West. (Toynbee 1923: 266–7)

Certainly Turkish intolerance towards its minorities increased as the nationalism that was the chief hallmark of Westernisation took hold in the imagination of its military and republican elites from the 1920s onwards.

BALKAN INDEPENDENCE: THE DREAM AND THE REALITY

The new Balkan states quickly adopted constitutions modelled on Western forms. But representative government was being attempted in countries unprepared for self-rule with borders that had been carved out arbitrarily by the great powers and populations whose sense of national awareness was often only dimly felt. A middle class, strongly entrenched in commerce and with a vested interest in promoting broadly based freedoms and the rule of law in order to safeguard its own interests and advance the common good, was almost everywhere absent. The peasantry were numerous but politically uninfluential. In 1866 only 4.2% of the Serb population was literate, Greece enjoying the highest level of literacy in the region (Vickers 1998: 15).

Often two parties, one based on the land-owning elite which could be described as 'conservative', and a rival forming around individuals prominent in the independence struggle who usually described themselves as 'liberal', took shape. But West European norms and practices were often mimicked by Balkan liberals and conservatives. What the great satirical playwright Ion Luca Caragiale wrote about Romania could easily refer to most of its neighbours: 'Political parties in the European sense of the word, formed by traditions, or by new or more recent class interests, and where programmes are based on principles or ideas, do not exist in Romania' (Constantiniu 1997: 239).

Romania and Serbia remained under narrow oligarchic control until the end of the 19th century and beyond. In Bulgaria, the liberal character of the independence movement meant that the Turnovo constitution of 1879 'placed the real power in the hands of an assembly that was to be elected by universal manhood suffrage' (Jelavich 1983a: 368). But the interference of Russia in Bulgarian affairs, as well as autocratic monarchs of foreign origin impatient with such radical heresies, quickly subverted the democratic spirit.

It was instead Greece that possessed the widest suffrage in the Balkans. But an enfranchised male population did not radicalise politics, perhaps owing to the high rate of emigration which could act as a curb on social tensions. Eleutherios Venizelos was the foremost turn-of-the-century spokesman of 'the incipient bourgeoisie' but, according to one observer, he 'had only a limited understanding of liberalism, confining it to ideas concerning rights of private property and profit-making' (Pollis 1992: 173). Liberal ideas could probably only make slow progress as long as the basic social unit in Greece remained the extended family and not the autonomous individual (Pollis 1992: 173). In Serbia and Albania the patriarchal *zadruga* system of large family cooperatives underpinned collective values that stifled individualism. Across the Balkans the notion of 'self' was often understood in terms of 'family', to which was added another layer, that of the organic modern state (Pollis 1992: 173). Patron–client relations under which influential families distributed rewards to their electoral followers, became the basis of the new politics.

Thus the modern state was refashioned in order to correspond to the traditional behaviour pattern of Balkan societies.

For nearly the first half century of independence, Romanian politics was dominated by the liberal political family, the Brătianus. They were good administrators and, despite their attachment to power, refrained from treating the state as their private property. A Romanian bourgeoisie emerged which 'made a national state and founded a national industry', (the largest oil reserves in Europe being discovered in Romania before 1914). But, according to one Romanian historian, the elite 'was unable to remove the damaging Turkish-Phanariot-orientated heritage from Romanian society or from its own conduct, especially in politics' (Constantiniu 1997: 319).

In its heyday, just after the First World War, the Romanian liberal 'system' adopted an imperious attitude to power. The historian Nicholas Nagy-Talavera has written:

> The liberal 'system' did not consider the Constitution and universal suffrage as sacred articles; more often they were seen as obstacles that needed to be circumvented ... The principle supports of the 'liberal system' were the crown, the bureaucracy and the police ...; as well as the old liberal props of the large banks, its press outlets, and the liberal party machine. (Nagy-Talavera 1999: 209)

When the British constitutional expert E. Dicey visited Bulgaria a decade after independence, he was struck by the chasm between the political elite and the peasantry:

> Except in the large towns, very little interest is taken in politics. To the great mass of the electorate it is a matter of utter indifference who their representatives might be. The difficulty is to get the electorate to vote at all; and in the majority of instances the representatives (in parliament) are virtually nominated by the government of the day. (Dicey quoted in Mouzelis 1986: 33)

Peasants who had experienced the Turkish yoke did not always find it heavier than rule by fellow Christian Slavs. In Bulgaria, landowning peasants who felt alienated by the parasitic urban oligarchy, would eventually sponsor a formidable political movement, Alexander Stamboliski's Bulgarian Agrarian National Union (Bell 1977: *passim*). But in Romania an inchoate peasant revolution in 1907, ruthlessly suppressed by the parties, broke peasant radicalism for over a decade. Even with the onset of universal suffrage in Romania after 1918, there wasn't a need to use extensive corruption or intimidation in elections.

Without them, a majority of the electorate was usually prepared to back the parties designated by the crown to form a new government and acquire the requisite parliamentary majority. According to Sorin Alexandrescu, '[T]he electorate behaved in the period of democratic modernism exactly as in the previous time, that of pre-modern feudalism' (Alexandrescu 1998: 87).

All of the Balkan states were monarchical and the origins and personalities of the crowned heads often played a key role in shaping political developments. A lot of faith was placed in monarchs whose origins were foreign because they were viewed as more disinterested in their approach to material wealth and power than local subordinates and capable of rising above factionalism. The failure rate of ambitious local rulers had been high throughout the 19th century. Capodistrias, the first leader of a free Greek state, had tried to introduce a centralist but 'enlightened' regime that would give the executive considerable power. But he was confounded by local notables and military men determined to defend their particular interests (Jelavich 1983a: 222). Prince Alexandru Cuza, the first leader of a united Romanian principality, fell foul of assertive nobles in 1866 for not dissimilar reasons. In Bulgaria, the able and wilful Stefan Stambulov had more success in beginning to create the infrastructure of a modern state during a premiership stretching from 1887 to 1894. He restored social order by suppressing banditry and creating a well-trained army. Railroads and ports were constructed and industrialization begun (Perry 1995: 236–70). But he was brought down by political enemies opposed to centralized rule. They enjoyed the barely concealed support of an unscrupulous monarch, Ferdinand I (Perry 1995: 239–40; Crampton 1997: 111). This German prince feared such an overmighty subject and his ruthless acquisition of power showed that cosmopolitan princes for hire to rule new states could be just as cruel as local Balkan despots.

Only Serbia refrained from importing a foreign monarch. The crown passed between two rival families, the Obrenovićs and the Karadjordjes, during the period from 1817 to 1903. Serbia's first prince Milos Obrenović executed his Karadjordje rival in 1817 and then sent his head to the Sultan as a sign of his fealty (Jelavich 1983a: 207). Milos 'turned himself into an Ottoman-style pasha ... and made himself one of Europe's richest men in the process, although he continued to sleep on the floor like any Serb peasant and never learnt to read or write' (Wheeler 1995: 5). He took possession of state lands and property that had been confiscated from Ottoman owners and he had the peasants work off their obligations on his private undertakings (Jelavich 1983a: 238). Milos's public money and private funds were not clearly separated. Sultanistic rule clad in Orthodox or nationalistic garb would reemerge with a vengeance under the Milosević husband-and-wife team in the Serbia of the 1990s. Their elevation of *l'état, c'est nous* into a ruling principle until 2000 faced little resistance, which suggests how political standards could suffer drastic reversals in the region. Enormous resentment at the behaviour of the last of the Obrenović dynasty boiled over into a bloody 1903 coup resulting in the execution of both the king and his wife. The Karadjordje, King Peter II, who ruled from 1903 to 1921 was more responsible. He translated J.S. Mill's *Essay on Liberty* while in exile. But the bruising Serbian experience was hardly an advertisement for native monarchy.

Foreign crowned heads had an additional advantage, that of securing European diplomatic support, with Europeanisation of society as a hoped for extra. King Carol I, who ruled Romania first as prince from 1866 to 1881, then as king until 1914, belonged to a Catholic branch of the Hohenzollern family. One rumour claims that he 'had never heard of Roumania when the offer [to be its prince had] reached him, but he took down an atlas, and, finding that a straight line from London to Bombay passed through Roumania, exclaimed: "That is a country with a future" and promptly decided to accept the crown' (Marriott 1958: 304).

Carol ruled well; he established an effective partnership with Ion C. Brătianu while giving the other parties a taste of office, and kept Romania aloof from neighbouring Balkan quarrels. Austrian influence prevailed in foreign policy; in 1894 when Dimitrie A. Sturdza became premier, he declared, at the request of Vienna's Bucharest representative, that 'we have to abstain from any act of interference in the internal affairs of the Hungarian kingdom' (Constantiniu 1997: 255). This effectively meant that the Romanians would refrain from taking energetic steps to help their co-ethnics in the Hungarian part of the Hapsburg empire, where attempts were being made to assimilate them. In the province of Transylvania, which held a central place in the nation-building myths of both the Romanians and the Hungarians, the Romanians were in a numerical majority. But they were denied autonomy by Budapest. In an age when pseudo-scientific notions about the hierarchy of nations were fashionable, the Hungarians justified their discriminatory policy by arguing that it was their vocation to absorb 'the less accomplished' peoples in their midst and raise them to a higher cultural plane (Gallagher 1995: 15). The Romanians in Transylvania, many guided by the Uniate Church, Orthodox in liturgy but part of the wider Catholic faith, saw themselves as inheritors of a Latin civilization that it was felt the Magyars with their Central Asian origins, could not easily appreciate.

Romania chose not to dabble in Transylvanian ethnic politics, which meant that attention could be paid to public works and early industrialization. Iaşi, the chief Moldavian city, even though it was superseded by Bucharest when it became the new state's capital, saw the erection of impressive public buildings in the French style before 1914. Urban development was pursued to the neglect of peasant welfare. Resources were diverted from the rural populace through policies of industrial protection which depressed the price of agricultural exports, a policy that would be continued in one form or another up until the end of the communist era.

A rare minister like Spiru Haret managed to divert resources in the early 1900s for rural education. He wished to make schools accessible and useful to the peasantry (Livezeanu 1995: 31–2). Haret, of modest social origins, obtained a place in political life through hard work (he was the first Romanian to obtain a doctorate in mathematics) (Constantiniu 1997: 255). He was thus a contrast with many other politicians who, when they thought of education, saw it as necessary primarily to inculcate national values. Bulgaria was not alone in having a school system 'geared to produce hundreds of educated and semi-educated "intellectuals" and lawyers each year who sought and were fit only for careers in the civil and military bureaucracies' (Bell 1977: 5). In the school curriculum history was designed to shape national consciousness and legitimate the nation-state. Balkan historiography developed as national historiography, offering practically no knowledge of the history of neighbours.

It is not surprising that the best-known intellectual in Southeast Europe in the period from 1910 to 1940 was a historian, the Romanian Nicolae Iorga (1871–1940). His self-proclaimed mission was to establish a place for Romania in universal history. Unlike Serbian intellectuals who in the 1860s began to be influenced by conservative Pan-Slavist thought from Russia that was deeply suspicious of the West, Iorga possessed a liberal view of nationalism during most of his public career. He shared the optimistic view of Mazzini that, once all nations enjoyed independence, they would be able to unite in a system based on friendship and international harmony. After going through an anti-Semitic phase occasioned by the spread of Jewish influence in commerce and the professions, he became a defender of Jews who were prepared to assimilate with Romanian culture (Nagy-Talavera 1999: 132). He contrasted Latin nationalism with its inherent diversity with the 'pagan' nationalism of the Germans based on common ancestry rather than attachment to common laws or a shared history (Nagy-Talavera 1999: 218).

However, it was ethnic nationalism based on allegedly common bloodlines, first popularised by the German Romantics and in pre-1914 Wilhelmine Germany recognised as the basis for German citizenship, which held most attraction for East European nationalist intellectuals. Even Iorga was at times swayed by it as when he published a book on the 'Latin' connections of the emphatically German-origin Romanian royal family (Nagy-Talavera 1999: 159). But he was one of the few well-known nationalist intellectuals in the Balkans who would consistently ridicule Hitler's ideas on 'national superiority'. Hitler's lack of respect for those nations he branded as lesser cultures was repugnant to Iorga and he would pay for his defiance of fashionable racial theories with his life in 1940 (Nagy-Talavera 1999: 314).

Iorga launched a South-East Europe Studies Institute in Bucharest in 1914, but distrust and ignorance of neighbours remained the norm. Hugh Seton-Watson, writing of the 1918–40 years argued that the 'lack of cultural relations between the East European states was one of the fundamental reasons for their failure to collaborate against common external enemies' (Seton-Watson 1945: 314). He complained of a 'false educational system ... which at its best encouraged chauvinism and at its worst helped to destroy all conceptions of morality ... one of the fundamental causes of the misfortunes of these peoples' (Seton-Watson 1945: 143).

Militarization combined with a nationalistic education system to create a chauvinist outlook. State budgets were tilted towards the military, a pillar of national identity. High military expenditure increased the likelihood of local wars erupting. In 1885 Serbia, taking advantage of a crisis stemming from Russian efforts to interfere in Bulgarian internal affairs, invaded Bulgaria but was decisively beaten (Perry 1995: 81). Military victory gave the Bulgarian army a central place in national life. Ivan Vazov, Bulgaria's national poet, wrote stirring national verses about the war in which Britain and Russia reversed their positions towards Bulgaria. Russia had been irked by the

1885 union of Bulgaria with the principality of Eastern Rumelia. It was determined to keep a weak Bulgaria tied to itself. Britain, on seeing that the Bulgarians were far from being Russian pawns, reversed its 1878 position and supported the acquisition of Eastern Rumelia. Austria-Hungary intervened to block a Bulgarian advance on Serbia and preserve the status quo that had existed before both Balkan states had gone to war (Pundeff 1971: 125–6).

DEEPENING SLAV QUARRELS

Great power interference was turning South Slav solidarity into endemic Balkan Slav rivalry. The Party of Right, founded in Croatia in 1861, pleased the Hapsburg rulers of that province by demeaning its Slav neighbours. Slovenes were 'mountain Croats' while the Serbs were 'an unclean servile race without culture' (Prpa-Jovanović 1997: 45). Ante Starčević, the party's founder was, like many later nationalist fanatics in the Balkans, of mixed race: his mother was Serb; 'nevertheless, he insisted that as long as the Serbs of Croatia did not grasp their essential Croat identity, they were lost' (Cohen 1998: 21).

Serbia, for its part, was burdened by its own superiority complex. If foreign imperial rule was to be ended in the South Slav lands, then it should occur in the way that Piedmont directed the freedom struggle in the Italian peninsula, with the other South Slav peoples falling in behind Serbian leadership (Judah 1997: 61). The primary national goal in the late 19th century which, according to Charles Jelavich, 'united the government, the church, the middle class ... the peasantry and the army' was the resurrection and expansion of the Serbian state (Jelavich 1962: 3). The Serbian Radical Party, dominant between 1903 and 1914, was 'attached to an isolationist and nationalist agenda with pronounced territorial ambitions' (Udovicki 1997a: 5). A cult of the 1389 battle of Kosovo developed 'as some sort of nationally-defining historical and spiritual event' (Malcolm 1998: xxx). The battle (which was not a crucial event in the Ottoman conquest of the Balkans) focused attention on the Islamic enemy (although Christians fought on both sides) and reminded Serbs of a glorious pre-Ottoman past (Malcolm 1998: 79). In the early 19th century, the Serbian linguistic reformer Vuk Karadžić began to emphasise the importance of the story of the Serbian leader, Prince Lazar, who fell at Kosovo by publishing different versions of the famous curse of Kosovo. Karadžić's 1845 version read:

Whoever is a Serb of Serbian blood
Whoever shares with me this heritage
And he comes not to fight at Kosovo
May he never have the progeny
His heart desires, neither son nor daughter;
Beneath his hand let nothing decent grow
Neither purple grapes nor wholelsome wheat;
Let him rust away like dripping iron
Until his name be extinguished.
(Sells 1996: 37)

The xenophobia contained in these lines was adopted in other Balkan lands with unfinished nationalist business to perform. Mihai Eminescu, Romania's greatest poet, published uncannily similar lines in his poem 'Doina':

If any shall cherish the stranger
May the dog eat his heart
May the weeds destroy his house
And may his kin perish in shame.
(Almond 1992: 31)

Until Karadžić's time, the Battle of Kosovo did not hold a central place in Serbian epic poetry: '[R]ather than Prince Lazar, the main Serbian epic hero was Marko Kraljević, a Serb vassal of the Sultan. Because he fought both for and against his masters in Constantinople, Prince Marko has served as a figure of mediation between the Serbian Orthodox and Ottoman worlds' (Sells 1996: 36).

But given the nationalist agenda of the Serbian state, a homogeneous identity was required which denied such coexistence. New myths emerged. Conversion to Islam was seen as based on cowardice and greed which justified harsh treatment against Albanian and Bosnian Muslims. The Slavs were seen as Christian by nature and abandonment of Christianity was tantamount to betrayal of the Serbian race (Sells 1996: 36).

The historical verse drama, *The Mountain Wreath* promotes these racially exclusive sentiments. The work of the Prince-Bishop of Montenegro, Peter II (1813–1851), it was published in 1847 under his pen name of Njegoš, and is considered by many Serb nationalists to be the central work of all Serbian literature (Sells 1996: 41). The work portrays and glorifies the extermination of Slavic Muslims at the hands of Serb warriors. The drama opens with the chief character, Prince Danilo brooding on the evils of Islam and the tragedy of Kosovo.

Danilo's lieutenants 'suggest celebrating the holy day (Pentecost) by "cleansing" (cstiti) the land of non-Christians. The chorus chants: "The high mountains reek with the stench of non-Christians". One of Danilo's men proclaims that struggle will not end until "we or the Turks [Slavic Muslims] are exterminated"' (Sells 1996: 41).

The drama proclaimed the view, influential among Serbian radicals in the 1990s, that by converting from Christianity to Islam, Slavs had changed their racial identity and joined the race of Turks who killed Prince Lazar. In the late 1980s, remains said to be those of Prince Lazar were exhumed and paraded around Serbia with the blessing of the Milošević state and the Orthodox Church (Judah 1997: 39). This was a calculated attempt to place religious fanaticism at the service of nationalist aggression and it produced a bloody outcome in the western Balkans during the 1990s. Croatia in the 1941–4 years also saw the alliance of Catholic integralism and fascism give rise to frightful bloodshed. Thankfully, nowhere else in the Balkans did such a destructive mix of religion and nationalist fundamentalism occur.

In Romania, sections of the nationalist elite were distrustful of the growing Jewish presence in the cities. Between 1859 and 1899, the Jewish population of Moldavia increased from 118,000 to 210,000 and that of Wallachia from 9,200 to 68,000 (Stavrianos 1958: 484). Jews were discriminated against in the 1866 Constitution which laid down that the only foreigners who could buy land were those belonging to the Christian faith (Gallagher 1995: 19). Some liberals who, in the 1848 revolution, had proclaimed the emancipation of the Jews in Wallachia, were prepared to dampen disappointment about the rate of post-independence progress by blaming the Jews for national ills (Kellogg 1995: 48–9). Ion C. Brătianu was one such figure. He was alarmed that the Jews comprised two-fifths of an urban population, amounting to 700,000 in a population of 5 million (Stavrianos 1958: 484). It was only pressure from the great powers at the 1878 Berlin Congress which compelled Romania to grant its Jewish population equal citizenship (Castellan 1992: 139–40). But Romania quietly flouted Article 44 of the Berlin Treaty concerning minority protection. It wasn't alone in this regard and the powers were not anxious to follow up non-compliance. On this question of anti-Semitic laws, Romania displayed the technique, noticeable in many other aspects of Balkan governance, of stalling for time or relying upon hair-splitting legalisms in order to wear down stronger external forces (Roberts 1963: 383).

In Romania the intellectual unemployment resulting from the expansion of higher education would fuel anti-Semitism, but in Bulgaria it was virtually non-existent owing to the much smaller size of the Jewish population. Bulgarians endeavoured to save their Jewish population in the Second World War, but even in Romania there was no mass anti-Semitism and by 1945 the largest numbers of Jews in Eastern Europe to have escaped Hitler's death camps were to be found there.

A century earlier, the first Balkan national states had been careful to make the Orthodox Church subservient to the state. Religion was nationalised which ensured that Orthodoxy's multinational traditions were soon lost sight of. The model being followed in Church–state relations was that adopted by Peter the Great of Russia. In 1721 he established what has become known as the Petrine model of state control of the Church (Ramet 1998: 277). The Orthodox Church became one of the main branches of the state administration with the Emperor as its 'supreme protector' (Hosking 1997: 227). After Greek independence, the Orthodox Church was organized along these lines with the Holy Synod controlled by the state under a government procurator (Runciman 1971: 68). In Romania

> the 1872 law on Church government allowed political interests to predominate in the election of metropolitans and bishops. Seats in the electoral college were given to all Orthodox parliamentarians who thus outnumbered the clergy. The Holy Synod, the principal governing body of the Church, was deprived of freedom of action. It could enact no law which might run counter to the laws of the state; and from 1892 priests received regular salaries from the state which strengthened the view that it was fitting for the church to offer loyal subservience to the government. (Hitchins 1994: 71)

The Orthodox Churches could usually be relied upon to endorse the power and authority of the secular ruler, which made a country like Romania relatively easy for a liberal-conservative oligarchy to govern in the first generations of independence. A nationalist historian like Iorga saw the multinational Orthodox centre at Mount Athos as having a negative influence on the history of the Romanians (Nagy-Talavera 1999: 84). For Iorga, Orthodoxy deserved respect only as long as it contributed to the well-being of the Romanian nation. He had more respect for the Uniate Church in Transylvania because of the service it had given to the national cause after 1750 (Nagy-Talavera 1999: 84).

One of the foremost scholars of nationalism, Ernest Gellner, saw its appeal as stemming from its ability to stimulate economic development.

He described '[N]ationalism as a conduit for economic growth insofar as it promotes communication through a literate, educated culture, and serves as a bond among like peoples' (Bookman 1994: 9). But in the Balkan states it remained largely an elite preoccupation and it failed to encourage a patriotic groundswell for material endeavour, except perhaps in Bulgaria which in the years after its 1885 victory over Serbia did witness some dramatic economic advances.

THE ROAD TO WAR

The scale of the economic challenges confronting the Balkan states all too often resulted in elites evading their responsibility to protect the material welfare of their citizens in favour of territorial aggrandisement. Pre-war military spending soared above all in Bulgaria which had the most strongly-felt irredentist claims. Prosperity is often a great disincentive to war and if living standards in the key Balkan trouble-spots had even been half those of multi-ethnic Switzerland, the region's inhabitants would probably have had much greater success in resolving some of their most pressing ethnic disputes.

In 1897 Bismarck had predicted that 'some damned foolish thing in the Balkans' would touch off a European conflagration (Stillman 1966: 47). The inconsistent and opportunistic behaviour of the outside powers active in the region remained the biggest source of danger even as the new states began to assert themselves. Russia and Austria-Hungary both turned against their favoured clients but were unable to bring them to heel. In 1886 Russian pressure forced the abdication of Alexander Battenberg, prince of Bulgaria, who had refused to be the vassal of St Petersburg. However, the regency under Stambulov successfully defied Russia. Stambolov even contemplated 'a personal union with Turkey', whereby the sultan would become tsar of Bulgaria with a dual Turkish-Bulgarian empire being formed to 'resist Russian encroachments' (Pundeff 1971: 127–8). Later in 1886 Russia severed all relations with Bulgaria and it was only following the demise of both Tsar Alexander III of Russia and Stambulov in 1894–5 that bilateral relations were normalised.

Austria was unable to contain South Slav unrest in its domains, thanks to the failure of its Serbian policy. The restoration of the Karadjordje dynasty in 1903 initiated a self-assertive foreign policy in Belgrade. Austria responded in 1906 by closing its borders to imports of Serbian livestock after 'discovering' diseased beasts. Before 'the Pig war' Serbia had shipped about 90% of its exports to Austria and the Austrian press predicted that 'she would suffocate in her own swine-fat' (Stavrianos 1958: 456–7). But in 1910, when both countries signed a new customs agreement, Serbia emerged strengthened. It found new markets for nearly 70% of its exports and it also started processing agricultural products because of the distance of its new markets. A 1906 arms contract with a French firm meant that Serbia was no longer relying on Austrian artillery, a factor of great importance less than a decade later (Stavrianos 1958: 457).

The rise of the Balkan states did not result in greater cooperation between them. Macedonia proved an apple of discord between Serbia, Bulgaria and Greece. Each of them coveted this ethnically highly varied as well as strategic territory. Macedonia commands a corridor which extends from Central Europe to the Mediterranean along the Morava and Vardar valleys. It is a route which has enabled successive invaders, Roman, Goth, Slav and Ottoman, to pass into the Balkans. In the caustic words of Joseph Rothschild, Macedonia's rival claimants 'encouraged their so-called "scholars" to "demonstrate" with historical, geographic, ethnic and linguistic "evidence" that the Macedonians were a branch of their own respective nations' (Rothschild 1958: 171). Greece and Bulgarian national interests dispatched groups of armed partisans to Macedonia in the 1900s to protect their respective interests there (Karakasidou 1997: 103). Besides national prestige, two other factors made Macedonia a desirable prize. It contained the great port of Thessaloniki as well as one of the most fertile parts of the Balkans (Stavrianos 1958: 517).

An International Macedonian Revolutionary Organization (IMRO), initially committed to establishing a South Slav federation in which Macedonia would rank alongside Bulgaria and Serbia, was founded in 1893. After a heroic revolutionary debut during the Illinden rebellion of 1903, IMRO had, by the 1920s, degenerated into a gangster band. It never resolved the ambiguity of whether it wanted Macedonia to be independent or part of Bulgaria (Rothschild 1958: 193). For most of its existence Macedonian peasants failed to see IMRO as their protector, nor did they identify strongly with any of the rival-state claimants to Macedonia. Usually their allegiance was to the village of their birth and, if they had wider horizons, it was to the Orthodox Church in order to distinguish themselves from Muslim or Catholic neighbours (Stavrianos 1958: 519).

The impetus behind political radicalism in Macedonia came from the large numbers who emigrated to Bulgaria after 1885. Macedonian hitmen were employed for the murder of Stambulov in 1895. Radicalised outsiders have consistently been a disruptive element in Balkan politics. Their hypernationalism—that of the Âromani immigrants to the Romanian Dobruja after 1918 or the post-1945 emigre Croats from western Herzegovina—disturbed interwar Romania and turned Tudjman's Croatia into a chief villain, as well as a prominent victim, of the post-1991 Yugoslav wars.

In 1908 the appeal of nationalism within the moribund Ottoman Empire was shown when officers known as the 'Young Turks' seized power from Sultan Abdul Hamid II. The movement was, in many ways, a reaction to Balkan nationalism. Although it had no coherent ideology, the desire to rejuvenate the Ottoman Empire and Ottomanise its inhabitants was evident. Bulgaria responded by throwing off nominal Ottoman control and proclaiming its independence on 5 October 1908, Ferdinand assuming the title of Tsar of Bulgaria. The next day, apparently by pre-arrangement, the annexation of Bosnia-Herzegovina was announced by Vienna which had exercised a protectorate over it since 1878. But such assaults on remaining Turkish authority in the area needed Russian acquiescence if the balance of power was not to be disturbed. Vienna thought it had the backing of the Russian Foreign minister but his Pan-Slav officials saw it as a humiliation for Russia (Wolff 1974: 90). A flood of recriminations ensued, shortly leading to a European crisis unlike any seen since 1878.

Russia became increasingly involved again in the Balkans after its Far Eastern ambitions were dealt a crushing reverse by Japan in 1905. Austria thought that its Bosnian *démarche* was worth the gamble if it succeeded in blocking permanently Serbian designs on this province. Italy was also flexing its muscles. It was intent on securing Turkish possessions in the Mediterranean and it seized the island of Rhodes as well as Libya before 1914 (Pundeff 1971: 133). Renewed fears that the powers were set on carving up the Balkans encouraged Belgrade, Sofia and Athens to draw up plans to collaborate in their own defence. A Bulgarian-Serbian treaty was signed in March 1912, 'a secret annexe of which provided for the partition of Macedonia along stipulated lines arbitrated by the Russian emperor if disagreement arose' (Pundeff 1971: 134). A Bulgarian-Greek alliance followed in May but it failed to agree a line demarcating Bulgarian and Greek territory in Macedonia. However, there was enough common ground to allow a four-pronged attack on Thrace to be mounted by Serbia, Macedonia, Greece and Bulgaria in October 1912. Turkey faced political chaos and the Young

Turks were unable to subdue an Albanian revolt. They, like peoples for long content to serve a multinational empire (such as the Scots after the decline of Britain's), had discovered their own national mission on the demise of the empire which had offered past glory and plunder.

Kaiser Wilhelm II of Germany had destroyed Bismarck's careful diplomacy and the great powers had gradually split into two hostile camps revolving around France and its allies Britain and Russia and Germany and its allies, Austria-Hungary and Turkey. These renewed tensions and suspicions meant that speedy action to dampen Balkan firestorms and prevent a major war occurring was increasingly difficult.

In a few weeks of fighting, the Turks were almost completely pushed out of Europe. But their defeat meant that the glue holding together the Balkan alliance dissolved. Bulgarian forces had concentrated on expelling the Turks from eastern Thrace while Greek and Serbian forces had occupied Macedonia, the principal objective for which Bulgaria had gone to war. When Bulgarian forces advanced to Thessaloniki, there was friction with the Greek forces already there. Serbia's forces, which had advanced beyond the line stipulated in the March 1912 treaty, demanded its revision on the grounds of 'effective occupation' (Pundeff 1971: 135). A further discordant voice was provided by Romania which insisted on a voice in the territorial settlement.

Macedonian extremists threatened King Ferdinand and his cabinet with assassination if they accepted a Russian arbitration, which was sure to result in their goal of a greater Bulgaria being snatched from them (Stavrianos 1958: 539). Public opinion was also intransigent. In a second Balkan war fought early in 1913, Bulgaria was overwhelmed by her erstwhile Christian allies. Turkey joined the fray to recover eastern Thrace. The peace of Bucharest, signed in April 1913, carved up Macedonia into three pieces. The smallest part, the Pirin region, was given to Bulgaria. Serbia took the Vardar valley with Skopje, Ohrid and Bitola. Greece was awarded southern (Aegean) Macedonia with Thessaloniki and other ports. Bulgaria was compensated with western Thrace, giving it an outlet to the Aegean, but Romania took southern Dobruja from Bulgaria. A separate Bulgarian–Turkish peace returned most of eastern Thrace to Turkey.

Macedonia failed to emerge as a state for another 75 years. However, Albania took shape after the Treaty of London in May 1913 forced the Ottomans to give up nearly all of their territories in Europe. The repressive nature of Young Turk rule had sharpened Albanian national consciousness in the previous three years. However, a self-governing Albania was really the fortuitous outcome of splits between the European powers and their local clients about how to apportion the mainly Albanian-speaking lands. Serbian, Greek and Montenegrin forces were in occupation of most of present-day Albania by the close of the First Balkan War at the end of 1912. Austria-Hungary feared that Serbia and Greece would partition Albania between them and that the main Albanian port, Durres, might become a Russian outpost on the Mediterranean through the Serbian connection. Meanwhile Italy saw the possibility of establishing a protectorate over a weak and friendless Albania. An ambassadors' conference in London chaired by Britain sat during 1912–13 and declared in the spring of 1913 that Albania was a 'Neutral Sovereign Principality under a Hereditary Monarch and Guaranteed by the Great Powers' (Castellan 1992: 383). The Balkan Allies against Ottoman Turkey were, however, awarded large swathes of mainly Albanian-inhabited territory, including Kosovo. Mainly Albanian-speaking areas went to Serbia and Montenegro while Greece received the large southern region, known as northern Epirus by Greece and Chameria by Albania.

But arranging borders which satisfied the contending parties was a nerve-racking business which increased the enmity between powers already divided into two hostile camps. Miranda Vickers has written that '[F]or weeks the peace of Europe hung upon the fate of Gjakova, a small Kosovar market town, which Austria claimed for Albania and Russia for Serbia' (Vickers 1995: 71). In the spring of 1913 war between Austria and Montenegro loomed over another disputed town: martial law was declared in Bosnia and troops prepared to march south towards Shkoder, an Albanian town occupied by Montenegrin forces. Vienna had felt entitled to act as an overlord in this part of the western Balkans ever since the Congress of Berlin; in 1878, to prevent the fellow Orthodox Christian South Slav states of Serbia and Montenegro having a common frontier, it had allowed the Ottomans to retain direct control of the Sandžak of Novi Pazar and its mainly Muslim population. This territory was acquired by Serbia in 1913 but Vienna was determined to prevent both it and its ally Montenegro encroaching any further on territory felt to be vital for Austrian security. It took a combined naval blockade by the powers of the Montenegrin port of Bar to persuade King Nicholas the ruler of Montenegro to withdraw from Shkoder and halt the massacre of Albanian civilians (Vickers 1995: 73). But as Sir Edward Grey, the British foreign secretary, admitted in parliament on 12 August 1913, it was the attempt to create boundaries that would prevent the powers clashing over Albania that was the primary impulse behind their intervention (Vickers 1995: 70). The European powers also selected a foreign prince to rule over Albania but, when settled conditions slowly emerged in the 1920s, it was (as in Serbia) a local chieftain, Ahmed Zogu, who would ascend the throne.

The 1912–13 Balkan wars had confirmed the reputation of the region as a zone of intense national rivalry and indeed hatred. Serbia, Montenegro and Greece subjected Albanians in Macedonia and Bulgarian-leaning Slavs there to heavy repression both during and after the Second Balkan War (Poulton 1995: 74–5). An international enquiry into the roots and conduct of the Balkan wars, established by the Carnegie Endowment for International Peace, documented the scale of the atrocities (Carnegie 1914: *passim*). Composed of eight well-known politicians, academics and journalists from the USA and each of the European powers with interests in the region, the commission's report makes sombre reading.

But there were brave and insistent Balkan voices that were prepared to swim against the chauvinist tide. Dimitrije Tucević, the leader of the Serbian Social Democratic Party, severely criticised the Serbian repression of Albanians in Kosovo which Serbia acquired in 1913 (Job 1993: 63). The razing of Albanian villages was described as the 'Third Balkan War' (Udovicki 1997b: 30). His party supported 'the unification of the Balkan countries with full political and cultural autonomy for all the constituent nations' (Udovicki 1997b: 30). Similar views enjoyed wide adherence in Bulgaria where they were expressed not only by a vigorous though divided Marxist movement but also by Stamboliski's peasant party (Rothschild 1958: 85).

The Bulgarian peasant was often unimpressed by the benefits of national government as this point made by a Bulgarian novelist, writing in 1892, makes clear:

> The peasant had but the vaguest idea of our transition from servitude to independent life; for him it matters little whether he pays tax to Akhmed or Ivan. In fact, Ivan is often more distasteful to him than Akhmed, for Akhmed could be more easily fooled or bribed; Akhmed did not take his son off as a soldier whereas Ivan does; Akhmed was naive and spoke Turkish, while Ivan is to all appearance a Christian like him, speaks Bulgarian, yet exacts more from him than did Akhmed. The meaning of state, rights and duties for the peasant add up to tax-payment and sending his son off as a soldier. His attitude to nature, life and livelihood are still those of fifty years ago (Stavrianos 1958: 423).

Pre-1914 European socialists were the most ardent champions of a Balkan federation. It was seen as stimulating capitalism and therefore socialism by turning the Balkan peninsula into one large market without trading barriers. A federation, by establishing a large state between Austria-Hungary and Russia, had the even more important benefit of reducing the chances of a Balkan conflict that would result in a world war (Rothschild 1958: 207).

Austro-Russian rivalry in the Balkans, over who should fill the vacuum left by the declining Ottoman Empire, became the most explosive element in European diplomacy after 1908. In Austria, the leaders of the Social Democratic Party, Karl Renner and Otto Bauer, advanced the principle of personal autonomy in order to try to disconnect the vexed question of nationality from territory. According to Robert King, '[A]ll other attempts to deal with the national question had been based on granting national and territorial rights in some form or other' (R. King 1973: 18). The belief that the heat could be taken out of conflicts of identity if national rights were accorded to persons rather than to territorial groupings would never be tried out in the Hapsburg Empire. Instead the mood of imperial officials in Vienna and especially Budapest hardened, especially towards minorities whose coethnics had formed separate states adjacent to them. Rather than agreeing with Russia to keep contentious Balkan questions 'on ice', there was a growing desire expressed in private by civil-military leaders in Vienna for a pre-emptive strike against Serbia to put it in its place and thus silence demands for a South Slav union (Anderson 1966: 307).

The clumsily executed incorporation of Bosnia into the Austrian empire was a sign of weakness rather than strength. Austrian efforts to develop the economy and infrastructure of Bosnia had sharpened the awareness of the Orthodox, Catholic, and Muslim Slavs sharing the territory. As the experience of much of Africa, the Middle East and Southeast Asia would show after 1945, such modernisation often provides an impetus for latent nationalism to develop. The Hapsburg Empire lacked a legitimising force able to rival nationalism. *Kaisertreue* (loyalty to the emperor who saw himself as heir to the Holy Roman Empire) was insufficiently attractive to act as a rallying symbol. The concept of a monarchical United States of Central Europe would remain stillborn as long as the Hapsburg monarchy was unable to infuse its concept of modern society with life (Bideleux and Jeffries 1998: 394).

Viennese efforts to promote Bosnian nationhood as a unifying factor which would insulate the territory from nationalist political movements in Serbia and Croatia never took root (Malcolm 1994: 147). Benjamin Kallay, the architect of Bosnian policy from 1882 to 1903 hoped that the Muslims would take up the idea of Bosnian nationhood (Rusinow 1995: 368). The customs, dress, architecture, and historical memories of the Bosnian Muslims could have become the basis for a new national identity. However, the strength of Islam militated against this. Islam is usually antinational; 'it asserts that Muslims should not commit themselves to any nation, since belonging to any community other than that of Islam is unworthy of a true believer' (Djilas 1991: 10).

The Bosnian Muslims had no sponsor nation to look to, unlike their Christian coethnics. So instead they held fast to a religious identity or else, in some cases, were drawn to a common South Slav one. For several centuries it had not been unknown for a family to separate itself into Christian and Islamic male members 'so as to have friends on the right side no matter what happened'.[5] This practice of family members aligning with different power formations still occurs in Balkan countries afflicted by acute turbulence such as Albania (Carver 1998: 91) and shows that identities can often be as supple as bamboo rather than as hard as granite.

After initial resistance to the 1878 Austrian occupation, the Muslims had accepted Hapsburg overlordship but without conspicuous enthusiasm (Zulfikarpasić 1998: 87). The Austrians retained the millet system with which Muslims had been more comfortable than the other South Slavs. The continuation of Turkish administrative arrangements was reflected in the fact that until the early years of this century, most Slavic Muslims in Bosnia still called themselves *Turcini*. The expansion of agriculture and industry, the creation of new banks, and the improvement of infrastructure were advances which Muslims benefited from, given their strong presence in Bosnian cities and towns where modernisation had the most impact (Zulfikarpasić 1998: 88–9). The demographic balance in Bosnia had shifted in favour of Christian Slavs after 1876 which meant that Austrian attempts to control its acquisition by working through the Muslims was unlikely to enjoy long-term success. (A province that had been 50% Muslim in the 1830s was 60% Christian by 1880 (McCarthy 1996: 82).) Foreign observers like the American journalist W.E. Carter who visited Bosnia in 1902 did not observe serious inter-ethnic tensions despite Christian–Muslim conflict in the 1870s. 'Members of the different religious faiths mix with each other on amicable terms and show mutual respect and mutual toleration ...' (Malcolm 1994: 145). But Croat and Serb nationalism was growing in popularity even before the 1908 crisis through the very network of school teachers, priests and educated newspaper readers which Vienna's modernisation push had fostered (Malcolm 1994: 149). Interethnic peace was fragile as long as Bosnia remained on a faultline where the interests of imperialism and rising nationalism sharply collided.

The quality of Austrian policy towards increasingly restive national-ists declined as the aged and increasingly reactionary Emperor Franz Josef II surrounded himself with blinkered officials who reinforced his hostility to reforming a ramshackle empire. The Austrian minister to Belgrade on 3 April 1909 communicated the degree of hatred there was in Serbia towards the annexation of Bosnia, but it did not have a sobering effect in Vienna (Stavrianos 1958: 531). Serbian officers, who had taken part in the 1903 revolution that had overthrown the pro-Austrian King Milan, formed the Black Hand in 1911, an armed secret society dedicated to Pan-Serb union (Jelavich 1983b: 111). Its founder, Colonel Dragutin Dimitrijević, better known by the pseudonym 'Apis' was chief of intelligence of the Serbian general staff by 1913. The Black Hand became active in Bosnia where it operated through a slightly older secret society, Narodna Odbrana (National Defence). Links were cultivated with a small number of revolutionary Bosnian youths unbeknownst to the Serbian government. Arms were provided to them in May 1914 by Colonel Apis, one month before Franz Ferdinand, the heir to the throne, was to pay a visit to Bosnia (Stavrianos 1958: 550).

At first sight, it might not appear obvious why Franz Ferdinand should be the target of South Slav assassins. He was known to be a critic of the Austro-Hungarian Dual Monarchy because it alienated other nationalities and therefore undermined Hapsburg rule. He is believed to have 'favoured the formation within the empire of a third state, consisting of territory inhabited by the Croats, Slovenes and Serbs ... in the hope that it would ... neutralise the Pan-Serb propaganda emanating from Belgrade' (Stavrianos 1958: 546). Reports forwarded to Colonel Apis about the political mood among the Hapsburgs' South Slav subjects claimed that Franz Ferdinand's ideas enjoyed growing sympathy among them. According to the Colonel's nephew, Dr Milan Zivanovich, Apis saw the creation of 'a South-Slav union within the Danubian monarchy' as a death threat to Serb nationalist goals which is why plans for the high-level killing were drawn up' (Stavrianos 1958: 552).

The Austro-Hungarian army was holding summer manoeuvres in Bosnia in June 1914 and Franz Ferdinand attended them in his capacity as Inspector General of the Armed Forces of the Empire (Malcolm 1994: 154–5). A visit to Sarajevo was arranged for 28 June 1914, St Vitus's Day, the anniversary of the battle of Kosovo and for several generations the most sacred day in the Serbian national calendar. Many acts of incompetence by the Austrian authorities on this day and in others preceding it show how lax they were in protecting the heir to the throne or showing sensitivity to Serb feelings. But if the flashpoint had not been in Sarajevo, it could well have occurred somewhere else (Jászi 1964: 126). In the seventeen months from January 1913 to 1 July 1914 the Austrian chief of staff, Count Conrad von Hotzendorf, according to his own statements, urged his colleagues of the need for a preventive war against Serbia no less than twenty-five times (Jászi 1964: 418 n. 19). The burden of restless nationalities seemed increasingly unsupportable at the end of a long reign which had seen the Hapsburgs lose wars against Germany and Italy and make sweeping concessions to Hungary. One contemporary observer Rudolf Kjellen remarked: 'A Great Power can endure without difficulty one Ireland, as England did, even three, as imperial Germany did (Poland, Alsace, Schleswig). Different is the case when a Great Power is composed of nothing else but Irelands, as was almost the history of Austria-Hungary ...' (Jászi 1964: 379).

Exactly one month after the murder of the Archduke and his wife, Austria-Hungary declared war on Serbia which led, in one week, to the eruption of a general European war. Vienna had seen its influence slipping away in the Balkans which it had largely seen as its sphere of influence. With Turkey virtually driven out of Europe, Austria-Hungary appeared the continent's new 'sick man'. The Balkan Wars had revealed its inability to prevent the South Slavs dismembering the Ottoman Empire (Bideleux and Jeffries 1998: 377). In July 1914 it was not hard for the Emperor to be persuaded by some of his chief counsellors that a war with Serbia was necessary. Count Stefan Tisza, the Premier of Hungary, was less easy to persuade. Hungary felt the pressure of restive minorities even more than its partner in the Dual Monarchy. He agreed only when he was assured that no Serbian territory would be annexed to the empire (Jelavich 1983b: 113).

On 23 July 1914 Austria-Hungary gave Serbia an ultimatum that the Belgrade government suppress irredentist ambitions and activities both inside and outside Serbia (Bideleux and Jeffries 1998: 377). Serbia accepted all but one of the conditions which would have involved the presence of Austro-Hungarian magistrates or policemen conducting their investigations on Serbian soil (Malcolm 1994: 157). The qualified

Serbian response was the pretext for a swift Austrian declaration of war. Austria had German support. Kaiser Wilhelm II referred to 'the last great battle between Teutons and Slavs' (Bideleux and Jeffries 1998: 378). Germany saw punishment of Serbia as a way of checking the growing strength of Russia. But it is clear that neither Vienna nor Berlin expected that a local war could escalate into an international conflict. Russia was determined to preserve Serbia. It had the support of its ally France when Austria was urged by its ally Germany to take a militant stand. Efforts by neutral third parties to avoid catastrophe proved unavailing as the armies of the great powers mobilised. War between Germany and Russia began on 3 August. After Germany entered Belgium to attack French defences from an unprotected flank, Britain issued an ultimatum demanding a German withdrawal from this neutral state. Upon its rejection by Berlin, a British declaration of war followed on 4 August.

The murders in Sarajevo were one of over a dozen assassinations of royal personages and presidents in Europe over the previous 35 years, most being committed outside the Balkans. Vladimir Dedijer has written that 'it was an incident which under more normal international circumstances could not have provoked such momentous consequences' (Dedijer 1967: 445). Compared with Belfast or Barcelona, Sarajevo in 1914 was not a cauldron of ethnic strife. The assassination was an opportunity for the Viennese war party to attack and incapacitate Serbia before South Slav tensions became too much for a sclerotic empire to handle (Dedijer 1967: 445).

The outbreak of the First World War was 'a consequence of the deepening division of Europe into mutually antagonistic power blocs' (Bideleux and Jeffries 1998: 378). But a radicalisation of feeling had slowly taken place especially among younger people who saw themselves trapped in political structures that cramped their prospects. Far more South Slavs in the Hapsburg Empire were willing to obey the orders of Vienna, pay taxes, and fight in the Emperor's service than take up the bomb or the revolutionary pamphlet. But it only takes a dedicated minority to challenge a soft state. Moreover, European public opinion was becoming increasingly receptive to nationalism as shown by the eagerness with which tens of millions of men marched off to war. Socialism and capitalism, the two chief ideological foes, had no interest in a general European war and leaders of capital and labour tried in vain to halt it. Gavrilo Princip, Franz Ferdinand's assassin, was a peasant's son who had broken free of rural isolation by receiving an education. Across Eastern Europe, thousands of other ambitious, talented, and frustrated young men from 'the insignificant classes' were being converted to nationalism thanks to an education which highlighted romantic and inflated images of their homeland. Intransigent nationalism would derive enormous strength from a war which would bring crashing down the multicultural traditions that had shaped the European world for centuries. Nowhere was this more true than of the Balkans.

NOTES

1. See 'Constantin Brancoveanu's "Cultural Monarchy" in 17th- and 18th-century Wallachia', www.rotravel.com/romania/sites/cultural/brancov.htm
2. Radio Free Europe (1999), *Balkan Report* Vol. 13, no 17, Prague: 5 May.
3. 'Gladstone's Ghost' (1999), *The Economist*, London: 29 May.
4. Ibid.
5. Brinje (1994): 18, quoting Sir Charles Elliott (1908), *Turkey in Europe*, London: Frank Cass, p. 344.

Chapter 2

SOUTHEAST EUROPE'S SEARCH FOR STABILITY 1914–1940

THE BALKANS AND THE GREAT WAR

The First World War added substantially to the store of resentments and rivalries which would prevent Balkan states and peoples cooperating in future decades. The existing states fought on different sides and invaded each other's territory. But until the autumn of 1915 Serbia was the sole belligerent in the Balkans. A state of 4.5 million people, it succeeded for a year in repulsing an empire of fifty million. But, contrary to some expectations, the Hapsburgs were able to retain the loyalty of the South Slavs and other nationalities fighting in their army.

If they were to enter the conflict at all, the priority of the Balkan neutrals was to join the winning side in the European war so as to obtain territory at the expense of each other or whichever of the regional empires crashed to defeat. One British observer wrote at the end of 1914 that 'the example of Romania during the Balkan war has up till now hypnotised neutral states, who think they only have to wait with their jaws well apart for cities, provinces, and whole countries to drop in'.[1] For Bulgaria the only question was which side was able to deliver it Macedonia. Sensing that the Central Powers were on course for victory, King Ferdinand aligned with Germany and Austria-Hungary in October 1915. Serbia was then overwhelmed during the following winter. The first ever aerial bombardment of civilians occurred when Austria bombarded refugees from Serbia as they trudged across the plain of Kosovo (Vickers 1998: 90).

Romania and Greece remained the only other Balkan states not aligned with the Central Powers. The Allies landed four divisions in Thessaloniki in the autumn of 1915 with the approval of Premier Venizelos but not that of King Constantine I (whose wife was a sister of the German Kaiser) (Jelavich 1983b: 118). In Romania the king and his ministers had also favoured rival alliances. On 3 August 1914 the Crown Council had rejected King Carol I's proposal that Romania join the Central Powers, deciding instead on a policy of neutrality (Alexandrescu 1998: 45). After lavish promises of territory from the

Allies, Romania eventually joined the war in August 1916. But, with a divided leadership unable to make a clearcut decision, Greece became an arena in which the warring powers struggled for control. In the summer of 1916, its northeastern territories were overrun by a German-Bulgarian force. When the cabinet voted to declare war on Bulgaria, it was overruled by the king. The Allies then tightened pressure on Greece; the fact that Britain had entered the war in defence of the neutrality of a small state like Belgium was lost sight of. At Thessaloniki in October 1916, under Allied protection, Venizelos set up a provisional government opposed to the king. Greece finally entered the war on the Allied side in July 1917, one month after Constantine had been forced from the throne after an ultimatum from a French general demanding his abdication under threat of Allied bombardment (Anderson 1966: 336). Greece was profoundly divided by a bitter feud whose effects would be felt even beyond the Second World War. An event that occurred in Athens on 26 December 1916 illustrated the deep enmities aroused:

> ... the Archbishop of Athens, standing on a cairn of stones, performed the medieval rite of excommunication. Eight bishops standing around him, representing royalist Greece, chanted: 'Cursed be Eleutherios Venizelos who imprisons priests and plots against his king and his country'. Each participant cried 'Cursed be he' and cast a stone upon the cairn. Sixty thousand Athenians took part in this ceremony, each bringing his stone and his curse. (Stavrianos 1958: 568)

To secure their backing for the Allied war effort Britain made lavish promises to Greece over Cyprus (and to the Jews in relation to Palestine) which would cause no end of trouble in the Eastern Mediterranean for the rest of the century.

During previous cycles of European tension and war, the powers had made promises to Balkan movements and states which they had often been forgetful of afterwards. It was only with reluctance that the British Foreign Office abandoned the idea of re-forming the Hapsburg Empire on the principle of autonomy for its subject peoples (Mazower 1998: 51). But the passions engendered by the war meant that the initiative was passing from a circle of elite policy-makers; academics, clerics, aristocrats and journalists who had promoted the cause of stateless small nations before 1914 saw their influence grow. In Britain, the most distinguished among them was R.W. Seton-Watson, a Scottish champion of the rights and freedoms of the South Slav, Czechoslovak, and Romanian nationalities of the Hapsburg Empire. In October 1916 he launched *New Europe*, a periodical which for four years successfully popularised the emancipation of the subject races of Central and Southeastern Europe (H. and C. Seton-Watson 1981: 179). In alliance with Dr Ronald Burrows, principal of King's College of the University of London, he promoted the study of East European languages, literature and history, the School of Slavonic Studies being launched at the University of London in 1915 (H. and C. Seton-Watson 1981: 142).

Senior British politicians now openly identified with Balkan causes. In October 1915, Sir Edward Carson quit the British cabinet over what he saw as Premier Asquith's 'betrayal of Serbia' (H. and C. Seton-Watson 1981: 199). Carson was a member of the council of the Serbian Society. On 7 December 1917, when the inaugural meeting of the Anglo-Romanian Society was held with the Lord Mayor of London presiding, Carson was the keynote speaker. He repeatedly asserted the British government's determination to stand by Romania, much of which had been overrun by the Central Powers in the previous months (H. and C. Seton-Watson 1981: 239).

A glance at the aims of the Anglo-Romanian Society shows that protecting British interests in the East in large part lay behind its formation:

> ... to promote close relations between the British Empire and Romania ... by mutual study of the life, literature and economic conditions of both countries; to support and make known Romania's just aspirations to the liberation of the Romanians of Austria-Hungary and their union with the Kingdom; and to spread a knowledge of Romania, its geopolitical position in the Near East and its importance for the welfare of the British Empire and the maintenance of peace in Europe. (H. and C. Seton-Watson 1981: 239)

The war dented British insularity, but deep-seated interest and concern for the Balkans among elite players would not long survive the return of peace. In the USA, the leaders of stateless nations such as the Czech Tomas Masaryk would also gain influential backers as American intervention in the European war drew closer. The USA would be a crucial arena for the advocates of new states, for it was from here that the decisive impetus for re-ordering Eastern Europe around national principles would come.

As early as 1915, the US President, Woodrow Wilson, had stated that '[E]very people has the right to choose the sovereignty under which they should live' (Ferguson 1999). In January 1918 (by which time the USA had entered the war on the side of Britain and France), Wilson issued his blueprint for peace based on 'Fourteen Points' in which the desirability of replacing the dynastic empires with states conforming to the nationality principle was made an imperative (Nicolson 1964: 39–40). The principle of self-determination for nations, for long the rallying-cry of nationalist movements representing stateless peoples, had been legitimised by a President of the USA who was now the central figure in the Allied war effort. Wilson was an upright Presbyterian of Ulster-Scots ancestry who, imbued with a 19th-century positivist outlook, believed that 'the whole world was steadily evolving towards "liberal" democratic nation-states and laissez-faire market economies' (Bideleux and Jeffries 1998: 410). He was convinced that the system of 'national' states which had taken hold in Western Europe could be extended to the east. The nationalist conflict in his ancestral homeland Ulster which, in 1914, had brought Britain to the brink of civil war, failed to shake his optimism. Nor did he seem to be aware that the pattern of relatively homogeneous West European states had only emerged gradually and painfully after much bloodshed and the ruthless exclusion of religious groups and other minorities which fell foul of the ruling group fashioning the new sovereign state. Nevertheless, imbued with the belief that the New World could redeem the sins of the Old, Wilson set up a group of four 'wise men' which in 1918 pored over maps in the New York City Central Library, in an effort to redraw the boundaries of Eastern Europe. Walter Lippmann, the head of the committee, pulled out, believing that the mission was an impossible one to fulfill. Viewing the handiwork he had begun, he remarked: 'Looked at from above, below, and from every side, I can't see anything in this treaty but endless trouble for Europe and I'm exceedingly doubtful in my own mind as to whether we can guarantee so impossible a peace' (Steele 1980: 158).

Wilson and some of his advisers would themselves soon have deep misgivings about having elevated the nationality principle to a central place in European affairs. But there was mounting pressure from below in Eastern Europe which the Allies would have found difficult to ignore. In July 1917, the Serbian government and the leaders of the Yugoslav Committee, made up of figures active in the name of South Slavs within the Hapsburg Empire, signed a declaration paving the way for a South Slav state: the Declaration of Corfu stated that 'all the South Slavs were one people and that, in accordance with the principle of self-determination, they wished to be united at the end of the war in one state' (Stavrianos 1958: 575). On the crucial question of centralism versus federalism little was said because agreement had proven impossible, an ominous portent for the future. Nevertheless, the Declaration offered a solid front to the outside world.

In April 1918, in the wake of Russia's collapse, Bessarabia's representatives convened and voted for union with Romania. To halt the disintegration of the Hungarian part of the empire, liberals brought into government in Budapest in the autumn of 1918 offered concessions to the nationalities. The minister of nationalities was Professor Ozskár Jászi, a genuine champion of the rights of subject peoples. He offered the nationalities full autonomy as the basis for a new Danubian confederation of free peoples, but it was too little too late (Stavrianos 1958: 574). On 18 October 1918, before the Budapest parliament, Alexandru Vaida-Voievod had read a declaration of Transylvania's independence from Hungary in the name of the Romanian National Council (Georgescu 1992: 171). His colleague, Iuliu Maniu who was in charge of foreign and military affairs for the council, assembled 70,000 Transylvanian soldiers in Vienna. With the imperial army collapsing, the Hungarian administration fell apart and the Romanians seized control of Transylvania. On 1 December 1918 before a crowd of 100,000 people at Alba Iulia the Council voted to unite Transylvania with Romania (Georgescu 1992: 171–2).

THE VERSAILLES TREATIES

In 1919–20 a series of treaties were signed with the defeated states whose ultimate objective was the preservation of peace and geopolitical stability in East-Central Europe (Nunez 1994: 520). Since it was widely believed that peace had been ruined by the ambitions of the dynastic empires, there was a groundswell of support for making an accommodation with the rising force of nationalism. The Allied statesmen at the peace conference showed by their actions that they hoped peace could be secured by encouraging the creation of Western-style culturally homogeneous nation-states in East-Central Europe.

The Treaty of Versailles, signed with Germany on 28 June 1919, has become the name by which the European peace treaties are collectively known. But there were also the St Germain Treaty with Austria (10 September 1919), the Trianon Treaty with Hungary (4 June 1920), the Neuilly Treaty with Bulgaria (27 November 1919) and the Sèvres Treaty with Turkey (20 August 1920).

Unlike the architects of the Congress of Berlin, the arbiters of Versailles favoured the idea of territorially powerful states in the Balkans and Eastern Europe generally. The Allies, especially France, saw the need for large states able to oppose revanchist efforts by the defeated powers and contain the menace of the Bolsheviks, the extreme socialists who had seized power in Russia in 1917 (Bideleux and Jeffries 1998: 410). Therefore, favourable allocations of territories were made to those states fortunate to be on the winning side when the First World War had ended. One of Wilson's Fourteen Points had stipulated that the Italian frontiers should be drawn 'along clearly recognisable lines of nationality' (Stavrianos 1958: 576). But this was waived to allow Italy to occupy the South Tyrol with its overwhelmingly Austrian population as well as parts of the Dalmatian coast where non-Italians predominated. Ethnic lines were ignored for strategic reasons. If the boundary between southern Hungary and Yugoslavia had been drawn on ethnic lines, it would have run very close to Belgrade, leaving the capital of the new South Slav state vulnerable to attack. Thus, it was decided to extend Yugoslavia northwards into the Hungarian plain, 200,000 Hungarians coming under Yugoslav rule. Strategic rather than ethnic considerations also led to Bulgaria being deprived of certain key areas (Stravrianos 1958: 577). No plebiscite was allowed to test the preferences of the inhabitants of these regions. Indeed, in contrast to Central Europe, the architects of Versailles refused to sanction plebiscites in any disputed part of Southeast Europe, an indication that for West European statesmen the views and fate of Balkan peoples counted for rather less than those in Central Europe.

Many new borders severed what had been natural economic units. Newly Romanian cities like Orádea and Arad were detached from their economic hinterlands in Hungary. Existing rail and trade networks were disrupted. The extensive river traffic on the Danube slumped as a result of the Balkanization of the Danube basin and the river lost its role as the main economic artery of Eastern Europe.

Hungary was the greatest net loser of the peace settlements. After Trianon, it was left with 28.6% of its former territory which was divided as follows: 31.5% to Romania (Transylvania and two-thirds of the Banat); 19.6% to Yugoslavia (Croatia, Slovenia and one-third of the Banat); and 18.9% to Czechoslovakia (Slovakia and Ruthenia). The remaining 1.4% consisted of miniscule cessions to Austria, Poland and Italy (Stavrianos 1958: 578).

Austria was forbidden to unite with Germany whose capacity to dominate East-Central Europe was actually enhanced by the break-up of the Hapsburg Empire and its replacement by a host of small, competing states. On 28 March 1919, the British Premier David Lloyd-George wrote to President Wilson:

I cannot conceive of any greater cause of future war than that the German people, who have certainly proven themselves one of the most vigorous and powerful races in the world, should be surrounded by a number of small states, many of them consisting of people who have never previously set up a stable government themselves, but each of them containing large masses of Germans clamouring for reunion with their native land. (Cohen 1998: 76)

At least 9.5 million Germans were to be found outside the borders of the post-1918 Reich, about 13% of the total German-speaking population of Europe (Ferguson 1999). Many were to be found in Central Europe and others in the Balkans, but the creation of a large new irredentist wave loyal to what had been Central Europe's strongest state had implications for all parts of Europe where dynasties had been replaced by states based on the national principle.

Solidarity and cooperation among the Allied powers was necessary if the Versailles system was to underwrite a stable Europe. But insular British leaders lost interest in the need to maintain European stability and quarrelled with their erstwhile French allies about points of detail (Lukacs 1953: 20). The absence of Western leadership was complemented by a shortage of goodwill among the new states of Eastern Europe. One exception was the Romanian statesman Take Ionescu who endeavoured to create a bloc of Allied powers stretching from Poland on the Baltic to Greece on the Aegean, the aim being to prevent any 'revisionist' efforts to undo the Versailles system (Scurtu and Buzatu 1999: 12). But such efforts to create a regional security system were foiled by debilitating quarrels. Disputes between Poland and Czechoslovakia and between Yugoslavia and Greece prevented a large *entente* emerging in Eastern Europe. The most serious quarrel was between Italy and Yugoslavia over the disputed city of Rijeka (known as Fiume before 1945). Occupied by the proto-fascist Gabriele D'Annunzio in September 1919, Rijeka was ceded to Italy under a bilateral treaty despite the fact that the city and much of its hinterland was Croat in population.

Yugoslavia spent large sums building a port to rival Rijeka which, even 'with its superior facilities, suffered a disastrous decline' (Stavrianos 1958: 56). Such 'beggar my neighbour' policies became a feature of much of the region's life. The regional alliance that emerged under French sponsorship, and known as the Little Entente, turned out to be a narrow military union embracing Czechoslovakia, Romania and Yugoslavia directed against Hungary (Borsody 1993: 34). The Little Entente states still traded more with their Hungarian and Austrian enemies than with each other (Rothschild 1974: 11). France traded little with her Balkan political protégés and the peace treaties contained no provisions for free trade zones, a development that would have to await the outcome of a second disastrous European civil war in the 1940s.

The League of Nations, meant to regulate the Versailles system by being a forum where disputes could be settled and inter-state cooperation promoted, never fulfilled its promise. The USA, the moral author of the peace, reverted to isolationism and refused to join the League. Wilson, though crushed by this rejection, was already appalled by realising while in Paris that 'no tribal entity was too small to have ambitions for self-determination'. Speaking to an Irish-American delegation in Paris on 11 June 1919, Wilson declared:

> When I gave utterances to those words [that all nations had a right to self-determination] I said them without the knowledge that nationalities existed, which are coming to us day after day ... You do not know and can not appreciate the anxieties that I have experienced as the result of those many millions of people having their hopes raised by what I said. (Moynihan 1993: 85)

In the new national states created during and after the Versailles treaties, around one in four of the population still belonged to national minorities (Mazower 1998: 56). In 1919, prompted by President Wilson, the architecture of the peace treaties required those states with large minorities to sign individual treaties guaranteeing certain rights to them (Nunez 1994: 519). These rights covered citizenship, equality of treatment under the law and religious freedom, as well as rights to certain forms of collective organization such as schooling (Mazower 1998: 53). The treaties were guaranteed by the League of Nations which established a procedure stipulating the rights of minorities, one allowing for petitions to be made (though not directly by the minorities concerned) if rights were felt to be violated. But the international power of the League proved to be largely fictitious (Lukacs 1953: 18).

The Allied powers had minorities themselves but they were unwilling to make the regime of minority protection applicable to them. This was a double standard that was also evident in the 1990s when the minority issue again appeared to be a pressing one, especially in the light of the warfare in Yugoslavia. In the Council of Europe states with minorities to which it was reluctant to grant formal recognition or collective rights, particularly France and Greece, delayed the introduction of a system of minority protection applicable to all members. Some of the Cold War victors, like the great powers at Versailles, were hoping for a collective body to protect minority rights in 'new' states but not in their own. The thinking of the British delegate at Versailles, Sir James Headlam-Morley, would have resonated with that of jealous guardians of West European state sovereignty 75 years later:

> It would be most dangerous to allow the inhabitants or citizens of any State direct approach to the League except through their own Government. If we allow this principle to be neglected, we should get into a position in which, for instance, the French in Canada, the Jews in America, the Roman Catholics in England, the Welsh, the Irish, the Scottish Highlanders, the Basques, Bretons or Catalans might approach the League and complain of injustices to which they are subjected. (Nunez 1994: 509)

From 1921 to 1969 Britain was not even prepared to permit the Catholic minority in Northern Ireland to use the Westminster Parliament in London as a forum where it could ask for relief from the repressive rule of the Protestant Unionist majority which had been given autonomy within the United Kingdom, so it is hardly surprising that British policy-makers were opposed to Europe-wide arrangements to safeguard minority rights. So was France, as indicated by the report sent by the French Foreign Ministry to the French delegate at the League of Nations on the subject of the petition filed in 1923 by Hungarian landowners in Romania over agrarian reform: 'The claim of the Hungarians is well-based in law, but the Romanians are our friends' (Nunez 1994: 522, n. 52).

Minority protection was unlikely to be taken very seriously as long as the states likely to break the various treaties were those in alliance with the great powers which dominated the Council of the League of Nations (Nunez 1994: 522). The intention of ethnic majorities in charge of new or enlarged states to establish a homogeneous polity based on supposedly Western norms was not regarded as unreasonable by French or British policy-makers. In 1922 Alexander Cadogan, later head of the British Foreign Office, wrote that although the governments of the new states were undoubtedly contravening the minorities treaties

> ... yet more harm would be done in the end by unnecessary interference than, even at the risk of a little local suffering, to allow these minorities to settle down under their present masters. As you know, so long as these people imagine that their grievances can be aired before the League of Nations, they will refuse to settle down and the present effervescence will continue indefinitely. (Finney 1995: 536–7, n. 8)

ASIA MINOR 1922: THE SHAPE OF THINGS TO COME

A reluctance to enforce League policy on minorities or revise and build upon the peace treaties in the light of new challenges, became a hardened reflex thanks in no small measure to the challenge to the Versailles settlement posed by a revived Turkey in the early 1920s. It had not been expected that a country dismissed as 'the sick man of Europe' for almost a century, would prove so disruptive. During the First World War the British had sponsored a revolt in the Arab-inhabited territories of the Ottoman Empire which were divided up into British and French protectorates by the Treaty of Sèvres in 1920. The Philhellene British Premier, Lloyd-George, dreamt of a new Greek empire in the Eastern Mediterranean and encouraged Venizelos to pursue Greek territorial ambitions in Asia Minor. As a Welshman, Lloyd-George empathised with the Greeks as a fellow nationality which had been mistreated by an imperial state (Goldstein 1991: 243). As a champion of the Allied cause from 1914, Venizelos was treated with more respect at Versailles than any of the other Balkan leaders. Georges Clemenceau, the French Premier, had met Venizelos while visiting Crete in the early 1900s and had told a friend then: 'In Crete I have discovered a phenomenon much more interesting than the excavations. He is a young advocate, Mr Venezuelos—Mr Venizelos? Frankly, I cannot quite recall his name but the whole of Europe will be speaking of him in a few years' (Stavrianos 1958: 475).

The lionising of Venizelos was one of the first instances of the external powers backing a local Balkan leader to an imprudent extent because he seemed to embody 'Western' qualities that were in short supply locally as well as being a reliable guardian of Western interests. Venizelos was seen as a 'reborn Gladstone' by British Philhellenes who were not unmindful of the fact that a new regional and untested power like Greece was required to protect the territory Britain had seized from a prostrate Turkey in the Middle East. Virulent Turcophobia was used by many of them to justify dismantling the Ottoman Empire. Thus the Earl of Cromer, Britain's pro-consul in Egypt, wrote in 1915: 'We are fighting in order that the Turkish hordes, who for five hundred years have camped in Europe, should be driven back into Asia' (Carabott 1995: 45).

Venizelos was sufficiently impressed by British enthusiasm for a Greek role in Asia Minor that he was even prepared to sacrifice territory that Greece had occupied after the fall of Ottoman Macedonia to realise such a goal. In a memorandum to the king written on 24 January 1915, he formulated the new policy of expansion in Asia Minor: 'I would not hesitate to recommend … the sacrifice of Kavalla, if only to save the Ottoman Greeks [of Asia Minor] and to ensure the foundation of a really big Greece' (Stavrianos 1958: 585).

From the Treaty of Sèvres, Greece acquired the region around the port of Smyrna, but Colonel Ioannis Metaxas, acting chief of the general staff in 1915, had warned Venizelos then of the logistical problems in the way of seizing a large part of Asia Minor. Out of a population of ten million, less than two million were Greeks. They were not a majority in any district which meant that Greece would be fighting for territory where the population was predominantly hostile. Given physical obstacles and the absence of roads, impeding military communications, and with the Turks having the advantage of fighting in their own country, 'Metaxas foresaw a repetition of Napoleon's experience in Russia' (Stavrianos 1958: 586). He concluded that Greek intervention could only be successful if the Allies fully participated in the operation and most of Asia Minor was partitioned among them, leaving a rump Turkish part unable to seriously menace the Greek positions around Smyrna (Stavrianos 1958: 586).

Internal Greek political disputes, Allied unwillingness to throw its full weight behind an Asia Minor adventure, and the emergence of an inspirational Turkish resistance leader, Kemal Atatürk, bore out the fears of Metaxas. In 1922 the Greeks were routed in Asia Minor. The humiliating treaty of Sèvres was shelved and in July 1923 the Treaty of Lausanne confirmed the outcome of the Greek–Turkish war. Smyrna and its hinterland returned to Turkey as did Eastern Thrace. Constantinople was confirmed as a Turkish city; Northern Epirus was restored to Albania; but the Dodecanese Islands (seized by Italy in 1911) would be vacated by her only in 1947 (Woodhouse 1998: 208).

In September 1922, a belligerent faction in the British government around Lloyd-George, had almost brought Britain and Turkey to war when advancing Turkish forces confronted British ones stationed at Chanak on the Asian side of the Dardenelles peninsula. The crisis was averted when the local British commander refused to deliver an ultimatum from London which would almost certainly have meant war (Fromkin 1991: 551). The failure of Lloyd-George's Greek policy soon led to his overthrow in a revolt mounted by a Conservative figure who as Premier in the 1920s and 1930s was determined to keep Britain out of Eastern entanglements. Stanley Baldwin confided to his wife that 'he had found out that Lloyd-George had been all for war and had schemed to make the country go to war with Turkey so that they should have a "Christians" ... war v. the Mahomedans ... On the strength of that they would call a General Election at once ... which, they calculated, would return them to office for another period of years' (Fromkin 1991: 553 n. 36).

Baldwin would be the dominant figure in British politics for the next dozen years. He avoided imperial adventures, concentrating (perhaps in reaction to Lloyd-George's behaviour) on domestic policy instead. Lloyd-George would be the first of a succession of European leaders—Hitler in wartime Yugoslavia and Stalin in postwar Yugoslavia spring to mind immediately—who would get their fingers burned by pursuing high-risk policies in Southeast Europe that were ultimately beyond their capacity to enforce.

Western encouragement for a reckless Asia Minor adventure had the most tragic human consequences. As a result of a convention signed by Greece and Turkey on 30 January 1923 under the aegis of the powers, an almost complete exchange of their minority populations occurred. Over 1,100,000 Greeks moved from Turkey to Greece and 380,000 Muslim Turks in the reverse direction (Finney 1995: 542). This was no repatriation, 'but two deportations into exile' (L. Carl Brown, 1984: 86). The distinguished British historian, Arnold Toynbee, who was one of the few policy advisers to adopt a neutral stance in the conflict, was in no doubt about who carried the responsibility for the tragedy:

> I acquired an affection not only for Smyrna (which had an indescribable charm of its own) but for Manysa, Bergama, Aivali, and other smaller places in the hinterland, and I made friends with a number of people of almost every denomination and nationality. These beautiful towns are now desolated, these amiable people killed, exiled, ruined, or tormented by the most appalling mental and physical agonies, and this through the wantonness of Western statesmen who hardened their hearts and stopped their ears against their own expert advisers. In these circumstances it gives me no satisfaction that in spite of myself I have in many cases prophesied right, and my only feeling besides sorrow for the victims is one of indignation that the real criminals should have got off so cheaply. After causing hundreds of thousands of fellow human beings to lose everything that makes life worth living, they have themselves lost nothing more irretrievable than office and reputation. (Toynbee 1923: x–xi)

Foreign manipulation had helped destroy almost beyond repair the peaceful symbiosis of Greek and Turk (Clogg 1992: 101). Britain and France came increasingly to favour the formula of exchanging populations in order to clear territory between neighbouring states which could not agree about where their boundaries should be fixed. The homogeneity of disputed territories was seen as a step towards peace, however unpalatable, a viewpoint that re-emerged among policy-makers charged with securing peace in war-torn Yugoslavia after 1991.

In 1925 rapid action by the League of Nations prevented a frontier clash between Greece and Bulgaria from escalating into full-scale war. It was one of the few successes of the policy of collective security associated with the League (Stavrianos 1958: 651–2). A League commission of enquiry under the British diplomat Sir Horace Rumbold concluded that the best way to reduce friction between these two unfriendly neighbours was not to accord greater protection to minorities, but to promote the exchange of populations (Finney 1995: 547). Thus, in the words of the historian Patrick B. Finney 'it was probably better to eliminate the minorities problem not by putting an end to persecution but by eliminating the minorities themselves' (Finney 1995: 547). By the end of the 1920s almost no Greeks remained in Bulgaria and western Thrace was almost completely cleared of its Bulgarian population (Finney 1995: 547).

After 1920 Serbia held the larger part of what had been Macedonia. Sir Miles Lampson, head of the British Foreign Office's Central Department argued that 'given ten years of undisturbed possession [by Yugoslavia] the Macedonian question will automatically cease to exist'. He advised that Britain should 'do nothing to upset the present Serbianisation of South Macedonia: it is the only way of avoiding trouble and is after all not at all a bad solution' (Finney 1995: 540).

Britain had swung around to the position that the absorption of minority populations by the majority nation-state was a better way of preserving peace than upholding the various minority treaties. In 1925 the viewpoint received the imprimatur of the British Foreign Secretary, Sir Austen Chamberlain, when he argued that the minority treaties served 'only to keep alive differences which otherwise might be healed in time': in these circumstances he doubted whether they were 'really anything but an evil for all concerned' (Finney 1995: 537 n. 9).

Chamberlain had established a warm friendship with the Italian dictator Benito Mussolini. Shortly after Mussolini's seizure of power in 1922 he had shelled the Greek island of Corfu and showed no inclination to withdraw from the mainly Greek-inhabited Dodecanese islands seized in 1912 after Italy's war with Turkey. Mussolini did not hide his contempt for the League of Nations which he saw as a brake on his vaulting ambitions. Yet Chamberlain declared at the 1925 Locarno conference designed to confirm Germany's post-1918 western frontiers that: 'For my part I frankly confess that I hold it as a misfortune for the peace of the world that the expectations which Italy has been encouraged to entertain when she entered the war were not more fully satisfied than they were' (Lamb 1977: 85). Later in 1926, he wrote in a Foreign Office memorandum that: 'If there be acts of his [Mussolini] which excite severe criticisms, no candid observer will deny that alike at home and abroad he has given a new life and a new standing to Italy' (Lamb 1977: 85).

Such a myopic attitude to undemocratic leaders, who were no real friends of Britain, would later be reflected in the dispatches of diplomats and their chiefs not just in their dealings with fascist leaders but with communists in Eastern Europe, especially if they displayed any sign of wishing autonomy from the Soviet Union.

MINORITIES IN THE NEW STATES

The minority question hung over the new or enlarged states of Southeast Europe and in the 1930s fatally undermined several of them. Writing in the 1940s after the Versailles system had been swept away, the historian Hugh Seton-Watson argued that: '[T]he problem can only be solved if it is possible to combine free use of the language of birth, and recognition of the personal nationality of the citizenry, with loyalty to a State which stands above the ethnical principle and includes men of different nations' (Hugh Seton-Watson 1945: 272).

The Austro-Hungarian Empire had rejected similar calls to depoliticise national feeling emanating from Karl Renner before 1914. Its post-imperial successors would turn an even deafer ear to calls for the adoption of a Swiss model of government whereby the different languages spoken in the state enjoyed official recognition. In 1918, the Transylvanian Romanians who drew up the Alba Iulia Declaration proclaiming union with the Kingdom of Romania, included important provisions for securing the acquiescence of the minorities making up over 40% of the territory's population. According to Paragraph 1 of Article 3 of the Declaration:

> All of the people have the right to public education, public administration, and the administration of justice in their own languages, provided by individuals chosen from among their own members. All people will receive rights of representation in the government of the country and in the legislative organ in accordance with their numbers. (Illyes 1982: 87)

The guarantee from local Romanians to the minorities in their midst was ignored by centralists in Bucharest who determined the shape of the union to the disadvantage not just of nonethnic Romanians but Romanians previously under foreign rule. Estonia was the only East European state where, on the surface, the state was prepared to make a genuinely far-reaching attempt to conciliate its minorities by treating them in a liberal fashion (Crampton 1994: 99).

It is not hard to see why majorities in multi-ethnic states were determined to dominate rather than conciliate minorities. They were often burdened by memories of discrimination meted out by imperial states to which these minorities had offered loyalty. When majorities-turned-into-minorities after 1918 found themselves subjected to the discriminatory measures which their elites had exercised beforehand, it was often regarded as sweet revenge by those now having the upper hand. Despite bombastic rhetoric about the completion of the historic mission to place a people in charge of its God-given homeland, there was underlying unease among ruling nationalists that the boundaries of their enlarged states might be transient. The survival of these boundaries was certainly seen as dependent on the outcome of great power machinations over which the East European successor states had little or no control. Therefore the prevailing instinct of the new elites was to consolidate the power of ethnic majorities by basing the state wholly around their interests. Building a state identity that included elements of minority culture proved unacceptable in the euphoric atmosphere after 1918. The name of the South Slav state that became Yugoslavia was indicative of that. The country's official name between 1921 and 1929, the Kingdom of the Serbs, Croats and Slovenes showed clearly that only these three groups were viewed as constitutive populations of the new nation. The 1921 Constitution 'did not formally discriminate against the [Muslim] minorities who made up almost 2 million of the country's 12 million inhabitants' but at least as far as the nation-building programme went, they were *personae non gratae* (Wachtel 1998: 71).

Minorities were often seen as threatening the cohesion and even survival prospects of countries like Romania and Yugoslavia when they claimed a separate national identity. In Bucharest and Belgrade the Versailles treaties with their provisions for minority protection were seen as encouraging the recalcitrance of minorities which ought to accept their fate and gradually assimilate with the majority. Thus, in 1919, Brătianu delayed the Versailles negotiations by refusing to guarantee the rights of minorities in the enlarged Romania. 'The

Minority Treaty was an attempt to weaken the unified nationalist outlook of the Romanian state', he argued (Illyes 1982: 89). Romania only signed when a more amenable government was formed, but the machinery for monitoring minority rights proved not to be a serious deterrent for governments embarking on the creation of a single nation-state in the multinational territories of which they had gained possession (Gallagher 1995: 24).

In Europe the beneficiaries of the peace treaties saw themselves joining the ranks of Europe's *Staatsvolk* (state people). This meant that they were culturally and politically pre-eminent in a state, even though other groups were present, sometimes in large numbers. The leaders of such ascendant nations equated the entire country with their own ethnic homeland and regarded the state as the particular expression of their own ethnic group. Thus nearly everywhere, the preference for the majority was shown in the way state jobs were filled. This became a priority when the majority state-building project ran into trouble in the economically depressed 1930s. In 1933, the Romanian politician Dr A. Vaida-Voevod tried to introduce measures which would have confined state employment, as well as other areas of the labour market deemed of national importance, to ethnic Romanians. However, he was obstructed by the Liberals who did not wish to see such a nationalist card falling into rival hands (MacCartney 1965: 326). Nevertheless, many Romanians were uneasy at the numerical domination the minorities enjoyed in all the cities of the new territories which Romania had acquired (Scurtu and Buzatu 1999: 49). So calls to reduce the influence of the minorities in the urban professions and rapidly promote educated Romanians in their place often enjoyed support beyond the ranks of political nationalists.

Restricting the access of minorities to education was seen as a way of eroding their identity and preventing a capable leadership forming among them. No other state went as far as the Yugoslav one which in the 1920s prevented Albanian-language schools functioning in Kosovo (Malcolm 1998: 267). In Romania, state education policy fluctuated. A liberal historian has made a strong case for the view that Romania was the only sizeable East European state to allow minorities educational autonomy (Pippidi 1993: 154). But the offensive against the minority schools network directed by Constantin Anghelescu, education minister from 1934 to 1937, suggests that assimilation was favoured in influential circles (Illyes 1982: 74–5).

Nicolae Iorga, Romania's most prolific historian, insisted when Prime Minister in 1931–2 that:

We have no plans to transform a good Hungarian or a good German into a hypocritical Romanian, because we believe that those who abandon all their past and sell their soul in exchange for some advantage will be, for the nation which is supposed to receive them, not a profit but a poison. (Pippidi 1993: 154)

Iorga argued that the minority nationalities deserved the opportunity to be educated in their mother tongue provided they showed loyalty to the state. He even spoke out in 1919 against the immediate nationalisation of the university of Cluj, the main higher education centre for the Hungarians of Transylvania. He recommended the creation of a modern technical university in Transylvania that would concentrate on mining, forestry and commerce rather than another humanistic one to rival those in Bucharest and Iaşi (Livezeanu 1995: 222). The minorities could have fitted in more easily to a technical university than to one producing graduates destined for law and the civil service. Down to the present the Hungarian demand for a university in their language and the Romanian refusal to allow it, are the main impediments preventing the normalisation of relations between the two peoples.

A state that viewed them as a serious menace to its own security could encourage minorities to move. In the mid-1920s, Greece expelled about 53,000 Bulgarians from Greek Thrace and Macedonia in order to make room for 638,000 Greek refugees from the littoral of Asia Minor (Rothschild 1974: 234). Henceforth 89% of the population of Greek Macedonia consisted of Greeks while Greek Thrace was virtually cleared of Bulgarians. In the 1930s ambitious plans were drawn up by Serb officials to change the national character of the population in Kosovo. The colonization programme occurring since 1918 both here and in Macedonia was to be stepped up and forceful measures were employed to promote the mass departure of Kosovo Albanians (Malcolm 1998: 278). But refugees and displaced peoples could keep national disputes at boiling point, as the uprooted Macedonians in Bulgaria were to prove in the first quarter of the last century.

Most minorities used non-violent means to try to obtain the group rights in the cultural and educational spheres seen as necessary to preserve their identity and hand it on to the next generation. The Bosnian Muslims in Yugoslavia and the Hungarians in Romania were represented in parliament by their own parties. Sometimes they collaborated with majority interests if they held the balance of power, but the gains extracted were often meagre. In the 1930s, the threat of worse discrimination and the desire of vocal elements to escape from a subordinate status radicalised minorities. As in the case of the Germans of Romania or the Croats of Yugoslavia, it sometimes predisposed their extremist leaders to combine with external forces to subvert the Versailles settlement.

The alienation of minorities and the refusal of most states to promote regional cooperation by strengthening economic ties with neighbours, made the new states vulnerable to predators as the international system grew increasingly lawless in the 1930s.

CENTRALIZATION

Not only minorities but ethnic majorities united in one state usually for the first time were confronted with the need to make major adjustments. The two largest states in the interwar Balkans were the unions of the Romanians and the South Slavs. It was bound to be difficult to unite areas with different national consciousnesses, administrative traditions, and religious loyalties (Lendvai 1969: 24). And so it proved. Constructing a common polity where members of the same ethnic family had enjoyed contrasting political experiences in the generations before 1918 was pursued in a half-hearted and unimaginative way. The decision to centralise government around the historic state-building core, Serbia and the Kingdom of Romania centred on Bucharest, proved to be a serious error. It resulted in two deeply fragmented states which it was not difficult to break up early in the Second World War.

Yugoslavia presented the greatest state-building challenge. At the start of its existence, there were four different rail networks, five currencies, and six legal systems all dating from before 1914 (Lampe 1996: 115). By the start of the century, the three main South Slav peoples, the Serbs, Croats and Slovenes, each possessed 'a widely distributed national consciousness and fully formed national ideology' (Rusinow 1995: 355). With the formation of Yugoslavia in 1919 all the South Slavs, except the Bulgarians, were now brought together in one state. The Croats, among whom the idea of South Slav unity had originated, expected the new state to grant what was denied to them by the Hapsburgs: national self-determination and a chance of promoting economic growth unhindered by long-distance interference (Prpa-Jovanović 1997: 53). But it soon emerged that the priorities of the Belgrade elite were different. Nikola Pasić, the dominant figure in Serbian politics, was only prepared to offer a unitary state solution to a multinational question (Thompson 1992: 2). Pasić's Radical Party had been accustomed to confronting or dominating opponents and the idea of power-sharing along regional lines was one that it could not easily have adjusted to (Lampe 1996: 127).

The incompatibility of views between Serb and Croat leaders emerged during negotiations on the island of Corfu in 1917 over the future of the South Slav territories. Ante Trumbić, the Croat who later became Yugoslav foreign minister, had a meeting with Stojan Protić, a representative of the Serbian government which was 'an educative experience for the Croats' (Tanner 1997: 116). 'We have the solution to Bosnia', Protić declared during one of their discussions: 'When our army crosses the Drina we will give the Turks [Muslims] 24 hours, well, maybe 48, to return to the Orthodox faith. Those who don't will be killed, as we have done in our time in Serbia'. Tanner recounts that the Croatian delegation fell silent in astonishment. 'You can't be serious', Trumbić said at last. 'Quite serious', the Serb replied.

The main impetus behind the South Slav union was Croatian and Slovene fear that their lands would otherwise be partitioned and handed over to Italy, keen to receive territorial rewards for its participation on the Allied side. It was an alliance of convenience rather than a love match between co-ethnics who trusted and knew one another, and one in which Serbia initially held most of the cards. In 1919 Pasić was ready to give up part of the Croatian coast to Italy to facilitate Yugoslav expansion towards the south and east where Serbia had territorial claims. But Trumbić, his foreign minister, refused to tolerate such a manoeuvre (Rusinow 1995: 19). However, in 1921 a Constitution for a centralized state was drawn up and approved in parliament. The Serbian Radicals obtained a majority for a document which imposed the laws and officials of Serbia on a greatly enlarged territory. The Bosnian Muslim deputies who held the balance of power were offered concessions in return for their votes, which concessions were afterwards withheld. Not one Bosnian Muslim or Croat was appointed as prefect for any of Bosnia's six provinces. All were Serbs as was the case in Vojvodina, where the Hungarians and Germans completely out-numbered the Serbs. Only in Slovenia was a disproportionate share of Serbian officials avoided (Lampe 1996: 130).

The French system of prefects appointed by the centre and entitled to control local government down to a minute level suited the Serbian political elite. The prefects were required to have fifteen years of previous government experience, a qualification that favoured candi-dates from Serbia's prewar bureaucracy (Lampe 1996: 130). There were Serbian public figures attached to genuine federalism who criticised

Pasić's approach. Jovan Cvijić advocated a Yugoslav federal community which he called the United States of Yugoslavia. He said of Pasić that 'he ... could not understand the mentality of Western Europe' (Prpa-Jovanović 1997: 52). But Hugh Seton-Watson, later to be one of the chief West European Balkan experts, had a more sympathetic view. By 'his preference for a uniform and centralising state over one based on a balance of regional autonomies', he argued, Pasić was expressing 'the dominant view of European liberals and radicals throughout the century' (Seton-Watson et al. 1976: 138). However, in a letter Hugh's father R.W. Seton-Watson wrote in 1915 to Alexander, the future King of Serbia, British pluralist arrangements were advocated over the French Jacobin model so popular from Portugal to Poland:

> The realization of the programme of Greater Serbia instead of that of Yugoslavia would ... signify the permanence of the old situation in which Serbs would be the toy of the Great Powers and the endless victims of foreign intrigues.
>
> It is possible that public opinion in Serbia is not completely aware even now of all that could be lost ...
>
> ... I write as a son of Scotland, which after two centuries of union with England, has lost none of its national identity. Perhaps for this reason it is easier for me to appreciate the desire of the Croats, that their relations with their Serb brothers should be regulated according to the same principles as the relations of the English and the Scots two centuries ago. (Seton-Watson et al. 1976: 309)

In Yugoslavia, the competing parties were based on the differing regions and except for the communists and several minor ones, none enjoyed a multinational appeal. This was not the case in Romania where the chief opponent of the Bucharest-based Liberals represented after 1926 a fusion of the Peasant Party of the Old Kingdom and the Romanian National Party of Transylvania (PNR), to form a party known as the National Peasant Party (PNT). But in both states, the monarchs supervising the ruling parties preferred centralized arrangements even though it rendered hollow their claims to be ruling over a united people. The 1923 Constitution, exclusively the work of the ruling Liberals, was centralist and nationalist (Macartney and Palmer 1962: 214). The 1918 Alba Iulia Declaration, with its clauses relating to decentralisation, was ignored. This had been the work of the Romanian National Party, the voice of Romanians in the territory opposed to Hungarian rule. In 1919, one of the few clean elections held in interwar Romania gave the

PNR and its allies a governing majority. In the first election held under universal suffrage, the demand for change was deeply felt. The government formed by Vaida-Voeivod showed its radical intentions. It wished to pass a radical land reform and open contacts with Bolshevik Russia in order to regularise the frontier between them. But in 1920 the crown dismissed the first government of reformers from outside the oligarchy. Elections were held 'in the old spirit' and by 1922 the Liberals were back in charge (Macartney and Palmer 1962: 213).

Only in Bulgaria were the powers of the crown, the military, and the old parties curbed, albeit temporarily, in the early 1920s. The Peasantist government of Alexander Stamboliski managed to slash the size of the army and introduce many reforms favouring small farmers before being overthrown in 1923 (Bell 1977: 208). In Albania, there was no backlash against centralist rule since it was only established with difficulty in the 1920s and 1930s. Ahmed Bey Zogu, the tribal chief who established control of the country in 1924 candidly admitted the obstacles a country unprepared for self-rule faced when it acquired independence after 1913. In 1928 he told the London *Daily Telegraph*:

> We are centuries behind the rest of Europe in civilization. The people can neither read nor write; there are few written laws which are obeyed, the blood feuds are still prevalent in many parts of the country. It is my determination to civilise my people and make them as far as possible adopt Western habits and customs. (Fischer 1995: 22)

It was perhaps no small achievement that by the mid-1930s, the authority of central government was recognised in most of Albania. The resulting political stability assisted the rise of national consciousness. But elsewhere in the Balkans the control exercised by one ethnic group over the public purse created mounting dissension.

In multinational Yugoslavia, Serbs controlled government and the army. Accounting for one-quarter of Yugoslavs, they made up between 75 and 80% of interwar members of the government (Prpa-Jovanović 1997: 54). Of 165 generals in active service, 161 were Serbs, two were Croats and two were Slovenes. All important diplomatic posts usually went to Serbs as did the top posts in state financial institutions (Stavrianos 1958: 625). These disparities of economic and political power meant that Serbs 'controlled a vast amount of patronage which they utilised effectively as a political weapon' (Stavrianos 1958: 625).

It was a similar picture in Romania. The financial and banking system was centralized in Bucharest and the Liberals simultaneously attempted to unify the provinces while diverting resources to the south and, not infrequently, into their own pockets (Wolff 1974: 126). Both the Romanian Liberals and Serbian Radicals operated by state subsidy to favoured institutions and favoured individuals, who expressed their gratitude by political contributions to the party coffers (Wolff 1974: 103). Opponents were coopted by bribes or neutralised by threats. Those who offered genuine opposition to the Liberals such as the PNT were dismissed as 'a band of mad dogs' by Brătianu which made them respond in kind (Scurtu and Buzatu 1999: 161). In Yugoslavia, the polarised pluralism of multiparty politics spilled over into violence when Stjepan Radić, the leader of the Croatian Peasant Party, was shot on the floor of parliament in June 1928, later succumbing to his wounds.

SOCIAL EXCLUSION UNDERMINES NATIONAL UNITY

Except for rare moments, most political strategies involved narrow elite groups and were fought over the heads of the peasant majority. Land reform occurred nearly everywhere, but it was carried out unenthusiastically, mainly to prevent the contagion of Bolshevism infecting the Balkans. In Greece, 38% of land was distributed, probably owing to the mass exodus of Turkish landowners from territories newly acquired by Greece. In Romania, the percentage of land distributed was 21% and, in Yugoslavia, one out of every four peasants received some land (Stavrianos 1958: 594). In Romania the aim behind land reform was often as much to cut down to size minority interests which held large estates as it was to improve the condition of the peasantry (Roberts 1951: 39). The reform was carried out in a piecemeal fashion and was not part of a wider developmental plan to make agriculture a viable part of the national economy. The pressure of rapidly increasing population was a difficult challenge for which there was no easy answer, but none of the agricultural ministries in Balkan states received adequate funding to provide basic services, never mind promote innovation or reform (Hessell Tiltman 1936: *passim*).

Across the Balkans, peasants were forced to bear much of the tax load even though their per capita income was far below that of city dwellers (Hessell Tiltman 1936: 112–13). This was done by levying light taxes on incomes and heavy taxes on mass consumption articles. Income tax in the various Balkan countries provided 19 to 28% of total tax revenue while taxes on commodities supplied 55 to 65% (Stavrianos 1958: 599; Roberts 1951: 82, n. 28).

Where industrialisation was pursued, the cost was borne disproportionately by the rural population. The heavy duties on imported manufacturing goods designed to shelter native industry resulted in retaliatory export duties on agricultural products (Stavrianos 1958: 600). Showcase industries, such as the ones developed in Romania in the 1920s and 1930s, failed to absorb the surplus population. No provision for credits was made so that peasants could improve their holdings and be protected against bad harvests (Wolff 1974: 128). Infrastructure improvements were completely neglected (especially in the new territories brought under Romanian rule) which would have enabled peasant produce to be brought more quickly to market and to ports for export (Hessell Tiltman 1936: 114–16).

Politicians showed barely concealed contempt for the peasantry. A peasant electorate was being forced to pay for the advancement of industry (Roberts 1951: 128). In Romania the nationalistic Liberals disavowed foreign investment and pursued ambitious and poorly thought-out policies that only widened an already large urban–rural divide. Clíches about the contented and bucolic peasantry were often used by prosperous city dwellers to impress a foreign audience, but sometimes a perceptive foreigner was well placed to detect the bourgeois urban contempt for peasant ways not far below the surface. The historian Robert Lee Wolff recalled an encounter with a Romanian businessman in the 1920s:

> [he] told me that the peasants were the strong backbone of the country, and that he would always be proud of their strength and their joyous rural life. A few sentences later he was calling them 'animals who can talk', and showing the utmost contempt for them and even Romania itself. (Wolff 1974: 188)

The peasantry usually showed scepticism towards political movements emanating from the cities whether it be the Liberals followed by their army of tax collectors and military recruiters or the ones who paraded the bombastic trappings of dictatorship in the 1930s (Mitrany 1951: 122). Only rarely did peasant alienation from urban neglect or oppression become dangerous. In Bulgaria a movement briefly achieved power in the early 1920s promoting an egalitarian rural democracy free from the domination of urban merchants and money lenders.

In the 1930s the experience of Bucharest with its high-rise buildings and new boulevards would contrast with the ever deeper misery much of the country had sunk into during the depression. But in the Balkan capitals there were also dangerous frustrations as the graduates pouring out of university with degrees in law or the humanities were unable to obtain remuneration in the already bloated public service (Hopken [1994]: 92). In Romania, an early outcome of 'the growth of a half-baked intellectual proletariat' was anti-Semitism (R.W. Seton-Watson 1943: 9). From 1922 Bucharest students regularly held strikes demanding restrictions on the number of Jews who could be admitted to university faculties and be allowed to practice in professions like law. But because of Article 60 of the Treaty of Versailles, the government was unable to grant what was called a *numerus clausus*, or a ceiling on Jewish enrolment (Nagy-Talavera 1999: 294). However, the Liberals discreetly exploited anti-Semitism in towns with many Jewish inhabitants (Nagy-Talavera 1999: 227). To put the blame on others for the obvious failures and injustices of the Romanian oligarchy enabled student discontent to be channelled in safe directions (Weber 1974: 511).

The centralist parties in Romania and Yugoslavia depended on ageing personalities who had not prepared a succession. The death of Pašić in 1926 enabled King Alexander to increase his authority as he played the divided parties off against one another. In Romania, the deaths in quick succession of King Ferdinand and his imperious chief minister, Ion I.C. Brătianu, in 1927 enabled the reform-minded PNT to come to the fore. Its newspaper triumphantly proclaimed in 1928 that '[T]he country has decided through a true plebiscite against dictatorship and for the rule of law ... Romania for the first time is becoming a civilized parliamentary state deserving to pass from East to West'.[2] But the fate of peasant reform in Bulgaria, where the more egalitarian social structure suited a bid to refashion government priorities around rural concerns, ought to have been a warning for rural radicals elsewhere in the region.

BULGARIA: NATIONALISM AND URBAN PRIORITIES CHALLENGED

The breakthrough of the Bulgarian Peasant Party (BANU) had occurred in 1918 when Bulgaria went down to defeat along with the Central Powers. This ended the reign of Tsar Ferdinand, 'an able but utterly unscrupulous ... ruler who sought to make Bulgaria great in order to satisfy his own megalomania ...' (Stavrianos 1958: 579). Alexander Stamboliski, BANU's leader, had opposed Bulgaria's participation in both the Balkan Wars and the First World War and had been sentenced to life imprisonment for opposing Ferdinand's war policies (Detez 1998: 306). He benefited from the tide of discontent against militarism and foreign adventures. In October 1919 elections held in a climate of social radicalism made BANU the largest party and Stamboliski became Prime Minister. He was a strong-willed and implacable personality who combined a fierce disdain for cities and industrialisation with an ardent desire for peace with his neighbours in order to secure the climate in which his radical reforms could go ahead (Rothschild 1958: 86).

Stamboliski represented Bulgaria at the Paris peace conference and signed the Treaty of Neuilly. Immediately afterwards he sent letters to his counterparts in neighbouring states urging that the past be forgotten and that all Balkan states collaborate for their common security and economic welfare (Stavrianos 1958: 648). He believed that only through economic growth could genuine independence be secured and he was not overly sad that the peace treaty required the size of the Bulgarian army to be greatly reduced (Bell 1977: 94). As a substitute for conscription he introduced a compulsory labour law which required a physically fit male to undertake at some time between his 20th and 40th birthdays an eight-month period of manual labour for the benefit of the state and to be liable to perform in his district up to 21 days of labour for the state every year until the age of 50 (the requirement for unmarried women was less and married women were exempt from the service). The physical and psychological results achieved were considerable. By the end of 1925 'about 800 bridges had been constructed, 600–700 miles of railway track laid, 1,800–1,900 miles of road built, swamps drained, canals dug, telephones strung, and forests planted' (Rothschild 1958: 91).

In 1920 voters gave BANU an outright majority and the radical pace of Stamboliski's policies increased. To bring nearer the dream of a peasant state, laws were passed in 1921 limiting the size of a peasant holding to 30 tilled hectares, and sharply curtailing the amount of farmland a city-dweller could own. Land not cultivated by the peasant's own family was liable to indemnified confiscation (Rothschild 1958: 90). In 1921 Stamboliski visited Prague, Warsaw and Bucharest seeking support for a Green International of peasant parties. A permanent bureau was established in Prague, Stamboliski envisaging it as a stepping stone towards a Green *Entente* of peasant states which would be a counterweight both to capitalist powers and Soviet Russia.

Ultimately Stamboliski would overreach himself. His increasingly strong-arm methods at home alienated the military and the conventional parties. His neighbours were slow to appreciate the advantages of a Bulgaria led by an internal reformer disavowing irredentism. In 1921 Stamboliski failed to persuade Pasić in Belgrade to take joint measures against the Macedonian terrorists of IMRO (Bell 1977: 200). In 1922, after IMRO attacks on its territory, Yugoslavia was poised to occupy parts of Bulgaria rather than cooperate with its government (Bell 1977: 201). Stamboliski successfully employed the good offices of the League of Nations to defuse the crisis.

The radical thrust of Bulgarian politics would have been consolidated if BANU had been able to enlist the support of the Bulgarian Communist Party (BCP). At its foundation in 1919, it was the only mass communist party in existence other than the Russian Bolshevik one. A membership of 21,000 in 1919 was drawn in large part from demobilised peasant soldiers (Rothschild 1958: 80–1). Negotiations for a coalition with BANU in the autumn of 1919 fell through over the allocation of the ministry of the interior. The Communists felt that there was a real chance they could take power in Bulgaria on their own. Moscow considered the revolutionary situation to be ripest in Bulgaria. In the Balkan Communist Federation set up in 1920, the BCP took advantage of Moscow's favour to dominate its activities (Rothschild 1958: 232). So the Communists spurned the prospect of an alliance with the peasant movement which had a large rural following in favour of change that no Marxist party could easily win over.

Stamboliski, in his turn, vastly overestimated his own strength. The Orange Guard, a party militia, intimidated the oligarchy but, as events were to show, it would be no match for the army. IMRO became a state within a state in the Pirin region, enjoying the allegiance of some of its population and of Macedonians resident elsewhere in the country (Pundeff 1971: 143). Macedonians, who made up one-third of Sofia's population, were influential in the army. In March 1923 when Yugoslavia at last saw the benefit of cooperating with Bulgaria and signed a treaty to stop IMRO terrorism, IMRO sentenced Stamboliski to death (Bell 1977: 203). His agreement to allow a buffer zone on the frontier enabling forces on both sides to pursue guerillas was a challenge to the nationalist obsession with sacrosanct national boundaries. Stamboliski's dream that Balkan cooperation would eventually produce a union allowing the states equal access to the Adriatic, Aegean and Black Seas was crushed in a coup mounted by elements of the oligarchy and the military with the crucial assistance of IMRO. In June 1923 Stamboliski was murdered in the most horrible manner and BANU suppressed by a fearful oligarchy. In 1925, thinking that the moment had come to strike at the elite, several Communists acting without any instructions from the leadership blew up Sofia

Cathedral, killing over a hundred notables. Mass arrests, judicial death sentences and unofficial murders of Communists and Agrarians followed. The Agrarians were neutralised and the Communists driven underground. But at least two of Stamboliski's reforms were retained and indeed were widely copied elsewhere: the land law limiting the size of private farms and the drafting of males into peacetime labour battalions, a device which the Nazis later claimed was an invention of Hitler's (Shotwell 1949: 106).

ROMANIA: REFORM SABOTAGED FROM ABOVE

In Romania, Stamboliski's ideas were broadly shared by Constantin Stere, a member of the 1928–30 PNT government. He was a novelist from Bessarabia who had been associated with the Russian populists (*narodniks*) who glorified the peasant and often opposed Marxist socialism. He argued that industrialism was a false route for Romania to take 'since the more advanced countries had already captured all the markets' (Wolff 1974: 104). He advocated a democracy with the peasant village at its fulcrum. Credits would be provided to encourage cooperation and enable a Balkan Denmark to emerge based on Romania's exceptionally fertile land (Wolff 1974: 104). But in office the PNT showed itself to be a middle class party with vestigial concern for the peasantry (Roberts 1951: 163). Its efforts at decentralization proved ineffective (Scurtu and Buzatu 1999: 179). Much of the Liberals' economic policy remained intact with its urban and big industry biases. Iuliu Maniu, the PNT leader, 'remained through his political career an oppositional force, excellent in criticism and combat, but without constructive solutions' (Constantiniu 1997: 326). He and his Transylvanian allies were felt to be out of their depths in the shifting sands of Bucharest politics. A Bucharest-born commentator summed up this political world as: '… not so much "Balkan" as southern, its temperament and rhetoric approximating to France and Italy … [It] must have been seen by the "German-trained" Maniu as well as other Transylvanians, as incomprehensible, a world in which it was impossible to have confidence' (Alexandrescu 1998: 280).

Maniu's generation, like that of Venizelos in Greece, another cautious reformer, was overtaken by the world depression which began in 1929. The price of raw materials dropped far more than those of manufactured goods. The value of Romania's mainly agricultural exports collapsed which led to a disastrous fall in the income of peasants, the bulk of the population here as in all other Balkan states.

It is likely that even without the economic slump the PNT would have lost out in a game of politics where the crown and the interests which had flourished under Liberal patronage enjoyed enormous discretionary power. In 1930 Maniu unwisely allowed Carol, who had been compelled to renounce the crown owing to his scandalous private life, to ascend the throne on a promise of future good behaviour. Maniu had allowed Carol to replace his own 10-year-old son Michael who had been king since 1927, on condition that he put aside his Jewish mistress, Elena Lupescu, and return to normal marital life. The failure to bring a selfish and corrupt royal adventurer to heel had grave consequences for Romanian public life in the 1930s. The Romanian journalist Pamfil Seicaru has pointed out that Carol could have been stopped in his tracks if the PNT had acted in a resolute manner:

> What would have happened if Iuliu Maniu had given the order, as Prime Minister, for Elena Lupescu to be arrested on the charge of entering the country with a false passport. Who would have rushed to defend her? The Liberal Party along with the other opposition parties would have applauded a measure that would have pleased public opinion. The King? In August 1930 he feared to provoke public opinion which the political parties could have whipped up with violent and well-organized agitation. On whom could Carol have depended in August 1930? Absolutely nobody. Can anyone imagine that the army would have defied the parties backed by public opinion to defend the King's paramour who had entered the country with a false passport? (Scurtu and Buzatu 1999: 359)

Carol steadily undermined an already fragile democracy by playing all the major politicians off against one another. The parties fell victim to the game of rivalry and backstair intrigue as Carol selected ambitious junior figures in the PNT and the Liberals to head quick-changing and heterogeneous coalitions. Inter-party rivalry and deep-seated factionalism weakened the main parties, enabling him to get his way. In Yugoslavia, King Alexander, a far more upright character, used similar methods as the politicians seemed incapable of keeping at bay the centrifugal tendencies that menaced Yugoslav unity (Prpa-Jovanivić 1997: 55). He reluctantly imposed a royal dictatorship in 1929 following the assassination of the Croat Stjepan Radić, who had been the chief critic of Yugoslav centralism. Many Croats saw this move as 'a more effective way of imposing Belgrade-style centralism' (Pavlowitch 1999: 275). But Alexander's firm opposition to Italy, which coveted Yugoslav territory, was welcomed by Croatian opinion. The Italian menace set a limit to any

Croatian separatism and, on the eve of the King's assassination in 1934, there were signs that he realised the shortcomings of an authoritarian approach to the complex problems of running a multinational state and that he may have been envisaging a return to conventional party politics (Lampe 1996: 164–7).

Romania witnessed the strongest popular backlash against democracy anywhere in Eastern Europe after 1930. The inglorious end of the 1928–33 period of mainly PNT governments created mounting impatience with democracy in the cities and among the educated youth. In the decade 1929–38 there were 283,583 students who attended institutions of higher learning: less than 10% got a degree and the bureaucracy was incapable of absorbing many of those who qualified (Weber 1974: 514). In Western Europe, the ability of Mussolini's Italy, Russia and Hitler's Germany to mop up unemployment, build spectacular public works projects and create a strong industrial base in the midst of a global depression evoked much admiration at a time when liberal politics seemed discredited. It is hardly surprising that in parts of the Balkans where the track record of the post-1918 regimes was far less impressive than the governments of France or Britain, the new order as proclaimed in Berlin and Rome seemed to offer hope of salvation for social groups lacking bright future prospects (Nagy-Talavera 1999: 359, 360).

In Bucharest restless students were attracted to a charismatic and manipulative philosopher, Nae Ionescu. Unlike most professors, he cultivated relations with the young whom he treated as equals if they shared his penchant for authoritarian solutions. Through this link and his newspaper, *Cuvintul*, 'he created a current of opinion hostile to the Western-orientated political parties' (Scurtu and Buzatu 1999: 31). Mircea Eliade, the young philosopher who gained an international reputation in later life, spoke for many of his generation when he complained in 1936 that:

> Democracy may be full of charm and comfort, but so far … it has not made us into a strong State, nor has it made us conscious of our greatness … If by leaving democracy Romania becomes a strong State, armed, conscious of its power and destiny, history will take account of that deed. (Linscott Ricketts 1988: 901)

The playwright Eugene Ionesco wrote in 1945:

> How different everything would have been if those two [Nae Ionescu and Eliade] had been good masters…

> If Nae Ionescu had not existed ... today we would have a fine generation of
> leaders between 35 and 40. Because of him they all became fascists. He created
> a stupid, horrifying, reactionary Romania. (Calinescu 1995: 410–11)

But the role specific individuals enjoyed in causing a generation of
Romanian youth to reject the Western liberal path can be over-estimated.
The low political standards exhibited by many of the post-1918 political
leaders had produced a backlash against a façade democracy based on
arranged elections and special privileges for narrow financial interests
presided over by a monarchy increasingly distancing itself from the
people. Carol had quickly revealed himself to be Europe's most corrupt
crowned head. In the early 1930s, accompanied by a trusted chauffeur, he
picked up prostitutes from the streets around the royal palace. The chief of
the Bucharest police overlooked the King's 'extra-curricular activities':
'Any prostitute, any illegal gambling den, any false money-lender was
required to pay him a tribute from which Carol took a cut' (Nagy-
Talavera 1999: 298–9).

Western leaders like Churchill were aware of Carol's lifestyle, which
was widely reported in the world's press. In no small measure, it may
have encouraged the British wartime leader effectively to offer up
Romania to the tender mercies of the Soviet Union during the Second
World War. There is an inglorious tradition of the leaders of the
Western powers deciding the fate of small Balkan states on the basis of
stereotypical views about a country and its leaders. Unfortunately, in
the 1930s Carol was Romania in the eyes of the global media and
indeed many diplomats, his behaviour being regarded as not untypical
for the country he ruled over. But many leading Romanians were
scandalised by it. When the PNT interior minister Ion Mihalache tried
to replace the chief-of-police, he refused point-blank to quit and in the
end it was Mihalache who was required to step down. From 1933 to
1937 Carol's Prime Minister was the compliant Gheorghe Tatarescu. Of
him it was said that when the King asked him to do something that it
was within his power to accomplish, his standard answer was: 'It has
been done Majesty' and when he was asked to do something that it was
impossible to realise, he declared: 'It will be done Majesty' (Scurtu and
Buzatu 1999: 195). Carol acted like a Phanariot, concerned with
transferring wealth and prestige from the public domain to his private
hands (Alexandrescu 1998: 113). Real power increasingly drained away
from the formal institutions and was located in a camarilla composed of
financiers, a few of Jewish descent, the industrialist Nicolae Malaxa of
Greek descent, and the right-wing economist Mihai Manoilescu. Real

decisions were often taken in the salon of Elena Lupescu over a game of bridge between the King and his cronies (Nagy-Talavera 1999: 283).

Maniu spoke out in 1933 against Lupescu, arguing that between the nation and the King there was 'a hydra which ... needed to be driven out' (Scurtu and Buzatu 1999: 277). His party newspaper later complained of the royal camarilla that '[N]o gangster film surpasses in manouevres and tricks, the activities of these jungle rogues' (Scurtu and Buzatu 1999: 306). But the really formidable challenger to the King's corrupt rule came from a native fascist movement which railed with increasing boldness against the rule of foreigners and the domination of foreign ideas and customs.

A latent struggle in modern Romanian thought between intellectuals who argued that prosperity lay in identifiying with Western liberal ideas and those who derived inspiration from native Orthodox traditions burst to the surface in the 1930s (Hitchins 1994: 292–335). A fascist movement, the Legion of the Archangel Michael, better known by the title of its political section, the Iron Guard, championed a nativist and authoritarian approach to organizing society. In Corneliu Z. Codreanu, a law graduate and son of a schoolteacher who was of German and Polish descent, it acquired a visionary leader. He mobilised impressive support without stimulation or assistance from Germany or Italy. He never hid his anti-Western views which were expressed to good effect in the campaign for the 1937 elections, the last largely free ones to be held in Romania for over fifty years:

> I am against the large Western democracies. I am against the Little Entente. I am against the Balkan Pact and I have no affection for the League of Nations ... which I don't believe in. I am for a Romanian foreign policy aligned to Rome and Berlin, alongside the national revolutionary states. (Constantiniu 1997: 348)

It was the emergence of messianic figures like Codreanu that prompted Sir Norman Angell, the British pacifist and Nobel Prize winner, to observe in the 1930s that: 'Political nationalism has become for the Europeans of our age the most important thing in the world, more than civilization, humanity, kindness, decency, pity: more important than life itself' (King 1973: 6).

But the visibility of demagogues like Codreanu and national extremist movements like the Macedonian IMRO had enabled important peace and cooperation initiatives in the Balkans during the 1930s to be lost sight of. Indeed, in Central Europe as the spirit of neighbourly cooperation was being replaced by belligerent nationalism, it was enjoying a new lease of life in the Southeast perhaps unparalleled before or since.

BALKAN COOPERATION

The momentum for Balkan cooperation was provided by Greece and Turkey. Venizelos, back in power as Greek Premier from 1928 to 1932, established cordial ties with Turkey, an unexpected departure after the bloodletting of the early 1920s. The ground was prepared in Athens by an effort to solve outstanding differences with Yugoslavia, Albania and Italy. Venizelos defied nationalist critics at home by assuring Turkey's leaders both privately and publicly that Greece had no aspirations to their territory and that he wished to settle outstanding issues (Stavrianos 1958: 666). In the spring of 1930 the two states signed a convention liquidating outstanding differences relating to the exchange of populations. More important, was the full-dress Treaty of Neutrality, Conciliation and Arbitration agreed in October 1930. Speakers at an accompanying banquet declared that a conflict which had lasted ten centuries was over (Macartney and Palmer 1962: 277). Venizelos made a triumphal visit to Turkey. To Kemal Atatürk the Turkish leader, he said: 'We have agreed on the future of the Middle East' (Woodhouse 1998: 220). The chief benefit of this reconciliation for both countries was that it ended the ability of Fascist Italy to play off one against the other and reduced the influence of a dangerously expansionist state in the Eastern Mediterranean (Macartney and Palmer 1962: 277–8).

In 1930 an unofficial Balkan conference was convened in Athens on the initiative of a political ally of Venizelos. It was attended by delegates of all the Balkan states, including Bulgaria. Delegates agreed on a number of resolutions in favour of cultural and economic cooperation. It was even agreed that foreign ministers of the six states present should meet once a year to exchange views. However, progress was stalled when Bulgaria raised the question of Macedonia and Yugoslavia refused to have the matter discussed (Macartney and Palmer 1962: 278). Nevertheless, there followed four further conferences in the next three years before a fifth was cancelled because of uneasy relations between Bulgaria and her neighbours (Woodhouse 1998: 221).

Regional cooperation was probably enhanced by the fact that Balkan solidarity was an issue no longer primarily associated with the radical left. The international communist federation, the Comintern, dominated by the Soviet Russian state, was promoting nationalist tensions in order to undermine the new multiethnic states of Yugoslavia and Romania which were seen as a barrier to Soviet communist expansion. The Fifth Comintern Congress in 1924 proclaimed the secession of all nationalities the binding line for all Communist parties (Lendvai 1969: 67).

The only Balkan communist party whose interests were suited by this line was Bulgaria. During the 1920s the Bulgarian Communist Party (BCP) used its commanding position in the Comintern and in the Balkan Communist Federation to promote a position on Macedonia that suited Bulgarian national interests. In 1928 the thesis was advanced by Georgi Dimitrov that the Greek refugees from Anatolia resettled in Greek Macedonia were adopting 'a Macedonian consciousness and abandoning their self-image as Greeks. They regard as their brothers not the Greeks but the Macedonians across the Bulgarian and Yugoslav borders'. Moscow supported the BCP when objections were raised by other Balkan parties about promoting a Macedonian identity that was felt to reinforce Bulgaria's claim over the region. Before 1939 Bulgaria was seen as having produced some of international communism's best Bolsheviks (Rothschild 1958: 302). The party's leader Georgi Dimitrov had achieved renown by defying the Nazis in 1933 when he was falsely accused of the Reichstag fire which had enabled Hitler to establish his dictatorship. It should not be forgotten that both Bulgaria and the Soviet Union were revisionist states keen to overturn the 1917–20 treaties which resulted in the loss of substantial territories. According to Joseph Rothschild, the Soviets may have believed that Yugoslavia, which had acquired most of Macedonia, was unviable as a state because of its complex ethnic mix (Rothschild 1958: 246).

In 1928, at its fourth congress, the Yugoslav Communist Party had endorsed the Comintern position that Yugoslavia should be dismembered since it was a country 'created in the Balkans by world imperialism for counterrevolutionary purposes aimed against the Soviet Union' (Vickers 1998: 113). Shackled to such an unpopular position, its influence slumped as did that of the Greek Communists. But the Yugoslav party adopted a more committed stance to Yugoslavia when Josip Broz Tito became its General Secretary in 1937. By now, it enjoyed the support of many educated young people committed to the Yugoslav ideal but opposed to the narrow rule of the royalist oligarchy. Relations between the various Balkan communist parties worsened as the BCP from 1935 onwards reverted to open revisionist propaganda about 'the oppressed Bulgarian districts of South Dobruja [in Romania] and the Western Province' [part of Yugoslavia after 1919] (Rothschild

1958: 255). In Greece an active Trotskyite movement emerged, stimulated by Moscow's championing of Bulgarian territorial demands in the region. The Balkan communist parties were going their own way, at loggerheads over the national question which their literature dismissed as a bourgeois anachronism. Thus, long before the communist parties when in power sought to obtain popular support by playing the nationalist card, rivalries over the demarcation of frontiers were fuelling ill will between them. As for Russia, it stood to benefit if Macedonia acted as a source of rivalry among the Balkan communist parties. Disunity enabled the Soviets to be 'the perpetual arbiter' and it ruled out the formation of a Balkan communist bloc which could pave the way for a Balkan communist federation able to diminish Soviet influence in the region (Rothschild 1958: 256).

Right-of-centre peace feelers even led to a meeting in Romania during 1931 between the then Premier Nicolae Iorga and Count Istvan Bethlen, who had led Hungary through the 1920s. It suggested that Budapest might be retreating from the bellicose threat of the Hungarian Regent, Admiral Nicolas Horthy in 1919, when he declared that 'the enemy Number One of Hungary is Romania because it has the greatest claim on our territory and is the strongest of our neighbours. That is why the principal goal of our foreign policy is to settle problems with Romania through recourse to arms' (Constantiniu 1997: 307). Iorga and Bethlen agreed that Russia posed a serious threat to both countries but they were unable to reach any broad agreement over Transylvania (Nagy-Talavera 1999: 295). Perhaps emboldened by a slight reduction in hostility between the two main non-Slavic states of Eastern Europe, France floated the idea of a Danubian Union in 1932. Foreign Minister André Tardieu advocated a customs union between Austria, Hungary, Czechoslovakia and Romania in order to forestall German expansionism (Seton-Watson 1945: 375). It was, in one historian's words, 'the most serious initiative of the interwar period toward bringing about cooperation among the peoples of the former Hapsburg Monarchy ...' (Borsody 1993: 35). It was a plan of economic cooperation based on the premise that political reconciliation in the Danube basin had to be preceded by economic rapprochement. But Austria and Hungary blocked the idea.

France and Britain soon displayed disunity over how to deal with the emergence of an aggressively revisionist Germany under Adolf Hitler. At a meeting between the three victorious European powers, France, Britain and Italy, held at Stresa on Lake Maggiore in April 1935, Mussolini was more supportive of efforts by the French to restrain

Hitler than the British. Franco-Italian desires to defend Italy's ally Austria from Hitler's aggressive designs and empower the League of Nations to prevent German rearmament received no encouragement from Britain. Mussolini and the French foreign minister, Pierre Laval, argued for a Central European Pact by which the smaller defeated states of the last war, Austria, Hungary and Bulgaria, would be freed from Versailles restrictions and allowed to strengthen their armed forces. To prevent friction between Hungary and neighbours which had acquired Hungarian territory, measures were required to promote a zone of nonaggression. But Britain, while not objecting in principle to a Central European Pact meant to restrain Nazi Germany, was unwilling to commit itself in any way to making it a reality. Laval complained that 'Britain had no intention of taking part in the effective defence of Austria' (Lamb 1997: 5). Later in 1935 Britain signed a treaty that allowed Germany to greatly expand her navy. In a very short time, France adjusted its stance to comply with Britain's fully-fledged appeasement policy (Borsody 1993: 59).

France had adopted a complacent attitude towards building an alliance system in Eastern Europe between former enemies in order to foster a climate of peace and security. Britain and France had neglected the Balkans in the 1920s. The French concluded alliances 'dictated by sheer national interest' while Britain shrunk from taking up any direct commitments in Central or Southeast Europe. Even between France and its main Eastern protégés, Poland, Czechoslovakia and Romania, there was surprisingly little trade. Foreign economic and political relations failed to synchronise (Bideleux and Jeffries 1998: 11). Indeed several of the states of the Little Entente (an alliance created in 1921) traded more with their old enemies Hungary and Austria than with each other. The cutback in military spending in interwar Britain and France also meant that concern to uphold the post-Versailles Balkan map was eroded. French industrialists, in collusion with corrupt Romanian officials, equipped the Romanian airforce with what some called 'flying hearses' and effectively sabotaged the creation of an effective Romanian airforce in the 1930s (Waldeck 1998: 37). Britain showed neutrality in the face of Italian aggression in the Balkans (Seton-Watson 1945: 412). The praise that Winston Churchill and Austen Chamberlain lavished on Mussolini failed to deter him from bullying and subverting states across the Adriatic Sea and may even have been an inducement.

Providing a new spur for Balkan cooperation was the rise of the revisionist powers. After 1933 not only Italy but Germany was committed to nullifying the Versailles Treaties and rearranging the map of Europe. On 9 February 1934, Greece, Romania, Yugoslavia and Turkey signed the Balkan Pact. The signatories agreed to guarantee the existing frontiers between them. Membership was open to any state prepared to accept the principles of the League of Nations and the postwar peace treaties. Bulgaria refused to accede on the grounds that to do so would imply renunciation of its claims to revision of the postwar treaties. Albania was in dispute with Greece over the status of the Greeks under Albanian rule in Northern Epirus (Woodhouse 1998: 228).

The next move after the 1934 pact was the modification of the Treaty of Lausanne by the Montreux Convention in July 1936. Under it, Turkey recovered full control of the Dardenelles and Greece obtained the right to fortify islands lying close to the Turkish coast. Cyprus was not yet a bone of contention between the two Aegean states. A British crown colony had been established on the island in 1925 after its formal annexation from Turkey. The Greek Cypriot majority agitated for *Enosis* or union with Greece. In 1931 an uprising occurred. Britain responded by dissolving the island's legislative council and deporting the ringleaders (Woodhouse 1998: 221–2). The Turkish Cypriots acquiesced in British rule. Atatürk stood aside. He confined the Turkish Republic to its heartland in Anatolia and renounced claims over other areas formerly in the Ottoman Empire. Under the terms of the Treaty of Lausanne, Turkey had no standing in law to object or even insist on consultations if Britain was to cede Cyprus to Greece or dispose of it in any other fashion (Woodhouse 1998: 222).

BULGARIA FINDS STABILITY

In 1938 the Balkan Pact was enlarged by admitting Bulgaria. By the Pact of Thessaloniki, the four existing Pact members lifted the military restrictions on Bulgaria imposed by the 1919 Neuilly Treaty in return for a promise that Bulgaria would not seek frontier revisions by force. A contrast can be drawn between the behaviour of Hungary, the chief revisionist small state in Central Europe, and Bulgaria, its Balkan counterpart. For nearly twenty years Hungary had not hidden its determination to recover by whatever means came to hand territories which it had ruled prior to 1918 and relations with most of its neighbours were frozen as a result. Meanwhile, Bulgaria with grievances nearly as pressing as those of Hungary was gradually able to put aside its revanchist outlook and envisage increasing cooperating with neighbours it had gone to war with several times in the recent past. There seemed to be a realisation in the Balkans among both beneficiaries and losers in the Versailles agreements that they must diminish quarrels among themselves to protect themselves against common dangers from aggressive powers like Italy and Germany. Such a realisation had not been felt among the Central European states grouped into the rival Little Entente and revisionist camps which rejected the 1932 Tardieu plan to create a customs union that would revive the Hapsburg system at least as an economic entity. Forward-looking thinking based on an appreciation of common threats did not fit the Balkan stereotype. Nor would the efforts of states in the region to refrain from being used as pawns by the Axis states before and in the early stages of the Second World War. But it is worth noting the statesmanlike behaviour of Balkan leaders in the 1930s when it was in short supply in most other parts of Europe.

Radical shifts in Bulgarian politics had facilitated a breakthrough in relations with its neighbours. In May 1934 Colonel Damyan Velchev, for many years commandant of the military cadet school, organized a coup. The party system had fragmented after the bitter conflicts of the early 1920s. Relatively free elections in 1931 had produced a varied coalition including remnants of the BANU. Perhaps its main achievement was to insulate the peasants against some of the worst effects of the great depression through debt relief, tax concessions, and state purchase of produce (Rothschild 1977: 348). Nevertheless, the depression, combined with the brittle and sometimes corrupt character of the parties permitted to engage in politics, paved the way for a military takeover.

A government headed by Kimon Georgiev, a lieutenant colonel of the reserve, was established in 1934. A support base for the regime was provided by junior officers and a group of intellectuals known as Zveno (the Link). The civil-military alliance was composed of militant patriots not fascists (Wolff 1974: 174). Indeed, the coup had been provoked by the need to head off a power-grab by pro-fascists under Professor Alexander Tsankov, the architect of Stamboliski's overthrow. In its hostility to fascism and the local oligarchy, Zveno bears comparison with the broadly based military movements such as those which swept Nasser to power in Egypt or that which secured the downfall of Portugal's right-wing dictatorship in 1974.

Its most notable achievement was the final suppression of IMRO. The Macedonian movement dissipated its energies in internal factional warfare in the course of which many IMRO leaders lost their lives (Oren

1973: 32). Moreover, by the 1930s it had degenerated into a terrorist band whose criminal activities, particularly in the drugs trade, had eclipsed any political vocation (Rothschild 1958: 192). In 1926 the authorities had provided money for village communes which would enable them to provide land for a proportion of the several hundreds of thousands of Macedonian refugees in the country. The money was raised in London with the backing of the League of Nations and it was an imaginative move which probably reduced the alienation of many Macedonians (Crampton 1997: 158). Not a few Macedonians were already becoming assimilated with the Bulgarian social mainstream. Unlike in Serbian-dominated Yugoslavia, Macedonians were able to rise fairly rapidly in politics and several acquired top ranking positions (Oren 1973: 30). Italy had been using the Macedonian Question to acquire sway in Bulgarian politics and a consensus was slowly emerging in Sofia that falling into the orbit of the Mussolini regime might have dire consequences for Bulgaria.

Following IMRO's suppression, the way was open for a normal-isation of relations with Yugoslavia, one of the goals of Velchev's group. But in April 1935, the middle ranking officers and technocrats of the Zveno group were pushed aside by the crown and senior officers. Velchev was a republican and the decision to establish ties with Moscow soon after the 1934 coup, raised unease in influential quarters. Zveno lacked a coherent social base and King Boris I proved to be a shrewder operator. Until 1938 he opted for non-parliamentary government. Then he allowed elections while prohibiting party labels, the resultant tame parliament allowing Boris to pursue a prudent course at home and abroad. Boris preferred neutrality without commitment to any great power. But he operated within narrow limits even at home, observing once that: 'My army is pro-German, my wife is Italian, my people are pro-Russian. I alone am pro-Bulgarian' (Crampton 1997: 169). Boris was probably the most capable of the Balkan monarchs in the 1880–1945 period.

Nissan Oren has summarised the King's abilities in the following way:

Boris was better informed of world events than any of the many political groups. His intimacy with German politics, his family connections with Rome, and his frequent tours of the west made him best-equipped to implement his own foreign-policy designs. Boris was not a dogmatic person. His natural wariness and endless patience gave him an advantage over his rivals ... To the end of his life he retained the confidence of several political figures whose ideological positions were at great variance with his own. His tact, personal charm and shrewdness helped immobilize many of his rivals at the most crucial junctures in the political development of Bulgaria. (Oren 1973: 61)

DARKENING SHADOWS OF WAR

In the 1930s the Axis states of Germany and Italy were putting mounting pressure on the Balkan states. Only exceptionally alert West European politicians such as Robert Schuman, the future architect of the European Union, showed concern, the French centrist deputy advocating federal arrangements (Price 2000: 20–1). Schuman paid a fact-finding visit to Yugoslavia shortly before King Alexander was murdered in Marseilles on 9 October 1934 at the start of a state visit to France. The deed was the work of the Croatian extreme nationalist movement, the Ustaša, the assassin a Macedonian IMRO gunman who had received support from the Italian and Hungarian governments (Stavrianos 1958: 629). Also murdered was the French foreign minister Louis Barthou, a strong opponent of appeasing Italy and Germany. Schuman had begged him privately not to go to Marseilles because of the volatility of the situation, but protocol decreed otherwise. Italy refused to extradite Ante Pavelić, the Ustaša leader, to France. When the matter was raised at the League of Nations and action against Hungary demanded, Italy warned that if Hungary was attacked by Yugoslavia and the Little Entente, Rome would go to her defence (Ridley 1997: 243).

But the threat that a new European war might be unleashed by the murder of a Balkan king in Marseilles was averted. Entertaining hopes of reaching an agreement with Italy against the rising German threat, France put pressure on Yugoslavia to be conciliatory to Mussolini, despite his regime's role in the murder of its king. His death destabilised the Balkans at a crucial time. Not only was he the only real unifying force in Yugoslavia, but he was the most consistent regional supporter of the Balkan and Little Ententes and the alliance with France (Stavrianos 1958: 741). He was succeeded by his cousin Prince Paul who was to act as Prince Regent until Alexander's son Peter came of age. Paul was a cosmopolitan figure who identified more with British and Russian aristocratic circles than with his own country, towards which he had a condescending attitude (Wolff 1974: 124).

Greece's ability to promote Balkan cooperation was handicapped by chronic cleavages between republicans and monarchists. The Liberal

Venizelos and the Populists led by Panayiotis Tsaldaris were supposedly the progressive and conservative poles of Greek politics. But they were personalized and parochial forces neglecting pressing issues of social policy and concentrating on narrow vendettas. The death of both of these patriarchs in 1936 left a political vacuum soon filled by the nationalist dictatorship of General Ioannis Metaxas which had little appetite for deepening regional cooperation.

Another serious blow for the Versailles system was the dismissal of the Romanian foreign minister Nicolae Titulescu in August 1936. He had been a champion of the League of Nations' principle of collective security and an ardent Francophile who desired a normalisation of relations with the Soviet Union (Constantiniu 1997: 355–8). He was removed just as the finishing touches were being put to an accord with the Soviet Union, the result of long negotiations with the Soviet foreign minister, Maxim Litvinov over the previous year (Hitchins 1998: 446). The Soviets had already signed such a treaty with France and Czechoslovakia in May 1935 and a resolution of disputes with Romania could well have increased the likelihood of a new alliance system emerging designed to check German expansionism. But Titulescu's pro-Western stance and realistic attitude to the Soviet Union was undermined by a fast-changing international situation in which pressure for accommodation with Germany increased.

In 1935–6 Mussolini's conquest of Ethiopia, despite League of Nations sanctions, had important consequences for the Balkans. Pierre Laval, the French foreign minister made it clear to Mussolini early in 1935 that his government would not stand in his way if he invaded Ethiopia (Ridley 1997: 248–9). Believing that a dangerous precedent had been established, the Entente states of Eastern Europe had enforced sanctions and suffered heavy losses in the process. The weakness and vacillation of their British and French allies were revealed when they allowed the League to drop sanctions in 1936, having failed to impose adequate economic penalties on Italy at the start (Stavrianos 1958: 741). Balkan states saw that they could not rely on the League of Nations for deliverance in the event of being attacked. In March 1936, following Hitler's occupation of the demilitarised Rhineland, the credibility of the French-led Entente collapsed and the defence system of France was revealed, to perceptive eyes, to be useless (Nagy-Talavera 1999: 312). At the time, Pierre Flandin, the French foreign minister, candidly admitted this: '[the] French alliance with the Little Entente was now valueless. In the future France could not hope to give effective assistance to Poland, Czechoslovakia, Yugoslavia, or Romania, in the event of German aggression ... In my opinion, the last chance of saving central and eastern Europe from German domination has been thrown away' (Lukacs 1953: 70).

In 1937 the death rattle of the Little Entente was heard when Czechoslovakia, increasingly menaced by Germany, proposed enlarging the military clauses of the pact to include a guarantee of full military assistance in case of aggression from any quarter (Stavrianos 1958: 743). By rejecting this proposal, Romania and Yugoslavia helped to seal the fate of the Little Entente. German economic penetration of the Balkans was already occurring as a result of increased trade. The Nazis, having gained full control of the national economy at home, could offer attractive terms to countries whose raw materials they coveted. Germany was prepared to buy Balkan agricultural products and other commodities at reasonable prices, and supply capital equipment in return (Pavlowitch 1999: 270). The ability of the countries of the Balkan Entente to take common measures to protect their security was inevitably reduced as they became increasingly dependent on an assertive Germany.

Even in the 1920s German planners had argued that escape from economic and political isolation was possible through a vigorous foreign policy and trade offensive directed at Southeast Europe (Ristović 1998: 3). Under the Nazis, when German schemes for a common European political space began to be aired publicly, the Balkans were not overlooked. By 1940 Britain and France were being accused of perpetuating unrest in the Balkans in order to prevent the creation of a pan-European entity (Ristović 1998: 2). German area specialists reacted strongly against the term 'Balkan' because of its association with a discredited oriental past. In the autumn of 1940, the German press proclaimed that 'the Balkans are dead' and 'Southeast Europe is born' (Ristović 1998: 2). The trade offensive was matched by an energetic attempt to promote German culture. In Bulgaria dozens of free scholarships were being offered for study in Germany by the late 1930s, many for technical subjects (Bruce Lockhart 1938: 169). Free or heavily subsidised trips to Italy were also 'a prominent feature of Italian propaganda'. Yet to the dismay of the British writer and ex-diplomat R.H. Bruce Lockhart, 'up to the spring of 1938, the British Council had given one scholarship to a Bulgarian and this solitary award went to a boy violinist' (Bruce Lockhart 1938: 170).

German official documents from 1940 argued for 'well-thought-out inclusion of [the Balkan] ... states into the constructive politics of the

Axis powers' (Ristović 1998: 2). But the ethnic variety of the Balkans was not exactly reassuring. In 1934, Rupert von Schumacher had complained that 'the Balkan peoples ... are not biologically or politically stable factors'. The comments of this academic authority of the region on 'the schizophrenic character of the Southeastern peoples', inevitably raises the question of how far 'racial purification' was part of the plan to 'de-Balkanize' the area (Ristović 1998: 4).

By March 1938, through his occupation of Austria, Hitler now controlled the main communication routes to the Balkan peninsula and Romania became an object of growing German interest. Germany would need secure access to, if not outright control of, Romanian oil supplies if it were to be engaged in all-out war. Hitler was already manipulating German minorities in the region, of which the Swabians in the Romanian Banat and the Saxons of Transylvania were among the largest (Seton-Watson 1945: 285). Anglo-French disinterest in Eastern Europe and an inability to envisage ways of halting German expansion culminated in the Munich Agreement of September 1938 which quickly resulted in Czechoslovakia disappearing from the map of Europe. The Balkan Entente survived but it was tacitly acknowledged that each member would deal separately with the powers (Pavlowitch 1999: 274).

The subsequent secession of Slovakia from the rump state in Prague in March 1939 had a strong impact in Belgrade. It convinced Yugoslavia's Prince Regent Paul of the need to make haste in trying to resolve the Croat question. The Croatian Peasant Party had been alienated from the Serb-ruled state for over a decade. The Croatian Ustaša was being groomed by Italy to subvert the Yugoslav state. Its core support was to be found among hardline nationalists centred on Zagreb university (Tanner 1997: 125). Disaffected intellectuals have usually been the first group to support secessionist moves in the Balkans and Ante Pavelić, the leader of the extremists, was briefly elected to parliament for a Zagreb seat in 1927 before going into exile to begin his plotting. But the Croatian Peasant Party retained the allegiance of the vast majority of Croats. Under its low-key leader Vladko Maček, it was even able to win solid local election results in traditionally Serb districts of Croatia and Bosnia (Tanner 1997: 125). Maček was committed to federal autonomy for Croatia but he showed allegiance to the dynasty and to the existence of Yugoslavia, reconciling many Serbs in Croatia to the idea of Croatian autonomy, without losing the bulk of his Croatian supporters. The agreement (*Sporazum*) signed between Paul's prime minister and Maček just a week before the Nazi invasion of Poland in August 1939 created an autonomous Croatian territory within Yugoslavia. The *Sporazum* resembled the Austro-Hungarian *Ausgleich* of 1867 meant to stabilise the Hapsburg Empire, but it may have been too little too late for Croats and a cause of alarm for many Serbs who were not granted a self-governing region of their own (Rusinow 1995: 377). It is impossible to know how the federal experiment would have worked out if the Second World War had not intervened. Nevertheless, it was a bold attempt to staunch a bleeding ulcer which threatened to cause a fatal haemorrhage in the enfeebled Yugoslav body politic.

An altogether contrasting approach by Belgrade was shown to the Kosovo question. The state felt no need to conciliate the large population of mainly Muslim Albanians. Instead it paid close attention to representations from Vasa Čubrilović, a senior historian at Belgrade university and a member of the Mlada Bosnia group implicated in the 1914 Sarajevo assassinations, who had bold answers for the Kosovo Albanian question. In a policy paper submitted to the government in 1937, he argued that the colonisation of Kosovo by Serbs and Montenegrins had failed and 'we are left with only one course—that of their [Albanian] mass emigration' (Malcolm 1998: 283–4). Čubrilović argued that expulsion and deportation needed to supersede emigration. He spelled out the means by which life in Kosovo would become as uncomfortable as possible for them:

> They [the state authorities] should take full advantage of the laws in order to embitter the existence of the Arnauts [the Turkish term for the Albanians] with us as far as possible: fines, arrests, ruthless application of all police prescriptions, punishing black marketeering, cutting forests, damaging fields, instigating dogs, forced labour and all the other means which a practical police are able to invent. (Križan 1994: 51)

Čubrilović insisted that expulsion and deportation needed to supersede emigration and he felt that the police state methods of 1930s Europe favoured his blueprint:

> The world today is used to things much worse than this and is so preoccupied with today's problems that this aspect should not be a cause of concern. At a time when Germany can expel tens of thousands of Jews and Russia can shift millions of people from one part of the continent to another, the shifting of a few hundred thousand Albanians will not lead to the outbreak of a world war. (Vickers 1998: 117)

The government was already taking energetic steps against the Kosovo Albanians. In 1935 a wave of land confiscations, far more extensive than previous ones, started up. It was based on a new rule that all land must be treated as state property unless the Albanians in possession had a Yugoslav document to prove ownership, something that had hardly ever been issued to them (Vickers 1998: 106). In the international arena, Yugoslavia had been discussing with Turkey from 1933 onwards the transfer of large numbers of Muslim Albanians to Anatolia. A treaty was actually drawn up and initialled in 1935 whereby Turkey would take 40,000 families, their lands passing immediately to the state. The process was meant to be completed by the mid-1940s (Malcolm 1998: 285).

The racism institutionalised in German state behaviour was lowering standards of political conduct in all directions. So was the emphasis on violence on a routine basis against all classes of opponents as shown by events like the 1934 Night of the Long Knives and the *Kristallnacht* pogrom directed against German Jews in 1938. Restraints on the use of state violence were fragile in the Balkans and in Romania would be swept away even before it became directly caught up in the 1939–45 European conflict. The elections of December 1937 had marked the collapse of government by political parties under royal direction. The strong showing of Codreanu's All for the Nation party meant that none of the parties around Carol obtained the 40% of the vote necessary for a parliamentary majority (Scurtu and Buzatu 1999: 333). Carol took power in February 1938 when he realised that he could not direct affairs by the old methods. On 24 February, a new corporatist constitution was approved by 4,289,581 votes to 5,843 in a referendum where voting was open and compulsory. The independence of the judiciary and the autonomy of the universities had been suppressed a few days previously and all political parties dissolved (Rothschild 1974: 311). A last-ditch effort to domesticate Codreanu had failed weeks before when Carol offered him the premier-ship on condition that the Iron Guard recognise Carol as its Captain (Alexandrescu 1998: 105). The xenophobic and anti-Semitic Codreanu was unlikely to jeopardise his credibility by bending the knee to a corrupt monarch who obstinately clung to his influential Jewish mistress, a woman widely seen as a combination of Messalina and Rasputin (Alexandrescu 1998: 135). Thereafter Carol resolved to crush the Iron Guard/Legionary movement by force. Imprisoned on trumped up charges in April 1938, Codreanu was 'shot while attempting to escape', along with some of his chief lieutenants, the following November. When the Iron Guard, in retaliation, murdered Premier Armand Calinescu, Carol's right-hand man, on 21 September 1939, the King ordered a massacre. In each county, the prefect was instructed to execute between three and five prominent Legionaries whose bodies were exposed in public squares, and numerous others were kept in prison (Constantiniu 1997: 368–9). Some prefects killed lunatics in the public asylum instead, realising that the King might be a transient figure even though the Iron Guard leadership had been devastated.

The chasm between the King and many of his people did not diminish. Even the official *Romanian Encyclopedia* (Vol. I 1938) could make the observation that 'between the governing elite, those in power, those with wealth and political influence and the rest, there exists a chasm which it is hard to bridge' (Constantiniu 1997: 319). The civic spirit, without which true democracy couldn't prosper, was absent in these conditions. Cyrus Sulzberger, the *New York Times* journalist, remembering a visit he made to Romania on the eve of the Second World War, wrote in a memoir that 'if there was any country that deserved to have a revolution, it was Romania at that moment' (Constantiniu 1997: 324).

The anti-Western backlash the Iron Guard had orchestrated in the 1930s bears some comparison with the religious and nationalist revolt that swept Iran in the 1970s. A corrupt and isolated dynasty, which preferred to see wealth reside in a few hands and orientated itself towards the West, drew the wrath of intellectuals and young people who felt excluded from the system. Orthodox fundamentalism pervaded the Guard just as radical Islam was the driving force behind the Iranian revolution. But the King obtained the consent of the Orthodox patriarch, Miron Cristea, who actually served as prime minister during the first half of the dictatorship, a sign of the willingness of the Church to align itself with secular power irrespective of its character. After recurring massacres, the Legion had become, in the words of one Romanian, 'a potato, the best part of which was below ground' (Nagy-Talavera 1999: 394).

The totalitarian state Carol created was a parody of the real thing. There was a single party, the Front of National Rebirth, with the King as its chief, his ministers attended parliament dressed in its uniform and gave the Roman salute. But this was 'a totalitarian regime with masons and well-known democrats' which made anti-Semitism according to the needs of the moment and tried to draw closer to Germany 'with Anglophiles and Francophiles still in the government' (Scurtu and Buzatu 1999: 354)

WAR REACHES THE BALKANS

Balkan states drew closer to one another in the initial phase of the war. Little advantage was seen to be had in aligning with Nazi Germany;

even an opportunist like Mussolini stayed out of the conflict for nearly a year until in June 1940 the moment to capitalise on Hitler's military successes appeared in danger of slipping away. Italy had given ample proof of its predatory interest in the Balkans by invading and occupying Albania on Easter Sunday 1939. The brutal way in which the Nazis dismembered Poland sent shockwaves through countries like Romania and Yugoslavia which, like Poland, had been designed to act as effective buffers against the revival of German and Russian might.

On 23 August 1939 Russia and Germany had signed a Pact of Non-Aggression which has gone down in history as the Molotov-Ribbentrop Pact after the two foreign ministers. Attached to it was a secret protocol which divided much of Southeast Europe into spheres of influence. One clause stated: 'As for the south east of Europe from the Soviet side, the interest of the USSR in Bessarabia is stressed. The German side declares a complete lack of interest in these regions' (Brogan 1990: 213).

Romania would be the first Balkan country to lose territory after the Second World War began. In April 1939 both Britain and France had given unilateral guarantees to Romania and Greece that they would undertake to give them 'all the support in their power', in the event of a clear threat to their independence (Barker 1976: 3, 5). But two Southeast European countries were being offered defence commitments by two struggling powers and long-standing allies which scarcely possessed the military means to fulfil them. It was a belated gesture after years of allowing a power vacuum to develop in the Balkans (Barker 1976: 6). Hitler had already been allowed to fill it economically. In October 1938 Sir Alexander Cadogan, the head of the British Foreign Office had candidly written in his diaries after the Munich Crisis: 'we must cut our losses in central and eastern Europe—let Germany, if she can, find there her *Lebensraum* and establish herself, if she can, as a powerful economic unit' (Cadogan 1971: 119).

In 1939–40 Romania turned increasingly to Germany, which was in a position to sell it heavy weaponry that a traditional ally like Britain did not have its disposal and whose economic domination of the country was steadily escalating. In the early 1940s Churchill would harbour resentment towards Romania and other Balkan states which had been offered security guarantees by Britain but instead moved into the Axis camp. The small states of the Balkans had little choice given that the might of Germany was already on their doorsteps and Britain was a faraway entity. But at least countries like Yugoslavia and Bulgaria manoeuvred to preserve as much independence as they could, especially once it became clear from the fate of Romania in 1940 that German guarantees of territorial integrity were not worth the paper they were written on.

Romania was in no position to resist successfully when, on 26 June 1940, Russia presented Carol with an ultimatum to hand over Bessarabia (and north Bukovina, formerly part of the Hapsburg Empire) within 24 hours. Romania, which had been describing itself as 'a neutral ally of the Axis' appealed to Berlin for help, but was advised to accept the diktat from a state which was a partner with Germany in the dismemberment of large parts of Eastern Europe. Bucharest conceded: the Romanian army was poorly armed and equipped. Many resources for military equipment had been diverted by the royal camarilla for its own use (Scurtu and Buzatu 1999: 359).

Bessarabia, a remote and badly governed territory, had a peripheral role in the Romanian national consciousness. This was not the case with Transylvania. Millions of Romanians still believe its unification with the Romanian kingdom in 1918 to be the seminal event in Romanian history. But deprived of true allies, Romania was at the mercy of Hungarian determination to acquire a territory which had been ruled by Budapest for several centuries. Afraid that a war between these two Danubian states would interrupt the flow of oil supplies from Romania vital for the war effort, Hitler decided to impose a settlement. On 30 August 1940 Romanian and Hungarian diplomats were presented with a settlement hurriedly worked out by Ribbentrop and the Italian foreign minister, Count Ciano. It gave Hungary one-third of her maximum demand, two-thirds of its territorial losses to Romania being restored to Budapest. Romania's Balkan allies were in no position to help. Under a military dictator, General Ion Antonescu who replaced the disgraced Carol on 6 September, Romania entered the Axis camp.

Hitler had no intention to further involve the Balkans in his wars of conquest. He wished to maintain the flow of Romanian oil and towards that end he backed the conservative Antonescu in his January 1941 power struggle with the Iron Guard, who were more ideologically congenial to the Nazis. But his hand was forced when, on 28 October 1940, his ally Mussolini invaded Greece. The Italian dictator had kept the Führer uninformed, knowing that he was likely to veto a scheme that did not accord with his war aims. Mussolini had already failed to reach an agreement with Yugoslavia and Bulgaria for the partitioning of Greece (Stavrianos 1958: 751). These countries had no desire to be surrounded on all sides by Axis countries with a record of treachery and double-dealing that surpassed anything seen in the Balkans. Mussolini's overtures were rejected and Athens was given warning of what was in store.

Italian forces were soon driven from Greek soil and the Greeks advanced into Albania, capturing its southern towns. Greece had quickly invoked the British guarantee of assistance offered before World War II if Greece was attacked (Macartney and Palmer 1962: 434). The island of Crete was occupied and squadrons of the British airforce were sent to the mainland. The British failed to persuade the Greek army to support an Albanian uprising against the Italians which might have resulted in Italy being driven from Albania completely. Many Greeks hoped to annexe Southern Albania (known to them as Northern Epirus) and to sponsor Albanian military action would make such an undertaking difficult (Wolff 1974: 196).

But the crucial aspect of the British engagement was that it made German intervention in the Balkans almost unavoidable. The threat posed to the Romanian oil fields was felt to be too great and only Hitler's forces could extricate their Italian allies from a self-inflicted defeat. Deteriorating relations with Russia also increased the visibility of the Balkans for the Germans.

Germany and Russia could agree on taking joint action to bury the results of the Versailles agreement. Molotov, in a speech to the Supreme Soviet in October 1939 had said, 'One blow from the German Army and another from the Soviet Army, put an end to this ugly product of Versailles—Poland' (Charlton 1983a: 11). But beyond that and the terroristic methods that were part of the practical politics of both regimes, the scope for cooperation was limited. A visit to Berlin by Molotov in November 1940 revealed widening divergences between the world's two main totalitarian states. Hitler was annoyed when Molotov showed no interest in the Nazi leader's offer to divide the British Empire between their two states. Instead Molotov concentrated on Balkan and Finnish territorial concerns, complaining that the German guarantee to Romania to preserve its post-1940 boundaries could be seen as a threat to Russia. He also expressed his interest in a mutual assistance pact with Bulgaria which recognised that 'Bulgaria is located within the security zone of the Black Sea boundaries of the Soviet Union' (Lukacs 1953: 328, 331; Stavrianos 1958: 753).

Russia was anxious to share control of the Black Sea Balkan region with Germany rather than to allow Hitler complete hegemony over an area adjacent to the strategic Bosporus straits. Stalin seemed to believe that the contest between Germans and Slavs, which produced violent outbursts and threats by Hitler in *Mein Kampf*, had been shelved. He overlooked the fact that by demanding territory and space in areas Germany had designated for *Lebensraum* he ran the risk of reviving Hitler's hatred of communism and perhaps even greater hatred of the Slavs (Borsody 1993: 45).

Eastern Europe's strategic importance had been underlined by the founder of the science of geopolitics, Sir Halford Mackinder, whose ideas were taken more seriously in Germany than in his native Britain. He had coined the famous formula in 1919:

> Who rules Eastern Europe commands the Heartland; Who rules the Heartland, commands the World-island; Who rules the World-Island, commands the World. (Davies 1996: 872)

The heartland was Eurasian Russia, seen as the location of the world's supreme natural fortress. Hitler, influenced by Mackinder's German disciple, Karl Haushofer, aimed to conquer 'the Heartland' so as to have the rest of the world at his feet (Trevor-Roper 1993: 81).

Molotov's obduracy seemed to convince Hitler that an alliance of convenience between two ideologically incompatible states had run its course and preparations must be made for a settling of accounts with Stalin. On 18 December 1940 Hitler ordered preparations to begin for the invasion of Russia (Operation Barbarossa). Five days earlier, directives for the invasion of Greece had been issued to the German high command. A number of overtures had been made to Greece to accept terms that could end the war with Italy. One of the conditions of receiving acceptable terms was that British forces must leave Greek soil. But even though 'the Greek government know the possibility of saving themselves to be open to them', peace feelers couched in these terms were rejected (Macartney and Palmer 1962: 435).

To neutralise Greece, Hitler had to extend his sphere of influence in Southeast Europe. Bulgaria was the key for a land assault on Greece and in January 1941, under heavy pressure, King Boris agreed to the entry of German troops (Stavrianos 1958: 754). Russia protested against the German advance into the heart of the Balkans but to no avail and in March Bulgaria adhered to the Axis's alliance system, the Tripartite Pact.

Berlin also saw the need to obtain the benevolent neutrality of Yugoslavia, an ally of Greece. The Nazis had been disappointed in the autumn of 1940 that the Yugoslavs spurned the invitation to seize the Aegean port of Thessaloniki, a suggestion which was also put to the

Bulgarians. The desire of Balkan states not to be dupes in Axis power-plays remained strong even as their freedom of action contracted. In late 1940 Turkey had offered an alliance to Yugoslavia which Prince Regent Paul ignored. A revived Balkan Pact involving these two states and Greece and Bulgaria might have persuaded Germany that it would be too costly and time consuming to subdue the Balkans with a vital Russian campaign looming.

By the spring of 1941 Germany was stepping up the pressure on Yugoslavia to enter the Axis orbit. On 25 March 1941 Yugoslavia signed the Tripartite Pact, having secured terms that would give it more freedom of manoeuvre than countries like Romania and Bulgaria. Two days later a coup in Belgrade resulted in the overthrow of Paul and the accession of his young nephew Peter. Yugoslavia urgently reassured Germany that it did not wish to alter its relationship with the Axis. However, Hitler claimed to see strong Russian involvement behind the coup and, calling together his generals, he announced that Yugoslavia had to be destroyed 'militarily and as a national unit' (Macartney and Palmer 1962: 442).

In fact if any power was responsible for the coup it was Britain. Since June 1940 British agents had paid out considerable sums of money to enemies of the Prince Regent in Serbian politics to plot against him (Tanner 1997: 139). Churchill had already directly telegraphed the Yugoslav premier, Dragisha Tsvetkovich, on 20 March, outlining a heroic role for Yugoslavia and mixing it with threats about 'her ruin' being 'irreparable':

> We know that the hearts of all true Serbs, Croats, and Slovenes beat for the freedom, integrity and independence of their country, and that they share the forward outlook of the English-speaking world. If Yugoslavia were at this time to stoop to the fate of Rumania, or commit the crime of Bulgaria, and become an accomplice in the attempted assassination of Greece, her ruin will be certain and irreparable ... I trust your excellency may rise to the height of world events. (Lukacs 1953: 366)

When the Prince Regent and his chief ally from the late 1930s, Milan Stojadinović, fell into British hands, they were interned in East Africa and Mauritius for the duration of the war. The Anglophile Paul had been forced by circumstances rather than political preference to accommodate with the Nazis and he had fought a hard bargain, but it seemed to make little difference for Churchill. Later the British leader would show scant regard for the fate of Bulgaria and Romania at the hands of the Soviets, perhaps because they had aligned with Britain's chief enemy at such a vital juncture in the war. In early 1941, Sir Alexander Cadogan, the head of the British Foreign Office, confided to his diary that 'All these Balkan peoples are trash ...' (Wheeler 1980: 245). Hitler had used the same word (*Gerümpel*) in *Mein Kampf* about the Balkan peoples (Wheeler 1980: 245). In the life-and-death struggle between Britain and Germany, later expanded to include the USA and Russia, there is no shortage of evidence which suggests that the Balkan peoples were seen as expendable. No effort had been made by the British after 1918 to encourage leaders like Stamboliski and Venizelos, committed to moving beyond narrow national interest to embrace a Balkan-wide vision for the development of the region's peoples. In the early 1930s, the British ambassador in Belgrade, Sir Neville Henderson, was prepared to endorse the royal dictatorship in Yugoslavia because he saw nothing better capable of emerging (Seton-Watson *et al.* 1976: 202). The viewpoint evident in the 1990s among Western, and particularly British, policy-makers that the Balkans seemed incapable of civilized forms of political behaviour and therefore the rules of modern conduct that applied to the rest of Europe need not be followed in their case, was already evident fifty years earlier.

The Balkan states had in fact gone far towards managing their differences in the 1930s and creating a system of regular conferences to solve some of them. In the early years of the Second World War, they strove to remain outside the conflict.

Upon hearing news of the Yugoslav coup, Churchill declared that Yugoslavia had found its soul. But Britain was in no position to assist Yugoslavia when Hitler made good his promise to dismantle the country. A massive air-attack on Belgrade on 6 April 1941, codenamed 'Operation Punishment', was accompanied by a declaration of war on Greece. Yugoslavia was rapidly overrun and by 2 June 1941 organized resistance had ended in all parts of Greece, including the island of Crete.

One historian believes that Hitler now had a golden opportunity to overrun the entire Middle East with its unparalleled oil wealth (Stavrianos 1958: 766). The Wehrmacht was winning impressive victories in North Africa under General Erwin Rommel. However, the opportunity was allowed to pass because, as a German diplomat observed, Hitler was moving 'along a mental one-way street against Russia' (Stavrianos 1958: 760). But Mussolini's foolish attack on Greece and the way it complicated and delayed Hitler's plans for a German invasion propelled the Balkans into the forefront of the war and may, in no small measure, have contributed to the eventual Axis defeat. It also meant that decisions would be taken about the future of the region by external leaders who saw it in terms of comic-opera kings, benighted peasants, or racially flawed peoples, terms that would not enable the Balkans to easily escape from the cycle of tyranny and instability which it had been subjected to ever since the age of nationalism had begun.

CONCLUSION

The failure of Britain and France to use their primacy after 1918 to reshape the European order along lines that would make it far less easy for conflicts of nationality to burst to the surface paved the way for a fresh fratricidal conflict two decades later. Exhausted by war, preoccupied by urgent domestic problems and lacking a common vision, Anglo-French leaders placed too much reliance on an East Central Europe of multiethnic states being able to provide the stability which had eluded the Europe of dynastic empires. But the nationalism of the democratic victors also prevented them from employing the leap of faith and imagination which would enable them to promote transnational arrangements, especially in the economic sphere, capable of taking the heat out of nationalist rivalries in regions such as the Balkans. The decorum of British and French public life and the strength of civil institutions masked the extent to which nationalism shaped elite views, particularly in the island power. But in their commitment to the nation as the cornerstone of political existence the successful states of Western Europe differed from the new and untried ones in the old imperial borderlands only in degree. Otherwise, the principle of the self-determination of nations would not have become the cornerstone of the shaky interwar order baptised at Versailles.

Britain and France soon placed little restraint on the new or enlarged victor states of Eastern Europe employing much the same tactics as the fallen empires in their treatment of minorities. The deportation of peoples as a means of halting the Greek–Turkish conflict of the early 1920s was actually overseen by the Allies who showed growing reluctance to allow their own creation, the League of Nations, to honour its own provisions concerning minority rights.

The League enjoyed some isolated successes, as in 1925 when it intervened swiftly to prevent Bulgaria being attacked by Greece. But as an instrument of collective European security, it would be fatally undermined by its own architects in the 1930s when Britain and France showed a preference for dealing directly with the dictators in charge of revisionist states determined to modify or overthrow the Versailles settlement. Earlier, these states had missed opportunities to stabilise the region by failing to throw their weight behind leaders like the Bulgarian premier Stamboliski, who had been committed to promoting Balkan cooperation before his murder in 1923.

The lack of forward thinking about the Balkans or the desire to take initiatives which would promote cooperation between rival states was palpable in the 1920s and 1930s. Low-grade advice from diplomatic officials was not infrequently received in the chancelleries of Paris and London. During the September 1923 Corfu crisis Lord Curzon, the British Foreign Secretary, complained in a minute that 'British ambassadors always seem to be shooting or on holiday when there is a crisis' (Lamb 1997: 45). No Western ambassador of note in the region stood out during the interwar years. Academics like R.W. Seton-Watson, well aware of the need for Britain and France to work assiduously to promote economic cooperation and fair treatment of minorities in order to isolate the forces of revanchist nationalism, lost the influence in policy-making circles that they had possessed during the First World War.

In the 1930s, without undue prompting from the Western powers, the Balkan states took measures to contain or settle some of their most pressing differences and prevent the region being destabilised by the aggressive revisionist states, Italy and Germany. Despite its limitations, the Balkan Entente proved more successful than the Little Entente of states from Eastern Europe as a whole which had benefited from the Versailles Treaty. The Balkan countries were conspicuous by their absence during the countdown to war from 1935 to 1939, largely as a result of the prudence of their leaders. The quality of leadership was, however, variable as weak-based democratic regimes gave way to dictatorships, usually of the royal variety.

The challenge of integrating new territories with different economic and social systems, as well as political standards, tested enlarged states like Romania and new ones like Poland and Yugoslavia to the limit. The 1929 economic crash, the failure of the Allies to promote functional cooperation along economic lines (thereby reviving at least the economic unity provided by the Hapsburg and Ottoman Empires), and decisions like Britain's to leave the gold standard in 1931, also contributed to the collapse of representative government in the Balkans.

However, the prevalence of stereotypical attitudes among West European diplomats and their political chiefs conveyed the feeling that democracy was viewed as an anomaly in the region. Such stereotypes proliferate when a power has no primary interests in a country and is disinclined to investigate the true state of affairs there.

In 1938, before the menace of Nazi Germany was really apparent to the British, the head of the British Foreign Office, Sir Alexander Cadogan, was relaxed about the prospect of Hitler establishing economic hegemony over the Balkans. A few years later, Britain's wartime leadership would be prepared to assign much of the region to the Soviet sphere of influence until, too late, it realised that Stalin's ambitions were not limited to creating a cordon sanitaire of dependent satellites on his western and southern flanks.

The Balkan states had mainly remained stony ground for the rival extreme ideologies of communism and fascism, an indication that the reputation of the region as fertile ground for extremists has not always been true. Only Romania developed an indigenous fascist movement that briefly became a formidable national force.

But because of its vulnerable geographic position, the region would fall victim to new tyrannies, though they had little local appeal. The Balkan states were caught in the middle of the conflict between Germany and Russia when both coveted the Danubian and Balkan lands for economic and strategic reasons.

NOTES

1. R. Storrs (1945), *Orientations*, London, p. 144, quoted in M. Anderson (1966), *The Eastern Question*, p. 316.
2. *Dreptatea*, 19 December 1928, quoted by Scurtu and Buzatu, (1999) *Istoria Românilor In Secolul XX*, p. 195.

Chapter 3

WHIRLWIND FROM THE EAST: THE ADVANCE OF COMMUNIST POWER, 1941–1948

By the second half of 1941, all the Balkan states (with the exception of Turkey) were under Axis control of one kind or another. Yugoslavia had been partitioned between Germany, Italy, Hungary and Bulgaria. Much of Slovenia was acquired by Germany which deported Slovene intellectuals and professionals and brought in German settlers, including many of the 100,000 or so German speakers who had evacuated Bessarabia when it fell to Russia in 1940. Macedonia was divided between Italy and Bulgaria. Montenegro was acquired by the Italians who annexed large parts of Bosnia and Dalmatia which, together with Albania, gave them control of the entire Adriatic coastline (Stavrianos 1958: 771).

Two rump states also emerged. Serbia, whose frontiers were reduced to those of 1912, was effectively controlled by the German military despite the existence of a puppet government under General Milan Nedić. Croatia, under the ultranationalist Ante Pavelić, the leader of the Ustaša movement, enjoyed more freedom of action. In May 1941 he installed himself as the Führer or *Poglavnik* of Croatia and promptly unleashed a reign of terror against Serbs and Jews. In 1942 Pavelić boasted that 'Great deeds were done by Germans and Croats together. We can proudly say that we succeeded in breaking the Serb nation which, after the English, is the most thick-headed, the most stubborn, and the most stupid' (Lukacs 1953: 783). The attempt to break the Serb nation involved massacring vulnerable and isolated Serb communities in Croatia and Bosnia. The Italian journalist Curzio Malaparte reported that Pavelić had shown him a basket filled with human eyes gouged from Serbian bodies 'given to me as a present by my dear Ustashas' (Beloff 1985: 74).

Most of Greece was given to Italy but Germany occupied the most strategic parts, including the main cities, and Bulgaria acquired eastern Macedonia and Thrace. Only Romania and Bulgaria remained nominally independent, but with a heavy German military presence designed to restrict the freedom of action of local rulers.

Hitler's 'New Order' was designed exclusively for the benefit of Germany and its interests. There was little place for Balkan movements that endorsed the Nazis' aims and methods. The Croatian Ustaša and the Romanian Iron Guard were tools of the Nazis whom those directing the German war effort distrusted. This was shown in January 1941 when Hitler took the side of the conservative Romanian general Ion Antonescu in his power struggle with the Iron Guard. The German Führer built up a good working relationship with Antonescu that was unique in his dealings with Axis satellite leaders (Waldeck 1998: 233). Antonescu was popular at home but his decision to send Romanian forces deep inside Russia produced increasing anxiety which turned to foreboding as Russia successfully counter-attacked at the end of 1942. From 1941 Iuliu Maniu demanded in letters to Antonescu that Romania should halt its advance after recapturing Bessarabia. Antonescu was irritated by such calls but he left Maniu at liberty despite German demands that he be silenced. In Bulgaria, another leader of a Peasant Party, Nikola Petkov was a focus of opposition. From King Boris downwards there was active resistance against Nazi attempts to send Bulgarian Jews to death camps and most of them survived. But in Thessaloniki, which had been occupied by the Germans because of its strategic importance, the largest concentration of Jews in the Balkans found no escape and it was wiped out in 1943–44.

Yugoslav communists organized resistance following the Nazi attack on Russia in June 1941. The communists enjoyed the advantage of being the only true national or all-Yugoslav party. Their leader Josip Broz, soon to be known as Marshal Tito, set up a guerilla movement known as the Partisans, apparently in deference to the memory of Russian 'partisans' against Napoleon (Thomas 1986: 426). Initially operating in Serbia, the Partisans withdrew and, after a two-hundred mile epic march in mid-1942, established a stronghold in the mountains of northwest Bosnia. Here they could rely on the support of Serb peasantry who were being persecuted by the Ustaša. They set up a parallel state and the ranks of the Partisan movement were swelled by Croat and Muslim recruits alienated from the foreign occupation forces or the local collaborationists.

The first acts of resistance were actually performed by the Četniks, Serbian royalists operating under the Yugoslav army officer, Colonel Draza Mihailović (Crampton 1994: 200). He established a base among the Serbian peasantry of western Serbia. His strategy was to prepare for a general uprising when the country appeared to be on the point of liberation rather than to risk annihilation by engaging the occupiers in immediate conflict. The British initially backed the Četniks. Their commitment to a royalist Yugoslavia appealed to Churchill. But enthusiasm in London for the Četniks waned owing to their reluctance to engage with the Hitlerite enemy and their preoccupation with trying to eliminate Tito's Partisans. The first Allied officer, the British Captain D.T. Hudson, had made contact with Tito's forces in October 1941 (Petrovich 1982: 38).

In 1942 the British Foreign Office enlisted the help of the Soviets to try and forge a united resistance movement under Mihailović's leadership. Believing in a monolithic world communist movement, they assumed that Tito was a Soviet cypher (Rothwell 1982: 205). In fact Tito was operating independently of Moscow and the first direct contact between Soviet forces and the Partisans would not take place until February 1944 (Maclean 1949: 433). The Foreign Office abandoned this ploy when the Soviets ignored its letters and 'when the absurdity of expecting Tito, with ten times as many men as Mihailović, to subordinate himself to his rival, finally sank in' (Rothwell 1982: 205).

A small British mission under F.W.D. Deakin was parachuted to the Partisans in May 1943 and its reports confirmed previous impressions that only the Partisans were seriously interested in engaging the enemy. In July Churchill sent Captain Fitzroy Maclean as his personal representative to the Partisans after large amounts of military aid had already been dispatched. Macleans's reports convinced Churchill and the chiefs of staff of the Partisans military usefulness. Henceforth Churchill was prepared to sideline the Četniks and throw his weight behind the Partisans (despite Foreign Office objections). Their communist complexion was secondary to the fact that they were effective in tying down Axis forces in the Balkans and thus performing a vital service to the Allied war effort.

BRITISH AND SOVIET INTERVENTION IN THE BALKANS 1941–43

Across the Balkans, Nazi repression, and a policy for the region based on economic plunder and ideological racism, won the New Order few friends and enabled a resistance movement like Tito's to survive against the odds. The invasion of Russia undermined Nazi authority even further and, at least in many South Slav inhabited parts of the Balkans, allowed Russian popularity to soar. This meant that local communists were bound to play an important role wherever resistance occurred. Even in Albania, where a communist party only came into existence in November 1941 (with Yugoslav help) local communists soon dominated the National Liberation Committee established in 1942.

Capitalising on a recrudescence of Pan-Slavism, Stalin launched a Pan-Slav Committee immediately after the German invasion. It disavowed the Pan-Slav imperialism of tsarist Russia, proclaimed the equality of Slav nations and promised 'No interference in the inner affairs of other nations' (Borsody 1993: 127–8). Stalin made a show of adhering to the Atlantic Charter which the American President Franklin Roosevelt and Churchill issued in August 1941, and which said in part: 'Firstly, their countries seek not aggrandisement, territorial or other; Second, they desire to see no territorial changes that do not accord with the freely expressed wishes of the peoples concerned; Third, they respect the right of all peoples to choose the form of government under which they will live ...' (Hammond 1982: 282).

The Soviet Union was fighting for its survival in September 1941 at the time Stalin adhered to the Atlantic Charter. Its promises were diametrically opposed to the policies Stalin would eventually carry out. But perhaps then the Allies could have been forgiven for suspending their critical judgment at this early stage in their relationship with the Russian leader. However, suspicions about his true intentions were not aroused when, in talks with his new allies, Stalin showed that he was no less determined than he had been during the lifetime of the Nazi–Soviet pact to regain territory lost after 1917. Moreover, the deep trauma induced by the unexpected German invasion in 1941 reinforced Russian determination to neutralise the Balkans as a potential threat to Soviet power. From the outset in talks with Britain Stalin and his Foreign Minister V.M. Molotov made clear their belief that it was the Russian entitlement to establish a zone of influence in the Balkans, especially in territory approaching the Black Sea. Stalin's ambitions in the region would escalate as the war turned in his favour. He saw that the Allies were often divided and confused about their policy towards the region, and Eastern Europe in general. They lacked any consistently-held alternative strategy to counteract Soviet domination.

The American President was reluctant to discuss postwar strategy with Russia or even with his closest ally, Churchill. He preferred to concentrate on winning the war and showed a disinclination to contemplate employing American armed strength to ensure a democratic peace in Europe. Neither Britain nor the United States bothered to give the Russians the impression that they cared deeply for Polish independence, a neglect presumably noticed in Moscow which allowed Stalin to draw the appropriate conclusions (Thomas 1986: 351). America's interest in Eastern Europe was 'weak, sentimental, idealistic, and theoretical' (Hammond 1982: 279). The US Secretary of State Cordell Hull often ignored Eastern Europe, expressing his preference at the Moscow conference of Allied foreign ministers in October 1942 for Eden and Molotov to discuss Polish and Yugoslav issues in his absence (Hammond 1982: 287). Upon his return to Washington, Hull was asked at a press conference what was meant by 'self-determination of liberated countries' which had figured in the post-summit declaration. He replied: 'The application of this principle of self-determination would be left to the military people in immediate charge' (Nadeau 1990: 66). To the Russians, this would have been eloquent testimony of the unpreparedness of the Americans to engage in the power politics that would attend the cessation of the world war.

At the Tehran summit of the Big Three in November 1943, Churchill wished to discuss the future shape of Eastern Europe, but Roosevelt was uninterested and Stalin evasive (Harriman and Abel 1975: 274). Roosevelt's behaviour at Tehran indicated his belief that the future of mankind at the war's end would lie in the hands of the USA and the Soviet Union. He did not conceal his opposition to the continuing existence of the British Empire from Stalin, with whom he was anxious to discuss the future of India (Colville 1986a: 3). Roosevelt showed no concern about the fact that much of Soviet territory had been acquired by force both before and after the triumph of Bolshevism, and the Russian leader must have been pleasantly surprised by his American counterpart's choice of priorities at their first meeting.

While the Soviet forces were reliant on aid from their Allies and still engaged in fierce combat with the Germans on Russian soil, the western Allies possessed important leverage which they would soon lose. Tehran was a missed opportunity, perhaps of historic magnitude, and Stalin, a master of realpolitik, may well have expanded his ambitions in Europe upon seeing the disunity of his Allies on vital questions concerning the peace.

The British, given their long if intermittent engagement in continental affairs, were bound to be more mindful of the new postwar European order than the USA. In the first stages of the British–Soviet wartime alliance, it appeared that Britain was ready to actively promote the idea of creating several confederations of states in central Europe and the Balkans. This was a revival of an old diplomatic strategy. Sir Orme

Sargent, the second-ranking official in the British Foreign Office, expressed the need to replace 'the pre-war congeries of weak, irresponsible and jealous national states in eastern Europe' with larger groupings (Wheeler 1980: 159). The fear of German revenge and of Soviet imperialism would, it was hoped, provide the incentive for 'the Middle Zone' (as Eastern Europe became known in the British Foreign Office during the war years) to abandon national egotism and pool sovereignty. Sargent even wrote on 29 January 1942 that: 'The peace and security of Europe as a whole, as contrasted with the wishes and prejudices of any individual state, will justify the use of force in just the same way as the American Civil War was justified in order to preserve the Union in the interests of the future of North America as a whole' (Wheeler 1980: 159).

With active British encouragement, the Greek and Yugoslav exiled governments had negotiated a formal agreement creating a 'Balkan Union' (Barker 1976: 131). On 15 January 1942 the Foreign Secretary, Sir Anthony Eden, presided over the signature of the agreement at a ceremony in the Foreign Office. In the words of Yugoslav expert Mark Wheeler it:

> called for the establishment of permanent consultative machinery by the two governments in the political, economic and military spheres. It was envisaged that foreign policy would be coordinated, that plans for a customs union and a joint economic development programme would be elaborated and that the defence establishments of the two states would be integrated by means of a combined general staff. It was expressly stated that the two governments looked forward to the accession of other Balkan states to the Union. (Wheeler 1980: 157–8)

The Foreign Office debated whether or not to say openly that it hoped Bulgaria and Romania would eventually join in, or whether this would provoke Soviet suspicion. Britain was officially at war with both countries since late 1941 and caution was advised. But, when faced with a direct question in the House of Commons on 4 February, Eden replied: 'What I can say for sure is that this Greek–Yugoslav treaty is definitely to form the basis of a Balkan confederation' (Barker 1976: 131).

During the middle years of the war, both publicly and in private communications, Churchill promoted the idea of a Europe that would not be organized primarily on the nation-state principle. In a message to Eden dated 21 October 1942 reproduced in Churchill's memoirs, the British Prime Minister wrote:

> It would be a measureless disaster if Russian barbarism overlaid the culture and independence of the ancient states of Europe. Hard as it is to say now, I trust that

the European family may act unitedly as one under a Council of Europe. I look forward to a United States of Europe in which the barriers between the nations will be gradually minimised ... I hope to see a Council consisting of perhaps ten units, including the former Great Powers, with several confederations— Scandinavia, Danube, Balkan etc ... (Borsody 1993: 110)

In a broadcast on 21 March 1943 Churchill made public his desire for a confederation 'of great states and groups of states. It is my earnest hope, though I can hardly expect to see its fulfillment in my lifetime, that we shall achieve the largest common measure of the integrated life of Europe that is possible without destroying the individual character and traditions of its many ancient and historic races' (Borsody 1993: 111).

In this declaration Churchill admitted that plans for a European Union could not succeed without the active backing of Britain, the USA and Russia, known as 'the Big Three'. This indeed proved to be the case. The US Secretary of State, Cordell Hull, showed scant understanding of the idea when it was put to him in 1942 (Borsody 1993: 112). There was no acknowledgement that the political arrangements which had made a vast territory like the United States a viable concern might be appropriate for Europe. Russian scepticism could be taken for granted. Stalin was firmly opposed to ideas of confederations of states even when they came from fellow communists like the Bulgarian Georgi Dimitrov, who advocated a communist Balkan confederation in the mid-1940s. The Foreign Office relegated its plan to oblivion. It stood in the way of the finalisation of the 1942 Anglo-Soviet alliance, but only later would British officials realise how much of an obstacle the union of its small western neighbours was seen by Stalin, impeding the Soviet political advance into Central Europe.

Consistent British advocacy of a postwar Eastern Europe organized along non-national lines might have impressed the Americans and forced Stalin to scale down his imperial designs on the region. Churchill had persuaded Roosevelt to accept other ideas which were even less in tune with the US State Department mind. But despite his visionary outlook, Churchill was a nationalist who lacked the imagination and the commitment for a scheme that would relegate the nation-state to a subordinate role in the affairs of Europe if confederalism or federalism became a reality. The only member of the cabinet who shared Churchill's enthusiasm for a remodelling of Europe was L.S. Amery, the Secretary of State for India, a relatively minor figure. He wrote in 1942: 'If we are first in the Balkans we should push on the setting up of a Balkan confederation there and then, while things are malleable and our influence is at its highest' (F.P. King 1973: 69).

Both Churchill and Amery belonged to a British Conservative Party in which long-standing opposition to federalising Europe has extended to end of the 20th century. Britain was ill-placed to promote a framework for a new Europe when it was so resistant to change in its own political arrangements (most of Ireland seceded in 1921 after the British Parliament refused to concede the relatively moderate demand for Home Rule in the previous forty years). The backing of Eden, the wartime Foreign Secretary, would have been needed if a confederal Europe was to move beyond the stage of 'a study project' (Wheeler 1980: 158). He soon got cold feet. In 1942 he ordered that the Balkan Union invitation to other states be downplayed. He held that Romania and Bulgaria (with which Britain was at war) must not be encouraged to believe 'that after the war they will live happily and without punishment on equal terms with the Allied Balkan states' (Wheeler 1980: 158).

In the summer of 1942 Eden was promoting the idea of the restoration of occupied national states in his talks with some of their exiled leaders. Thus, he assured Eduard Beneš, the Czechoslovak President, that not only would Britain recognise the pre-Munich frontiers of Czechoslovakia, but it would support the Czech plan for expelling the German and Hungarian minority populations (Borsody 1993: 114). This remark showed that Eden could not see beyond traditional solutions for settling national differences, ones that had drowned different corners of Europe in blood during successive centuries. More far-seeing policy advisers like Sir Orme Sargent in the Foreign office who argued in 1941–42 that Britain had a chance to impose its own vision on the postwar order at a time when Stalin, preoccupied with survival, had not worked out any definite plans for a future European settlement, went unheeded (Wheeler 1980: 302, n. 128).

Britain would show that it had no coherent strategy for the Balkans except to act there in defence of its own great power interests, ones that lay outside the area in the Middle East and India, and to concentrate on bringing the war to a rapid conclusion. Britain's supranational ideas, vaguely held and casually advanced, were dropped as soon as the Soviets actively opposed them (Borsody 1993: 117). If Britain felt that a resuscitated nation-state system could be a barrier before the international force of communism backed up by the Soviet Red Army, it was an act of self-delusion which played into Stalin's hands.

Sir Llewellyn Woodward, the historian of the British Foreign Office in the Second World War, wrote that many British officials, like their political leaders, thought between 1941 and 1945 that 'nothing would be lost, and a great deal might be gained, by assuming Russian sincerity' (Woodward 1970: xlvi). In 1941, the chief of the secret service was apparently told by Churchill to concentrate all his resources on the Axis because the Soviet Union was now an ally (Thomas 1986: 312). A former Communist, the Yugoslav Milovan Djilas, who dealt with Stalin at close quarters in the mid-1940s, was astonished that at this time the British 'did not realise that the Soviet Union was no normal, no legitimate state by any accepted standard' (Thomas 1986: 317). It took a long time before the central role that ideology played in shaping the aims and tactics of the Soviet state came to be understood by British policy advisers (Charlton 1983b: 26). Some English public schools with their emphasis on empirical approaches to learning and neglect of theory may have left diplomats ill-equipped to grapple with the intricacies of the Soviet mind. Expertise on the Soviet system was simply lacking in government circles. In 1936 Fitzroy Maclean was 'assured that the Moscow Embassy was a dead end'. He was the first British diplomat 'who had ever asked to go to such a notoriously unpleasant spot' (Thomas, [quoting internal Foreign Office source] 1986: 79).

Stalin was able to grasp that American ignorance of his system was astonishing. The weakness of non-Marxist Socialism in the USA ensured that there were no counterparts to the British Socialists Clement Attlee and Ernest Bevin, able to warn from long experience about the totalitarian aims of the Soviets. Senior American politicians like Wendell Wilkie, Joseph Davies (former ambassador in Moscow) and Henry Wallace (Commerce Secretary in the mid-1940s) were prepared to give the Russians the benefit of the doubt and view the Soviet system as one that could be reconciled with liberal democracy (see Thomas 1986: chapters 9 and 10). The naivety of western observations was fuelled by ignorance of Soviet ideology or else a desperate optimism inspired by the war (Thomas 1986: 116–7). Some Soviet officials were puzzled by the restraint of their Allies long after Stalin's plans to establish direct control of at least half of Europe had started to be activated. In 1945, Maxim Litvinov, Deputy Commisar For Foreign Affairs asked the American journalist Edgar Snow, 'Why did you Americans wait until now to begin opposing us in the Balkans and Eastern Europe? ... You should have done this three years ago. Now it's too late and your complaints only arouse suspicions here' (Thomas 1986: 104).

When working out the terms of their alliance with Britain, Soviet negotiators had insisted that the 1941 frontiers, established as a result of the joint conquests carried out in the east with Hitler, be recognised as permanent (Barker 1976: 125). To accede to Stalin's demand would be to contravene the Atlantic Charter of 1941, seen as the blueprint for a Europe liberated from tyranny. Part 2 spoke out against 'territorial changes that do not accord with the freely-expressed wishes of the people concerned'. Part 3 defended 'the right of all peoples to choose the form of government under which they will live' (Borsody 1993: 105).

In 1942 when Anglo-Soviet negotiations were in train, Churchill reminded his Foreign Secretary that 'We have never recognised the frontiers of Russia except de facto. They were acquired by acts of aggression in shameful collusion with Hitler ... I regard our sincerity [as] invoked in the maintenance of the principles of the Atlantic Charter ...' (Barker 1976: 130). However, Eden held out for compliance, arguing that 'Stalin might have asked for much more, e.g. control of the Dardenelles, spheres of influence in the Balkans ...' (Barker 1976: 130). A reluctant Churchill agreed even though it was clear that he knew he was accepting acts of aggression comparable to those of Hitler in 1938–39. Churchill was obliged to say that the clauses on self-determination in the Atlantic Charter did not apply to the territory of enemy states. Hugh Thomas has remarked: 'Since there was no chance that any British Government led by Churchill would contemplate that this Charter should apply to the territories of allied empires, it became hard to know indeed where he thought it was applicable' (Thomas 1986: 180).

But the core problem, according to one Central European historian, was not the line of frontiers but the form of government that would emerge in the Middle Zone (Borsody 1993: 126–7). Britain was slow to wake up to Soviet intentions or else assumed that the Kremlin would not be in a position to carry out its most aggressive ones. Belief that Russia could evolve from tyranny to democracy was then widespread. As late as 1944–45 Churchill made several statements in which he suggested that the ideological differences between the USSR and the Atlantic democracies were receding into the background (Lukacs 1953: 590; Borsody 1993: 145). In America, business leaders were prone to be particularly impressed by the Russians. Donald Nelson, director of the War Production Board, but previously Vice-President of Sears Roebuck, considered 'that there is, in some ways, more free enterprise in Russia than here in the United States' (Thomas 1986: 243). Lord Beaverbrook, a Canadian capitalist and imperialist who wielded much influence via his British press empire, was prepared to give Stalin the benefit of the doubt on most issues. It was his admiration for power, according to one source, which enabled him to acquire such a positive view of the Russian leader (Thomas 1986: 318).

Trust in Stalin's intentions was reinforced in May 1943 by the announcement in Moscow that the Communist International was being wound up. The Comintern, as it was better known, had tried to promote communist revolution on a global basis in order to strengthen the Soviet system. In dismantling the Comintern, Stalin wished to reassure his partners in the alliance that Russia would not use its military successes 'to promote indiscriminate revolution' (Thomas 1986: 116). If the aim was to lower the guard of the Atlantic democracies, Stalin succeeded. Senator Tom Connally, Chairman of the Foreign Relations Committee of the US Senate, for example said that Stalin's decision meant that Russian Communism would no longer interfere in the affairs of other nations (Thomas 1986: 116). Stalin's decisive motivation was beginning to appear as Russian imperialism disguised within Communist ideology (Charlton 1983b: 26–7). For the Austrian lifelong Marxist Ernst Fischer, the real significance of the Comintern's dissolution was that 'the old concept of world revolution had in fact been superseded by a new concept—that of Russia as a world empire' (Fischer 1974: 401). It is not insignificant that the 1943 decision coincided with a partial halt to the persecution of the Russian Orthodox Church and a decision by Stalin to characterise the struggle against German Nazism as a patriotic Russian war.

Wartime western leaders, whatever their undoubted achievements in helping to defeat Hitler, lacked the imagination, or the empathy with the problems of Eastern Europe, necessary to check a new wave of aggression in the region. A plan involving supranational forms of government might in the end have failed, but it probably would have made Soviet domination less easy to accomplish, and could well have persuaded Stalin to scale down his demands. But Western statesmen failed to appreciate the destructive qualities of nationalism and the ability of a totalitarian leader like Stalin (whose creed of proletarian internationalism was avowedly anti-national) to exploit it for his own ends. A similar lack of understanding by Western leaders who had created a European Union to manage the economic and financial arrangements of 12 west European states would help plunge Yugoslavia into warfare in the 1990s. If wartime leaders and their advisors had been clearer about how Europe had been plunged into a destructive civil war twice in less than fifty years, it is likely that there would have been a stronger impetus behind new arrangements based on the pooling of sovereignty in the postwar era. But the true federalists were scattered idealists and uninfluential academics and politicians spread over many countries who lacked the ear of the powerful in the few remaining democratic states.

THE BALKANS IN 1943: MILITARY OPTIONS

The absence of clear political plans for Southeast Europe reduced the attractiveness of Allied military operations in the area even when opportunities seemed to present themselves. At a military conference on 19 November 1942 Hitler anticipated Balkan invasion possibilities which he feared the Allies might pursue, warning that an approach from the direction of the Black Sea, such as a landing in Romania, would be disastrous for Germany (Lukacs 1953: 480). Much of Yugoslavia and Greece was occupied by Italian forces. When Italy withdrew from the war in July 1943, after Mussolini's overthrow, the Axis position in Southeast Europe was significantly weakened. The historian John Lukacs reckons that by October 1943, much of the western Balkans 'were either controlled by anti-German forces, or formed a vast, mysterious no-man's land of high mountains and long valleys' (Lukacs 1953: 530).

Lukacs argued that the western Allies could have 'virtually walked into Fortress Europe' through certain poorly defended strategic corridors in the Balkans during late 1943. In the short-term Hitler profited from their reluctance to commit forces to the region. German forces remained in charge of much of northern Yugoslavia down to the spring of 1945. But in the long run it was Stalin who benefited. Russia was pushing for a second front to be opened up by the Allies but he preferred it to be in western Europe. Lukacs argues that in 1943–44 Churchill made about half-a-dozen futile attempts to put Allied forces into the Balkans but that the opposition of the US President and the American Joint Chiefs of staff prevented any agreement on action being taken (Lukacs 1953: 678).

Churchill probably realised that an Allied Balkan offensive could only be successfully promoted in Anglo-American war counsels if Turkey could be persuaded to enter the war against Hitler. In December 1943 Churchill had a meeting with the Turkish leader Ismet İnönü in which he begged him to 'take the country into war as the only way to start a

Balkan campaign which might keep the Soviet Union out of South-eastern Europe' (Rothwell 1982: 113). Even though, according to the Foreign Office, Greece had 'an overwhelmingly moral claim to the Dodecanese', Britain was prepared to set it aside 'because of the need to offer Turkey a reward if it would enter the war' (Rothwell 1982: 197). During the first half of the war Britain never pronounced in favour of the restoration of Albanian independence in case Greece required to be appeased with a grant of territory in Southern Albania, known to the Greeks as Northern Epirus. Thus the tendency to move Balkan territory from state to state, perhaps moving peoples in the process, remained a primary reflex among the Great Powers sixty years or more after the Congress of Berlin had created such a damaging precedent.

Though Turkey feared Russian designs on the strategic Bosporus straits, it was also wary of war. The intense nationalism which was a guiding principle for the new republican state was based on a suspicion of European powers. The Turks 'saw no reason to risk their very existence which had cost them so dear in what was primarily a war of the European powers' own making' (Deringil 1989: 3). Kemal Atatürk's successors sought no territorial gains and feared that all Turkey might achieve by entering the war would be to serve as a battleground for the Great Powers.

Turkey was not reassured by Churchill's entreaties when it recalled that E.H. Carr, the foreign editor of *The Times*, had publicly advocated in 1941 that the Soviet Union be allowed to 'interpret and apply ... the guiding principles of the Atlantic Charter in east Europe' (Rothwell 1982: 93). Sir Orme Sargent, deputy head of the Foreign Office, observed in 1942 that Carr's proposal, couched in an editorial carried in the most influential mouthpiece of British opinion, was bound to have a disastrous effect on Turkey, which was unlikely to give up its neutrality to facilitate the creation of a Soviet-dominated Balkans (Rothwell 1982: 93). But serving officials in the Foreign Office were already voicing not dissimilar sentiments to Carr without necessarily being pro-Soviet. Pierson Dixon, one of the chief officials in the section of the Foreign Office handling relations with Southeast Europe wrote in October 1942 that there was certain to be an 'element of coercion' in the peace settlement in the Balkans. 'Those countries will have to be lopped or stretched to fit the bed in which we decided, after taking their interests into account also, that the Balkans can easiest lie' (Rothwell 1982: 194). Turkey had become the first Balkan country to shake off the unwelcome tutelage of the Powers and the peculiar way in which they had interpreted what the best interests of Turkey were. Churchill thus fought in vain to bring the strategically placed Eurasian country into a war which could only have a very uncertain outcome for it.

The United States still lacked the nagging doubts possessed by Churchill about Russia's intentions towards its western neighbours. On 10 August 1943 Roosevelt told his military chiefs: '[T]he British Foreign Office does not want the Balkans to come under Russian influence. Britain wants to get to the Balkans first'. But Roosevelt, in his own words, could 'not believe that Russians would desire to take over the Balkan states' (Nadeau 1990: 76). Until Roosevelt's presidency ended with his death in April 1945, the US government preferred to give Russia a free hand in Eastern Europe.

There was scant American investment in Eastern Europe. Roosevelt's domestic ascendancy meant that he could pay far less attention to East European lobbies in the USA such as the Poles. His generals were loathe to take military decisions for purely political purposes. General Dwight D. Eisenhower, the American soldier who was the Commander of Allied Forces in western Europe in 1944–5, 'resented any suggestions that political factors should be considered in military planning' (Hammond 1982: 286–7). In the spring of 1945 Eisenhower decided that General George Patton's army should halt at Pilsen in western Czechoslovakia and should refuse to liberate Prague, which Patton could easily have done. According to the US historian Thomas Hammond: 'This event, more than anything else, convinced the Czechoslovak people that the United States had abandoned their country to the tender mercies of the Russians. It may also have provided Moscow with additional evidence that the United States was not vitally interested in eastern Europe' (Hammond 1982: 287). Certainly if the top US military commander showed no concern about being the first to liberate a city whose capitulation before Hitler in 1938–9 marked the symbolic triumph of totalitarianism in the 1930s, then they could not be expected to show an interest in operations in Southeast Europe.

The Soviet Union and its local supporters were also bound to benefit from the agreement between Britain and the USA in late 1944 to forbid the use of the large allied military force in Italy in any second country other than Greece. Besides benefiting Tito's partisans, the Allied decision not to land troops in the western Balkans enabled the communists to sweep to power in Albania, the only pre-war Balkan country without a communist party. Enver Hoxha's National Liberation Movement filled the breach as Albania's tribal leaders and feudal beys compromised themselves by aligning with the Italian occupiers in control from 1939 to 1943. Much of the non-communist opposition was entangled with the German occupation of 1943–44. Hoxha's forces had no difficulty in championing the Albanian nationalism which had been kindled during King Zog's rule. Britain, which had refused to recognise Zog or any other government-in-exile, channelled military aid to Hoxha. Recriminations later ensued among British liaison officers with the Albanian resistance about the extent to which British aid secured the triumph of communism in Albania, and the motives behind it (Hibbert 1991: *passim*; Vickers 1995: 155–6). But the author of an authoritative study of Albania in wartime reckons that the Albanian 'partisans would have won in any case, because of their significant base of support in the south and because of the strength of their Yugoslav allies' (Fischer 1999: 267).

Albania was as peripheral to Western policy makers in wartime as it would be in subsequent decades. The few US commentators who were aware of gathering Soviet strength in the Balkans were usually not advocates of any containment policy. An influential columnist such as Walter Lippmann argued in 1943 that not much could be done by the Atlantic powers to influence the fate of Eastern Europe after the war (Lukacs 1953: 480). Indeed, in the last months of his Presidency, Roosevelt was more upset by Britain's forceful intervention in Greek politics, for what was widely seen as old-fashioned imperialistic reasons, than he was by anything Stalin did in Poland or Romania before April 1945 (Charmley 1993: 593).

US influence in wartime strategy was increasingly decisive as its commitment to the war effort increased prior to the 'D-Day' Normandy landings of June 1944. After the Battle of Stalingrad in 1942–3, which forced the Germans onto the retreat in Russia, the USA emphasised the maintenance of very friendly relations with the Soviet Union (Borsody 1993: 119). It is understandable that admiration for Russian valour and sacrifices in resisting the might of Hitler's juggernaut drowned out concerns about any future Russian occupation of Eastern Europe among American public opinion and also policy makers unfamiliar with the complexities of European affairs. At the November 1943 Tehran conference of the Allied leaders, Harry Hopkins, one of Roosevelt's principal advisers, brought with him a memorandum which recognised that '... since without question she [Russia] will dominate Europe on the defeat of the Axis, it is even more essential to develop and maintain the most friendly relations with Russia' (Borsody 1993: 119). American diplomacy refrained from advocating the partition of Europe, and its chief practitioners rejected Churchill's advocacy of European federalism as well as its direct opposite, the establishment of spheres of influence. Instead, the Americans promoted a 'One World' concept centred around a United Nations organization meant to harmonise the postwar order; Washington saw 'Big Three' unity as vital for making the new internationalism work (Borsody 1993: 122–3). It did not see European unity as necessary for its global programme to take practical shape. American lack of interest in East European political affairs (perhaps understandable in light of its commitments in the Pacific, the Asian mainland and western Europe) meant that alarm signals about Soviet intentions in the Middle Zone of Europe did not surface until Russian forces had reached Berlin and Vienna in 1945.

SPHERES OF INFLUENCE: 1944

It was only in the last weeks of Roosevelt's life, in the spring of 1945, that Churchill was prepared to convey in full measure his sense of alarm about the impending fate of Eastern Europe to his American ally (Charmley 1993: 623). British policy in Southeast Europe had been shaped by the nature of the Allied war effort. The need for 'Big Three' unity as the June 1944 invasion of western Europe approached had been a basic concern that Churchill would have found it difficult to override even if he had wanted to. Soviet progress on the eastern front in 1943–44 greatly strengthened Stalin's hand across Eastern Europe.

British–US setbacks in Italy where Allied forces were bogged down in the Appenines through 1944–5 also reduced the room for manoeuvre of the Atlantic democracies in Eastern Europe (Borsody 1993: 151). Following Mussolini's overthrow in 1943, the Allies rejected his military successor's offer of total cooperation and allowed Hitler to disarm thirty Italian divisions in the Balkans and to seize the Italian islands of the eastern Mediterranean (Cretzianu 1957: 181). The Allies' failure to exploit military possibilities in the Balkans as they were painfully inching their way up the Italian peninsula was damned by at least one senior American commander. General Mark Clark wrote in his memoirs *Calculated Risk*: '... save for a high-level blunder that turned us away from the Balkan states and permitted them to fall under Red Army control, the Mediterranean campaign might have been the most decisive of all in postwar history' (Cretzianu 1957: 182).

The way in which the military concerns of the 'Big Three' overshadowed the need to maintain the political integrity of the countries in the Middle Zone was perhaps never clearer than in the first months of 1944.

Poland was the critical issue. The London-based government of Stanislaw Micolajczyk was unwilling to accede to the new borders with the Soviet Union whereby they lost one-third of their eastern territory and gained compensatory territory from Germany to which Poland had slim claims. Churchill bluntly told the Poles in February 1944 that 'he did not intend Anglo-Russian relations to be wrecked by the Polish Government if they refused what he considered to be a reasonable offer'; if they refused he would 'conclude a direct agreement with Stalin' (Charmley 1993: 560). He had his doubts about taking such a stand as when he told John Colville, his private secretary, on 4 March 1944 that he felt like 'telling the Russians, "Personally I fight tyranny whatever uniform it wears or slogans it utters" (Charmley 1993: 560). Perhaps he realised that he was in much the same position as Neville Chamberlain was when he put pressure on the Czechoslovak government to hand over territory to Nazi Germany. Churchill's predecessor has been widely condemned for failing to understand the nature of the Nazi regime and the insatiable ambition of the man at its head. It is unclear whether the capacity of relatively humane leaders like the British and American ones to recognise evil had advanced greatly during the subsequent war. Churchill's fluctuating views about Russian intentions in Eastern Europe begs the question whether he understood the nature of Soviet politics and the mindset of the Russian dictator in a more realistic way than Chamberlain had read the mind and intentions of Hitler.

Despite rhetoric about common European political arrangements after the war, Churchill was an old-fashioned nationalist reluctant to move beyond a Europe of nations and states. Perhaps the tiring business of trying to resolve quarrels within exile governments, such as the Yugoslav and Greek ones, had reduced his enthusiasm for settling internecine and parochial disputes on a continental level. In early 1944 Paul-Henri Spaak, then the Belgian Foreign Minister, and later one of the architects of the European Union, did not get very far when he raised the idea of a British-led European Union with Eden (Charmley 1993: 566). In May 1944, Duff Cooper, British ambassador to the French Liberation Forces in Algeria and a future British ambassador to Paris, wrote a document arguing that the rise of Soviet power was a threat to European stability. He complained about 'the hand-to-mouth' nature of British diplomacy, disguising itself under the euphemism 'pragmatism', and he urged British sponsorship of 'a Union' of the 'nations situated in the western seaboard of Europe', starting with a Franco-British alliance (Charmley 1993: 565, 566). Duff Cooper's call for radical thinking about the shape of democratic Europe went unheeded by his political masters. Spaak, writing in 1952, exclaimed that a historic opportunity had been missed:

> What a pity Europe was not 'created' in 1945—a great chance was lost ... ruins lay everywhere ... everything had to be begun again, everything could have been begun on a new basis. Instead, Russia was left to consolidate her conquest and organize Eastern Europe, while western Europe was going to work again in the old way, resuming outdated traditions. (Borsody 1993: 154)

A pattern already established, of Britain conceding to Soviet wishes in Eastern Europe and then having second thoughts before the needs of wartime strategy required a fresh meeting of minds with Stalin, was firmly in place by 1944. The least resistance in regard to Soviet demands was usually shown in regard to Romania. In March 1944 the Romanian government was informed through Romanian emissaries who had arrived in Cairo that the first requirement it had to meet in order to make peace with the Allies was the surrender of the Romanian army to the Russians, whose advance had pushed right up to the Romanian frontier (Lukacs 1953: 583). When Alexandru Cretzianu, the Romanian emissary in Cairo, expressed the fear that such an approach would lead to Romania becoming a Soviet satellite, he was admonished by Lord Moyne, the Resident British Minister in the Middle East, for being alarmist (Lukacs 1953: 584).

While thought was being given to proposing the creation of spheres of influence in Eastern Europe, the British were increasingly anxious to promote their interests in Bulgaria. Indeed one Foreign Office view expressed in March 1944 was, that in a choice between Hungary and Bulgaria, the latter should have undoubted preference in view of the need to keep the Russians well away from the Bosporus Straits (Rothwell 1982: 209). This view was taken up by the Post-Hostilities Planning Committee consisting of representatives from the three armed services chaired by the Foreign Office which in February 1944 had noted that:

> Should Russia obtain control of Bulgaria she would be in a position to establish airfields within 100 miles of the Straits. Moreover, the Russians have a traditional connection with Bulgaria, and occupation by them might lead to permanent control. Occupation by British forces would tend to strengthen British influence not only in Bulgaria, but also in Greece and Turkey. Moreover, the Soviet Union is not at war with Bulgaria whereas the United Kingdom is. (Rothwell 1982: 210)

Rothwell writes that '[T]he inclusion of Bulgaria within Britain's East Mediterranean sphere was taking shape as a definite war aim during the first half of 1944' (Rothwell 1982: 210). The Post-Hostilities Planning Committee had defined Britain's vital strategic interests as (i) threats to Middle Eastern oil; (ii) the Mediterranean; (iii) 'vital sea communications'; and (iv) maintenance of the concentrated industrial areas of Britain (Thomas 1986: 310). It felt that the British should not oppose any reasonable demands of the USSR where they do not conflict with these vital strategic interests.

Bulgaria's entry into the German orbit had been apparent when in March 1941, King Boris signed the tripartite Pact and German troops were allowed to enter the country. But Bulgaria's refusal to declare war on the Soviet Union in June 1941 showed that its monarch still retained important freedom of action from Berlin. Boris successfully argued that peasant conscripts would not make good warriors away from their home areas, especially if they were fighting a traditional ally. Boris persuaded Hitler to allow his army to stay in the Balkans and he even managed to prevent the creation of a volunteer legion for duty on the eastern front (Crampton 1997: 173, 175). Bulgaria and the Soviet Union also retained full diplomatic relations right up until September 1944 (though in December 1941 Boris had declared war on the western Allies).

King Boris died suddenly on 28 August 1943 shortly after returning from a difficult encounter with Hitler. Foul-play has long been suspected and it may well have been that the Nazis feared Boris was poised to switch sides as Romania would do in 1944. The 1943–44 governments attempted to extricate the country from the disastrous alliance with Germany but without success (Oren 1973: 89). The Organization of Special Services (OSS), in charge of US special operations in occupied Eastern Europe, paid a great deal of attention to Bulgaria at the time, but British interest in Bulgaria was fickle. The problem might well have lain at the very top. Nissan Oren has written:

At best, Bulgaria commanded Churchill's complete disinterest; at worst, Churchill's attitude towards Bulgaria was colored by a strong feeling of repugnance. Bulgaria had won his lasting enmity as early as the First World War, when she joined the Central Powers and thus contributed to the failure of his favorite campaign, that in the Dardenelles. (Oren 1973: 75)

As the war dragged on Churchill and his colleagues were increasingly exhausted and the Prime Minister's views on Russia's intentions oscillated between optimism and pessimism, sometimes within a few days of one another (Thomas 1986: 693). But by early May 1944

Churchill was harbouring darker thoughts about the intended role of the Soviets in Eastern Europe than he had expressed previously.

On 4 May he minuted Eden about 'the brute issues between us and the Soviet government which are developing in Italy, in Rumania, in Bulgaria, in Yugoslavia—and above all in Greece. Are we going to acquiesce in the Communization of the Balkans and perhaps of Italy? ... If our conclusion is that we resist Communist infusion and invasion, we should put it to them pretty plainly ... evidently we are approaching a showdown with the Russians' (Barker 1976: 123).

But instead of Moscow being reminded of the principles that the Big Three had agreed to uphold in the Atlantic Charter, a division of the Balkans into spheres of influence for Britain and Russia respectively was proposed. On 17 May 1944 Eden consulted the Russians about the possibility of extending the current 'understandings' into something more specific: Britain had 'recognised' Soviet 'predominance' in Romania; now in return, the Soviets might like to acknowledge that Greece was within the British sphere (Charmley 1993: 567). John Charmley has written: 'that the Soviets agreed to such a proposal occasions as little surprise as the fact that neither Eden nor Churchill mentioned it in their respective memoirs' (Charmley 1993: 567).

On 18 May Churchill wrote to Roosevelt to obtain his blessing for this proposal. Indeed, the Russians had made this a requirement of their approval because they were aware of the preponderant role the USA now played in the western alliance and they wished to receive the unanimous commitment of their main allies for a proposal that was so favourable to Russian interests (Wolff 1974: 252; Borsody 1993: 134; Charmley 1993: 566).

Churchill tried to allay the suspicions Roosevelt was likely to have about such secret diplomacy done over the heads of the nations involved. He argued that we 'do not of course wish to carve up the Balkans into spheres of influence, and in agreeing to this arrangement we should make it clear that it applied only to war conditions and did not affect the rights and responsibilities which each of the Great Powers will have to exercise at the peace settlements and afterwards in regard to the whole of Europe' (Wolff 1974: 253). Roosevelt and the State Department were unconvinced by Churchill's special pleading; Roosevelt told Churchill that he saw the division of the Balkan region into spheres of influence 'as a likely outcome' despite the declared intention (Charmley 1993: 567). However, Roosevelt did not impose any veto, being 'essentially indifferent to the details of any settlement in Eastern

Europe as long as they did not become issues in the presidential election' (concerns shared by a successor when he was reluctantly embroiled in the Balkans exactly fifty years later) (Charmley 1993: 587).

British reassurance about Russian intentions in the Balkans was expressed with unusual certainty by Eden at a meeting of the war cabinet in July 1944. He stated: 'It is doubtful whether there is any deliberate "communising" of the Balkans at the present moment ... Nor can any accusation be levelled at the Russians of organizing the spread of communism in the Balkans' (F.P. King 1973: 73). These views may have been coloured by the fact that the Communist-led resistance of Tito's Partisans in Yugoslavia had assisted the British war effort and Britain was on better terms with them than their royalist counterpart, the Četniks. Tito had 'impressed most of the British liaison officers ... as a man who would choose country rather than creed if a choice was essential' (Thomas 1986: 434). But at a summit with Roosevelt in Quebec during September 1944, Churchill's misgivings resurfaced and he spoke in terms very different from his Foreign Secretary. Speaking in favour of 'a strike in the Adriatic armpit' around Trieste, he recommended such a military plan because of 'the rapid encroachment of the Russians into the Balkan peninsula and the dangerous spread of Soviet influence there' (Barker 1976: 124). But Roosevelt was unconvinced and Churchill did not press the issue, reporting back to his war cabinet that there had been 'almost complete agreement' at the summit (Barker 1976: 124).

GREECE AND BRITISH POLICY IN THE BALKANS

British concern about the future of Southeast Europe increasingly revolved around Greece as the Soviets advanced towards Central Europe at a faster rate than their western allies. With mounting unease, Churchill watched the growing influence of the National Liberation Front (EAM), a coalition of left-wing and anti-monarchist forces set up by the Greek Communist Party after the occupation of 1941. The Greek centre-right was in complete disarray over the quarrel between monarchist and republican interests which had paralysed politics for much of the interwar period. The military arm of EAM, the National People's Liberation Front (ELAS) 'threatened not only to dominate the resistance movement but to dictate the nation's political future' (Iatrides 1981: 17). Britain was concerned about its interests in the Eastern Mediterranean and the Middle East if a pro-Soviet government took power in Athens. The exiled Greek government in Cairo relied upon the

British for its contacts with occupied Greece and Britain paid scant regard to the wishes of a faction-ridden group of exiles when the Greek situation began to increasingly preoccupy Churchill.

Lincoln MacVeagh, the Cairo-based US ambassador to the Yugoslav and Greek exiled governments, in a report to Washington sent in August 1944, was critical of the British handling of Greek affairs. He described 'the low ebb to which British prestige has fallen owing to the opportunist shifts of British policy toward the resistance movements, the repeated British military fiascos in Greece, Crete and the Dodecanese, and the many mistakes in psychology which the British have committed in their handling of the Greek military, and other problems' (Iatrides 1980: 577).

Churchill wished to land troops in Greece as soon as the Axis withdrew in order to pave the way for the restoration of King George II. In Moscow during October 1944, Churchill raised the future of Greece with Stalin in conjunction with that of other Balkan states (except Albania), and also Hungary. His wartime memoirs describe the scene in vivid detail:

> The moment was apt for business, so I said, 'Let us settle about our affairs in the Balkans. Your armies are in Rumania and Bulgaria. We have interests, missions, and agents there. Don't let us get at small purposes in small ways. So far as Britain and Russia are concerned, how would it do for you to have ninety per cent predominance in Rumania, for us to have ninety per cent predominance in Greece, and go fifty-fifty about Yugoslavia?' While this was being translated I wrote out on a half-sheet of paper:

> **Rumania**
>
> | | |
> |---|---|
> | Russia | 90% |
> | The others | 10% |
>
> **Greece**
>
> | | |
> |---|---|
> | Great Britain (in accord with USA) | 90% |
> | Russia | 10% |
> | Yugoslavia | 50–50% |
> | Hungary | 50–50% |
>
> **Bulgaria**
>
> | | |
> |---|---|
> | Russia | 75% |
> | The others | 25% |

> I pushed this across to Stalin, who had by then heard the translation. There was a slight pause. Then he took his blue pencil and made a large tick on it, and passed it back to us. It was all settled in no more time than it takes to set down.

> Of course we had long and anxiously covered our point, and were only dealing with immediate wartime arrangements. All larger questions were reserved on both sides for what we then hoped would be a peace table when the war was

won. After this there was a long silence. The pencilled paper lay in the centre of the table. At length I said, 'Might it not be thought rather cynical if it seemed we had disposed of these issues, so fateful to millions of people, in such an offhand manner? Let us burn the paper'. 'No, you keep it', said Stalin. (Churchill 1954: 227–8)

Churchill insisted that the agreement only dealt with 'immediate wartime arrangements'. But according to Robert Lee Wolff, 'I think we must conclude, however reluctantly, that the Prime Minister knew in his heart that it would be extremely difficult to lessen Russian influence anywhere once it had established itself, and that his wish to burn the paper arose from apprehension that it might leak out, and that its true momentous impact upon the lives of people in the Balkans might be realized' (Wolff 1974: 261).

For John Charmley the percentages agreement was at fault not because of its cynical nature, but because 'it was as naive a document as ever sought to pass muster as realpolitik' (Charmley 1993: 588). Churchill, as on previous occasions when he had transacted business with Stalin over the fate of Eastern Europe, was troubled by the outcome. Robert Lee Wolff has recounted that he drafted a letter to Stalin which he did not send but in which he wrote:

These percentages which I have put down are no more than a method by which in our thoughts we can see how near we are together, and then decide upon the steps necessary to bring us into full agreement. As I said, they would be considered crude, and even callous, if they were exposed to the scrutiny of the Foreign Office and diplomats all over the world. Therefore they could not be the basis of any public document, certainly not at the present time. They might however be a good guide for the conduct of our public affairs. If we manage these affairs well, we shall perhaps prevent several civil wars and much bloodshed and strife in the small countries concerned. (Churchill 1954: 231)

To his cabinet, Churchill gave the same assurance about the percentages agreement as he had given to Roosevelt. He provided details of what reciprocity between the British and the Soviets over Greece and Romania would involve in practice:

... Britain will take the lead in a military sense and try to help the existing Royal Greek Government to establish itself in Athens upon as broad and united a basis as possible. Soviet Russia would be ready to concede this position and function to Great Britain in the same sort of way as Britain would recognize the intimate relationship between Russia and Rumania. (Churchill 1954: 233)

No doubt to justify the Soviet Union being allowed 'to take the lead in a practical way' in Romania and Bulgaria, Churchill reminded his cabinet colleagues that 'she had been wantonly attacked with twenty-six divisions' by the former and had 'ancient ties' with the latter (Churchill 1954: 233).

On his return from Moscow, Churchill had a stormy meeting with the Polish Premier on 14 October who was reluctant to accept the proposed new frontier for his country or the inclusion of Communists in the government. Churchill lost his temper with Micolajczyk:

> You are absolutely crazy ... unless you accept the frontier you are out of business forever ... We will be sick and tired of you if you go on arguing ... You are callous people who want to wreck Europe. I shall leave you to your own troubles ... You have only your own miserable selfish interests in mind ... In this war what is your contribution to the Allied effort? What did you throw into the common pool? (de Zayas quoted in Ponting 1994: 47–8)

Churchill forgot the Polish fighter pilots who provided the most successful squadron in the Battle of Britain and who were doing conspicuously well in the gruelling Italian campaign (Ponting 1994: 664). It was a performance perhaps more in keeping with that which Hitler reserved for the leaders of neighbouring countries that he wished to intimidate than with Churchill's normal behaviour towards a fellow democrat with whom he was engaged in a common fight for freedom. His treatment of the Poles is mentioned to show that if democratically-minded Romanians and Bulgarians had had governments installed in Allied countries, it is unlikely that they would have escaped such brow-beating, especially if they were proving resistant to plans for their countries which Churchill was working out with Stalin over their heads.

Churchill might have been warned by the Soviet reaction to the uprising staged by the Polish Home Army in Warsaw on 1 August 1944. The Red Army, already encamped on the opposite banks of the river Vistula, did nothing to help the Home Army whom Stalin described as a 'handful of power-hungry adventurers and criminals' (Thomas 1986: 360). Britain and the USA were prevented by the Soviets from dropping supplies to the Warsaw rebels. The 'flower of the Polish underground, perhaps 200,000 people, were killed by the Germans' (Thomas 1986: 360). Averell Harriman, the US ambassador in Moscow, urged the State Department to point out that Stalin's attitude imperilled postwar cooperation among the Allies (Harriman and Abel 1975: 340). He wrote to Harry Hopkins in September 1944:

> I have evidence that they [the Soviets] have misinterpreted our generous attitude towards them as a sign of weakness and acceptance of their policies ...

unless we take issue with the present policy there is every indication that the Soviet Union will become a world bully wherever [its] interests are involved. (Colville 1986a: 5)

Harriman's deputy in the Moscow embassy, George Kennan wrote in 1946 that the fate of the Warsaw Uprising should have been the pretext for 'a fully-fledged and realistic showdown' with Stalin over his intentions for Poland. The cause of 'aid to the brave Home Army' was one which could have struck a chord with Western public opinion (Thomas 1986: 361). But the leading American policymakers were convinced that Stalin was not to be judged by his original ideology, a view similar to that held by appeasers of Hitler in the 1930s, who preferred to believe that after writing *Mein Kampf* he had gradually mellowed (Colville 1986b: 73).

Roosevelt neglected East European affairs and it was left to Churchill to work out a postwar strategy for this part of Europe. Various matters raised his suspicions about Stalin's intentions. British Intelligence informed him that the Katyn massacre, in which 14,000 Polish officers were shot in cold blood, was the work of the Soviets not the Germans. The British Prime Minister's enthusiasm for the Soviet Union after June 1941 was eroded by the surly treatment which members of the British armed forces received in Russia. Britain shipped 5,000 tanks and 7,000 aircraft to Murmansk, losing many ships and men in the dangerous Arctic convoys, but it received little thanks from the Soviets. The British and American military missions in Moscow were often snubbed and sidelined (Colville 1986a: 2).

But Churchill's understanding of both the nature of the Soviet system and East European politics in general remained limited (Charmley 1993: 621). Public statements, and discussions with his cabinet, indicate he believed that cultivating good personal relations with Stalin could bridge the ideological gulf between them. Up to the spring of 1945, he believed that: '[S]o long as Stalin lasted … Anglo–Russian friendship would be maintained.' He told cabinet colleagues after the Yalta agreement that: 'Poor Neville Chamberlain believed that he could trust Hitler. He was wrong. But I don't think I am wrong about Stalin' (Thomas 1986: 698).

Churchill failed to realise that the occupation of Greece, after the unpopular dictatorship of General Ioannis Metaxas, had wrought a profound change in the political mood of the country. As a committed royalist he was adamant about restoring the unpopular King George II to the throne even though it played into the hands of the King's communist adversaries. The King was tarnished because of his association with the pre-war dictatorship. In March 1944 the Greek forces in Egypt mutinied against the King and his government. British troops quelled the mutiny and some 10,000 Greek soldiers—about half the entire Greek armed forces—were interned in British-run camps (Murtagh 1994: 29). Later Churchill reluctantly accepted the idea of a new government under the centrist politician Giorgis Papandreou which pledged to hold a plebiscite on the monarchy after liberation (Ponting 1994: 671). The British Foreign Office and most of the war cabinet supported a regency under a figure who could attempt to unite Greek opinion, but Churchill was ready to risk a collision, even with the USA, in order to have his way (Charmley 1993: 599–600). On 15 October 1944, twenty-four hours after German troops quit Athens, British troops arrived followed by Papandreou and his government. The communist ELAS forces controlled most of the country outside Athens. The British brought the Greek Army back from Egypt purged of all but its royalist elements and amalgamated it with the ex-German-controlled 'security battalions', which until a month earlier had been fighting the Greek guerillas (Ponting 1994: 672). On 4 December 1944 Churchill ordered Brigadier Ronald Scobie to treat Athens 'as if you were in a conquered city where a local rebellion is in progress'. For much of December the city was convulsed by fighting between ELAS and British forces. Churchill was in Athens on Christmas Day 1944 during what were the opening stages of a civil war which would erupt with much greater intensity in the second half of the 1940s. On meeting the Greek Orthodox Archbishop Damaskinos, he warmed to him and agreed that he could become Regent, as had been the Foreign Office advice to him for some time (Charmley 1993: 601–2, 603). Back in London, Churchill confronted the King on 29 December and demanded that he appoint the Archbishop as Regent pending a plebiscite. When the King resisted, Churchill warned him that Britain would recognise the Regent anyway and the King capitulated (Ponting 1994: 674).

Churchill's penchant for conducting high politics in terms of personalities in the Balkans was shared by Stalin. When they met in Moscow in 1945, the Russian leader took to the Romanian businessman Petru Groza who had agreed to be the Soviet front man in Romania.

By 'the winter of 1945–46, the British were not only the most influential foreign power in Greece but in effect the rulers of the country, appointing and dismissing prime ministers, dictating all departments of state from defence to employment ... Police, army and education were supervised by British experts' (Thomas 1986: 545). Hugh Thomas has written that:

> Sir Reginald Leeper, the Australian-born diplomatist ... who was British Ambassador in Athens, seemed to behave more like a colonial governor than an ordinary ambassador. Believing that for geographical and economic reasons, Greece could never be independent and, rejecting a permanent British occupation, he suggested that the country could join the British Common-wealth as a dominion. (Thomas 1986: 547)

The West would accuse the Russians of behaving like arch-imperialists in Eastern Europe once the Cold War started. But Britain's behaviour in Greece only weakened the formidable case that anti-communists could marshal. Churchill's government also tried desperately to prevent Macedonian unification occurring through a South Slav union involving Yugoslavia and Bulgaria (Rossos 2000: 139–40). In 1944 the Foreign Office believed that encroachments on Greek territory would soon follow along with a Soviet push towards the Aegean and Bosporus straits. In the end, and not for the first time, both London and Moscow would reach surprising agreement about the desirability of keeping the Balkans disunited rather than under the control of a powerful South Slav state (Rossos 2000: 142).

Stalin was careful not to criticise British actions in Greece before 1946. On 30 December 1944 the Soviet Union ostentatiously appointed an Ambassador to the official Greek government. Ecstatic at Stalin's cooperative role, Churchill started to describe EAM/ELAM as Trotskyites (Rothwell 1982: 220–21). If they had been that, they would not have followed Stalin's orders or held out so much hope in Russian backing for their attempt to come to power in Greece, backing which would be withheld even as the Cold War got underway.

Since the Soviets had remained aloof from Greece, Churchill reflected that there was nothing that could be done about heavyhanded Russian actions in Romania. After Antonescu had been overthrown in a coup masterminded by young King Michael on 23 August 1944, the Russians had quickly occupied the whole country. If the Romanian anti-Nazis had known what Britain's broad intentions were for their country, they might not have risked their necks to overthrow a pro-Axis dictator, an action which enabled the Russians to push much faster into Eastern Europe than they had expected to do. The collapse of the German presence in Romania enabled them to occupy Bulgaria two weeks later and put paid to British hopes of influencing that country's postwar future. A British military mission soon arrived in Bucharest to be part of the Allied Control Commission which was to implement the terms of the armistice Romania had signed with the Allies. But the British were sidelined by the Russians who argued that parity required them to take the lead in Romania since no Russian representatives had been included in the Allied Control Commission set up in Italy a short time before.

Soon the Russians began to act ruthlessly against Romanian democrats. But when the British mission's political adviser, Ian Le Rougetel energetically protested about Russian methods, Churchill expressed alarm. On 4 November 1944 he minuted Eden that Le Rougetel 'doesn't understand that our interests in Romania do not exceed 10% and we are mere spectators' (Porter 1990: 304). On 8 November the Foreign Office had thought it necessary to send a telegram marked 'Strict secret' to Le Rougetel pointing out details of the percentages agreement Churchill had agreed in Moscow during the previous month (Porter 1990: 305). But two days later Churchill was still complaining to Eden that the British mission in Bucharest was behaving as if it was in Greece. Later on 18 January 1945, Churchill complained to Eden about efforts by British officers in Romania to prevent the deportation to Russia of tens of thousands of German-speaking citizens whose ancestors had been in Romania since the Middle Ages.

Churchill wrote to Eden: 'Why are we making a fuss about the Russian deportations in Rumania of Saxons and others. It is understood that the Russians were to work their will in this sphere. Anyhow we cannot prevent them'. Churchill returned to the subject a few days later: 'I cannot consider that it is wrong of the Russians to take Roumanians of any origin they like to work in the Russian coal-fields' (Ponting 1994: 665).

Churchill also gave firm orders to serving British officers to deny point-blank to Romanians that the country had been ceded to the Soviet sphere of influence. Archibald Clark Kerr, the British ambassador to Moscow in 1945, who was with the Allied Control Commission in Bucharest in 1944–5, later remarked that one of the most unpleasant acts he ever had to carry out in his diplomatic career was to lie to a man of Maniu's stature (Porter 1990: 305). In early 1945 American officials were being asked by Maniu to tell him if 'spheres of influence' existed so that he could make the best possible arrangements for the country with Russia. In the words of Hugh Thomas: 'They could give no reply' (Thomas 1986: 408).

Iuliu Maniu enjoyed immense political prestige in Romania in 1945, having defied the royal dictatorship as well as the German-influenced

Antonescu one. Elections had to be delayed until the end of 1946 to ensure that the communists could rig the results. But investigations after 1989 show that Maniu's Peasant Party emerged as a clear winner in many areas (Tarau and Bucur 1998: 300–22). It is not unnatural that Romanian democrats would accept the word of British officers about their country's intentions towards Romania despite growing evidence that it had in fact been abandoned to Stalin. The coup mounted by the King in August 1944 proved of enormous benefit to the Allies and according to some military historians may have shortened the war by as much as six months (Constantiniu 1997: 442). It deprived the Germans of Romanian oil supplies, and the loss of this vital resource, as well as bauxite and chrome mined elsewhere in the Balkans, dealt a fatal blow to the German military machine according to Albert Speer, who was in charge of German war production (Porter 1990: 296). Stalin was prepared to decorate Michael with the Soviet Union's highest military award, the Order of Victory for the decisive contribution Romania made to the war 'at a moment when the defeat of Germany was not yet certain' (Porter 1990: 296). He lavishly praised the King to Churchill at the Potsdam summit in July 1945 (Rothwell 1982: 519, n. 31). Romania played a far more vital role in the Second World War than in the First World War in securing victory for an alliance including Britain. But whereas its territory was greatly expanded in 1919, its fate after 1945 was to effectively lose its independence and have an alien social system imposed on it.

If Great Britain had not put its own strategic interests in the eastern Mediterranean ahead of the concern about the democratic future of the region, and officers like Le Rougetel had instead been encouraged to defend the democratic forces which had brought Romania out of the war, Stalin might have thought twice about imposing Soviet-style rule on the country. After all, the communist party in 1939 had numbered less than one thousand members, it had been unable to mount any significant wartime resistance to the Antonescu regime, and the role it played in the 1944 coup was of secondary importance (Markham 1996: 141).

Soviet concern about the weakness of Romanian communism was shown in the mid-1940s in various ways. Members of the Iron Guard were enrolled into the party *en masse* and attempts were even made to entice ex-King Carol back to the country to head a puppet monarchy (manoeuvres which the British blocked by asking the authorities in Portugal where Carol was living, to carefully supervise his movements) (Rothwell 1982: 381).

YALTA, FEBRUARY 1945

The Allied leaders convened in the Crimean resort of Yalta between 4 and 11 February 1945 to map out the contours of a postwar Europe. Anglo-American preparations were perfunctory. Roosevelt paused only briefly at Malta for talks with the British and he pointedly avoided seeing Churchill alone until the fifth day of the conference. He would not agree on any preliminary discussion of strategy or foreign policy and, to Averell Harriman's horror, he spoke to Stalin about his hostility towards Britain retaining a colonial empire (Colville 1986a: 4).

The Declaration on Liberated Europe that was part of the agreed Yalta communiqué, published on 11 February, pledged that 'the three governments will jointly assist the people in any liberated European state or former Axis satellite state in Europe ... to form interim governmental authorities, broadly representative of all democratic elements in the population and pledged to the earliest possible establishment, through free elections of governments responsible to the will of the people' (Borsody 1993: 140).

The document had been drawn up by the US State Department and was accepted by the Russians. It had originally been part of a broader proposal to establish a European High Commission, composed of Britain, the Soviet Union, the USA and France whose aim was to establish representative governments and find solutions to emerging economic problems in all the former occupied and satellite states, excepting Germany. Hitler, in the words of George Kennan, had accomplished 'the technical task of the unification of Europe ... central authorities in a whole series of areas; in transport, in banking, in procurement ... why could not this situation be usefully exploited after the Allied victory?' (Thomas 1986: 475). However, Roosevelt decided against presenting the proposal for a European High Commission to the Yalta Conference. According to Stephen Borsody, this was a missed opportunity 'to ensure in some form, at least, direct participation of the Western Powers in assisting the East European nations to establish popular governments' (Borsody 1993: 141).

But the Yalta declaration offered more hope for democratic forces in Eastern Europe than the secret percentages agreement; however, terminology such as 'democracy' and 'free elections' meant different things to the Allies. The British and Americans interpreted such language 'in terms of their own political traditions'. But to the Russians 'democratic' and 'free elections' were terms that did not permit untrammeled free choice (Wolff 1974: 266–7). The western Allies were slow to realise this and only a few perceptive observers like the American Minister in Moscow in 1944, George Kennan, were aware of the propensity of the Soviets to lie in order to further their current objectives and long-term strategy (Thomas 1986: 126). At the Potsdam summit in July 1945, Stalin showed how seriously he took the democratic safeguards contained in the Yalta agreement when he said that: 'A freely elected government in any of these [East European] countries would be anti-Soviet and that we cannot allow' (Hammond 1982: 296).

Andrei Vyshinsky, the Soviet deputy foreign minister, along with other Communist diplomats, was already explaining to their Western counterparts that Eastern Europe would soon see a new version of democracy, neither Western nor Russian but indigenous (Thomas 1986: 71). Yugoslavia's Tito was also talking about the imminent emergence of 'people's democracies'; original forms of democracy which were not to be confused with the bourgeois democracies already in place in the West. Writing in *The Times* on 4 October 1945, E.H. Carr claimed that 'the Russians are entitled to point out that democracy on the Western pattern has been tried and failed in these countries in the past ...' (Haslam 1999: 126).

The Yalta Agreement in fact held no safeguards for genuinely free elections. But in a speech to the House of Commons on 27 February 1945 Churchill was reassuring about the future of the nations in the Middle Zone. Regarding Poland, he said that: 'The Poles will have their future in their own hands, with the single limitation that they must honestly follow ... a policy friendly to Russia'. More broadly, he declared: 'The impression I brought back from the Crimea ... is that Marshall Stalin and the Soviet leaders wish to live in honourable friendship and equality with the Western democracies. I feel that their word is their bond ...' (Borsody 1993: 144–5). Similar words of reassurance were expressed by Roosevelt but both Allied leaders were as wrong as Chamberlain had been in 1938 about the future of Czechoslovakia and Hitler's good intentions, although history has been much harsher towards Chamberlain than to his successor.

Stalin at Yalta had derived reassurance from the disunity and lack of a clear strategy for Europe which Roosevelt and Churchill exhibited. The American President chose Yalta to announce that he intended to withdraw American forces from Europe within 18 months of the war coming to an end. He was more concerned about Western colonialism and imperialism which he enlarged upon in front of Stalin to the discomfiture of the British. Lord Gladwyn, a British official present at

Yalta, recalled that Roosevelt's 'one idea was to play up to Stalin, and oil him up as much as he possibly could. He did everything he could to appease the Russian dictator' (Charlton 1983a: 23).

About Roosevelt, George Kennan further observed in a similar vein that: 'In the latter part of the War we had led Stalin to believe that western Europe was being reduced to so pathetic a state in terms of military and economic power and self-confidence, and that the United States was motivated by such a sweeping naivety with regard to Soviet power, that without any further military action at all, the Soviet Union could soon dominate the United States from the whole Eurasian landmass and pretty much have its own way throughout the world' (Urban 1976: 31).

The vast expansion in American military power had not been accompanied by an increase in the size or expertise of the American State Department. Averell Harriman, the US ambassador in Moscow pressed the State Department in the spring of 1944 to define its attitude towards the countries of Eastern Europe, but his call for greater postwar planning to deal with problems there largely fell on deaf ears (Harriman and Abel 1975: 305). Back home in Washington during July 1944, the US diplomat Lincoln MacVeagh, who had served in Southeast European diplomatic posts almost without interruption since 1933, expressed his frustration in his journal about the lack of interest in the State Department about political matters in that part of the world:

> ... I fear that the understanding of the Greek situation, which is a critical one in a critical part of the world, will be but very summary and inadequate on the part of the Department's 'policy makers' – the Under Secretary, the assistant Secretaries and the Office Directors. But they don't want it otherwise. They have neither the time nor the inclination (nor the belief that it is necessary) to understand anything well. I often resent the criticism of the Department in the press, but when you get beyond certain men in our missions in the field and the desk officers in Washington, the good correspondents, such as Cy Sulzberger, are, I fear, far ahead of any personnel the Department can boast of in their knowledge of foreign affairs. (Iatrides 1980: 567)

Britain, at least over Greece, was the beneficiary of Washington's lack of interest in the affairs of Balkan countries. But it was Stalin who took the most advantage, and an ailing Roosevelt could hardly be expected to respond to menacing Russian actions in this part of Europe, if his foreign policy advisers themselves showed apathy towards the dangerous build up of tensions in the region.

Within weeks of Yalta, the escalating Russian takeover of Romania was to dash Churchill's confidence in being able to do business with

Stalin. On 27 February, the day Churchill delivered his reassuring speech to the British parliament about Stalin's intentions, Andrei Vyshinsky, the Soviet deputy Foreign Minister and Stalin's trouble-shooter in the new satellites, arrived with orders to impose a government fully compliant to Moscow. Vyshinsky threatened Romania with extinction unless the King appointed the 'fellow-traveller' Petru Groza as Prime Minister (Lukacs 1953: 657). The Americans, who had an energetic chief of mission in Bucharest, Burton Berry, protested strongly, but after the King acceded to Vyshinsky's threats on 6 March, the clamour died down (Markham 1996: 125–6). On 13 March Vyshinsky gave a speech to the new Romanian government in which he declared that: 'A new page has been turned in the history of Romania, a page in which it will be written in gold letters, the friendship of Romania for the Soviet Union and Marshall Stalin' (Markham 1996: 145). But a more accurate indication of Vyshinsky's true feelings towards Romanians was shown by his remark that: 'They are not a nation, but a profession' (Djilas 1962: 140).

Churchill once again engaged in one of his *volte-faces* which had characterized his erratic policy towards the Middle Zone countries and which revealed his lack of a clearcut strategy for the region. On 5 March 1945 he rebuked Eden for trying to interfere in Romania, arguing that it might lead to accusations that: 'we have broken our faith about Roumania after taking advantage of our position in Greece. And this will compromise the stand we have taken at Yalta over Poland. I consider that strict instructions should be sent to our representatives in Roumania not to develop an anti-Russian political front there. This they are doing with untimely energy without realizing what is at stake in other fields' (Carlton 1981: 254). But on 7 March Churchill was telling his Foreign Secretary that 'our honour is at stake'; his private secretary, John Colville observed that both men feared that 'our willingness to trust our Russian ally may have been in vain and they look with despondency to the future (Colville 1981: 569–70).

The British Foreign Office decided not to invoke the Declaration on Liberated Europe, signed at Yalta, over Romania. But a change in British policy towards that country was noticeable from the emergence of the Groza government onwards. '[T]he wartime attitude of special indifference to Romania' was 'replaced by one of no more and no less indifference to the fate of that country than to that of the rest of Eastern Europe "dubiously" liberated by the Soviet army' (Rothwell 1982: 375).

In his post-Yalta contacts with Washington, Churchill increasingly advocated both diplomatic and even military resistance to forestall Russian attempts to colonize Eastern Europe. He was particularly concerned with Soviet behaviour in Poland and in the first of ten telegrams sent to Roosevelt in March about Eastern Europe, he proposed that Stalin be asked to live up to the promises made at Yalta (Borsody 1993: 149; Charmley 1993: 622–3). But Roosevelt, in declining health and preoccupied with the war in the Far East, was unimpressed. (One of the last actions Roosevelt took before his death was to order the suppression of an American officer's report blaming the Soviets for the Katyn massacre of Polish officers) (Rothwell 1982: 161). Churchill pleaded with him on 13 March that 'we can ... make no progress at Moscow without your aid and if we get out of step the doom of Poland is sealed'. Churchill warned that soon he would be questioned in parliament about the lack of progress since Yalta and 'I shall be forced to tell the truth'. The fact was that 'Poland has lost her frontiers'; the question which would be asked in the Commons was 'Is she now to lose her freedom' (Charmley 1993: 623–4).

Since Britain had gone to war with Hitler over Poland six years earlier, concern with its fate was high among British MPs, representatives of citizens who had sacrificed much in subsequent years of warfare which had almost resulted in the conquest of Britain. But there was no such British interest in the Balkans which had played a peripheral role in the war during most of its stages. Lack of public concern, lack of empathy with the fate of the region, and accumulated prejudices about its inhabitants may, in no small way, have influenced the attitude of British leaders towards the fate of Romania and neighbouring states occupied by Soviet forces.

THE END OF THE WAR APPROACHES

Harry S. Truman, a former Senator from Missouri and US Vice President only since January 1945, was thrust from obscurity by Roosevelt's death on 12 April 1945. He had only been granted two interviews with the President during that time. He found himself thrust into a political and military maelstrom, without any adequate preparation. Not surprisingly, little was expected from a US Mid-Western politician who had made certain narrow domestic issues his speciality in an unspectacular political career. The loss of Roosevelt and the elevation of an untested and outwardly parochial figure in his place was treated with foreboding in

Anglo-American policy circles where the fear grew that the Atlantic democracies could be supplanted by Soviet power.

The political vacuum at the heart of American power occurred at a crucial moment in international politics and contributed in no small way to the tragic events unfolding in Eastern Europe. It would not be filled immediately, but Truman dashed the worst fears about him by turning out to be an internationally minded President. He had served in France with the US Army in the First World War which had convinced him 'of the duty of Americans to play their part in international politics if civilization was to be preserved' (Thomas 1986: 187). On 23 April 1945, in a meeting with Molotov, he said that the USA was tired of waiting for the Soviet Union to carry out the terms of the Yalta Agreement which were supposed to give the East European nations a chance to establish democratic regimes. When Molotov attempted to change the subject, Truman cut him off: 'That will be all, Mr Molotov, I would appreciate it if you would transmit my views to Marshal Stalin'. According to Charles Bohlen who had acted as interpreter: 'they were probably the first sharp words uttered during the war by an American President to a Soviet high official' (Thomas 1986: 188).

Many American officials were still influenced by the wartime alliance with the Soviets and the realisation of the immense sacrifice in Russian lives that had been necessary for Hitler to be repulsed. The nature of Soviet plans for Eastern Europe was slow to be grasped in Washington policy making circles, especially among liberals associated with Roosevelt's 'New Deal' reforms. Truman himself belonged to the reformist camp and he appointed as Secretary of State a lawyer and businessman James Byrnes who, during his eighteen months in this position, showed naivety and lack of foresight in dealing with Stalin. Coming from the state of South Carolina, where the Black population were denied voting rights, he was not in a strong position to persuade the Soviets to permit genuinely free elections in Eastern Europe.

The approaching end of the war also resulted in a change of political leadership in Britain that on the surface appeared to benefit the Soviets even more than Truman's elevation. A general election in June 1945 resulted in a landslide victory for the Labour Party. It was committed to a sweeping programme of domestic reforms including nationalisation of much of industry and the public utilities. Left-wing ideas had been in the ascendant in Britain during the war. The popular historian, A.J.P. Taylor told a radio audience in December 1945 that 'nobody in Europe believed in the American way of life, that is, in private enterprise'.

E.H. Carr, the foreign affairs analyst of *The Times* and future historian of the Russian revolution, used this influential platform to express his impatience with complaints about Soviet aggression. To Carr, it seemed absurd that 'questions of recognising, or not recognising, regimes within the Soviet zone should be allowed any longer to cloud relations between the major powers' (Thomas 1986: 319–20, 321).

But the indulgence towards the Soviet Union which had led even the hard-headed diplomat at the head of the British Foreign Office, Sir Alexander Cadogan, to refer to the Soviet leader affectionately as 'Uncle Joe' suffered a reverse with the British Labour electoral victory. Clement Attlee, the new Prime Minister and Ernest Bevin, the experienced trade union leader who became Foreign Secretary, were pragmatic socialists who had acquired a deep distrust of pro-Soviet Marxists both at home and abroad. The somersaults in Soviet policy that characterised Churchill's last years as Premier were replaced by a hardheaded attitude towards Soviet power. For Attlee, the Russians were 'ideological imperialists' and he thought the Americans had insufficient appreciation of this (Thomas 1986: 293). Bevin, aware of the cruel repression Stalin and his followers had visited on the peoples of the Soviet Union, was not fooled by the fact that, as believers in socialism, they might share common aims. He tried to keep the door open for improved relations with Moscow but he developed a hatred for the executioners of Stalin's policy, especially Molotov, with whom he almost came to blows at the Paris peace conference in 1946 (Rothwell 1982: 234–5). In September 1945, a meeting in London of the foreign ministers of the major powers had failed to resolve differences between the Soviet Union and its western allies about the shape of postwar Europe. In October 1945, J.C. Ward of the Foreign Office's Economic and Reconstruction Department, saw Russia's appetite as being insatiable:

> The Russian agitation against any idea of a regional association of western Europe, their demand for the trusteeship of Tripolitania and their suggestion that they should acquire a formal stake in the security of the western Mediterranean by stationing a warship at Tangier, all suggest that the day has gone when we could buy the Russians off by handing over to them the countries of Central Europe and the Balkans. (Rothwell 1982: 240)

In the summer of 1945 Stalin was presumed to be behind the efforts of Tito's Partisans to take advantage of the Nazi defeat and occupy parts of northeast Italy and southern Austria. In 1943 the Partisans had announced that the Italian province of Venezia Giulia, along with the city of Trieste, had been annexed to Yugoslavia (Wolff 1974: 305). Churchill had responded that these claims should be left to a postwar peace conference. But he was determined that the British should hold the head of the Adriatic, including the city of Trieste. A head-on clash between New Zealand forces and the Partisans in May–June 1945 appeared a strong possibility. The Partisans had taken most of the province of Istria, Italian-ruled after 1918 despite its South Slav majority, while New Zealand forces occupied the city of Trieste itself (Wolff 1974: 305). But Stalin was reluctant to show enthusiasm for Yugoslav territorial ambitions in case it led to a premature clash between erstwhile allies. Moscow's restraining influence on Tito led, on this occasion, to the crisis being defused (Thomas 1986: 435).

Britain persevered in trying to keep open lines of communication with Tito even as he pursued communist policies that appeared even more hardline than those of the Soviet Union itself (Rothwell 1982: 392–3). Perhaps this helps to explain why, in the spring and summer of 1945, the British authorities chose to repatriate between twenty and thirty thousand Yugoslav refugees to the Partisans. The facts of the repatriation were first brought to public attention by the publication of Aleksander Solzhenitsyn's *The Gulag Archipelago* in 1973. A much larger number of Russians, Cossacks and members of the military corps who had fought on the German side under the renegade General Andrey Vlasov, were returned (Thomas 1986: 323). This followed a decision by the British cabinet in September 1944 to return to Russia all Soviet citizens found in German combat uniforms. The question was re-opened following the publication of such books as Nicholas Bethell's *The Last Secret* and Nikolai Tolstoy's *Victims of Yalta*.

Some of the strongest criticism of the repatriation of Yugoslavs came from Milovan Djilas, a senior figure in the Yugoslav communist leadership in 1945. Writing nearly 35 years later, by which time he had become the main political dissident in Tito's Yugoslavia, Djilas related that:

> The great majority of the people the British forced back from Austria were simple peasants. They had no murders on their hands. They had not been Ustashis or Slovenian 'Home Guards'. Their only crime was fear of Communism and the reputation of the Communists. Their sole motivation for leaving the country was panic. If the British had handed over to us 'Quisling' leaders such as Nedic, and police agents who had collaborated with the Nazis in torturing and killing people, or had done it on their own, there could be no question of the morality of the British action. But this is not what they did. They forced back the lot—and this was profoundly wrong.

Djilas expressed astonishment that 'the British ... should have been so thoroughly remiss in examining the sort of justice that was likely to be meted out to the repatriates'. He related that in 1945: '[T]here were no properly constituted courts. There was no way in which the cases of 20–30,000 people could have been reliably investigated. So the easy way out was to have them all shot, and have done with the problem'.

The Yugoslav leadership in 1945 was unable to understand why the British had acted as they did:

> We believed in the ideological context prevailing at the time, that the British would have a good deal of sympathy with these refugees, seeing that they had fled Communism. We thought the British would show 'class solidarity' with them, and some of us even feared that they would enlist them for future use against Communist governments, especially our own. Yet, to our great surprise, they did none of these things but delivered them into our hands. (Urban 1979: 40)

Djilas expressed his surprise at the naivety of the British about the reality of Soviet power in Eastern Europe (Thomas 1986: 317). It took the British Foreign Office's northern department (which dealt with Russian affairs) some time to abandon the cherished hope that the foundations of postwar European policy ought to be the Anglo-Soviet alliance. In the USA the inclination for arranging compromises with the Soviet Union to preserve as much of the wartime alliance as possible remained strong in 1945–6. For Secretary of State Byrnes cooperation with the Russians to launch the United Nations, the first meeting of whose General Assembly was scheduled for January 1946, 'was a higher priority than the form of government in the countries bordering Russia in southeastern Europe' (Black 1982: 86–7). It is perhaps little wonder that Victor Abakumov, Russia's new minister of state security in 1946, said in that year:

> It is our good fortune ... that the British and the Americans in their attitude towards us have still not emerged from the postwar state of calf-love. They dream of lasting peace and building a democratic world for all men. They don't seem to realise that we are the ones who are going to build a new world, and that we shall do it without their liberal democratic recipes. All their slobber plays right into our hands and we shall thank them for this, in the next world, with coals of fire. (Thomas 1986: 110–11)

THE SUBJUGATION OF BULGARIA

At the Potsdam conference of the Allied powers which ran from 17 July to 2 August 1945, where Stalin was not inappropriately dressed 'like the

Emperor of Austria in a bad musical comedy', important decisions were taken about the Polish borders, and the nature of the occupation of Germany (Thomas 1986: 80). But Stalin refused to make any concessions about relaxing Soviet domination of the Allied Control Commissions in Romania or Bulgaria (Schuyler 1982: 143). Nevertheless, what appeared to be increasing Western resistance to Stalin's plans in Eastern Europe encouraged Romania's King Michael, in August 1945, to start 'a royal strike' in the hope that it would lead to the removal of the Groza government. Sir Orme Sargent, the head of the Foreign Office was warning at that time of the need for greater 'co-ordination of Anglo-American policies in Eastern Europe and the joint avoidance of "promises, express or implied, to the peoples of these areas which it might be feared, could not be carried out"' (Thomas 1986: 304). The warning was issued just after Bevin, at the September 1945 London meeting of the foreign ministers of the powers, had singled out Bulgaria and Romania and told Molotov that 'the chief difficulty' in relations with Russia lay there (Rothwell 1982: 236).

In New York, on 26 October 1945 President Truman gave encouragement to democratic demands in Eastern Europe by promising: 'we shall help the defeated enemy states establish peaceful democratic governments ... we shall refuse to recognise any government imposed upon any nation by the force of any foreign power' (Thomas 1986: 196). Since the detonation of the atomic bomb over Hiroshima and Nagasaki in August–September 1945, the USA was now the world's most powerful state. The hopes of anti-communists fighting a rearguard action in parts of the Balkans hitherto neglected by the USA, were galvanized by belated American interest in their fate. The heads of the US missions in Bucharest and Sofia were also encouraged by the firmer line emanating from Washington.

In August 1945 Maynard Barnes, the US representative in Bulgaria, had tried to obtain the postponement of elections until they could comply with the Joint Declaration on the Liberation of Europe made at Yalta, but he was slapped down by the US State Department which complained that he had exceeded his authority (Black 1982: 80). Bulgaria was the only Balkan country where, before the war, the Communists had enjoyed a popular base. The arrival in force of the Red Army during September 1944 allowed the political initiative to pass completely into their hands. A newly formed people's militia butchered thousands of officials of the former conservative royalist regime (Crampton 1994: 225–6). British estimates of the extent of the communist terror were of between 40 and 50,000 killed and there were much higher estimates, for example from the veteran American reporter of Balkan affairs Reuben Markham (Thomas 1986: 419). What amounted to an attempt to decapitate the old political system deserved a robust international response but, in the chaos of Europe in 1944–5, the mass Bulgarian killings went largely unheeded.

Bulgaria had stayed out of the Russo-German war and, but for its occupation of adjacent parts of Yugoslavia, had not been involved in the global conflict. Nevertheless, in December 1944, 22 ex-ministers and 3 Regents, 8 close advisers of ex-King Boris and 68 ex-parliamentarians were sentenced to death. The prosecution was given double the number of executions it had demanded, Bulgaria's right-wing being destroyed in the process (Crampton 1994: 226; Thomas 1986: 869 n. 96).

Nevertheless, the pre-war peasant movement BANU remained an active force and in Nikola Petkov it had a fearless leader prepared to defy communist tyranny. Petkov had been a believer in cooperation with the Communists and he supported the overthrow of the old regime (Black 1982: 93). But he soon decided to work in alliance with the US representative Barnes to preserve at least a semblance of democracy. As in Romania, the Western Allies had some leverage. Their consent was needed before the peace treaties (eventually to be signed in Paris in 1947 in relation to the occupied countries) could be drawn up and international legitimacy bestowed on the postwar regimes. But the two energetic officials representing the USA in Bulgaria and Romania found that their superiors were usually not interested in ensuring that the terms of the Yalta agreement were adhered to. Washington refused to support Barnes's call for the postponement of elections in Bulgaria; on 18 November 1945 the communist-led Fatherland Front got 88% of votes cast which gave them all the seats in parliament.

General John Crane, the US member of the Allied Control Commission (ACC), sent a dispatch to Washington early in 1946 complaining that the agreement at Potsdam whereby members of the ACC could go where they liked without previous notification had been frequently breached during his 14 months in Bulgaria. He wrote that the Russians denied him entry into any place where there were Russian troops, a big restriction, for there were 'Russian troops everywhere'. He concluded: 'Is not our country of sufficient strength to demand and enforce its demand for reasonable treatment of a mission such as this? … I am afraid we are following the policy of appeasement of the late Mr Chamberlain' (Thomas 1986: 422).

Following the abolition of the monarchy in September 1946, elections for a Grand National Assembly took place on 27 October. Perhaps because of orders from Moscow not to overplay their hand, the Communists allowed the opposition to win 20% of the seats (Crampton 1994: 227). Georgi Dimitrov, the veteran communist and former head of the Comintern, became Prime Minister. In parliament, Petkov defied the Communists 'with almost reckless bravery' (Wolff 1974: 300). In January 1947 he goaded Dimitrov as follows:

'Let me remind you that I have never been a citizen of a foreign country nor have I been in foreign service' to which Dimitrov replied: 'I was a citizen of the great Soviet Union ... an honor and a privilege', and the exchange continued:

PETKOV: 'You became a Bulgarian subject two days before the elections. This was officially announced from Moscow'.

DIMITROV: 'I'll teach you a lesson soon'.

PETKOV: 'For more than twenty years you were officially a foreign subject and in the service of a foreign state'.

On 6 June 1947 the communist militia arrested Petkov on the floor of parliament. He was tried before a 'People's Court' for conspiring to overthrow the state and a death sentence was handed down. On 23 September Petkov was hanged, Dimitrov later claiming that he might have been spared but for Anglo-American protests which constituted interference in Bulgaria's internal affairs. Dimitrov conveniently forgot that it was only international protests which had saved him from being executed by the Nazis in 1933 after the Reichstag fire (Rothwell 1982: 388). The British, in an official note, called Petkov's execution 'a judicial murder'. But the USA recognised the Bulgarian government a week after it, a good example of the failure of the two countries to coordinate their activities in the Balkans at this time (Wolff 1974: 302).

Maynard Barnes had resigned as head of the US mission in Bulgaria in protest at his government's decision and he left the foreign service (Black 1982: 89). Burton Berry, his US counterpart in Romania, had been equally critical of the State Department's quiescence in face of the communist takeover and in 1946 he asked to be transferred to another post (Percival 1997: 90).

THE SUBJUGATION OF ROMANIA

It was the British who in Romania made the running in determining Western policy towards the new communist-led regime. The preservation of democracy there proved not to be a British priority. Maniu, the leading anti-communist whose political career had begun as a member of the Hapsburg parliament in Budapest, was seen as a relic from the past. He and the other pre-war party leaders were viewed as obstacles standing in the way of preserving good relations with Moscow (Percival 1997: 167). Britain's fraught economic situation meant that there was also a strong incentive to restore commercial links with the regime in Bucharest irrespective of its character. According to Mark Percival, 'Britain's food shortages in the late 1940s are an important factor behind London's lack of interest in Romanian political developments' (Percival 1997: 108). However, there was a failure to realise that Britain would hardly be in a position to benefit from Romania's oil wealth and agricultural surplus if complete Soviet control was established.

Some British diplomatic resistance was mounted against the fatalistic approach of the Foreign Office to Romanian events. In late 1945 the Foreign Office Research Department argued that the Groza government's transparent lack of support meant that it was weak and Britain should maintain a firm line to ensure that it complied with democratic procedures (Percival 1997: 83). This was also the view of Ian Le Rougetel, the head of Britain's diplomatic mission. He argued that 'the USSR did not want to break with the UK over Romania and there was consequently no need to appease Groza' (Percival 1997: 83). Le Rougetel had served in Romania in 1939–40 and his dispatches did not usually reflect the stereotypical views of the department in London towards the country and its political leaders. Le Rougetel was aware that Maniu had been one of the few politicians to defy openly the royal and Antonescu dictatorships. He would probably have endorsed R.W. Seton-Watson's estimation of him published in the *Manchester Guardian* in 1944 that 'his personal integrity, democratic views, and moderation in foreign policies [were] beyond dispute' (Saiu 1992: 19).

But Maniu's indecision and procrastination also proved exasperating, even to Le Rougetel. His refusal to join the government immediately after Antonescu's overthrow in 1944, when no other well-known younger figures from the democratic camp were available, greatly reduced his influence and the willingness of the British to take his views into account. Nevertheless, Le Rougetel urged his superiors to try and influence unfolding events. In late 1945 he was urging London to suggest 'offering the Soviets a base at Galati in return for disinteresting themselves from the political complexions of the Romanian government' (Percival 1997: 84). There was hardly an East European country where the communists were weaker than in Romania and it is conceiveable that Stalin might have been persuaded to accept a bargain whereby the Soviets would effectively control Romanian defence and foreign policy while allowing the country a large degree of internal autonomy. It was exactly such an arrangement that Moscow permitted to evolve in Finland where the communists were much stronger than in Romania and which had been an integral part of Russia up to 30 years before. But, if Stalin was to stop short of the sovietization of Romania, it probably would have involved his erstwhile allies making concessions to Russia over some other matter, and this they showed no inclination to do.

There were a number of Western initiatives that benefited the Romanian democratic cause but fell far short of a sustained policy of assistance. One was the willingness of the West to allow free elections to take place in Greece in 1946 (when the result was uncertain) in the hope that this might encourage a similar response by the Soviets in the countries to the north. The other was the decision of Byrnes to send a well-known liberal New Dealer, Mark Ethridge, to visit Romania and Bulgaria and make an independent appraisal of political conditions there. Ethridge spent several weeks in both countries in late 1945 and his report on Romania (a copy of which Byrnes presented to Stalin) concluded:

1. The Groza government was not broadly representative of the Romanian people.
2. Elections conducted by the government would be a farce.
3. The situation has progressed too far to be rectified solely by the Romanian authorities.
4. The only acceptable solution would require the agreement of the three Allied Powers, at top level, to the installation of a truly representative government, which would then be called upon to hold elections under the watchful eye of a fully tripartite ACC. (Schuyler 1982: 147)

King Michael's decision to boycott the government in August 1945, to show the world that a regime imposed by the Soviets in March was illegitimate, had prompted the Americans to take a more proactive stance. So had the decision, at the London conference of Allied foreign ministers by Washington's representatives in Bucharest and Sofia, Berry and Barnes, of 'insisting upon telling the whole truth about Russian actions in the Balkans' (Saiu 1992: 142). But given the lack of any clear-cut American interest in Romania and, in the absence of any effective coordination with the British, the initiative soon swung back to advocates of a policy of least resistance. In December 1945, at the Moscow conference of foreign ministers preparing for the peace treaties signed in Paris in 1947, Britain and the USA decided to recognise the Groza government. The agreement contained face-saving democratic language, but the Foreign Office briefing to the British delegation showed that the British had no illusions that such guarantees would count for much. According to Mark Percival, the briefing argued that it would 'be better to accept that there was no chance of serious reorganisation of the Romanian or Bulgarian governments in the immediate term, and that policy should be to create conditions for the gradual re-emergence of democracy in the long-term . . .' (Percival 1997: 85). Britain was more keen to recognise Groza than the USA, but Washington's position was not really dissimilar (Schuyler 1982: 149–50).

Once recognition went ahead, Britain made hardly any attempt to stop the violation of the Moscow agreement. It was a sign that the agreement 'amounted to an abandonment by Britain of the principles of the Yalta Declaration as far as Romania was concerned' (Percival 1997: 86). Adrian Holman, the new British minister, reported in August 1946 that the UK policy seemed to be strengthening the government at the expense of the opposition (Percival 1997: 90). The British minister had acquired a jaundiced view of the Romanian Premier when Groza 'tried to do a deal with Holman to use state funds to buy the latter's private Rolls Royce' (Rothwell 1982: 378). But the incident may have just confirmed in him a negative view of Romania and the ability of its people to aspire to proper Western styles of conduct. It would not be the first time that Western policy makers seized upon such incidences of misrule or corruption in the Balkans to damn a whole country.

Thereafter, Holman's reports were increasingly negative about the opposition as well as the government. In the autumn of 1946, with elections due in November, London felt no obligation to concede to Maniu's request for British election observers to be sent. The Foreign Office pleaded the lack of available personnel (Percival 1997: 91). In October 1946, when 'Maniu supplied the British Legation with orders which had come into his possession from the Inspector General of the Police and of the Prefecture of Salaj county to ensure that the government won the elections, for instance by keeping two separate registers of elections, one for all those eligible to vote and one for those who could be expected to vote for the government', the British response was low-key (Percival 1997: 160–1). London saw the King rather than the non-communist parties as a guarantee of continuity. But following the communist electoral landslide (which investigation of the communist archives after 1989 has revealed was secured by the methods which Maniu in vain alerted the British about), no British support was forthcoming for royal attempts to resist a communist takeover. King Michael considered refusing to open parliament because of the fraudulent nature of the elections. A statement by Britain and the USA that the terms of the Moscow agreement (relating to free elections) had been violated, was an essential precondition for any attempt by the King to refuse to deal with the post-election government (Percival 1997: 161–2). However, neither the British nor the Americans were willing to issue such a statement. Holman wrote in his review of the year that it was 'no easy task for the British and American representatives ... to explain ... the reason which had prompted His Majesty's Government ... to modify their policy at this critical juncture'. This passage of Holman's review was removed from the final version printed in London (Percival 1997: 162–3).

The only concrete support from the West that Romania received before sovietization was complete was food aid. In February 1947, General Courtland Schuyler, the American member of the ACC, had learnt that much of northeast Romania was in the grip of imminent famine. The harvest had been poor and Soviet troops had confiscated food reserves peasants normally kept for such an emergency. Schuyler made a tour of a badly stricken area and, on his return to Bucharest, he suggested to his Soviet counterpart on the ACC, General Ivan Susaikov that they both appeal to their governments to rush food and medical supplies to the area; Schuyler relates the response he got:

> He looked at me for a moment, laughed and replied, 'Of course I won't join you. We have famines in parts of Russia almost every year. The weak die and the strong survive. That is Nature's way. Besides', he added, 'these people were our enemies two years ago. They brought this on themselves. Let them now get themselves out of it'. (Schuyler 1982: 154)

The USA diverted a ship on its way to Germany with several million army rations to Constanţa. A shipment of grain followed and the food was diverted to the worst affected areas. The contempt which the Soviet occupiers had for the Romanians they were supposedly liberating was noticeable also to Milovan Djilas when he stopped in the city of Iasi en route to Moscow early in 1947. He relates in *Conversations With Stalin*:

> We were most taken aback by the arrogant attitude of the Soviet representatives. I remember how horrified we were at the words of the Soviet

commander in Iasi: 'Oh this dirty Romanian Iasi! And these Romanian corn-pone eaters (mamalizhniki)!'. (Djilas 1962: 139–40)

The Romanian democratic opposition was completely friendless when elite figures started to be arrested in 1947. Maniu and leading members of his party were put on trial in October. Some had been apprehended attempting to flee the country. Reporting the trial, Holman commented that the evidence against the Peasant leaders was 'extremely strong' and that the defendants could be found guilty in an English court. At a time when a Romanian exile was pleading in London for the British to give Maniu an honour in order to remind the world of his pro-Allies role in the war, Holman urged that no gesture be made. A sign of the disarray the Western allies were in came when Holman advised that Britain should avoid becoming associated with US protests because the US legation was so 'deeply involved' in plotting with Maniu (Percival 1997: 166).

It is possible to criticise both Maniu's and Britain's role in the last year's of Romania's freedom. Maniu had been naive to assume that Britain would disregard wider considerations of Anglo-Soviet relations and strive to safeguard Romania's freedom. British officials were disingenuous in 'expecting Romanian politicians to carry out pro-Allies actions' without any guarantees that they would result in Britain taking trouble to safeguard Romanian interests in its negotiations with Moscow (Percival 1997: 150–1). The enforced abdication of King Michael on 30 December 1947 saw the removal of the last feeble barrier preventing the sovietization of Romania. British officials had naively assumed that the King could be a force for moderation even if his country and its government was completely in communist hands. Years later the exiled King bitterly criticised the duplicity of countries which he had expected might stand by Romania, not least because of his role in thwarting their German foe as a result of the August 1944 coup (Ciobanu 1997: 179–80). His abdication resulted in little comment from London, where officials soon resolved to try and accommodate themselves to the new political realities in Romania.

RUSSIAN INTENTIONS AND YUGOSLAV RESISTANCE

The weaknesses of American and British policy towards Eastern Europe already examined in this chapter enabled Stalin to establish control over a ring of countries which the Red Army had entered in force in its Western push against the remnants of Hitler's forces. Despite some fears expressed in diplomatic circles, Stalin did not intend to absorb the new communist satellites into the Soviet state. Instead, he preferred to create nominally self-governing dependencies answerable to the Soviet Union in all essential respects. A prototype already existed in the state of Mongolia, dependent on Moscow since the 1920s, though few realised this in the 1940s (Thomas 1986: 341). Territorial adjustments between the Soviet Union and its neighbours confirmed by the Paris peace treaties of 1947 were all to the benefit of Moscow. Stalin promoted adjustments in the borders between satellites in order to strengthen his hold over them. Initially, the Soviets appear to have felt that an 'independent' Transylvanian state in the Danubian basin might suit their interests. When the former Hungarian premier, Count Istvan Bethlen, was captured by them early in 1945, it was reported that they proposed to him that he assume the governorship of such a puppet state (his ancestors had ruled a flourishing Transylvania in the 17th century) (Burks 1961: 164–5). But when Bethlen refused, the Soviets decided to leave the territory in Romanian hands: Romania's retention of Transylvania was intended to increase the pitifully low standing of the communist party there, Romania being strategically more important to Russia than Hungary was.

It was Stalin who handpicked the rulers on the Western edges of his empire. Whim and personal prejudice dictated the selection process rather than any clearcut ideological motives. Thus in Hungary a loyal Muscovite like Matyas Rákosi became the local strongman while, in Romania, Ana Pauker, who had also spent a lengthy period in the Soviet Union, was rejected in favour of a home communist Gheorghe Gheorghiu-Dej who became party boss in 1946. Pauker was disadvantaged by being a woman and a Jewess, but Rákosi was also Jewish. The chief requirement of the leaders of the new 'Peoples Democracies' was that they show a readiness to bow to the supreme and absolute authority of the Kremlin at all times.

During the heyday of the Comintern, Stalin had tried to transform national communist parties into mere instruments of Soviet foreign policy. These parties were 'expected to conform to the momentary interests of the Soviet Union and its appraisal of the international situation' (Djilas 1991: 55).

The limits of Soviet power were shown by the failure of Stalin's bid to force Yugoslavia down to the same level of other East European countries which had been occupied by the Red Army (Djilas 1962: 172). Stalin was probably not unduly bothered when the leaders of the

Yugoslav revolution took over the royal palaces and aristocratic villas in the exclusive Belgrade suburb of Dedinje for themselves (Djilas 1983: 12). He was keen to probe the weaknesses of his fellow communists the better to bring them under his power. But, from the outset, he found it hard to bring Tito to heel or establish hegemony over the Yugoslav party. Tito had led an indigenous revolution which had largely triumphed without the help of the Red Army. The Partisans were devoted first to Tito and only then to Stalin and the 'Russian mother party'. The Soviets could not call on any other leader to challenge Tito's control of the party. This was because of Moscow's own bloodletting in the late 1930s. It is reckoned that Stalin killed more Central Committee members than the Yugoslav police in the interwar period or the Axis during the war (Lendvai 1969: 144). Members who had belonged before 1940 amounted to less than a fraction of one percent. Both Tito and Stalin shared the aim of seeing communism triumph in Yugoslavia. But in the war years Tito had openly defied Stalin, who had preferred to see the royalists enjoy a titular authority, at least initially. The event which most clearly showed that Tito had his own plan was the meeting of the Anti-Fascist Council for the National Liberation of Yugoslavia held in the Bosnian town of Jajce on 29 November 1943. Paul Lendvai has described its significance:

> The Council was transformed into a provisional legislature, and its executive into a provisional government headed by Tito, who received the title of Marshal. Moscow, however, was informed only forty-eight hours before the fact. The cable also omitted to mention the trifling matter that the meeting would declare the royal government-in-exile illegal and forbid King Peter to return to Yugoslavia. On the eve of the crucial Tehran Conference of the three great powers, this was regarded by an 'unusually angry' Stalin as a 'stab in the back for the Soviet Union'. (Lendvai 1969: 78)

Tito's actions showed that he believed in the principle of sovereign equality for communist states which the Soviet Union upheld for propaganda purposes but never practised (Campbell 1967: 20). Fitzroy Maclean, the chief British liaison officer with the wartime Partisans, had already concluded that Tito was 'a principal, not a subordinate with an odd lack of servility' (Maclean 1949: 308). Stalin had been angered by Tito's speech at Ljubljana on 27 May 1945 in which the latter had asserted that 'we will not be dependent on anyone ever again ... We do not want to be small change; we do not want to be involved in any spheres of influence' (Djilas 1983: 91). The Soviet ambassador complained that 'we regard Comrade Tito's speech as unfriendly'.

The Russians also reacted angrily when Milovan Djilas complained about serious assaults which the Red Army had perpetrated on Yugoslav civilians in 1944–5 (Djilas 1962: 87–8). During their brief 5-month stay around Belgrade, Soviet forces were responsible for 1,219 rapes, 121 rapes with murder, and 1,204 robberies with violence. No other country dared to produce such statistical evidence of Russian excesses (Lendvai 1969: 12). Friction was also caused by Russian efforts to recruit a wide number of people, including Četniks and White Russians, into Soviet intelligence. Stalin was confronted by a leader who saw himself as perhaps the world's most important communist after the Soviet leader himself.

British and American diplomats saw no sign of any looming Yugoslav–Soviet split (Rothwell 1982: 393). The opening of diplomatic papers for the late 1980s may reveal similar Anglo-American complacency about the danger posed by Tito's successor Milosević for the future survival of Yugoslavia. There were clues that might have alerted perceptive diplomats in the mid-1940s, if they had been encouraged to pay close attention to the Balkans at that time. But it is not surprising that the schism in the communist movement took the West unawares. Between 1945 and 1948 Yugoslavia played the role of the communist world's boldest front-line outpost in the escalating confrontation with the West. Collectivisation of agriculture and industry was pushed ahead more forcefully than in most other East European states. Tito pushed his dispute with the west over Trieste to the absolute limit. In 1947 it was Belgrade rather than Moscow which provided vital logistical support for the Communists in Greece when the civil war between left and right resumed there. In 1946 Yugoslavia had mounted attacks on US aircraft it claimed were violating its airspace, bringing one down on 19 August with the loss of all on board (Lees 1996: 14). But both Britain and the USA stopped short of breaking with Tito. The United Nations Relief and Rehabilitation Agency (UNRRA) fed millions of people in Yugoslavia, serving as the only source for civilian clothing and medical supplies, as well as providing livestock and farm implements to revive food production. UNRRA spent $415.6 million in Yugoslavia which was one-fifth of its budget, most of the aid being American in origin (Lees 1996: 18–19).

Anglo-American assistance to the Yugoslav communists during and after the war undoubtedly made it easier for Tito to mend his fences with the West after being expelled from the Communist bloc. But Tito's radical anti-imperialism in 1945–7 was one of the key factors persuading the USA to abandon its inactive approach to the sovietization of Eastern Europe.

The famous 8,000 word 'Long Telegram' dispatched from Moscow in February 1946 by George Kennan, the American minister there, alerted US officials about how Soviet expansionism threatened American interests across the globe. Kennan argued that a sprawling Russian state plagued by age-old insecurity about the intentions of its neighbours and other powers was 'promising ground for a doctrine such as Marxism which viewed conflicts as insoluble by peaceful means' (Thomas 1986: 676). Marxism had combined with Russian nationalism to create an aggressive and expansionist state with vast resources at its disposal prepared to undermine the United States rather than establish a *modus vivendi* with it (Thomas 1986: 677).

Kennan's memorandum was widely circulated among policy makers in Washington. Within a very short time a far more vigorous American response to Soviet encroachments was evident. In March 1946 the Truman administration protested to the Soviet Union about the stationing of troops in Iran against the wishes of its government. Iran was not a country in whose affairs American interest had previously been evinced (Kuniholm 1980: 322–3). It is significant that Washington proceeded without coordinating its actions with Britain which had a major commercial interest in a country seen as vital for the defence of India (Thomas 1986: 691). India was on the verge of independence, undermining Britain's will to retain a dominant role in the Middle East which it was increasingly beyond its financial capacity to do.

Churchill's famous speech delivered at Fulton, Missouri on 5 March 1946 just four days before Washington issued its warning to Moscow over Iran could be seen as a bid by Britain's most eminent statesman to urge her paramount ally to fill the vacuum that had opened up in the Mediterranean and the Middle East. Churchill warned that the countries of Central and Eastern Europe were under increasing Soviet control. The unlimited expansion of Soviet power and ideology was clearly desired by Moscow. The much quoted passage in his speech referred to the 'iron curtain' which had descended across the centre of Europe 'from Stettin in the Baltic, to Trieste in the Adriatic. In the face of persistent Soviet aggression, the old international balance of power was losing its validity. A new Anglo–American alliance, if necessary involving common citizenship, was required to provide a defence of free institutions, otherwise a new Dark Age could return (Thomas 1986: 703–4; Borsody 1993: 175).

Stalin had never been spoken to in such frank terms by Churchill or Roosevelt during their wartime alliance; otherwise a modified Soviet approach to Eastern Europe might have emerged. The Soviets attacked Churchill's speech as the opening salvo of a war of aggression directed at them by former allies. The international conflict between the Communist world and the non-Communist world, known as the Cold War, soon became a recognised fact of life (Hammond 1982: 3). The role of the chief Western participants in this conflict deserves much critical scrutiny. But it is difficult to accept the view that their rather belated reaction to Soviet expansionism compelled Stalin to be more ruthless in Eastern Europe than he might otherwise have been (Hammond 1982: 6–12). Before the Fulton speech, overwhelming evidence from Poland, Romania and Bulgaria shows that Stalin was determined to impose undemocratic regimes fully subservient to Soviet interests. The pace of sovietization may have been stepped up after Fulton, but the machinery for establishing obedient one-party states was already in place across much of Eastern Europe.

Another year would elapse before the USA produced concrete evidence that it was ready to resist Soviet expansion beyond traditional Russian zones of influence. It was the southern Balkans which would provide the first arena of US Cold War activity. Lincoln MacVeagh, the long-standing US ambassador to Greece, had been warning in dispatches to Roosevelt and Truman of the strategic importance of the region. On 15 October 1944 in a memorandum to Roosevelt he wrote:

> ... I realise that Yugoslavia,—and Greece to an even greater extent,—are very small potatoes still in the typical American view of foreign affairs. But I should like to stress once more my belief that eventually what goes on in the Balkans and Near East generally will have to be recognised as of prime importance to us despite the fact that the countries involved are small and remote. (Iatrides 1980: 627)

In the same report he warned:

> Evidence is equally plain right here of Britain's inability to defend alone her Empire against powerful pressure under conditions of modern war. I doubt if in any other part of the world it can appear so clearly as here,—along its principal artery,—that, militarily speaking, the British Empire is anachronistic, perfect for the eighteenth century, impossible for the twentieth. Every day brings its evidence of weakness and dispersion, or consequent opportunism, and dependence on American ... strength.

When the Greek Civil war had resumed in 1947, MacVeagh sent a top secret telegram to Washington on 20 February in which he warned:

... We feel situation here so critical that no time should be lost in applying any remedial measures, even if only of a temporary character ... If nothing but economic and financial factors were to be considered, full collapse from Greece's present position might take several months. However, deteriorating morale both of civil servants and armed forces, as well as of general public, owing to inadequate incomes, fear of growing banditry, lack of confidence in Government, and exploitation by Communists, creates possibility of much more rapid denouement.

MacVeagh urged that 'our determination ... not to permit foreign encroachment, either from without or within, on independence and integrity of Greece' be made plain to everyone, 'including the Soviet Union' (Iatrides 1980: 712).

MacVeagh's telegram was incorporated in a memorandum which Under Secretary of State Dean Acheson submitted to General George Marshall, the new Secretary of State. Its receipt virtually coincided with the arrival of two aides-memoires from the British Embassy announcing Britain's inability to extend further assistance to Greece and Turkey after 31 March 1947 and requiring immediate consultation for the purpose of shifting to the USA the burden of such assistance (Iatrides 1980: 713). Within days, on 12 March, President Truman received authorisation from Congress for a programme of assistance to Greece and Turkey, worth $4 billion. US policy makers were convinced that if Greece fell to communism so too would Italy, and Soviet power would extend from the central Mediterranean deep into the Middle East.

American aid was orchestrated by Dwight Griswold, a former governor of Nebraska. His high-handed attitude to the Greeks was not unlike that of the Soviet commissars installed in northern Balkan countries. MacVeagh was warning privately in 1948, shortly after being withdrawn from Greece, that 'to wave the big stick ... give[s] support to the Communist charge that our "imperialism" is making slaves of the local inhabitants' (Iatrides 1980: 737). American military advisers and operatives of the newly-created Central Intelligence Agency poured into the country. American military aid was about to turn the tide against the Communist guerillas. But the tendency of Washington to treat Greece as an insignificant client state stoked up enduring Greek resentment about Western interference in domestic affairs. MacVeagh's 1944 complaint about British overbearance in Greece would apply with equal force to the Americans just a few short years later:

Bitterness, as regards the British, resentfulness of their lack of tact towards smaller peoples, distrust of their capacity to devote sufficient means to any project, and suspicion as to their political intentions, are so wide-spread as to be practically universal among the Balkan peoples today. (Iatrides 1980: 457)

However, it was the Soviet Union that would be the first great power to suffer an embarrassing reversal in the Balkans during the nuclear age. Soviet efforts to weaken Tito by promoting internal dissensions in Yugoslavia proved unavailing. The struggle which the Partisans had waged simultaneously against occupiers, collaborators, and Croatian and Serbian extremists enabled the Communists to present themselves after the war as the sole unifying force in the country (Djilas 1991: 14). Communist power in Yugoslavia was far more broadly based than in countries like Romania or Albania, where the new rulers had enlisted extreme rightists and whole clans in order to boost the numbers in initially tiny parties. With the exception of the Albanians in Kosovo who held aloof from the Partisans, the latter were representative of most of the ethnic components of Yugoslavia nearly two years before the war's end. The Croats of Dalmatia formed no less than five divisions, attracted to the Partisans by the twin pressures of Italian occupation and the atrocities committed by the Četniks. Bosnian Muslims, Slovenes, and Croats from Croatia joined in increasing numbers. By the end of 1943, non-Serb nationalities accounted for two-fifths of the Partisan forces (Lendvai 1969: 65).

So it was difficult for Soviet agents to foment dissent on ethnic lines. But it was the perceived national ambitions of the Yugoslavs in the region, not the way they were interpreting Marxist-Leninist ideology, which produced the break with Moscow. Stalin feared that Tito was intent on creating a powerful Balkan federation of 40 million people which would produce a rival pole of attraction for the communist faithful elsewhere. Indeed negotiations had taken place as early as November 1944 between the Bulgarian and Yugoslav communists over the creation of a South-Slav union. The Yugoslavs proposed that Bulgaria should become a separate republic in federal Yugoslavia while the Bulgarians held out for a dual state in which they would be a joint partner with Yugoslavia (Wolff 1974: 314). In 1947 Tito and Dimitrov, the Bulgarian leader, signed an agreement putting an end to frontier travel barriers and arranging for a future customs union. Tito then embarked on a triumphal tour of East European capitals.

In January 1948 Soviet annoyance at these freelance Balkan initiatives spilled over when Dimitrov predicted that a Balkan federation would arise and the peoples of the regions would be the ones 'who will decide whether it will be a federation or a confederation, and when or how it will be formed' (Wolff 1974: 320). Dimitrov also predicted that Greece would be a member.

On 29 January 1948 the Soviet daily *Pravda* openly disagreed with Dimitrov, expressing its doubts that the Balkan countries needed any 'problematic and artificial federation or confederation or customs union' (Wolff 1974: 320). Stalin summoned the top Bulgarian communists to Moscow where a Yugoslav delegation had already been discussing political and military cooperation. When he met with them, he criticised the independent behaviour of both countries. Dimitrov was humiliated by Stalin when he attempted to justify his statement (Djilas 1983: 173–7). Although the truth will probably never be known, his death in Moscow during 1949 may have been the direct result of Stalin's extreme anger with the role he had played in the Soviet–Yugoslav quarrel. Tito had absented himself from the delegation on the grounds of illness. Edvard Kardelj, the chief Yugoslav ideologist, was advised to stop helping the Greek Communists. Stalin told him: 'They have no prospects of success at all. Do you think that Britain and the USA ... will permit their arteries of communication in the Mediterranean to be severed? Nonesense. And we don't have a navy. The uprising in Greece must be wound up as soon as possible' (Djilas 1983: 169).

While insisting that any Balkan union must be on Soviet terms and under its supervision, Stalin during the 18 months before the break with Tito egged on the Yugoslavs in their efforts to cement a federation with Albania. In January 1947 Stalin told Djilas: 'We have no special interest in Albania. We agree that Yugoslavia should swallow up Albania' (Djilas 1962: 142–7). But that encouragement may have been a provocation meant to entrap the Yugoslavs and it is how the Belgrade leadership came to view it (Hodos 1987: 7).

On 10 February Stalin outlined his own ideas for East European unity: Romania and Hungary should unite, and Bulgaria and Yugoslavia, after which the latter should annex Albania. After this session, the Yugoslavs agreed among themselves that they should postpone the idea of a federation rather than accept one on Stalin's terms. Apprehension about Soviet intentions grew when, on 11 February, Kardelj was virtually ordered to sign an agreement that Yugoslavia would consult the Soviet Union in future on all questions of foreign policy (Lees 1996: 50–1).

Stalin had been particularly irked by the Yugoslav decision in January 1948 to move two divisions to Albania and move part of its air force there to repulse any attack by the opponents of the Greek communists

(Lendvai 1969: 83). Yugoslavia claimed that it was acceding merely to a request from Tirana where communists favouring amalgamation with Yugoslavia were then in the ascendancy. Albania, despite its small size, was of vital importance to Yugoslavia. Inside a Yugoslav–Albanian federation, Yugoslavia's Albanian majority in Kosovo could be united with the rest of the ethnic Albanians in one single republic, thereby solving an intractable problem which would return to afflict Yugoslavia in the 1980s (Djilas 1962: 144).

Matters moved towards a break when, on 1 March 1948, the Yugoslav Central Committee rejected Stalin's demand for an immediate Yugoslav–Bulgarian union. Tito bluntly stated that this would be to allow a Trojan horse to enter the Yugoslav party (Lendvai 1969: 84). Tito was no communist heretic. He wanted to be a partner not a servant. His pride as a national leader who had made a revolution single-handedly was incompatible with Stalinist hierarchy. On 18 March Soviet advisers were withdrawn from Yugoslavia. With Tito challenging Stalin's monopoly of running the Communist movement, a split was impossible to avoid. On 28 June Yugoslavia was formally expelled from the Communist Information Bureau (Cominform) and anathemas were placed on the head of Tito. Stalin warned: 'I will shake my little finger and there will be no more Tito' (Crampton 1994: 260). Instead, in the first schism to shake the post-1917 international communist movement it was Russia that lost out. The feud soon acquired 'the character of a national conflict ... between the then only Communist great power and a small Balkan country' (Lendvai 1969: 85). Russia's quarrel with Yugoslavia showed Stalin at his most incompetent, according to Robert Conquest (Lees 1996: 79). Without the neurotic and overbearing attitude of the Soviets, a Balkan federation could have begun to take shape in the 1940s, which might have prevented some of the national rivalries of the later communist period and indeed beyond.

CONCLUSION

By necessity, this chapter has concentrated on the actions of the major powers towards the Balkans. The future of the area, and that of Eastern Europe in general, would be determined for almost the rest of the century by decisions arrived at by a small number of political leaders briefly united in an effort to defeat Hitler and Nazism.

Stalin proved to be the most far-seeing and calculating of the Big Three. The 1940s revealed that the principal Western leaders, Churchill and Roosevelt, lacked an empathy with the problems of Eastern Europe necessary to check a new wave of aggression in the region. The Soviet Union wished to subjugate the entire area but Britain and the USA failed to acquire an effective counter-strategy. Churchill was unable to convince the Americans that the Balkans was a suitable theatre for military operations in 1943. He never really used his powers of eloquence, or moral authority as the leader of the only other European country to successfully resist Hitler, to persuade the Americans that a democratic Eastern Europe whose eastern borders were clearly demarcated, should be established as a key peacetime objective.

If the fate of Eastern Europe had been raised in a purposeful manner with Stalin before German military power had been broken, a new triumph of tyranny could have been avoided across much of the region. Top Russian officials themselves suggested that Stalin would have acted with more restraint if the Western allies had been firmer. He was prepared to allow Finland to enjoy internal freedom as long as it took Soviet security interests into account. This suggests that there was a theoretical possibility that some of his other Western neighbours might have achieved a Finnish-style solution.

The Finns achieved their democratic breathing space without relying on the Western powers. It may be that a ruler like Romania's King Michael was over-reliant on the West and that he could have made terms with Moscow stopping short of full sovietization if Britain in particular had been open about its intentions towards his country.

Throughout the war years a pattern had grown up of Britain conceding to the Soviets in Eastern Europe and then Churchill having second thoughts, but then, after failing to acquire US support for a tougher approach towards the Russians, deciding reluctantly to accept a flawed compromise. Particularly in the Balkans, the USA had no economic interests, or large immigrant populations able to lobby for American efforts to preserve the self-determination of their former homelands.

The Western alliance had no alternative strategy to Soviet hegemony in Eastern Europe which it could easily mobilise around. Britain was prepared to trade territory and allocate spheres of influence in the Balkans in order to protect its own empire in Asia. But this was a futile policy. Much of the rationale behind Britain's aggressive actions in Greece vanished with Indian independence in 1947. But Britain's neo-imperial role in Greece in the 1940s made it all the easier for Stalin's power-grab in countries to the north to be successful.

Britain's supranational ideas for a federal or confederal Europe were ones that held out better prospects for reconstructing Europe after the second of two European civil wars fought around nationalist quarrels. But a post-nationalist Europe, embraced by an increasing number of West European states in the 1950s, went against the instincts of the British political elite; even Churchill's infatuation with the idea was basically insincere and inevitably shortlived.

The failure to coordinate policies in Eastern Europe extended into the Truman and Attlee eras. In the Balkans, the list of civil and military officials from Britain and the USA sick-at-heart over the policy of minimal engagement there eloquently testified to the bankruptcy of western policy in the region. The Cold War eventually broke out in the late 1940s over how far into Europe Soviet domination could extend. The West belatedly realised that turning a blind eye to what Stalin was doing in countries like Romania and Bulgaria was not satisfying his appetite for new conquests, only whetting it. Clumsy Anglo-American efforts to resist communism in Greece by advancing reactionary monarchists tarnished the cause of freedom and stored up trouble for the future. In Yugoslavia the Soviet Union stumbled even more heavily when it branded the national form of communism championed by Tito as heresy but then failed to extinguish it.

The Yugoslav leader showed the fissiparous tendencies present within communism and the way that conflicting national objectives could bring communist states to the point of confrontation far more quickly than democratic ones. But for the Soviet–Yugoslav quarrel, a communist-led South Slav union might have emerged under Yugoslav auspices. A quarrel with Moscow over its economically exploitative policies might have been hard to avoid with or without Stalin's baleful presence. But a communist Balkan union could have defused the Albanian question by allowing mainly Albanian-speaking territories to be united and also taken the heat out of the Macedonian question by uniting Bulgarian and Yugoslav territory. Branka Magaš has argued that a new future could have been mapped out for the region if unification had been pursued before the communist parties started to speak in the name of their respective 'states' (Magaš 1993: 30). But of course, such a union might well have generated tensions of its own around personality, regional frustrations and the disfunctional character of communist economics. So one should not be categorical in assuming that a rare opportunity to push the Balkans in the direction of post-nationalist functional co-operation was definitely lost in 1948. But when relations were mended between Belgrade and Moscow, the opportunities for co-operative initiatives devaluing national sovereignty were over. With the exception of Bulgaria, each of the communist Balkan states jealously cultivated their sovereignty. In the words of Pierre Hassner, 'the Balkanization of communism has prevailed over the Communization of the Balkans' (Fejtö 1974: 158).

Chapter 4

TYRANNY FROM WITHOUT AND WITHIN: THE BALKANS
1949–1973

The Cold War separated Greece from the rest of the Balkan states which, in turn, found themselves cut off from remaining western influences. Henceforth, Soviet norms and values shaped the political, economic and social structures of the satellite regimes in Romania, Bulgaria, and Albania.

Yugoslavia, despite its political orientation towards the West in the 1950s, always retained many features of the Soviet-style command economy and did not cease to be an authoritarian regime. This command economy, based largely on heavy industry, was more prevalent in areas of Yugoslavia without previous industrial traditions or a commercial middle-class of any significance. Problems would arise from this at the end of the communist era which would pull much of Yugoslavia in a direction different from that of other Balkan states. But up to the 1980s, the region it was in was one of the key frontlines in the Cold War 'from which Western Europe could be politically and even militarily intimidated, and indeed kept off balance' by the Soviet Union (Gati 1990: 24).

An increasingly apprehensive United States government decided to fill the power vacuum in the Eastern Mediterranean left by the retreating British in 1947. Truman convinced Congress that American security depended upon preventing further Soviet encroachments in the Balkans. Other measures were taken to contain Soviet ambitions in Europe as a whole. In June 1947, the US proposed the Marshall Plan to rebuild Western Europe economically and enable it to withstand communist pressure. In June 1948 the Western powers swallowed their doubts about the German people's affinity to democracy and decided to build up a strong anti-communist West Germany. In June 1949 the North Atlantic Treaty Organization (NATO) was founded as a defensive military alliance concerned with keeping communism at bay. Finally, far less publicity attended Truman's decision in June 1948 to broaden the role of the newly established Central Intelligence Agency (CIA) to include covert operations against the Soviet Union and its satellites in the fields of propaganda and economic warfare (Hodos 1987: 1).

The United States's commitment to the 'rollback' of the Iron Curtain was reaffirmed publicly in 1953 by John Foster Dulles, Secretary of State under President Dwight D. Eisenhower (Ulam 1995: 179). Already from 1949, the CIA had resorted to secret flights over Eastern Europe to gather intelligence. An Office of Special Operations (linked to the CIA and headed by Frank Wisner, a New York lawyer who had begun his intelligence career as an agent in wartime Romania) had been created in 1948, one of its aims being to stimulate sabotage and resistance behind the Iron Curtain (Kovrig 1991: 39). More significant was the decision, in 1950, to launch Radio Free Europe which was designed to keep alive resistance to totalitarianism and provide East Europeans with information withheld from their censored media (Urban 1997: *passim*).

The resolve of western countries to band together against Soviet expansionism was greatly strengthened by the 1948 Soviet–Yugoslav split. It 'shattered both the communist claim and the western illusion that those who shared the same Marxist-Leninist ideology could not develop significant differences among themselves; that the usual conflicts of national interest among sovereign states did not apply to communist states' (Gati 1990: 17). Soviet military preparations were drawn up to end the Tito heresy by force but, in September 1949 Britain and the US 'put Moscow on notice that an attack on Yugoslavia would have serious consequences' (Djilas 1983: 259).

THE SOVIET COMMAND ECONOMY IMPOSED ON THE BALKANS

Stalin's tendency to treat the nominally independent states behind the Iron Curtain as colonial vassals subject to his territorial whims did enormous damage to Soviet interests. It left his successors with difficult legacies which they scarcely knew how to handle.

Huge resentments had been stoked up in the 'People's Democracies' at the claims for reparations made by the USSR against countries with which it had been in conflict after 1941. Paul Lendvai has written that some estimates put the total loot acquired by Russia in Romania at $2 billion alone in the years 1945–6:

> Plant and equipment were dismantled, merchant marine and rolling stock expropriated, stores of industrial and semi-manufactured goods removed and shipped off to Russia. (Lendvai 1969: 285–6)

It is estimated that the net gains which the Soviet economy enjoyed at the direct expense of its satellites in the 1945–56 period totalled $20 billion (after the deduction of credits) (Lendvai 1969: 11). The

Soviets do not appear to have paused to think that the seizure of good created by the labour of ordinary citizens who were not responsible for declaring war on the Soviet Union, would generate deep ill will at a time when the Soviet system needed to acquire popular legitimacy in countries where communism had a flimsy popular base.

In the twilight of Stalin's dictatorship, no analysis was made of policy options towards the region. This would have only been to throw into question Stalin's judgment and indeed the cult of personality that surrounded him. Instead, East-Central and Southeast Europe found itself subordinated to Stalin's personal and ideological whims and to the Soviet Union's policy interests. The Soviet Union took advantage of the fact that many millions saw it as the centre of 'a universally-binding revolutionary creed' whose will dare not be questioned (Lendvai 1969: 351). Only Tito was in a position to insist on the right to national independence and equality within the communist world (Campbell 1967: 98). Soviet apologists saw Titoism as a diabolical virus 'which because it kept a Marxist character and cited Lenin in defying Stalin ... attacked the vulnerability of the puppet regimes in ways that no Western propaganda or diplomacy could do' (Campbell 1967: 98). Within Yugoslav communist ranks, there was considerable dismay over Tito's break with Moscow. During the years 1948–53, 16,288 Cominformists, pro-Soviet communists, were arrested and convicted. Of these '44.42 per cent were Serbs with many being veterans of the Partisan war for whom faith in Stalin and the Soviet Union had been part of their wartime creed' (Thomas 1999: 32).

Stalin's satellite system felt threatened by Tito's high reputation in some of Yugoslavia's fellow satellites. His attempt to create a socialist federation of nations in the Danubian basin was viewed as a rival pole of attraction in the Soviet world. If less paranoid minds had been at work in Moscow in the late 1940s, they might have viewed the efforts of the only communist satellite leader with genuine popular appeal as a visionary attempt to consolidate Marxism-Leninism in different terrain capable of saving them from many future problems.

Stalin was always more interested in Balkan hatreds than in Balkan reconciliation (Djilas 1983: 191). His desire to manipulate inter-state tensions and national rivalries explains why cleavages which had bedevilled relations between royal Balkan states acquired a new intensity under their communist successors. He failed to provide 'a workable system of political and economic inter-state relations in the

Soviet bloc' (Gati 1990: 27). The Council for Mutual Economic Assistance, which was meant to synchronise the economies of the communist states, was not allowed to carry out this role by Stalin.

Instead of countries being encouraged to specialise in areas of economic production which their climates and natural resources suited them for, 'each East European country was directed both to duplicate the Soviet experience and develop what it needed on its own' (Gati 1990: 20). The emphasis on heavy industry at the expense of other technological sectors (and of agriculture) proved to be harmful in the long term for the satellite states, especially the Balkan ones where the resource-base for heavy industry was found only in a few areas. Following the Soviet model and creating a numerically strong industrial proletariat in the metal and extractive industries was an ideological goal which took precedence over normal developmental goals. The attachment of the Romanian and the Albanian regimes to both the Stalinist political and economic models made them problem cases for Moscow when the Soviet leadership's priorities changed after 1953. Insisting on the exclusive validity of the Stalinist model was a form of self-protection meant to repel pressure for liberalisation and reform.

THE YEARS OF STALIN'S PURGES

After 1948 a series of purges marked the repudiation of the belief that different national roads to socialism were possible, and its replacement with 'a Stalinist concept of imperial conformity' (Hodos 1987: 2). George Hodos has argued that the purges would have taken place even without the break with Yugoslavia, which merely speeded up the process. Already there was ample evidence from Moscow itself that the ageing dictator was beginning to profoundly distrust his closest associates. So he was even more likely to be acutely suspicious of his foreign agents in the satellite countries, especially if their careers in the party had not involved close interaction with the Soviet Union (Hodos 1987: 2–3).

Albania was the first country in which members of the communist leadership were put on trial for political heresy or treason. A section of the party led by the interior minister, Koçi Xoxe had indeed worked closely with Belgrade to bring about a Yugoslav–Albanian union in which Albania would be the seventh republic of the enlarged federation. Within a year of Tito's expulsion from the Cominform, the Yugoslav wing of the party was in prison or in camps and the nationalist wing, under Enver Hoxha, was fully in control. For the next four decades the purge would be used by Hoxha to crush enemies real or imagined. Of the 31 members of the Central Committee elected at the first party congress in 1948, 14 were liquidated and 8 forcibly removed from political life (Lendvai 1969: 196). After 1948 Tito was reluctant to make Albania an arena of confrontation with Stalin. Plans for unity were dropped, but Hoxha's fertile suspicions were fed by attempts mounted by Britain and the USA in the early 1950s to detach Albania from the Soviet orbit. Albania was geographically cut off from the rest of the Soviet bloc, but several invasion efforts foundered because Kim Philby, the head of the British MI6's Washington bureau, was a Soviet double agent (Bethell 1995: 298).

Initially, Stalin had been 'curious and suspicious about the only leader of a Communist regime in the Soviet bloc who escaped from any historical ties or contacts with the Soviet Union' (Halliday 1986: 6). But these despots were from not dissimilar backgrounds, both men born into lands of vendettas and skulduggery on the troubled edges of the Ottoman and Russian empires. Stalin's familiarity with the ethnic particularisms of the Caucasus gave him a clear start over his rivals in the internecine world of Bolshevik politics after 1917. Hoxha grew up in a land of endemic clan rivalries, but despite communist efforts to modernise a traditional society, the clan would remain at the heart of the political system.

Romania was the other Balkan state which, after Albania, was most reluctant to destalinise, and here a local Stalinist ruler was allowed to have his way 'because his plotting and scheming did not seem to endanger Soviet aims' (Hodos 1987: 93–4).

Gheorghe Gheorghiu-Dej, the dominant figure in communist Romania from 1948 to 1965, showed his fidelity to Moscow by delivering the chief denunciation of Tito at the Cominform conference held in July 1949. In the following year, he ordered the deportation of thousands of ethnic Serbs, living on Romania's border with Yugoslavia, to a distant area in the east of the country. But this 'home communist', who had spent the 1933–44 years in a Romanian prison, may have feared that he was vulnerable in the purge years on account of his distant ties with Moscow. From 1948 he was locked in a struggle for supremacy with Ana Pauker and Vasile Luca, 'Moscow communists' who lacked his advantage of being an ethnic Romanian; to bolster his position, he offered up as a sacrifice Lucreţiu Pătrăşcanu, minister of justice from 1944 to 1948. The latter had aroused the suspicion of the

Russians at the armistice negotiations in September 1944 when, instead of accepting Moscow's terms, he closely questioned some of them (Deletant 1999: 157). He was also guilty of 'chauvinism', a cardinal sin in Stalin's lexicon because in July 1945 and June 1946 he had made two speeches, blaming Hungarian elements for ethnic tensions in Transylvania (Deletant 1999: 171). Pătrăşcanu, a lawyer and one of the few talented intellectuals with a lengthy party history, had also cast doubt on Dej's fitness to steer Romania into the communist future. His liberal education and undogmatic intellect were seen as manifestations of bourgeois irregularity once his isolation in the party became apparent (Hodos 1987: 96). Arrested in 1948, he wasn't placed on trial and executed until 1954.

Dej feared for his own position during the first stirrings of destalinisation. He needed to remove a dangerous rival who had stubbornly refused under torture to confess to a catalogue of imaginary crimes. By now the 'Moscow Communists' Pauker and Luca had been purged and Moscow was still allowing its loyal Stalinist servant a degree of autonomy in implementing the show-trial strategy.

In Bulgaria, the designated victim, the deputy premier, Traicho Kostov, also upset Moscow's scenario by denouncing in open court the charges ranged against him. Like Pătrăşcanu he had fallen foul of Moscow by displaying independence of mind towards the Soviets on at least one occasion. In his case he had questioned the impact of Soviet economic policy on Bulgaria at a Kremlin meeting attended by Stalin (Djilas 1983: 166–7). In 1946–7 the Soviet Union had bought up much of the Bulgarian tobacco crop and its famous attar of roses at very low prices. When the Bulgarians tried to market the rest of their tobacco and rose essence, they were shocked to discover that they were competing against their own products, offered by the Russians on Western markets at less than prevailing world prices (Lendvai 1969: 222). The fact that Kostov was the principal Bulgarian opponent of Tito's plan for a South Slav union made no difference to his fate (Hodos 1987: 17). But preparations for his trial were delayed because the ailing Dimitrov refused all pressure to implicate Kostov, his closest associate for 30 years. Only after Dimitrov was removed to Moscow and confined to a hospital from which he never emerged again, could the trial proceed as planned (Hodos 1987: 21).

Everywhere except in Albania, purge victims were usually rehabilitated with the blessing of Moscow. Xoxe remained a traitor because he proposed to end Albania's independence. Support for this view even came from Albania's leading writer Ismail Kadare after he fled from the communist regime in 1990. What was significant about Xoxe to a writer widely-tipped as a future Nobel laureate was that he was 'of Slavic origin, sworn enemy of the intelligentsia, cruelty incarnate, ugly, short, unpolished' (Kadare 1995: 124).

Without the purges it would still have been an uphill struggle for the leaders of parties usually imposed by force to obtain popular legitimacy. But, in their wake, the political credibility-gap was widened and the instability of many of the satellite regimes deepened. Trouble also ensued with the partial rehabilitation of Tito in the mid-1950s; earlier, leaders had been required to vie with each other in denouncing Tito's betrayal of socialism and his involvement with imperialism (Fejtö 1974: 53). The Peoples Democracies' ability to command popular respect was further eroded when, one by one, they were required to make their peace with yesterday's top renegade.

But it was the irrational economic system imposed by Stalin which probably most damaged communist prospects in the Balkans and central Europe. The requirement to adopt a system of planned industrialization based on the unbalanced development of heavy industry irrespective of local conditions, proved a recipe for economic obsolescence.

The operation of the Stalinist command system, in its pristine form, has perhaps never been better described than by Paul Lendvai:

> In the Stalinist economic system, millions of economic decisions were taken on the basis of faulty data derived from an irrational pricing system and coordinated by a centralized high command through a myriad of orders. The main features were: political interference at all levels, suppression of initiative, and the fact that the orders issued from the center were not binding on those above, but had to be implemented without question by those below. (Lendvai 1969: 96)

Of all the communist states, the Balkan ones were probably most damaged by Stalinist orthodoxy, because their mainly agricultural economies were least equipped to cope with its demands. Stalinism not only greatly weakened the USSR and its satellites *vis-à-vis* the USA and Western Europe but its emphasis on self-sufficiency persuaded dogmatic communists in the Balkans to revive the nationalist political cultures of their societies. In nearly every case, it resulted in quarrels with the Soviet Union about what should be the priorities shaping communist policy in their countries.

YUGOSLAVIA: BETWEEN EAST AND WEST

The new collective leadership installed in the Kremlin following Stalin's death in March 1953 knew that the relationship with the satellites based on terror and servility could not go on indefinitely. Once Nikita Khruschev established his authority as the new Soviet party leader, he looked for a way in which Soviet domination of the bloc could be combined with an increasing degree of pragmatic flexibility (Gati 1990: 35).

In particular, Khruschev made it an early priority to try and mend the quarrel with Yugoslavia's Marshal Tito which had badly weakened Soviet authority within the communist family. The new Soviet leadership feared that Stalin's anti-Tito vendetta might push Yugoslavia into the Western camp. Indeed President Eisenhower entertained hopes of enticing Yugoslavia into NATO and Dulles, his Secretary of State, hoped that Tito could 'be convinced to inspire, if not lead, a Titoist liberation movement in the satellites' (Lees 1996: 122).

The Americans relied on the lever of aid to consolidate their links with Belgrade. Western aid, predominantly American, in the form of loans, grants, and surplus sales totalling $2.5 billion, was given to Yugoslavia during a critical period. It helped to save the country from economic collapse, if not outright famine in some places (Lendvai 1969: 101). Almost one-third of the package consisted of military supplies meant to strengthen Tito's army in the event of a Soviet-led invasion which Stalin was preparing before the outbreak of the Korean War in June 1950 directed his attention eastwards. In May 1953, on Yugoslavia's airforce day, Tito (flanked by US diplomats and their country's military hardware) referred to the USA, Britain and France as 'our allies' (Lees 1996: 129). On 9 August 1954 Yugoslavia signed a treaty with Greece and Turkey in which each of them pledged political and military aid if one of the others came under attack, the form it took to be determined by consultation (Vukadinović 1994: 188). All three countries felt threatened by the Soviet Union and since 1952 Greece and Turkey had been members of NATO.

But Moscow's wooing of Belgrade caused Tito to scale down his rapprochement with the West. Khruschev's visit to Yugoslavia in 1955 when he effectively atoned for the sins of his predecessor, led to a normalisation of relations between these two estranged communist states. Tito easily saw the advantage of remaining independent from the contending power blocs. Thereafter, enthusiasm for trilateral Balkan cooperation faded and the Balkan Pact was quietly shelved.

If the stand-off between Moscow and Belgrade had continued, it is unlikely that the USA would have interfered unduly in Yugoslav internal politics or tried to dominate its foreign policy (Campbell 1967: 163). Throughout the Cold War, Washington was not squeamish about backing authoritarian regimes if they kept their distance from, or were hostile to, the Soviet Union. But to insist that Tito forfeit his monopoly of power by introducing democratic mechanisms might only have resulted in the weakening of his authority (Beloff 1985: 161). The USA and its European allies never asked Tito to reconsider his one-man role at the head of what was still very much a police state. When the former top communist Milovan Djilas was imprisoned in 1954 after failing to persuade his colleagues to move from communism to western social democracy, his case was ignored by the Western powers (except by left-wingers in the British Labour Party). Radio Free Europe also refrained from broadcasting to Yugoslavia in order to provide uncensored news to Yugoslavs. The psychological impact of this radio station may have been very important. It helped its target audiences to refrain from identifying with the regimes that oppressed them even when the West continued to negotiate with them (Korné 1999). The failure to create a Yugoslav department of Radio Free Europe may have weakened the long-term opposition to communism in a country where communist dogmatists would make a comeback in the 1980s when the Tito era finally ended (Korné 1999: ii).

The West obtained consolation from Tito's willingness to modify the communist economic system, apparently in important ways. In 1954 most land was back in private hands (though with a ten hectare upper limit on private holdings) (Lendvai 1969: 87). The regime's ideologist, Edvard Kardelj, explained the new departure in a 1954 Oslo lecture. Both 'classic bourgeois democracy' and centralist, bureaucratic state socialism were being rejected. Yugoslav socialism was to be based on 'direct democracy guaranteeing the maximum amount of workers self-government through managerial bodies' (Fejtö 1974: 55). A guarded admirer described the Yugoslav path as 'a unique series of experiments in economics and social development' undertaken by a communist regime plotting a course separate from Moscow (Lendvai 1969: 90).

Under the Yugoslav system of 'self-management', factories were supposedly owned by workers and their councils rather than by the state (Silber and Little 1995: 34). This was an essentially syndicalist idea, dressed in appropriate quotes from Marx and Lenin (Lendvai 1969: 87). It elicited respectful attention from economists and social scientists in the West keen to explore ways of reconciling two social systems whose antagonism had the world poised on the brink of war. But it was only after the Tito era ended that the often inefficient and contrived nature of the self-management system came to be widely recognised. The political decentralization permitted in the context of one-party rule allowed ambitious party leaders in Yugoslavia's self-governing republics and provinces to shape self-management around their own short-term political requirements. As a result, innumerable 'political' factories went up in the 1960s and 1970s which fuelled an economic crisis that in turn led to political rivalry along inter-republican lines which would blow apart the Yugoslav federation after 1989.

Tito's brilliantly executed balancing-act between East and West brought practical economic assistance mainly from the West which helped to shore up a jerry-built economic edifice. In 1956 he declared that 'I feel at home in the Soviet Union because we are part of the same family: the family of socialism' (Beloff 1985: 158). But his Western backers were not alarmed by his re-emphasising the theme of 'proletarian internationalism'. Washington was satisfied that Tito remained his own man when he refused to join the Soviet-led military alliance called the Warsaw Pact, created in 1955. The pact allowed Soviet troops to remain on the territory of any member state to protect it against foreign (i.e. Western) aggression (Gati 1990: 83). Tito did not wish to get entangled in an alliance system which, he was well aware, was ultimately designed to protect Soviet interests. Instead he carved out a new source of influence by rallying the non-aligned countries which wished to remain aloof from the contending Cold War blocs. Yugoslavia's leadership of the non-aligned movement, composed of neutralist countries like India and Egypt, gave Yugoslavia a degree of international stature which no Balkan country has ever enjoyed since the era of national states began after 1830. The USA was suspicious of the true neutralism of this bloc and, in the mid-1950s, it stepped up military and economic assistance to Belgrade, in the hope that Tito's energies could be deflected elsewhere (Lees 1996: 147). In the second half of the 1950s the Eisenhower administration began to reflect that Tito had derived more from the West's strategy than the USA had (Lees 1996: xv). Congress was increasingly reluctant to release further funds as it appeared that Yugoslavia's willingness to cooperate with Western defence plans was further away than ever (Lees 1996: xiv). In 1958 both countries agreed to suspend the military aid programme. But the USA saw Yugoslavia's detachment from the Soviet orbit as an important victory and economic assistance channelled through international finance organizations was supported in order to preserve Yugoslavia's independence. Leading Western officials such as Britain's Sir Duncan Wilson, author of a favourable biography of Tito, and George Kennan, US ambassador from 1961 to 1963, as well as influential figures of the 1980s such as Lawrence Eagleburger (second secretary in Belgrade, 1962–65 and US ambassador in 1977–81) and Brent Scowcroft (assistant air attaché in 1959–61) could be found ready to back favoured treatment for Yugoslavia, (in some cases after Tito's departure) (Woodward 1995: 155).

WESTERN MISCALCULATIONS IN GREECE AND CYPRUS

Generally, the West behaved with more circumspection in Yugoslavia than in other Southeast European states where it felt it had major security interests: Greece and later Cyprus. Following the defeat of the Greek communists in the 1947–9 civil war, the USA played virtually a pro-consular role in Greek affairs. State security organizations had been created and run by Americans, some of them Greek-Americans, until native Greeks whom Washington trusted could be put in their place (Murtagh 1994: 18). Greece was one of the first counties where the USA applied the Cold War logic that there were only pro-communists and anti-communists and that the pedigree of the latter was unimportant if they were capable of containing Marxism. Washington thus embraced the Greek Right, which included a pro-fascist wartime collaborationist element which acquired influence in an army purged of liberals as well as radicals (Murtagh 1994: 19). Right-wing parties were in the ascendancy that were committed to the survival of the same Balkan oligarchical politics widespread in the region before 1945. Greece retained a heavily politicised and centralized state bureaucracy which was recruited through an archaic education system (Close 1995: 126). Deputies of the parliamentary Right mediated between the bureaucracy and the public, being ever ready to intercede with the former on behalf of their clients. The Right's partisanship, hunger for the political spoils and lack of administrative ability surrounded Greek politics with uncertainty. A semblance of stability was provided with the emergence of the Greek Rally under General Alexander Papagos. In 1952 he succeeded in uniting the Right and attracting enough centre voters to win a large electoral majority and achieve the goal of single-party government. His reputation as a nationalist enabled Papagos to strengthen relations with Turkey. A defence treaty was signed in 1953 and the position of the Turkish minority in Greece was improved. The Americans, inordinately concerned with any revival of leftist influence in Greece, did not show equivalent vigilance in ensuring that bilateral ties between two states crucial for the security of NATO's Eastern Mediterranean flank remained in good repair. Meanwhile, Britain was prepared to stoke up Greek–Turkish state rivalry if turning two NATO members into unfriendly allies could help maintain its control of the island of Cyprus.

Cyprus lies 40 miles from the south coast of Turkey and 70 miles from the Lebanon. In 1960 its 600,000 inhabitants were 80% Greek and 18% Turkish. The Turks are descendants of Anatolian immigrants who arrived after the Ottoman conquest in 1571. Until 1974, the two peoples 'were interspersed throughout the island, some living in mixed villages, others in exclusively Greek or Turkish communities. They coexisted peacefully but remained socially distinct, participating in each other's ceremonies and cooperating in a variety of economic arrangements, but rarely inter-marrying or taking joint political initiatives' (Souter 1984: 657–8). Since the 1930s the Greeks had been overwhelmingly committed to *enosis* (union with Greece) while the leaders of the Turkish minority swung behind the idea of partitioning the island. *Enosis* was endorsed by the Papagos government, but Britain was unwilling to cede control even to a NATO ally like Greece. It wished to develop the island as a strategic base so as to defend its remaining interests in the Middle East which, with the handover of territories elsewhere, revolved around having a steady supply of oil from the Persian Gulf. Sir Anthony Eden, British Foreign Secretary from 1951 to 1955 and Prime Minister from 1955 to 1957, summarised the position as follows: 'No Cyprus, no certain facilities to protect our oil. No oil, unemployment and hunger in Britain. It is as simple as that' (O'Malley and Craig 1999: 7, n. 16).

Ernest Bevin, Eden's predecessor as Foreign Secretary, had offered Cyprus self-government under a liberal constitution but without the option of moving to complete independence. In 1946 he admitted in an internal memorandum that 'we have starved the Cypriots, treated them very badly, and must mend our ways' (O'Malley and Craig 1999: 9). Harsh colonial conditions had encouraged the rise of the communist-led AKEL party which, in 1946, won control of 4 of the island's 6 town councils. The strength of the Cypriot Left dissuaded the USA from persuading Britain to work out a compromise that could allow Cypriot self-determination while protecting minority rights. Anglo-American nervousness increased when the head of the island's Greek Orthodox church, Archbishop Makarios III, assumed the political leadership of the Greek majority in 1950. Instead of being a counterweight to AKEL, Makarios was prepared to work with the local left and mobilise world opinion (at which he proved extremely skilful) in order to bring about a colonial withdrawal. Addressing a large AKEL audience in the early 1950s, Makarios said that: 'In our effort to win the freedom we desire we shall stretch out both our right hand and our left to take the help offered by East and West' (words presumably noted by the CIA) (O'Malley and Craig 1999: 12). Tito could be allowed to play this balancing role because his non-aligned communism benefited the West, but there was no desire to allow a prelate, who soon attracted great animosity in Washington as well as London, to play a similar role.

In 1951 Athens offered Britain four bases in Greece and any facilities it wanted in Cyprus if it would pave the way for self-determination. A meeting between Eden and Papagos in 1953 went badly. Eden warned the Greek Premier that *enosis* would never happen and he even goaded him by asking why he did not ask for Alexandria or New York where there were also many Greeks (Mayes 1981: 53).

In 1954, Henry Hopkinson, the British colonial minister said in parliament: 'it has always been understood and agreed that there are certain territories in the Commonwealth which, owing to their special circumstances, never expect to be fully independent ... I have said that the question of the abrogation of British sovereignty cannot arise ...' (Mayes 1981: 54–5).

In Athens official anger was shown when the Greek government issued a stamp in which a page of Hansard (the official report of British parliamentary debates) was obliterated by a large ink blot. Soon Greece decided to raise the Cyprus question at the United Nations and in 1955 Greek-Cypriot civil disobedience spilled over into an anti-British guerrilla campaign led by General George Grivas. Britain had already decided to weaken the Greek position by encouraging Turkey to take an interest in Cyprus. Under Atatürk and his successor, İsmet İnönü, a policy of strict non-interference in areas outside Turkish state boundaries had prevailed. But a nationalist flavour re-entered Turkish political life in 1950 with the election of Adnan Menderes, who appealed to conservative domestic interests—especially in the Islamic camp. C.M. Woodhouse, a member of the British intelligence service and later a Conservative MP, admitted in his memoirs that Harold Macmillan, a leading figure in the Eden government, 'was urging us to stir up the Turks in order to neutralise the Greek agitation' (Hitchens 1997: 43). A Turkish foreign ministry official, interviewed on Britain's Granada television in 1984, recalled being approached by the British chargé d'affaires in Ankara at an early stage of the *enosis* campaign and being told that the Cyprus situation 'was getting out of hand ... What was Turkey going to do about it?' (Hitchens 1997: 3).

In June 1955 Eden decided to hold an international conference in order to change the perception of the Cyprus problem as an internal one and instead highlight growing antagonism between Greece and Turkey (O'Malley and Craig 1999: 19, n. 8). Selwyn Lloyd, a cabinet colleague, suggested in July 1955 that: 'Throughout the negotiations our aim would be to bring the Greeks up against the Turkish refusal to accept enosis and so condition them to accept a solution which would leave sovereignty in our hands' (O'Malley and Craig 1999: 21, n. 15). When the conference opened in London on 29 August 1955, the Turks threatened to treat any change in Cyprus's status as an abandonment of the 1923 Treaty of Lausanne and promised to issue counter-claims against Greece in western Thrace and the Dodecanese islands. Greek astonishment at Turkey's unexpectedly hardline stance was compounded by the eruption of riots in Istanbul, Izmir, and Ankara during the conference. Turkish mobs attacked Greek as well as Armenian and Jewish property causing $300 million worth of damage. The riots appeared carefully synchronised, taking place simultaneously in these far-flung cities (O'Malley and Craig 1999: 23). At his trial in 1960, following his overthrow by the Turkish military, Menderes was accused of having fomented the riots in order to impress the British government with his intransigence. The long-standing Greek presence in the cities of western Turkey drew to a gradual end as a result of these pogroms. Even worse was the collapse in Greek–Turkish relations that followed twenty years of relatively good bilateral ties. Britain had prodded the Turks into getting involved in the Cyprus dispute without paying much heed to the explosive consequences; Britain's interests in the Middle East took precedence over maintaining NATO amity in the alliance's vital southeastern flank.

1956: EASTERN AND WESTERN IMPERIALISM AT WORK

Britain's Middle Eastern interests assumed critical importance after the Egyptian leader, Colonel Gamel Abdul Nasser, nationalised the Suez Canal in July 1955. Eden saw an unpredictable Arab nationalist regime in charge of this vital waterway as a direct threat to Western interests comparable to the rise of Hitler. He obtained the agreement of France, increasingly beleaguered fighting a colonial war in Algeria, to prepare for an assault on Egypt. Israel was to mount a diversionary attack on Egypt to give the pretext for an Anglo-French intervention meant to force both sides to push back from the canal. This plan was put into action at the end of October 1956. In the words of Bennett Kovrig, this 'ill-conceived and cynically-timed adventure effectively incapacitated the Western Alliance and comforted the Kremlin at the moment of greatest challenge to both East and West in Europe in postwar history' (Kovrig 1991: 102).

Neither the British nor the French were deflected from their assault on Egypt by the popular uprising in Hungary against Soviet-led communist rule. In October 1956 even the newly-installed party chief Imre Nagy was swept along by popular fervour and called for a withdrawal of Soviet troops, declaring his country neutral on 1 November 1956. By now, Soviet forces were seeking to regain control of the country to impose a reliable native communist regime. Anglo-American disunity over Suez meant that the likelihood of any Western military intervention was remote. The priority of defending the integrity of the Soviet bloc was uppermost (Kovrig 1991: 87); Khruschev hoped that the global uproar created by the Suez affair would eclipse the propaganda damage suffered by the Soviet Union as it felt obliged to send in the Red Army to maintain its grip on a supposedly fraternal socialist country like Hungary.

To bring Eden to his senses, the USA started selling sterling, causing a currency crisis in Britain, and refused to help with its shortfall in oil supplies. Eisenhower even refused to see the British Defence Minister Selwyn Lloyd when he arrived in Washington to try and explain the UK position (O'Malley and Craig 1999: 45). Dulles, in a phone conversation with the President on 30 October 1956 remarked: 'What a great tragedy it is, just when the whole Soviet policy is collapsing the British and French are doing the same thing in the Arab world' (Kovrig 1991: 94). Only during the sharp transatlantic disagreements that became public in 1993–4 as NATO dithered over how to halt the war in Bosnia being waged mainly against unarmed civilians, would Anglo-American disunity again plunge to such depths.

The low key US response to the Hungarian uprising acutely contrasted with the tone of American propaganda on Radio Free Europe (RFE) and the statements of contenders in the 1952 US presidential election, when East Europeans were promised help with liberalising their countries short of direct NATO military intervention. Since 1950 the CIA had been training East Europeans for paramilitary operations in the satellite states, but it was not given the go-ahead to mount covert operations in Hungary during the critical autumn of 1956 (Kovrig 1991: 92–3). According to George Urban, a future director of RFE, the Munich-based station created the impression that action was unlikely to be far behind US words of support for Hungarian anti-communist freedom fighters (Urban 1997: 213–15). One of these Hungarians, Ferenc Kobol, said to the author James Michener that:

> Words like 'freedom', 'struggle for national honour', 'rollback', and 'liberation' have meanings ... Believe me when I say that you cannot tell Hungarians or Bulgarians or Poles every day for six years to love liberty and then sit back philosophically and say, 'but the Hungarians and Bulgarians and Poles mustn't do anything about liberty. They must remember that we're only using words' ...
>
> If America wants to flood Eastern and Central Europe with these words, it must acknowledge an ultimate responsibility for them. Otherwise you are inciting nations to commit suicide. (Michener 1975: 238)

The Hungarian Stalinist regime of Matyas Rákosi, which had been swept away in the first stages of the Hungarian revolution, had its counterparts in Albania, Bulgaria and Romania. These Balkan communist chiefs must have been relieved by the outcome of the crisis. It suggested that if the West was unwilling to risk a confrontation to roll back Soviet power in Hungary, it was even less likely to aid anti-communists in the Balkans where, in the Second World War, the western Allies had already been averse to taking bold policy initiatives.

After the Cold War, George Urban also saw the Western behaviour at the time of Suez and Hungary as presaging how it would respond to the internal wars which erupted following the break-up of Yugoslavia:

> Looking back over the last four decades, it is hard to avoid the conclusion that very little has changed. The sorry spectacle of the fumbling Dwight D. Eisenhower and ham-fisted Anthony Eden—which filled Western television screens in those not very distant days—offered a preview of what was to follow in the Balkans thirty-five years on, with George Bush, James Baker, John Major, Douglas Hurd, Cyrus Vance, Malcolm Rifkind, Douglas Hogg, (Lord) David Owen, and Boutros Boutros-Ghali leading western policy in Bosnia into first human disaster and then lasting ignominy ...
>
> In 1956—as later in the Balkans—the West was unready for action but expert at obfuscation. Caught by surprise by every change in the fortunes of communism, it remained a spectator. It was caught unawares by Yugoslavia's

expulsion from the Cominform, by the 1953 Berlin uprising, by the 1956 Polish upheavals, by the Hungarian revolution, by the construction of the Berlin Wall, by the 1968 occupation of Czechoslovakia, by the rise and suppression of Solidarity, by the invasion of Afghanistan, by the demolition of the Berlin Wall, by the collapse of East Germany, and finally by the fall of the Soviet empire itself. (Urban 1997: 244–5)

But the Soviets could not rely on low profile and unimaginative western policy towards Eastern Europe in order to extend their control over restless satellites. The model of bilateral relations established by Stalin, requiring unconditional subordination to key Soviet policies, was still very much intact. But satellite leaders all had cause to resent the periodically clumsy and overbearing interventions in their states' affairs mounted by Khruschev. Since terror had largely been discarded as a weapon of control, they were in a stronger position to ignore or override Soviet orders.

NATIONAL STALINISM IN THE BALKANS

In 1956 the Soviets certainly did not expect that Romania, hitherto one of the most placid of satellites, would shortly challenge Moscow's right to control the evolution of the communist bloc. In the aftermath of the Hungarian revolt Gheorghe Gheorghiu-Dej, who had been in unchallenged control of party and state since 1952, took with him to Budapest 2,000 Hungarian-speaking party activists in order to help reorganize the Hungarian communist party. Silviu Brucan, a high state official in the Dej era, is in no doubt that Moscow's request for help was proof not only of the confidence the Soviet leaders placed in Dej but also of their high appreciation for his political skills (Brucan 1993: 53).

In 1958 the Soviet Union had sufficient confidence in Dej to remove all its troops from Romania. Six years later, the Romanian security and intelligence services became the first such agencies of a Warsaw Pact country to get rid of counsellors from the Soviet KGB. Indeed, Romania's foreign intelligence service was the only one to shake off direct Soviet supervision before the collapse of communism in 1989 (Deletant 1999: 285). But, by Dej's last years in power, relations with the Soviet Union had changed. Romania was plotting an increasingly independent course in economic and foreign policy and managing to place limits on the degree of Soviet interference it would allow.

The mutual dislike felt by Khruschev and Dej, which started to come to the fore in 1957, may have helped to engineer the rift. Romanian communists found it hard to forget that the USSR had plundered the country in the late 1940s and forced them to sign trading deals heavily weighted in favour of Moscow. The unequal treatment was still continuing. Between 1956 and 1960 East European countries as a whole received Soviet loans and credits of more than $2 billion: Romania's share of the total was a mere $95 million (Lendvai 1969: 286). Paul Lendvai has written that Khruschev's impetuous behaviour, 'lacking imagination and consistency and pervaded by hostility and features of betrayal, did not deter but enflamed the seething resentment the Romanian leaders had harboured so long' (Lendvai 1969: 305). Dej, like Hoxha in Albania, feared that Khruschev might try and remove him as a relic of Stalinism (Deletant 1999: 281). It was resistance to destalinisation which would lead both countries 'to the brink of desatellization' (Fejtö 1974: 34).

Matters came to a head after Khruschev decided to revive the Council for Mutual Economic Assistance (Comecon) and turn it into an instrument for planning and economic specification in the eastern bloc. He had grown alarmed at the slow progress in economic integration occurring, especially when compared with the spectacular advances being made by the European Economic Community (EEC). In order for a socialist economic community to emerge which would rival the capitalist West, he proposed in 1962 that a supranationalist planning authority be created. A Comecon-wide investment plan would be drawn up to decide which sectors of economic activity each country should specialise in. This meant a clear move away from the pattern established under Stalin whereby each country strove to industrialise and make itself largely self-sufficient without paying undue attention to the profitability of newly-created industries (Fejtö 1974: 158–9).

Romania had potentially some of the best arable land in the Soviet bloc. But its leaders did not want it merely to be a supplier of agricultural produce to the rest of the bloc. This was the role wine-producing Moldavia (formerly the Romanian province of Bessarabia) had within the Soviet Union. The retention of a numerically large peasantry and the failure to swiftly industrialise the country and create an industrial proletariat which would identify with a wholly state-run economy potentially weakened the basis of communist rule.

The Yugoslav model, whereby Tito still channelled huge resources into heavy industry while keeping his distance from Moscow, was one that the Romanian communists could not fail to ignore. In the late 1950s both countries embarked on the construction of the huge Iron

Gate navigation and power project which had long been dreamt of on both sides of the Danube. This ambitious project was worked out on a bilateral basis without any Soviet help or reference to Comecon (Campbell 1967: 107).

When Khruschev refused to desist with his integrationist ideas, the Romanians dug in their heels. In March 1963 the central committee unanimously agreed that Romania based 'her co-operation with other socialist countries on the principles of national sovereignty and independence, equality of rights, fraternal aid, and national interests' (Fejtö 1974: 160). Since these principles had been written into the declaration of the world's communist parties gathered at their 1960 conference in Moscow, Romania was able to use them to advantage. At the July 1963 Comecon summit, the Soviets and their supporters reluctantly agreed to shelve their plans for economic integration.

Romania was demonstrating to the world that it was possible to attain substantial independence in spite of adverse geopolitical conditions (Lendvai 1969: 2). A number of factors were on the side of the country's leadership. A period of détente followed the 1962 Cuban missile crisis and the USSR was reluctant to crack down heavily on a wayward ally because of the impact it might have in the West as well as in newly independent states. Romania remained firmly orthodox in its internal course, which reassured the Kremlin. Moreover, the extent of Soviet tolerance for communist dissent in the Balkans would prove greater than in the northern tier of satellites where Soviet core interests lay (Gati 1990: 79). Economically, the Balkans were also of marginal importance to the Soviet Union. In the mid-1960s the combined share of the four Balkan communist states in Soviet foreign trade totalled only 15.3%, which was less than that of East Germany alone (Lendvai 1969: 532).

Dej was assisted in his bid for partial independence by the fact that Khruschev was an increasingly weakened leader. He had enjoyed few major policy successes, if the Soviet Union's achievements in space are put aside, and was subject to frequent attempts to oust him, one of which succeeded in October 1964. The increasingly bitter quarrel between the Soviet Union and China also increased Romania's leverage. When Khruschev once again attempted to get Dej to fall into line behind Soviet centralism, his response was to get his central committee to pass a resolution on 27 April 1964 which was at once viewed as a virtual declaration of independence (Fejtö 1974: 162). Victory seemed to go to Romania in August 1964 when Anastas Mikoyan, a top member of the

Soviet Politburo, publicly stated that friendship between his country and Romania was based on 'mutual respect for national independence and sovereignty ... and non-interference in internal affairs' (Fejtö 1974: 163).

Dej had been asked by Khruschev to choose between the Soviet Union and what had been the Soviet model until the end of the 1950s. He chose the latter which could be summed up as neo-Stalinism at home and Titoism abroad (Crampton 1994: 313). For Albania, the decline of Soviet power was revealed by the humiliating break with China which enabled Enver Hoxha to seek a new protector. Mao's China, like Albania, was refusing to jettison the Stalinist legacy. Albania took its side in the feud rocking the socialist family. In November 1960, after a stormy four-hour meeting with Hoxha in Moscow, a furious Khruschev reportedly said to him: 'I find it easier to get on with Macmillan than with you' (Fejtö 1974: 153). Hoxha, and his then right-hand-man Mehmet Shehu fled Moscow before the end of the world communist summit they had been attending, preferring the safety of travelling as much of the way as possible in the capitalist West than on trusting their fate in a Soviet plane (Halliday 1986: 227). In 1961, the 22nd Soviet party congress denounced the anti-Soviet attitudes of the Albanian leader but China's Chou En-lai defended Hoxha: 'Any public ... condemnation of a fraternal party ... is an attack on the unity of the socialist camp'. On the same day the Albanian central committee declared: 'We shall not retreat, and we shall not give way before the slanderous attacks, blackmail and pressure of Nikita Khruschev and others' (Fejtö 1974: 155).

Albania retreated into isolation, being the first state in the world to suppress organized religion. In 1967, Hoxha insisting that 'the only religion for an Albanian was Albanianism' (Lendvai 1969: 205). Even China was eventually found wanting after US President Nixon's visit to Peking in 1971. According to Hoxha, Mao was never a Marxist but was merely good at disguising his attachment to atavistic Chinese philosophical trends (Halliday 1986: 253). On the 40th anniversary of the liberation in 1984, Hoxha told the Albanian people:

> The Titoites, the Soviet revisionists and those of the countries of Eastern Europe, and Mao Zedong's China had ulterior, hostile, enslaving aims. We tore the mask from them and told them bluntly that Albania was not for sale for a handful of rags, or for a few rubles, dinars or yuan. (Halliday 1986: 255)

If what Hoxha accused Mao of is true, then the Albanian leader might in fairness also be seen as a primarily indigenous figure for whom the trappings of Marxism-Leninism were a handy disguise for traditional tyranny. François Fejtö viewed Hoxha as the heir to bloodthirsty Ottoman lords like Ali Pasha who used to rule in the name of the Sublime Porte (Fejtö 1974: 129). Periodic purges ensured that he remained one of Europe's most durable communist leaders. In 1981 Premier Mehmet Shehu met a violent death, from his own hands according to Hoxha, but more likely as a result of a shoot-out in the Politburo. Hoxha claimed that he had committed suicide after being subjected to severe criticism for arranging the betrothal of his son to a woman whose family contained 'six to seven war criminals', thus undermining the credibility of the party (Halliday 1986: 327–8). The truth or otherwise of this tale is immaterial. It shows how deeply clan mentalities lay at the base of a communist regime; indeed in 1962, of the 58 members of the central committee, no fewer than 28 were related, and 8 were married to each other (Carver 1998: 91). Thus, behind an egalitarian façade, a small number of families wielded power and enjoyed inordinate privileges.

It has been alleged that a factor contributing to the split was disagreement over how to handle the Kosovo issue (Halliday 1986: 330). Hoxha had not actively promoted the irredentist cause among the Albanian population in Kosovo. Albania remained surprisingly tight-lipped during the long years when Tito's iron-fisted interior minister, Alexander Ranković cracked down on the Yugoslav province's Albanian majority. Following Ranković's disgrace in 1965, a thaw occurred and anti-Albanian discrimination greatly eased. But when Albanian discontent at the pace of economic development led to rioting in 1981, it was an opportunity for a profoundly nationalist regime to express its backing for the unification of Albanians in one state. But Albania was reluctant to trade the isolation which had nurtured a cruel and eccentric regime like Hoxha's for a policy of active irredentism which could have destabilised it. Refugees from Kosovo were usually detained if not handed back to the Yugoslav authorities. The Hoxha regime was determined to minimise contact between its population and co-ethnics from the more open society in Kosovo where private property was permitted and religion was not banned (Meier 1999: 30).

It is perhaps revealing about the underlying nature of Hoxha's regime that the Western regime with which it enjoyed closest relations in the late 1960s was the Colonels' right-wing dictatorship in Greece. Diplomatic relations with Athens were renewed for the first time since 1939, and it was to Romania that the Greek dictator Papadopoulos paid his first foreign state-visit. The Bulgarians emphasised 'peaceful co-existence among states of differing social systems', Balkan communists perhaps feeling that their own regime's global profile was bound to improve with a quasi-fascist regime in the neighbourhood (Wolff 1974: 610). But it may well be that tyrants of the left found it much easier to get down to business with their right-wing counterparts than with pussyfooting democrats and perhaps, as communist Romania eventually showed, there were deeper affinities between the forces of radical left and right at work as well.

THE BULGARIAN EXCEPTION

Bulgaria was the only satellite state never to challenge Soviet hegemony. In the 1960s the Soviet ambassador sat on the platform on all major political occasions and, on festive occasions, the streets and public buildings were hung with giant portraits of the members of the Soviet Politburo side by side with those of their Bulgarian counterparts (Lendvai 1969: 206). Indeed on two occasions (in 1962–3 and in 1973) Todor Zhivkov even proposed that Bulgaria be incorporated into the Soviet Union as the sixteenth of its federal republics (Brown 1992: 125 n. 9).

The history of the Bulgarian Communist Party (BCP) may explain the absence of a Titoite or Hoxhaist heresy. Within a few years of the Russian revolution, Bulgaria would possess one of Europe's largest communist parties. Persecution at home in the 1920s forced thousands of militants to flee to the Soviet Union where they were the second-largest group of political exiles after the Poles (Oren 1973: 25).

In the Second World War, the BCP had grown too week to emulate the resistance exploits of Tito's Partisans. Relentless surveillance at home and rivalry between Dimitrov and left-wing rivals, who had gained control of the BCP when Dimitrov was abroad, blunted its effectiveness. After his prestige in the worldwide communist movement was reinforced by his performance in the 1933 Reichstag trial, Dimitrov was able to crush his numerous rivals. In the Stalinist terror of the late 1930s several hundred Bulgarian communists were liquidated. Those 'working in the Ukraine were accused of no less a crime than that of having conspired to annexe the southern Ukraine to Bulgaria' (Oren 1973: 37).

During the war, King Boris had denied the BCP a rallying-point by being careful not to declare war on the Soviet Union. In September 1944, power fell into its hands suddenly and unheroically in a coup mounted by a few junior officers with the acquiescence of the minister of war. Thereafter the Kremlin choreographed the communist takeover, allowing local communists little discretionary power. By executing BCP general-secretary Traicho Kostov in 1949, 'Stalin intended to reveal the depth of the abyss to everyone under him on the Bulgarian communist scene. If Kostov could become a traitor overnight, there was no immunity for anyone' (Oren 1973: 108).

Bulgaria, from 1950 to 1954, was ruled by Vulko Chervenkov, a ruthless Stalinist functionary. Chervenkov was a model satellite boss in the eyes of Kremlin hardliners. From 1925 to 1946, he had lived in the Soviet Union. He graduated from a Soviet secret police academy and his complete dependability (allied to his genuine interest in Bulgarian and Russian literature) enabled him to be placed in charge of the educational and propaganda system of the Comintern (Brown 1970: 24; Oren 1973: 111).

Chervenkov initiated the changes which turned a country of tens of thousands of peasant smallholders into one dominated by about 975 huge collective farms at the end of the 1950s. The impact of collectivisation on the peasant psyche may have been more devastating in Bulgaria than in any other part of the Balkans. The peasantry's attachment to the land and its egalitarian outlook had bred a strong political consciousness in which anti-urban feeling was much in evidence. In the 1950s the countryside became a colony of an elite urbanising the country at a furious pace. Peasant production was harnessed in order to promote the capacity required for industrialization which placed the BCP in a long line of Balkan rulers intent on squeezing as much wealth from the countryside as possible (Oren 1973: 115).

On the international front, Bulgaria pursued a militant anti-Western line. Protestant American missionaries and educators had exercised strong, though limited, influence on middle-class families (Barker 1948: 14). But this source of westernisation was curtailed even before 1950 when Bulgaria demanded the recall of the US ambassador Donald Heath; in the Kostov trial, he had been accused by the prosecutor of sabotage and espionage. After refusing the demand, Washington broke off diplomatic relations. In 1956 after Kostov was partly rehabilitated, the Sofia authorities informed the US that the charges against Heath were also groundless and diplomatic relations were restored in 1959.

Revolutionary aggression extended to the treatment of politically uncongenial neighbouring states and minorities. In 1949, after Vladimir Poptomov, a communist who also had an IMRO background, was appointed foreign minister, the Macedonian question was rekindled. Official propaganda asserted that the Macedonian people were identical to, and inseparable from, the Bulgarian people (Oren 1973: 120). The Sofia press portrayed Yugoslavia's Tito as a 'fat, idle boaster' and cartoons depicted him as a Goering-figure 'dreaming about new orders' (Kareeva 1998: 47).

Relations with Turkey were disturbed in 1950–1 when around 150,000 Turks were pushed out of Bulgaria. Many were from the southern Dobruja, the most fertile part of Bulgaria, which was almost emptied of its Turkish population; a few thousand Roma were also added to the exodus (Oren 1973: 122).

Stalin's death was followed by signs of restiveness in Bulgaria, though not on the scale of other satellites. In May 1953 a riot and strike occurred among the tobacco workers of Plovdiv. Though small it was the first recorded instance of popular resistance to Soviet methods anywhere in the bloc in the post-Stalin era (Brown 1970: 25). It undermined the impression that the Bulgarians en masse passively accepted communism (Brown 1970: 25). In 1954 Chervenkov's power started to drain from him. He retained the premiership but gave up the leadership of the party. He may well have 'misjudged the power balance within the Soviet leadership, selecting Georgi Malenkov as his patron' (Rothschild 1989: 213). Certainly, he now started to lose the power of patronage that control over the nomenklatura entailed (Brown 1970: 25).

Todor Zhivkov, the new 43-year-old general secretary of the BCP, was not considered outstanding leadership material. A home communist of the younger generation, he slowly became a rallying-point for communists of a similar background. From 1954 to 1962 he slowly built up his authority in the party. Chervenkov lost the premiership in 1956 to Anton Yugov, a home communist who, as minister of the interior, had directed the reign of terror against the monarchist elite in the mid-1940s.

The respective rise and decline of Bulgarian hardliners and pragmatists reflected the pace of events in the Soviet 'motherland'. Chervenkov was back as minister of culture following the revival of Soviet orthodoxy occasioned by the crushing of the 1956 Hungarian revolt. But in 1961 he was ousted from all leadership positions following 'Khruschev's resumption of the attack on Stalin's methods and heritage' at the 22nd Congress of the CPSU (Rothschild 1989: 214). At the November 1962 Congress of the BCP, Premier Yugov was stripped of his authority and Chervenkov was expelled from the party. The Congress had been postponed for three months, which suggests that there were sharp inner party disagreements. Indeed, it was again interrupted for several days when Zhivkov abruptly went to Moscow for consultations. It is clear that the Kremlin came down on the side of Zhivkov who now added the post of premiership to that of party chief. The independence of Yugoslavia, the defection of Albania, and the waywardness of the Romanians possibly underscored the need for the Soviet Union to have a reliable Balkan dependency.

Bulgaria gained economically from the close Soviet connection, or at least it was not exploited to the same degree as other satellites. In the late 1960s a western source estimated that the Russians had injected $2 billion, financing one-quarter of Bulgaria's total economic investment (Lendvai 1969: 247). Bulgaria also benefited from Comecon schemes for economic specialisation introduced in the early 1960s. It specialised in the transport sector where by 1973, one-third of its industrial output was located. Its industrial products were mainly low quality but at least the emphasis on low grade chemical and metal production which helped to sink the Romanian economy was avoided in Bulgaria (Crampton 1997: 200).

Zhivkov enjoyed Soviet favour which he repaid with public displays of obsequiousness. But he was more than a colourless local appendage running one of Moscow's more malleable satellites. He had shown cool nerves and tactical skills of a high order by 'removing men of greater stature who were initially far more powerful' (Brown 1970: 173). Nevertheless, during the rest of the 1960s he found it hard to clear out dissidents from the lower echelons of the party.

In 1965, an attempted coup, involving three generals, was nipped in the bud. It suggested that the appeal of the more outwardly egalitarian model of Chinese communism went quite deep in Bulgaria, whose social structure was the most egalitarian in the Balkans (Drezov 2000: 198). The leader of the conspiracy, Ivan Todorov-Gorunya, reportedly committed suicide to avoid arrest. He had been the political commissar of the best known of the wartime partisan groups. He later went on to be a deputy minister and a dominant figure in the Vratsa district, where the partisans had acquired a wartime following (Brown 1970: 175).

It is interesting to speculate what the Soviet response would have been if the coup had succeeded. Would Moscow have regarded Zhivkov as someone too closely connected with the recently deposed Khruschev to be worth rescuing or would the Soviets have intervened with force, if necessary, to correct the situation not unlike the way that France intervened in some of its nominally independent ex-colonies? It is hard to imagine that the Kremlin would have been indifferent to the situation. Indeed, three weeks after the coup was uncovered Mikhail Suslov, Moscow's chief seeker-out of heresy, was in Sofia to see how great was the danger of deviation.

The threat to the regime from the Marxist-Leninist left was much greater than that posed by pro-Western dissidents so noticeable in Central Europe's bloc countries. For the 1963–74 period, the secret police were monitoring over 1,200 communist party members who were engaged in left-wing opposition activities to the Zhivkov regime (Drezov 2000: 198).

Upon combining in his own person the government and party leadership in 1962, Zhivkov expanded his control over the security and intelligence services centred on the interior ministry. He extended this control to the army after the 1965 scare which was followed in 1968 by the uncovering of another conspiracy among pro-Chinese party dissidents. Political and economic controls were relaxed for a while in the mid-1960s. Literature and the arts saw the greatest degree of relaxation and restrictions on travel were eased, though not to the extent seen in Hungary or Poland (Brown 1970: 188–9). In 1965, a system of 'planning from below' was designed to give local enterprises and their managers greater responsibility, but the reaction to the Czechoslovak crisis in 1968 prevented Bulgaria moving in the liberal direction of communist Hungary (Crampton 1997: 198). In 1971 a new constitution confirmed the country's status to be that of a socialist state and Zhivkov now became formal Head of State. But he was careful not to promote a cult of personality at least comparable to that seen in Romania. Bulgaria's deep traditions of social egalitarianism would have made that a risky project. Zhivkov was an autocrat who became de facto ruler for life, but he was accessible and still possessed the common touch. Until the final years of his rule he possessed enough shrewdness not to allow power to go completely to his head (Rothschild 1989: 215).

The humiliating conclusion to Eden's 1956 Suez gamble resulted in Britain scaling down its political ambitions in the Middle East and its military operations in the Eastern Mediterranean. British obduracy was now less likely to stand in the way of a settlement to the Cyprus question. But British leaders found it difficult to strike the right note in their dealings with the parties to the dispute, especially on the Greek side. When the British Colonial Minister, Alan Lennox-Boyd visited Athens in December 1956, the historian and fellow Conservative C.M. Woodhouse wrote that '(H)is breezy, offhand manner, which might have appealed to African chiefs, offended the Greeks' (Woodhouse 1982: 69).

From 1955 to 1963, years when Constantine Karamanlis was Prime Minister, Greece enjoyed political stability. Karamanlis was a moderate on the Cyprus question and the Menderes government in Turkey gradually assumed a less intransigent attitude. Both Greece and Turkey were alert to the Soviet threat. In 1959 their nervousness about the strength of AKEL on the island made them prepared to limit Cyprus's independence in the interests of Western self-defence (O'Malley and Craig 1999: 75).

By now Britain was increasingly a bystander in negotiations for self-government. The USA, with its leverage over Greece and Turkey, was starting to take the lead. The preparedness of Makarios to accept independence rather than union with Greece (for fear that partition would be a condition of *enosis*) opened the way for a settlement (Kyle 1984: 7).

On 15 August 1960 Cyprus became an independent state within the British Commonwealth. A powersharing settlement divided the civil service on a 70–30 ratio between Greek and Turkish speakers. Turkish Cypriots enjoyed a power of veto over legislation on defence, foreign affairs, elections, municipalities and taxation (O'Malley and Craig 1999: 91). This was consociational democracy, which has been used in other divided societies such as Austria, the Lebanon and Belgium as an alternative to simple majority rule. For it to have worked in Cyprus the respective community leaderships would have had to show a degree of commitment to it. But Makarios was still wedded to *enosis*, while Turkish Cypriot politicians, despite the moderate leadership of Fazil Kutchuk, favoured partition.

On 30 November 1963 Makarios proposed constitutional revisions which would have destroyed the powersharing principle. He may have been taking advantage of the disarray in western capitals that followed US President Kennedy's assassination. Within a month the most serious inter-communal fighting to date had erupted and on this occasion it was the Turkish Cypriots who bore the brunt of it (Mayes 1981: 167–8). In March 1964, a UN peacekeeping force arrived and progress was made in restoring a temporary peace in mixed districts from which many Turkish speakers had fled (O'Malley and Craig 1999: 107). But the USA preferred partition. On a visit to the island in 1964, George Ball, the Under-Secretary of State, told Lt.-Commander Martin Packard, the British naval officer seeking to restore inter-communal trust, that partition was the only option (Murtagh 1994: 67). To Washington's consternation, the Cyprus question was destabilizing NATO. Turkey had mobilised its forces for invasion on several occasions in 1963–4. On 5 June 1964 US President Lyndon Johnson sent a note to the Turkish Premier warning that if Turkey invaded Cyprus unilaterally, it could not depend on NATO to defend it against any Soviet retaliation (O'Malley and Craig 1999: 109). Concern about the continued strength of the pro-Soviet AKEL encouraged Washington policymakers to believe that partition and the transfer of most of the island to the control of anti-communist Greece was the best formula to strive for. US officials were also profoundly exasperated with Makarios who was viewed as a left-leaning and completely untrustworthy figure. George Ball, and Dean Acheson who emerged from retirement to try to broker a settlement in the mid-1960s, viewed Makarios in deeply negative terms. For Acheson he was that 'bloody and bearded old reprobate' (Chace 1998: 414). Adlai Stevenson, US ambassador to the UN, viewed Cyprus's President (according to his colleague George Ball) as 'a wicked, unreliable conniver who concealed his venality under the sanctimonious vestments of a religious leader'; according to Ball, Stevenson assured him that the only way to deal with Makarios was 'by giving the old bastard absolute hell' (Ball 1982: 340–1).

Makarios had alienated these pillars of the US liberal establishment, who would shortly be replaced by hardline Cold Warriors when Richard Nixon entered the White House in 1969. In 1965 he had rejected the Acheson plan which tried to reconcile the main demands of all the interested parties. It would have united most of the island with Greece except for the long Karpas peninsula in the northeast, which would have been given to Turkey. Inside the area to be part of Greece, there would be one or two Turkish cantons enjoying local autonomy; for accepting *enosis*, Turkey would acquire from Greece a four-mile-square island off the former's south coast (Mayes 1981: 176–7).

New tensions surfaced in the summer of 1965 when Makarios attempted to revoke many Turkish-Cypriot rights. The archbishop appeared a quintessentially Byzantine intriguer of the kind who would be familiar to Western negotiators in the Bosnian war of 1992–5, when they were exhausted and outmanoeuvred by local power brokers like Radovan Karadzić. Makarios's personal political agenda of remaining the island's leader sometimes appeared to take precedence over his stated policy of *enosis*. In 1964 Ball reacted with fury when, in response to the killing of about 50 Turkish Cypriots at Limassol, Makarios declared: 'there have always been these occasional incidents; we are quite used to this' (Ball 1982: 345).

In Washington, President Johnson, alarmed at the gap in NATO security presented by Cyprus, adopted an imperious manner which far outdid the British in its brutal directness. When failing to convince Alexander Matsos, Greece's Washington envoy, of the merits of the Acheson plan, Johnson became abusive and threatening. Peter Murtagh has related the following stormy encounter in the White House:

'Then listen to me, Mr Ambassador', Johnson thundered, 'Fuck your parliament and your constitution. America is an elephant. Cyprus is a flea. Greece is a flea. If those two fleas continue itching the elephant, they may just get whacked by the elephant's trunk, whacked good ... We pay a lot of good American dollars to the Greeks, Mr Ambassador. If your prime minister gives me talk about democracy, Parliament and constitution, he, his parliament, and his constitution may not last very long'.

'I must protest your manner', Ambassador Matsas spluttered but Johnson continued shouting.

'Don't forget to tell old Papa-what's-his-name [a reference to Prime Minister George Papandreou] what I told you. Mind you tell him, you hear'.

Matsas reeled away from the White House and back to his Embassy ... a full and explicit report ... [was] cabled immediately to Athens. Not long after it was dispatched the phone rang.

'Are you trying to get yourself into my bad books, Mr Ambassador', asked the US president. 'Do you want me to get really angry with you? That was a private conversation me and you had. You had no call putting in all them words I used on you. Watch your step'. (Murtagh 1994: 90–1)

Johnson had spoken frankly to Turkey but he was more mindful of the Turkish position over Cyprus. Turkey, as a bridge between Europe and Asia and a barrier between the Soviet Union and both the Mediterranean and the Middle East, was strategically far more vital to the USA than Greece was (O'Malley and Craig 1999: 120–1). The USA found itself adopting the 19th century strategy of bolstering the Turks' authority and also of actively intervening in Athens politics whenever interests of state appeared to justify it. The communist threat, repressed with difficulty in the 1940s, resulted in massive US military aid.

Extremely close ties were established between the CIA and the informal power centres of the court and the army which often proved far more influential than the government of the day. Queen Frederika, a granddaughter of the last German Kaiser, was a reactionary who constantly meddled in politics. She expected regular gifts from the Americans, the CIA annually receiving 'Frederika's Christmas gift list' (Murtagh 1994: 47). The CIA also enjoyed close ties with members of a secret group of right-wing officers known as Idea—an acronym for 'Sacred League of Greek Officers'. A leading member was Colonel Giorgis Papadopolous, who had been on the payroll of the CIA since 1952 when it helped to establish the Greek Secret Service (KYP). Thereafter Papadopolous acted as the chief liaison officer between the CIA and KYP (Barnes 1999).

A civilian counterweight to these alternative power-centres emerged during the premiership of Constantine Karamanlis (1955–63). Although on the political right, he was a less partisan figure who took some steps to normalise Greek politics in the wake of the civil war. He won two elections in 1956 and 1958 which were seen as fair by Greek standards (Murtagh 1994: 52). But his ultimate failure to establish the primacy of the elected government over the palace led to his departure from politics.

The crisis which would culminate in the military's seizure of power in 1967 can perhaps be traced back to an incident which occurred in London in April 1963 when the King and Queen of Greece were on a private visit. Outside their hotel, Frederika was confronted by Betty Ambitelos, a Welsh woman pleading for the release of her 49-year-old Greek husband, imprisoned in Greece since 1947; he was one of almost 1,100 political prisoners, a further 900 being held in internal exile. The royal couple fled from Ambitelos and her supporters and sought refuge in a private house. Lord Home, the Foreign Secretary, offered a fulsome apology for any distress caused (Murtagh 1994: 60–1). Karamanlis resigned in June 1963 when the palace refused to accept his advice and postpone a state visit to Britain (in the interval, a popular opposition MP, Grigoris Lambrakis, had been murdered by the Greek secret police) (Woodhouse 1998: 147–50).

Four years of political instability followed. The monarchy and armed forces sought to assert their authority over the government of Giorgis Papandreou, leader of the Centre Union Party which won two elections in 1963 and 1965. Henry Labouisse, the US ambassador, opposed interference with the electoral process for partisan ends and threw his weight behind a peaceful transfer of power from the right to the centre-left (Murtagh 1994: 71). But, as with Britain in wartime Yugoslavia when rival agencies tried to neutralise their respective strategies, the American embassy in Athens found itself at loggerheads with the CIA. The CIA service chief boasted in 1964: 'I have 60 full-time members of my staff which makes me more important than the ambassador' (Murtagh 1994: 82).

In 1967 new Greek elections were scheduled for 28 May in a bid to break the political deadlock. Two months before voting, the new king, Constantine II had approached the US ambassador, Philipps Talbot, and sounded him out about the likely American response to a military takeover. The ambassador responded that the USA would not support any 'extra-parliamentary solution'; soon after a cable was dispatched from the State Department urging Talbot to 'warn the king more strongly against a possible deviation from the Constitution' (Murtagh 1994: 110).

In April 1967 middle-ranking officers pre-empted the generals and the palace by staging a coup of their own. More than 10,000 people were arrested and 6,000 were deported to Yaras, an Aegean island where many were tortured by secret police chief, Brigadier Demetrios Ioannides (Barnes 1999). The US response to the takeover by Colonel Giorgis Papadopolous was muted. Ambassador Talbot suspended heavy arms shipments but in the 1967–8 financial year, US military supplies to Greece still amounted to $65 million, suggesting the embargo was largely a sham (Murtagh 1994: 201). The June 1967 Arab–Israeli war dissuaded the USA from taking a hardline with 'the Colonels' regime'. The 'Six Day War' underlined the importance of Greek land and sea space in the Mediterranean—and the need to retain the cooperation of whoever was in charge in Athens.

The British Labour Government of Harold Wilson was then under heavy American influence, which helps to explain why London imitated the 'cool but correct' policy of Washington towards the Athens junta. In 1969 Britain broke ranks with other West European governments by selling planes, ships and other military equipment to Greece. C.M. Woodhouse, the historian, complained of 'the inordinately tolerant British government' (Woodhouse 1998: 298). But strenuous opposition to the dictatorship was mounted by private individuals such as the ex-naval officer Martin Packard and the former head of the BBC, Sir Hugh Greene. The hostility of the smaller European democracies resulted in Greece quitting the Council of Europe in 1969 in the face of certain expulsion (Woodhouse 1998: 297). But the ostracism of Western Europe was largely nullified by the backing which US President

Nixon and his Greek-American Vice-President, Spiro Agnew, were prepared to give to the junta. Both the USA and the colonels were vexed by the strength of the left on Cyprus and by Makarios's neutral stance in the Cold War. Nixon was furious to discover in 1969 that Cyprus was one of four non-communist countries still shipping to North Vietnam. When Makarios refused to join the US-led economic boycott, Nixon cut off American aid (O'Malley and Craig 1999: 132).

It is unlikely that the CIA would have kept the depth of anti-Makarios feeling in the White House from its main Greek associates. One of the most prominent was Brigadier Ioannides who seized power in his own right in 1973. The Archbishop claimed in a 1976 interview that when he had met the Brigadier in 1964, the officer had proposed a radical solution to the Greek–Turkish deadlock:

> He wanted to 'see me secretly to suggest to me a project that would have settled forever the problem of Cyprus'. He entered, he kissed my hand very respectfully, then, 'Your Beatitude, here is my project. To attack the Turkish Cypriots suddenly, everywhere on the island, and eliminate them to the last one'. I was astonished, speechless. Then I told him that I could not agree with him; I told him that I couldn't even conceive of killing so many innocents. He [Ioannides] kissed my hand again and went away very angry. (Hitchens 1997: 39)

There had been several attempts by the colonels to eliminate Makarios. Ioannides was determined to secure *enosis*, despite evidence that revulsion towards the military dictatorship in Athens was reconciling many Greek-Cypriots to independence (Souter 1984: 663). Neither the USA nor Britain broke off diplomatic relations with Greece, or even withdrew their ambassadors, even though many people were killed in a student occupation in Athens and in nationwide anti-junta protests on the eve of Ioannides's seizure of power. In July 1967, Richard Crossman, a minister in the Labour government, had noted with alarm a Defence Ministry paper brought before a cabinet committee in which the government was urged not to intervene if the Greek army staged a pro-*enosis* coup on Cyprus. Crossman observed: 'A Commonwealth country is attacked by a Fascist dictatorship and though we have 15,000 armed men there we stand aside' (Crossman 1976: 449). Under the 1960 Treaty of Guarantee with Britain, one that London not Cyprus had insisted upon, Britain had agreed to uphold Cyprus's independence and its constitution (Kyle 1984: 8).

On and after 15 July 1974, when Makarios was overthrown by the National Guard led by its Greek officers, Britain failed to reverse the coup. Makarios was rescued by British forces but, in subsequent days, the pro-Athens regime of Nicos Samson carried out a reign of terror which was quickly followed by a Turkish invasion. During the coup and invasion, some 3,500 people died and 2,000 went missing. One-third of the population was displaced: 180,000 Greek Cypriots and 65,000 Turkish-Cypriots (Souter 1984: 664). A report of the British Foreign Affairs Select Committee concluded that Britain had 'a legal right, a moral obligation and the military capability to intervene but did not do so'. The Foreign Secretary, James Callaghan, was criticised for refusing to divulge why Britain had acted the way it had during the 1974 crisis (O'Malley and Craig 1999: 160).

Far greater controversy surrounded the role of the USA and whether Henry Kissinger, the National Security Advisor, effectively in charge of US foreign policy, knew in advance about the Greek coup and whether the CIA was involved.

Certainly the US embassy in Athens reacted in a nonchalant way to the coup. Henry Tasca, the US ambassador, had felt that his posting to Greece was beneath him. He had even complained to King Constantine that they had 'promised me Italy and we had to go to Greece instead' (Sulzberger 1987: 143). A cable sent to Washington on 18 July with Tasca's concurrence argued that the Greek military was solidly behind Ioannides, that he had achieved parity with the Turks and that 'any Turkish invasion of the island would unite all of the Greek nationals behind Ioannides' (Murtagh 1994: 250). In a memorandum prepared on 7 August 1974 by Tom Boyatt, head of the Cyprus desk at the US State Department, he wrote: 'It would be hard to imagine judgments more divorced from reality than these' (Murtagh 1994: 251). The role of the CIA and Kissinger was recounted in detail in the 11-page secret memorandum which remains classified to the present day (Murtagh 1994: 247). Britain sought likewise to block the ability of the committee of MPs to get an accurate picture of the government's role in July and August 1974. O'Malley and Craig wrote:

> The normal powers of a select committee, such as the ability to send for people, papers or records, were initially blocked, then conceded only after considerable pressure. The committee was not empowered to travel outside the UK, and had to resort to interviewing Cypriot refugees living in London. And when the MPs cross-examined the key witnesses, Callaghan and Roy Hattersley, his junior minister, their answers were evasive and contradictory. (O'Malley and Craig 1999: 159)

Arnold Smith, the Commonwealth's Secretary-General, demanded British action at the UN, but he was told by British diplomats that

Britain would not use the Security Council to obtain a resolution to roll back the coup unless Kissinger agreed in advance (Hitchens 1997: 92). Kissinger (in a 1975 interview with the *New York Times*'s C.L. Sulzberger) 'implied ... that the CIA might have encouraged the junta to stage the unsuccessful Cyprus coup'; he also 'indicated that Washington had instructed Tasca to caution the junta against this move, but that Tasca didn't follow instructions "all the way"' (Sulzberger 1987: 148). Nixon's National Security Advisor has been widely seen as at best negligent and at worst sympathetic to the political aims of the plotters (the view put forward in O'Malley and Craig's book) which reflected the trajectory of US policy towards Cyprus in the previous decade. Certainly his stated wish to gather in the facts after 15 July 1974 enabled Nicos Samson to briefly gain control of the island and step up a manhunt against pro-Makarios and left-wing forces. According to the book by O'Malley and Craig, authors who have had access to declassified material as well as interviewing many of the key actors, 'the Americans seemed to be doing everything they could to help the Turks make up their mind that intervention was the only way they could get satisfaction' (O'Malley and Craig 1999: 178). The United States showed no apparent worry that the sovereignty of a left-wing island might be replaced by partition between two unfriendly but firmly anti-communist states and indeed it was reluctant to see Makarios recognised anew as Head of State (O'Malley and Craig 1999: 178). But fresh efforts were made to prevent the real danger of war between two NATO states. When Greek ships were reported in Cyprus waters, those ships were attacked by dozens of Turkish warplanes, ships which turned out to be from the Turkish navy: it was hard to distinguish a Greek destroyer from a Turkish one because both had the same supplier, the US (O'Malley and Craig 1999: 193).

On 23 July 1974, the day a ceasefire was negotiated, the military junta in Athens was overthrown to be replaced by an interim government under Constantine Karamanlis, who returned from exile. A tense stand-off between Britain and Turkey occurred when plans were discovered to bomb Nicosia airport, where British troops, part of a UN peacekeeping force, were stationed. Prime Minister Wilson recalled in his memoirs that if Turkey had not backed down, 'we would undoubtedly have been involved in hostilities which might well have escalated. Apart from the lunacy at Suez, this is probably the nearest Britain came to war with another nation since 1945' (Wilson 1979: 64).

On 14 August 1974 after ceasefire talks between the guarantor powers and representatives of the Cypriot communities broke down in Geneva,

Turkey expanded beyond the bridgeheads it had acquired in July and occupied 36% of the island, much bloodshed occurring in the process. The CIA was unwilling to forestall it and Callaghan, the Foreign Secretary, told the Greek Cypriots that since Britain was no longer a superpower, it 'could only take decisive action as part of a UN initiative, or in support of the Americans' (O'Malley and Craig 1999: 208).

An uneasy peace prevailed on the island for the next quarter-of-a-century. Turkey is now the largest military power and in 1983 Rauf Denktash, leader of the Turkish Cypriots, declared the independence of the Turkish Republic of North Cyprus (a state only recognised by Turkey). On Makarios's death in 1977, he was succeeded as President by Spyros Kyprianou. The UN recognised his government as the only legal one which has enabled it to impose an economic embargo on the Turkish zone.

Washington's preferred option of partition was realised but at the risk of damaging US relations with Greece, perhaps irreparably. Karamanlis took Greek forces out of NATO while staying within the alliance (Woodhouse 1998: 306). The left-wing Andreas Papandreou succeeded him as Premier in 1981 and proved a thorn in the side of the USA for much of the next decade. In 1998 Nicholas Burns, the US ambassador to Greece, apologised for past American policies and conceded that, in the name of anti-communism, the CIA had meddled often disastrously in the internal affairs of Greece (Barnes 1999).

YUGOSLAVIA: THE PERILS OF COMMUNIST FEDERALISM

The Soviet Union did not take advantage of Western disarray in the Eastern Mediterranean to meddle in Cypriot affairs even though it was able to influence AKEL, the island's largest political force. Setbacks in Egypt and Syria had perhaps taught the Soviets that the Middle East was a region where they had to tread cautiously. Moscow's attention was more closely focused on Yugoslavia in the early 1970s. Tito's state was the Marxist prodigal son, but its architect and mainstay still had a strong sentimental attachment to the communist world. In the 1970s evidence was building up that Tito had failed to create a common set of values and interests capable of holding his multinational state together. In 1971 an upsurge of nationalist feeling in Croatia upset his carefully-crafted policy of balancing Yugoslavia's ethnic components. Leonid Brezhnev, the post-1964 Soviet leader, offered Soviet military help if it was needed (Beloff 1985: 176). Tito declined, purged the

Croatian party of leading liberals, and contained the crisis. But in 1973 he accepted a credit from the Soviet government reportedly of $1.3 billion, a sum far greater than Yugoslavia was then receiving from the World Bank (Beloff 1985: 176). Yugoslavia was still careful to preserve its impartiality in the Cold War. Tito frustrated Fidel Castro's bid to turn the non-aligned states into 'natural allies of the socialist camp' (Meier 1999: 2); in 1984 Yugoslavia ignored the Soviet boycott of the Olympic Games in Los Angeles.

But whenever Tito moved publicly closer to the Soviet Union, his system's authoritarian rigidity was emphasised. In 1954, following Stalin's death, he seems to have offered Milovan Djilas as a sacrifice to the Kremlin as a rapprochement was taking shape (Doder 1979: 191). In the previous autumn Djilas, the then speaker of the parliament and Vice-Premier, had started publishing articles expressing the opinion that the Leninist type of party and state were obsolete (Fejtö 1974: 57). Tito, having permitted publication, then sided with his wayward lieutenant's conservative critics and he was purged (Lees 1996: 135). Djilas was critical of the unscrupulous ambition, pride and ostentation which he detected in 'the new class' emerging in Yugoslavia. In his later writings, he 'reached the conclusion that the socialist system as practised in the communist states did not and could not allow true freedom and provided no answers for men's needs' (Campbell 1967: 141). But ironically Djilas had played a key role in helping to create Yugoslavia's 'New Class'. Along with Edvard Kardelj, he had launched the self-management idea. A sceptical Tito was only won round when he recalled Lenin's slogan of the Russian civil war, 'factories to the workers' (Doder 1979: 97).

It was Djilas who had played the principal role in delineating the new internal borders of Yugoslavia in 1944–5, some of whose republics would produce acquisitive and conflicting communist elites. These borders overlaid historic boundaries which still exercised a pull for national loyalties. It was therefore not going to be easy to create viable administrative arrangements for a multinational state in which no single nationality was in the majority. The country had no common language. 80 percent may have spoken Serbo-Croat, but the language existed in two major literary forms which made 'the whole sphere of public communications even in Serbo-Croat an arena for nationalist contestation' from the 1960s onwards (Magaš 1993: 17).

In the late 1940s a second Yugoslavia had been launched when it was envisaged that the granting of Home Rule to its different ethnic components would disarm conflicting nationalisms, particularly those of the Serbs and the Croats. The creation of a socialist commonwealth which would be, in Herder's phrase, 'a garden of nationalities ... bound together by commitment to a common way of life', engendered real enthusiasm among many of the Partisans who had fought against invaders and local nationalists (Doder 1979: 101). Having overwhelmed their formidable wartime opponents and survived the wrath of Stalin, the optimism which Tito and his comrades possessed about being able to solve the national question is perhaps understandable. The regime's theoreticians envisaged that the new Yugoslav working-class would be the basis for a common identity which eventually would relegate ethnic loyalties to the periphery of society. Institutions meant to promote elite consensus and the establishment of a social contract with the working-class in which the Yugoslav state would be the guarantor of acceptable living standards would, it was hoped, put an end to endemic Serb-Croat rivalry and prevent any new nationalist disorders troubling Yugoslavia.

But even when Tito was in his prime, the optimistic rhetoric failed to match the reality. August Cesarec, an early communist, had argued that, in order to marginalize exclusive nationalism '[t]he task for us is to erect an insurmountable barrier, to dualize time and divide it into the black past and the white future' (Djilas 1991: 59, 183). But later, with communism in power, Tito showed that he feared the capacity of a divisive past to blow away his communist experiment. Instead of coming to terms with Četnik, Ustaša and even Partisan atrocities, his regime preferred to keep the past 'under the surface, unattended, unhealed, unappeased' (Stokes 1994: 94). An authoritarian regime finds it more difficult to promote honest remembrance and reconciliation than a democratic one. The West German state promoted reconciliation with its neighbours and a public acknowledgement of the high crimes committed by its immediate predecessor with admirable consistency that produced a remarkable transformation in the collective outlook of state and society. Instead, just as communist East Germany preferred to blame Hitler's excesses on bourgeois capitalism, their Yugoslav counterparts likewise pointed the finger of blame for the occupation and civil war horrors in 1941–44 Yugoslavia on the old class enemy. The coercive violence which it was prepared to unleash against opponents of its monopoly of power meant that the strategy of promoting internal dialogue, (perhaps something like the Truth Commissions attempted in countries like post-*apartheid* South

Africa) in order to expiate the past, was simply beyond its capacity (Stokes 1994: 94). Public holidays celebrated Partisan glories, but the '"private" history held by individuals and families in Serbia … preserved the memory of a different and more complex reality' (Thomas 1999: 22).

When the communists decided to retain the name 'Yugoslavia', it meant that it was still defined as a Slavic country. Until the late 1960s, the Albanians of Kosovo were treated in a colonial fashion with mass arrests and beatings a common response to the slightest flutter of unrest (Meier 1999: 27). Workers' control turned out to be a screen behind which rival communist bureaucracies based in each of Yugoslavia's six republics and two autonomous provinces competed for influence and resources. As increasing power was delegated from the centre to the federal units, intellectuals and creative artists, instead of emerging as a force promoting a common Yugoslav identity, were preoccupied more and more with their own national cultures.

Ultimately, it was Tito himself, 'a sincere Yugoslav, an internationalist and a cosmopolitan, unencumbered by his Croat or Slovenian origins' who became the chief integrative force for Yugoslavia (Tepavać 1997: 65). His wartime achievements made the personality cult which grew up around him less synthetic than that of any other leader in the communist world. His long rule witnessed a transformation in living standards which ultimately strengthened the legitimacy of the Yugoslav ideal: life expectancy rose from 46 in 1938 to 68 in 1972: figures for the purchase of consumer durables such as refrigerators, cars, washing machines, and televisions showed a 100% jump for the period from 1945 to 1968 (Doder 1979: 65). Ordinary citizens were shielded from the negative effects of a dysfunctional economic system longer than anywhere else in the communist world.

The social contract meant to underpin Yugoslav stability was combined with an emphasis on the military as the guardian of the state. Tito was careful to develop the closest of ties with the army upon which he lavished at least 6% of the national budget until the early 1970s (Meier 1999: 5). The army remained a stronghold of orthodoxy, viewing 'socialism and the unified Yugoslav state as prerequisites for its own existence' (Meier 1999: 5). From the 1960s promotion in the officer corps was increasingly based on political conformity not ability (Sikavica 1997: 135). Officers were not permitted to travel abroad privately. Nine out of ten came from the villages. One Yugoslav sociologist is quoted as describing them as:

...peasant boys who like order and clarity. They are perplexed by modern complexities and pluralistic trends in our society make them uncomfortable. Tito is a strong and forceful personality, and they like him and trust him. (Doder 1979: 148)

The personality cult around Tito was 'maintained without any reference to Marx, Engels or Lenin' (Doder 1979: 113). Tito's birthday on 25 May, not the international workers' day of 1 May, was the principal ceremonial event of his regime. But Tito himself retained a powerful attachment to the Marxist cause he had served in the interwar years as an agent of the Comintern. His system had made concessions to capitalism in the 1950s but his overall record suggests that he did not see capitalism as a viable or appropriate economic system for Yugoslavia. For forty years, his system was characterized by a zig-zag between authoritarianism and liberalism (Tepavać 1997: 72). But it is clear that he distrusted competitive democracy which would challenge the communist monopoly of power and, ultimately, his personal rule (Djilas 1995: 91). He would quite possibly have disagreed with Lord Owen, the UN peace envoy in war-torn post-1991 Yugoslavia, who wrote in 1995:

> Maybe if Djilas's advocacy of democracy had been given the hearing it deserved in the 1950s and implanted in the 1960s, the present ... war could have been avoided. (Owen 1996: 36)

CONCLUSION

Eastern Europe was a permanent centre of international tension between 1945 and 1989. After the early years of the Cold War, outside attention shifted away from the Balkan states towards Central Europe. But the imposition of the Soviet side was an unmitigated disaster for the Balkan region. A rigidly hierarchical social system was replaced by one in which initiative was suppressed and advancement was based on ideology, not expertise or merit. This system of 'anti-selection', found in all communist countries formed around a *nomenklatura*, resulted in a crude programme of ill-development: the Balkan states were saddled with stone-age industries which swallowed valuable resources and produced little of long-term value for the region. These negative features were least apparent in Yugoslavia: here there was genuine regional pluralism thanks to federalism. But the mediocrity of many top officials, recycled under the federal system, culminated in disastrous results during the 1980s.

The West was slow to grasp the impact of sovietization on society and political culture in Eastern Europe. Writers like George Orwell had few parallels among public officials. Leading officials were unable to avoid the temptation of behaving in an overbearing manner in parts of Southeast Europe that fell into their sphere of influence. Towards Greece and Cyprus, Britain and the USA periodically behaved with a stunning lack of foresight. Eden stirred up Greek–Turkish disagreement over Cyprus to defend transitory British interests. There is strong evidence that, under Nixon and Kissinger, the US government colluded in the partition of Cyprus. As before, colossal blunders committed in the Balkans did not result in censure or punishment. To take the example of Cyprus in 1974: the British Foreign Secretary saw no need to explain to the Foreign Affairs committee of parliament the basis for his minimalist approach to the crisis. But perhaps because it was the Balkans, no strong action was taken (a similar lax approach was shown by the British political elite to policy errors in Northern Ireland which is the nearest counterpart to an unresolved conflict of nationalism in Western Europe).

The national communism of the Balkans engendered much wishful thinking in the West. Charles de Gaulle was on a state visit to Romania when his goverment was assailed by the May 1968 student demonstrations in Paris. But he and Ceauşescu were able to condemn American imperialism in South-East Asia and stress the need for states like theirs to insist on their national independence at a time of superpower confrontation (Durandin 1995: 426). But de Gaulle never had a coherent strategy towards the Balkan countries. With the key one, Yugoslavia, relations were strained. De Gaulle refused to forgive Tito for having executed Mihailović in 1946. His wartime Free French forces had decorated the royalist chief in 1943, and he was someone de Gaulle always regarded as his counterpart in seeking the liberation of his country. During his eleven years in charge of France, de Gaulle always firmly resisted Yugoslav overtures and he never once entertained Tito on a state visit (Gard 2000: 29). France's dalliance with communist Romania would in its turn prove short-lived. While it lasted, it was clear that the Quai d'Orsay had delusions about what a leader of Ceauşescu's stamp really wanted. In the 1970s it became harder for de Gaulle's successors to avoid the conclusion that when communist leaders embraced nationalism, it was a political survival strategy rather than a desire to liberalise Soviet communism. They still usually maintained the obsolete Soviet command economy.

Ultimately, national communism spawned more irrationality and excesses than the Soviet variety: Bulgaria stayed closer to the Soviet path than its neighbours, (except for lapses into intolerant nationalism in the 1980s) which may explain why it is in a better position than most of them to recover politically and economically. Hoxha's isolationist dictatorship was stone-age communism at its most absurd. Eventually, there would be a reversal to sultanistic rule in Yugoslavia in the late 1980s.

Under Tito, Yugoslavia had retained a strongly socialist economy and Tito enjoyed a personal standing no other communist leader in history has been able to emulate. His system may have been a tempting example to others in the bloc, demonstrating how far it was possible to go without undermining communism. In Romania, Dej could see that Yugoslavia was more stable than Hungary, East Germany or Poland. There was no workers' unrest: a social contract bonded the party elite closer to society than elsewhere. Perhaps but for his death in 1965 the Romanian system might have been liberalised much further than Ceauşescu was prepared to go in the late 1960s.

By the late 1960s the Balkan countries were following widely differing 'national paths to socialism'. The optimism of Paul Lendvai who wrote in 1969 that 'the air in the Balkans ... is electric with a sense of change' proved unfounded (Lendvai 1969: 350). Even in Yugoslavia, the Soviet-style command economy was retained in uneasy symbiosis with some aspects of private enterprise; poorly-formulated policies of investment and development often with heavy industry at their core, only resulted in widening the developmental gap between the north-western republics of Slovenia and Croatia and much of the rest of the country.

No qualitative improvements in the nature of communist rule occurred in any Balkan state. Indeed in Romania, ever-increasing boldness in foreign policy was matched by a retreat to hardline communism under the personal dictatorship of Nicolae Ceauşescu which swept away most of the liberalising measures of the mid-1960s. Superficially, it appeared that the Balkanization of Communism had prevailed over the Communisation of the Balkans. But, in reality, the communist social system, transforming what had been mainly agricultural societies, wrought more damage in the Balkans (with the exception of Yugoslavia) than in Central Europe. Ideological goals— curtailing private ownership, removing bourgeois values and purging the social groups that stood for them—surpassed normal developmental goals. Political culture was dominated by proletarian symbols with miners and steelworkers at the pinnacle of the low grade heavy industrial economy which had been installed in Romania and, to a lesser extent, in Bulgaria by the 1970s. Romania's industry in particular concentrated on bulk rather than quality, exporting to unreliable Third World markets. The high technology sector was neglected despite the abundance of scientific talent. No experiments in market economics were allowed; no underground market economy emerged; the service sector was increasingly starved of resources. Midway through the Cold War, the Balkan communist economies were not so much under-developed as chronically ill-developed.

Chapter 5

NATIONALISM WITHOUT REFORM: THE BALKAN COMMUNIST STATES, 1974-1989

During the Cold War each of the Balkan states adopted different paths in their international relations, which did not encourage co-operation between them. Bulgaria remained a Soviet ally, Romania acquired semi-independence from Moscow, Albania was consistently anti-Soviet after 1961 while forging an alliance with China that collapsed in acrimony in the mid-1970s, Yugoslavia emerged as a pillar of the non-aligned movement, while Greece and Turkey were pillars of NATO.

Despite these external divergences, it is important not to exaggerate the policy differences between the Balkan communist states, especially in the economic realm. All of them, to a greater or lesser extent were committed to the socialist economic model which promoted heavy industry, neglected agriculture, and encouraged the formation of a numerically dominant working-class. The energy supplies for industrialization were usually not to be found locally. Soviet oil and gas was available to Comecon states at below world market prices. But it was still hard for the Balkan communist states to shield themselves from the chill winds of global recession following the quadrupling of world oil prices in 1973 by the Organization of Petroleum Exporting States. The oil price shock did not cause any of them to reconsider their economic strategies. Yugoslavia, Romania and Bulgaria borrowed heavily on the international money markets to finance major industrial projects. Albania, outside the world economy, improvised as best it could in the last decade of Hoxha's rule in order to expand its industrial base. Pouring resources into antediluvian industry, or incurring expensive international obligations for the same end, proved costly policy failures for each of them. It was ordinary citizens who had to bear the cost of their rulers' blinkered thinking. In each of the Balkan states, elites with shrinking policy objectives increasingly took refuge in nationalism in order to stifle dissent and obtain acquiescence for austerity programmes which, as in the case of Romania, had a high human cost. But it was in Yugoslavia that the reversion to nationalism went furthest and had the most alarming consequences, given the multi-ethnic nature of that state.

YUGOSLAVIA: THE COLLAPSE OF A DREAM

Tito probably went to his grave a convinced communist despite his opulent lifestyle. Nevertheless, he was willing to experiment, sometimes boldly, within prescribed political limits. He was the only post-1945 communist leader sufficiently confident of his authority to decentralise power.

Tito's attraction to ever more elaborate forms of federalism suggests that he believed regional pluralism within the one-party context was capable of overcoming the dangers of fragmentation. Multi-party politics could have polarised politics along ethnic lines, but his own autocratic approach lacked any effective instruments for preventing or managing conflicts of interest moving along nationalist lines. One aim he always pursued with single-minded consistency was to defuse Serb–Croat rivalry by promoting smaller republics in order for them to act as counterweights to the two largest South Slav units. Accordingly, Bosnia, Macedonia and Slovenia did well out of Tito's system. After 1966, the Muslims, the largest grouping in the federal republic of Bosnia, were elevated to the status of a national group; Tito 'hoped that by adding a third, perhaps mediating group [to the Serbs and Croats], more rational, less nation-based policies would be developed within the republic and perhaps even at federal level (Friedman 1996: 187). Strong commitment to the Yugoslav ideal was shown by the Muslims of Bosnia. Ethnographers noticed that Muslim villagers in Bosnia displayed less interest in their genealogies compared with Bosnian Serbs or Croats, one anthropologist concluding that this made them more resistant to an ethnonationalist discourse, emphasising common blood (Bringe 1995: 31). Meanwhile, in the cities of Bosnia 40% of marriages were mixed by the start of the 1990s (Friedman 1996: 179). Children of rich Muslims and members of the old aristocracy were prominent in the communist party (Zulfikarpasić 1998: 13). But it is worth recalling that of the 4 million Muslims in Yugoslavia by the 1980s, less than two million declared themselves to be of Muslim nationality (Bringe 1995: 11). Albanians, the largest element, were far more likely to adhere to their Albanian national identity which had been strengthened during the punitive Ranković years. By contrast, for the Bosnian Muslims, religion was their chief distinguishing characteristic, though their lifestyle was mainly secular, which made them ideal candidates for a post-nationalist Yugoslavia or indeed Europe. It is worth mentioning that the Muslims who, according to the 1991 census, made up 45% of the population in the Sandžak region lying within Serbia and

Montenegro identified with their Bosnian co-religionists, though being more traditional in outlook.

Indignant Serb intellectuals, who felt that Serbia was the biggest loser under Tito's nationality policies, complained that 'Titoism was fertile in producing artificial nationalities' (Ekmecić 1994: 87). But Serbia's main city, Belgrade, was the federal capital which enabled it to play a pivotal role in the state. Serbs from Bosnia and Croatia's Krajina region played a prominent role in the affairs of these republics as well as in the regime at central level.

Moreover, the bulk of the officer corps of the Yugoslav People's Army (*Jugoslovenska narodna armija*: JNA) would always be drawn from Serbia and Montenegro. In 1970 Serbs made up 57.4% of the officer corps, a figure which rose to 60% in 1990: by contrast, Muslims, 8.4% of the population in 1970, made up only 4% of the officer corps in that year (Friedman 1996: 184). A potential challenge to the authority of the JNA in its centralized form emerged in 1968. The invasion of Czechoslovakia revealed shortcomings in the preparedness of the army to forestall a similar move. It was decided to form territorial defence (TD) forces that would be better able to organize Partisan-style popular forms of self-defence. These were funded and controlled by individual republics and provinces. A debate ensued within the army about how much independence they deserved to enjoy. Conservatives, who argued that the decentralization which had occurred in party matters would lead to republican armies capable of going down the separatist road, prevailed (Magaš 1993: 329). In the event the Yugoslav army was the one institution which saw the least degree of innovation and reform under Tito. Given the ethnic composition of its officer corps, this would have fateful consequences for the state when it was overtaken by a fundamental crisis in the 1980s.

Inter-republican rivalries grew sharper as power began to be transferred from federal to republican institutions. After 1962, the centralized management of the communist party's personnel was discontinued so that it was attention to local, not pan-Yugoslav, interests which was required if an ambitious figure was to rise in the party (Bebler 1993: 78). Decentralization went furthest under the 1974 constitution which invested each Yugoslav republic and province with theoretical 'statehood'. This was a definite advance in the status of the non-Slav minorities, the Albanians and the Hungarians, as the provinces in which they were strongly represented became Federal members in their own right alongside the republics. For national minorities living within the eight Federal units, full cultural and political rights (use of their national language in state affairs; proportional representation at municipal and higher levels) were guaranteed (Magaš 1993: 338). Tito, at the age of 82, was made president for life and, after him, the head of state was to be a collective body: the federal presidency would comprise one member from each republic and province, plus the president of the communist party and the federal minister of defence (Thompson 1992: 1–2). The federal government was still meant to determine the broad direction of policy, but, more than ever, there was an emphasis on achieving unanimity among the republics and provinces before decisions could be implemented, which proved to be a recipe for administrative gridlock.

The 1974 constitution turned Yugoslavia into a constitutional oddity, a state which was suspended between being a federal and a confederal one. Even before Tito's death in 1980, it was clear that the republics were able to determine appointments at all levels, including even the federal ministers. Dusko Doder, writing in 1979, has related:

> Those Yugoslavs who have opted out of the tribal mold now find themselves at a disadvantage. 'I'll never make ambassador', a senior bureaucrat in the Foreign Ministry told me privately. 'I left my republic twenty years ago and I've lost all contact with people there. Today you have to be nominated by your republic for ambassadorships'. (Doder 1979: 227–8)

As he approached the end of his long life, Tito's authority and ability to mediate between rival interest groups became increasingly vital in order for the system to function. Tepavać has described well the shortcomings of this arrangement:

> When a problem arose between two or more republics, republican leaders learnt to approach Tito separately instead of meeting together. Tito often would satisfy the parties individually, sometimes at each other's expense, and without resolving the underlying issues. (Tepavać 1997: 75)

So at the end, Tito was Yugoslavia's only effective instrument in a land aptly described as 'one country with six republics, five nationalities, four religions (including Communism), three languages, and two scripts' (Roberts 1991: 176). A.J.P. Taylor, the British historian, described him as 'the last of the Hapsburgs', governing an array of people by dividing them and playing one off against the other (quoted by Cohen 1998: 55). Averell Harriman, evidently one of the few Westerners to press Tito about the future, obtained a reply which suggested that he was not sanguine about what might follow after him: 'It is quite impossible for me to name a single successor. In the end, there is no one to protect the country from its divisions' (Cohen 1998: 108).

So indeed it would prove. The gulf between several of the republican leaderships grew increasingly large as they started 'to fall back on ethno-national identity as a source of strength and security' (Gow 1994: 460). When its effects were already obvious, Milovan Djilas warned of 'a bureaucratic nationalism based on economic self-interest' which he saw as more dangerous than classical nationalism (Kaplan 1993: xxiv).

Aleksa Djilas, the son of Milovan, believes that Tito was willing to accommodate many national demands because their existence enabled him to demonstrate his indispensability as the supreme arbiter of the system (Djilas 1995: 91). The extensive autonomy given to the national sub-components of the state blocked its decision-making capacity (Denitch 1994: 105). The republics duplicated services and subsidised their own producers. Important hydro-electric programmes, which would have lessened Yugoslavia's dependence on costly oil imports, were held up in the 1970s by disagreement on the share-out of benefits between Bosnia, on the one hand, and Serbia and Montenegro on the other (Beloff 1985: 198). The inordinate length of time it took to complete a rail line connecting Bar on the Montenegrin coast with Belgrade was due largely to such rivalries (Bookman 1995: 23).

Titoism provided few public outlets for an expression of Yugoslav identity except in ritualistic or symbolic forms. Politics was the business of politicians whose arena was increasingly the competing republics. Under an authoritarian system, civic initiatives which would allow citizens to operate independently of the party were simply outlawed, so civil society remained a private affair. On balance, Tito may have been more afraid of liberal reform than of nationalism; otherwise, he might not have allowed so many constitutional innovations that encouraged the rise of sub-state nationalism.

Perhaps his biggest single error was to leave the fate of the party and state in the hands of conservative nonentities during the 1970s. They rose to the fore after the purge of liberals first in Croatia and then in Serbia during the early 1970s.

In Croatia, the liberalism permitted after Ranković's fall in 1966 produced demands for a loosening of controls from Belgrade which permeated not only the society but much of the party also. In 1967, Croatian intellectuals, unhappy with the publication of a new dictionary of Serbo-Croatian, which emphasised the Serbian form of the language, demanded an amendment to the constitution to decouple Croatian from

Serbian (Tanner 1997: 196). Matters came to a head in 1971, by which time the Croatian communist party was being swept along on a tide of popular nationalism. There is scant evidence to corroborate claims being made to Tito, especially by members of his military entourage, that separatism was on the agenda. But in September 1971, while on a visit to Moscow, Tito was lectured for three hours by the Soviet leaders and, according to one source, virtually ordered to remove 'anti-Soviet leaders' from office (Tanner 1997: 200). This was the most serious internal crisis since the break with Stalin in 1948 and the Soviets may have felt that they now enjoyed a rare chance to exercise leverage in Yugoslav affairs. Tito, after lengthy attempts to moderate the agenda of the Croatian party, decided to purge it of its liberal leadership in November 1971. Prison sentences were meted out to recalcitrant nationalists who would not retreat into silence, such as Franjo Tudjman, an ex-general in the JNA who had decided to seek political fulfilment by championing Croatian causes.

The purge of reform communists in Croatia meant that the weight of the Serbian minority in the party's affairs was even more prominent than before. Driving nationalism underground meant that it would take a far more intransigent form than before when, after Tito's death, the political monopoly enjoyed by the communist party started to be broken.

If Tito had been forced into a corner by the 'Croatian Spring' of 1971 and pressure from Belgrade centralists, as well as the Soviet Union, it is hard to justify his decision to carry out a comprehensive purge of liberal reformers in the Serbian communist party in 1972. The existence of a strong liberal rallying-point in the federal capital itself may have filled Tito with unease. If the Yugoslav system was to be liberalised (and like the Hungarian party in the 1980s forsake its authoritarian past for a new social democratic orientation), then a strong nucleus of reform in Serbia was essential. Tito destroyed this option in 1972 when he eliminated 'an entire generation of liberal communist reformers ... from political life' (Denitch 1994: 56). They were replaced with conservative nonentities and obedient apparatchiks who talked in 'wooden language', speaking the jargon associated with the 1974 constitution and self-management to an increasingly bored and contemptuous Yugoslav audience (Dimitrijević 2000: 421). The 'negative selection' which resulted in ambitious but often mediocre personalities filling the top positions, enabled nationalism to enjoy a gradual revival in Serbia.

In some quarters, much has been made of the fact that in the 1969 elections, the only ones in the Tito era that gave voters a choice between more than one candidate, Serbian and Montenegrin voters preferred old-guard candidates with a Partisan background while 'all the other Yugoslavs favored reformist candidates' (Anzulovic 1999: 96, 200 n. 72). A survey carried out two decades later in 1990 by the Institute of Political Studies in Belgrade found the value structure of the Serbian population to be an authoritarian one: 27.4% of respondents believed that 'in the state, as in a family, everyone must know who is the oldest, that is, there must be one commander who is listened to by everyone' (Obradović 2000: 442–3). Serbs were at that time just about to endorse, through competitive elections, the Serbian communist party (under a new name) on a programme, *inter alia*, designed to maintain the state at the centre of their economic lives. According to Nebojša Popov, a Belgrade-based social scientist writing in the late 1990s, Yugoslavia was a powerful illustration of the way that 'the party state (Communism) produces mass passivity even apathy'. He quotes Miklos Biro to make his point: 'The whole economic system functioned on the principle of *receiving*, not *earning* ... Everything was received—salary, apartment, position, credit, money.' A person's position depended on displaying political conformity rather than individual abilities or actions (Popov 2000a: 98). The liberal reformers who stood in the 1969 elections and whom Tito purged in 1972 must have appeared unsettling for those citizens in Serbia who preferred a system based on paternalism and conformity. Why they were so numerous in Serbia and Montenegro, and whether explanations need to be found beyond the strength of the military-industrial complex in these parts of Yugoslavia and the relative weakness of industries exporting high-quality products to western markets, is a subject upon which more research is required. It is perhaps too easy to think in terms of a clash between western Yugoslavia with its central European culture and economic orientation and the collectivist mentality of those parts of Yugoslavia squarely in the Balkan peninsula. Serbia's per capita income was closer to that of Croatia than to the southernmost republic Macedonia, and later Serbian attempts to recentralise Yugoslavia brought it into conflict with republics poorer than itself as well as richer ones like Croatia and Slovenia (Hoare 1999: 100).

In the era preceding the upsurge of Serbian nationalism, the 1974 constitution was not defended with any enthusiasm by the cautious Serbian leadership. In 1974 a bid was made by conservative elements to integrate the provinces of Kosovo and Voivodina with the Serbian republic without eliminating them; however, it foundered on the resistance of other republics (Pešić 2000: 31). But resentment over the fact that the Serbs, once 'a people of state', had lost their unitary character under Tito's decentralist arrangements, would steadily escalate. As in Croatia, Serbian grievances were quietly ventilated by intellectuals who were ready to make converts among politicians not averse to seeking legitimacy by promoting popular nationalism. Not a few intellectuals viewed the constitution as a diabolical plot against Serbia's interests, unity, and even very right to exist as a nation.

Tito's reluctance to build on early links with the European Economic Community (EEC) limited the country's reformist options in the 1980s. His sentimental attachment to the communist east meant that 'he repeatedly turned down offers to get into the European Free Trade Association' (Denitch 1994: 58). Bogdan Denitch believes this 'would have permitted Yugoslavia to get into the European Community at the same time as Spain, Portugal and Greece did. Had Yugoslavia done so, it could have mobilised European aid in the transition from authoritarianism to democracy' (Denitch 1994: 58).

Doubtless, there are elements of wishful thinking here, but Yugoslavia had advantages which could have facilitated its entry into what became the European Union long before other Communist states. Despite its abundant shortcomings, the economy enjoyed far closer links with its successful west European counterparts than did any Comecon state. Moreover, there was a strong reservoir of goodwill towards Yugoslavia, particularly from social-democratic leaders in the West impressed by the transformation of the country from its wartime state. But Tito disdained western social democrats (Meier 1999: 2). He preferred to tramp the world stage as a champion of non-alignment even though the practical benefits for Yugoslavia are debatable. He saw no need to open up his hybrid political and economic system to the West any further than he had done in the early 1950s, as long as Western financial aid continued to be readily available.

Western loans flooded into Yugoslavia in the 1970s, by which time the self-management system was based not on commercial profitability but on complex bureaucratic arrangements. In 1973, after the quadrupling of world oil prices, Western banks, awash with funds, were avid to find borrowers. In 1977, when a law gave the eight federal units the right to raise their own funds and look after their own interest accounts, it meant the lifting of any remaining restrictions on borrowing from overseas (Beloff 1985: 199). Nora Beloff has written:

> In the West, where the old heavy industries were in deep depression, governments and traders were euphoric in finding insatiable customers: 'Who,

except the Yugoslavs in these difficult times, would be building a new steel mill?' asked a merchant-banker in the City of London in 1980, explaining why he was syndicating a loan for yet another mill in the unprofitable heavy-industry complex of Smeredovo in Serbia. (Beloff 1985: 199)

Yugoslavia's debt soared from $5.7 billion in 1975 to $19.2 billion in 1981 (Meier 1999: 10). In 1981 international lenders started to pay more critical attention to Yugoslavia when the country was unable to meet some of its debt repayments. Visiting Western officials 'were shaken to discover the quantity, unaccountability and elusiveness of their Yugoslav creditors' (Beloff 1985: 200). In 1983, as a condition for new credits, the Yugoslav republics were obliged to give supervisory powers back to their federal bank, but they still retained a veto over its transactions.

Yet Yugoslavia continued to enjoy an easy ride from Western governments and financial institutions. In 1981 West Germany made available a credit package of DM 1.4 billion, 600 million of which was handed over without restrictions of any kind. Neither West Germany nor any other western lender linked financial assistance with 'any kind of reciprocity or commitment to specific behaviour' (Meier 1999: 12). Yugoslavia's pivotal role, on the Cold War front-line, as a guarantor of stability in a fractured Europe, meant that international organizations such as the IMF and the World Bank were politically conditioned to respond to its requirements with a far less critical eye than they would direct at other supplicants. Powerful Western policy-makers, such as Lawrence Eagleburger, who shaped the State Department's East European policies between 1981 and 1992, were able to exercise important leverage on behalf of Yugoslavia when they wanted to. These factors need to be borne in mind when assessing claims, such as those from Susan Woodward, that it was IMF pressure in the mid-1980s for austerity measures to be introduced that opened the floodgates for ethnic tensions (Woodward 1995: 68).

When the hardline Serbian communist, Slobodan Milošević began his rise to power in the mid-1980s by appealing to Serbian nationalism, it generated little concern in Belgrade's diplomatic community. Victor Meier, the long-standing Balkan correspondent of the *Frankfurter Allgemeine* from 1975 to 1993, has recalled conversations with Western diplomats 'who were inclined, at that time, to believe that Milošević's centralism was possibly better for Yugoslavia than no centralism at all' (Meier 1999: 41). James Scanlan, US ambassador in the mid-1980s 'unequivocally took Milošević's side' and later returned to Belgrade to serve as the local manager of the pharmaceutical firm of US-based Serbian businessman, Milan Panić (Meier 1999: 41).

A large and strategically-placed segment of the Yugoslav communist party was reluctant to move in a liberal direction even as the rest of the communist bloc discarded Leninist controls. Milošević would not have found it so easy to promote Serbian hegemony if this concept had not been particularly appealing to many in Serbia proper, as well as the provinces of Voivodina and Kosovo, and the republic of Montenegro, each of which came under Serbian control in the late 1980s. The leadership of the army, it turned out, was prepared to rally behind a leader who moved away from incoherent and quarrelsome federalism, even though the decisive leadership Milošević offered was very different from Tito's brand. Those Serbs who had no love of communism found the nationalism of Milošević refreshing. Through control of the media, he cleverly positioned himself as a moderniser, inciting an 'anti-bureaucratic revolution' against federalist red tape which, he claimed, Serbs had suffered the most from. He even attracted dissident Marxists of the Praxis school who were widely admired in the west, as well as Četniks. But in Slovenia, and later Croatia, adherents of federalism were determined not to succumb to Serb-inspired Belgrade centralism. The Slovenian section of the party was convinced by the late 1980s that communism had collapsed as a world economic and political system (Obradović 2000: 438). The clash between Milošević and his opponents in the federation might be seen as one between western Yugoslavia with its central European culture and economic orientation and the collectivist mentality of those parts of Yugoslavia squarely in the Balkan peninsula. But it should not be forgotten that Macedonia, the southernmost republic, also emerged as a bastion of federal sentiment opposed to Milošević's Greater Serbia programme. Macedonia, which in the time of royal Yugoslavia had been known as South Serbia, had acquired various badges of nationality after 1945, a recognised language and history and, in 1967, separate status for the Macedonian Orthodox Church (Poulton 1995: 118). Not surprisingly, support for Tito's vision of a Yugoslavia without any privileged nations was higher in Macedonia than almost anywhere else in the state.

ROMANIA: THE WEST AND A TYRANT'S FOLLIES

The wishful thinking of the United States towards Yugoslavia was dwarfed by its willingness to be taken in by the diplomatic alchemy practised by the leaders of communist Romania. For nearly fifty years Romania endured a totalitarian brand of communism in which individual liberty was trampled under foot and civil society flattened. But in the West Romania's autonomous foreign policy convinced top officials that Romania was an agent of disunity in the Soviet camp and therefore worth cultivating. Until the 1980s Radio Free Europe was occasionally asked by the State Department to play down a number of human rights abuses so that 'US policy-makers could obtain or maintain Ceauşescu's goodwill' (Urban 1997: 115).

Relations with the USA had started to revive in 1964 when Romania relaxed its arsenal of repression. Virtually all political prisoners were released (about 11,000), the jamming of foreign radio broadcasts stopped, and cultural contact with the West was revived (Lendvai 1969: 314). The USA had made such concessions to basic human rights a condition for improving bilateral ties but, thereafter, the West was reluctant to concern itself unduly with the internal politics of the Romanian regime.

A change at the top occurred in 1965 with the death of Gheorghiu-Dej. Lendvai has described him as 'a latter-day successor of Petru Rares and the other medieval Romanian princes who, by virtuoso performances in intrigue, deceit and manoeuvring, divided their powerful adversaries and survived in the face of overwhelming odds' (Lendvai 1969: 304–5). Ceauşescu, his 47-year-old successor, quickly gained a reputation as a maverick communist whom it might be in the interests of the West to cultivate. Romanian nationalism was emphasised with ever greater fervour in order to strengthen the regime's popular standing. New party statutes in May 1965 abandoned all reference to the 1917 Russian revolution or to the Soviet fatherland of the proletariat, hitherto the ultimate source of legitimacy for all communist regimes (Gallagher 1995: 57). Henceforth the Romanian nation was at the centre of all major pronouncements and at the July 1965 party congress the leading role was transferred from the working-class to the socialist nation (Schöpflin 1974: 92).

For nearly 25 years Romania was to be ruled by one of the most rigid and implacable leaders of the 1917–89 communist era. Nicolae Ceauşescu was a boorish and suspicious autocrat who disallowed any deviation from strict communist norms and who (egged on by wife and eventual co-ruler Elena) imposed enormous suffering on his people to try and satisfy grandiose ambitions.

Roger Kirk, the United States's last ambassador to communist Romania, has described well a leader whose intolerance would eventually spark off a popular revolt and result in he, and his wife, being executed by some of their former underlings:

> Although he had no particular charm or charisma, he was able, even without mass killings or wholesale arrests, to inspire fear and obedience in those around him and indeed in virtually an entire nation.
>
> He had a peasant's shrewdness and mistrust of others, impressive native intelligence, an excellent memory. And a good head for detail. He was a master at controlling and manipulating others. He was vengeful, suspicious and without scruples in pursuit of his ends. As his power grew, he became more and more impatient with subordinates, humiliating them and often threatening to fire them on the spot. He did not like being contradicted, and he would not long keep around him those who disagreed with him or ventured their own opinions. (Kirk and Raceanu 1994: 36–7)

An autonomous foreign policy was an indispensable adjunct of Romania's national communism. In 1966 Romania successfully resisted Soviet plans to strengthen the powers of the Warsaw Pact over the armed forces of its members (Feijtö 1974: 317–8). In 1967 Romania refused to follow other Warsaw Pact members and freeze diplomatic relations with Israel after the Six Day War; in 1968 Ceauşescu's image as a reform-minded Marxist received a tremendous boost when he refused to join the Soviet Union and the other Warsaw Pact states in sending forces to crush Czechoslovakia's experiment in liberal communism. In January 1969 Ceauşescu met with Tito and both of them denounced the doctrine of 'limited sovereignty' which the Kremlin allowed the satellites and which became known as 'the Brezhnev Doctrine' (Harrington and Courtney 1991: 285–6).

Little noticed at the time was the fact that Ceauşescu never endorsed 'the Prague Spring' nor stated that it was worthy of emulation in his own country. He made sure that the leading reformist tracts published in Prague by Czech party liberals and their intellectual supporters, never got into the Romanian press and were not even reproduced in the confidential bulletins prepared for party officials (Tinu: 1998). However irritated they might be by Romania's acrobatics, the Soviets knew that Ceauşescu was an orthodox communist who had no inclination to retreat from Marxism-Leninism. Indeed, part of his skill as a leader manoeuvring between East and West was that he knew when to stop short of unforgivable provocation. This was shown in May 1967 when Chou En-lai, the Chinese Premier attempted to use Bucharest as a rostrum for fierce attacks on the Soviet Union while on an 8-day visit. The Romanians censored his speeches ruthlessly and no joint communiqué was issued, only a press notice stating that 'during the exchange of opinions each side expressed its respective viewpoints' (Lendvai 1969: 327).

Rewards were not slow in coming from the West. In September 1967 Corneliu Manescu was unanimously elected President of the UN General Assembly, the first representative of a communist country ever to attain this position. De Gaulle in 1968 personally bestowed the *Légion d'Honneur* on Ceauşescu (Bethell 1995: 283). In 1978 he became the first Communist Head of State to be invited to stay as a guest of Great Britain's Queen Elizabeth II at Buckingham Palace. During the visit he was made a Knight Grand Cross of the Order of the Bath, a signal royal honour in Britain; on 22 December 1989, as his regime was collapsing, the Foreign Office advised the Queen to take away the honour 'as a mark of revulsion at abuses in human rights in Romania' (Bethell 1995: 213). But, earlier, in 1983 the Foreign Office had agreed to the forcible return to Romania of the dissident Stancu Papusoiu, 'the first forcible removal of any individual from Britain to Romania or Russia since 1947' (Bethell 1995: 285–6). Sèrgiu Celac, Ceauşescu's interpreter in the 1970s and later ambassador to Britain, reckoned that the 1978 British visit was a more important propaganda coup for him than any other foreign visit (Percival 1994: 86). Romanians such as Dan Hurmuzescu, who had worked undercover for the British secret service in wartime Romania and later served 17 years in prison under Dej, beseeched the British embassy not to allow such a visit: it sapped the morale of Ceauşescu's opponents who believed it would consolidate the dictator's authority at home (Sweeney 1991: 119).

In 1971, while on a visit to North Korea, Ceauşescu found a brand of communism that particularly suited his implacable character and, upon his return home, he determined to model Romania on the fanatical and regimented character of Kim Il-Sung's regime. This was also the era of US President Richard Nixon and relations with the West blossomed even as Ceauşescu endeavoured to make his Balkan state an outpost of East Asian communism. Henry Kissinger, Nixon's powerful National Security Advisor, was a major influence on US ties with Bucharest. He abandoned the previous US approach of treating communist Eastern Europe as a monolithic bloc and opted instead for a policy of differentiating between different forms of Marxist rule. According to C.L. Sulzberger, he argued that 'it is the essence of geopolitics to be able to distinguish between different degrees of evil' (Sulzberger 1987: 86). This policy of differentiating between communist states on the basis of their relations with the Soviet Union and willingness to co-operate with western countries, continued into the mid-1980s. On 21 September 1983, Vice-President George Bush was still re-affirming American willingness to 'engage in closer political, economic and cultural relations with countries like Hungary and Romania which show continuing openness and independence' (Funderburk 1994: 188).

Romania proved helpful to President Nixon by facilitating a number of diplomatic initiatives such as the clandestine negotiations with North Vietnam in 1969–70 and, more especially, the President's groundbreaking trip to Mao's China in 1971 (Sulzberger 1987: 83). Romania was viewed as a valuable interlocutor with the Soviet world and organizations like Yasser Arafat's Palestine Liberation Organization. There seems to have been little pause for thought about how the Russians viewed the unlikely US–Romanian friendship or whether Moscow might even be benefiting from it.

It was during the 1969–74 Nixon Presidency that Romania joined such international institutions as the General Agreement on Tariffs and Trade (GATT), the International Monetary Fund and the World Bank, membership of which was withheld from other communist states (Kirk and Raceanu 1994: 4). Nixon visited Bucharest in 1969 and received Ceauşescu in Washington in 1970 and 1973. During his presidency and that of Gerald Ford (1974–76), the respective secretaries of state, ministers of foreign affairs, and several other cabinet ministers visited each other's capitals virtually every year (Kirk and Raceanu 1994: 4). David Funderburk, US ambassador to Romania from 1981 to 1985 and later to be a Republican Congressman, reckons that the friendship between Nixon and Ceauşescu transcended ideology: 'Both of them had a similar attachment to power, its acquisition and retention' (Funderburk 1994: 115). In disgrace after the Watergate scandal, Nixon continued to regard Ceauşescu as a great man, regularly sent him greetings on his birthday, and travelled to Romania to see him in 1982 (Funderburk 1994: 116).

Nixon was largely responsible for the most substantial US concession made to Romania, the granting in 1975 of Most-Favoured-Nation (MFN) trade status. It provides for parity of treatment on tariffs, the USA having withheld MFN status from Romania and other communist countries in 1951 (Kirk and Raceanu 1994: 4–5). MFN enabled Romania to obtain high technology goods from the USA and this, and other trading agreements with the West, allowed Romanian inspectors and other personnel into a range of industrial plants

(Almond 1988: 25). According to critics of its policy, the USA did not stop to wonder who was the chief beneficiary of allowing a communist state access to its markets, and much sensitive technology. Certainly, the Bucharest–Washington entente had no appreciable impact on political conditions in Romania which steadily worsened from 1971 onwards. The Communist Party tightened its grip on society; by 1987, 25% of the adult population were members, twice the proportion for the Soviet Union (Berindei 1998a: 10). An intelligence service known as the *Securitate* supervised the population and decided their fate: where they lived and worked, whether they were promoted or penalised, and whether they got into trouble with the law (Berindei 1998b: 12). A 1981 law permitted imprisonment for mistakes committed in the workplace. In 1983 intellectuals were warned that artistic creativity could not exist without a revolutionary message, a far cry from Ceauşescu's 1965 guarantee to 'our men of letters and our artists' that 'they are at liberty to determine how they should paint, write and compose' (Feijtö 1974: 450).

Revelations provided by Ion Pacepa, the head of the external branch of the Romanian intelligence service, after he defected to the USA in 1978, should have punctured Western complacency about Romania, but the existing policy was slow to change. European states like West Germany were prepared to appease Ceauşescu rather than use their economic strength to show their disproval for his despotism. In May 1983, during a visit to Bucharest, Bonn's Foreign Minister, Hans-Dietrich Genscher agreed that West Germany would pay Romania DM 7000 for each member of the Saxon community allowed to resettle in his country (Harrington and Courtney 1991: 507). Pacepa argued that Romania was playing a double-game towards the West with the complicity of the Soviet Union (Funderburk 1994: 45). He insisted that within the limits allowed by Marxism-Leninism and its treaty obligations under the Warsaw Pact, Bucharest occasionally diverged from Moscow, the aim being to obtain Western technology and loans in order to press ahead with building a communist system (Funderburk 1994: 74). Sharing Pacepa's view, Ambassador Funderburk was told by a Romanian official that Romania's decision to defy the Soviet boycott and participate in the 1984 Los Angeles Olympics, had actually been agreed months in advance with the Russians. The Soviet Union, argued Mark Almond, obtained valuable intelligence and economic advantages from Bucharest's close Western ties:

Perhaps Ceauşescu does not share everything with Moscow, or even as much as Moscow would like; but much of what he has been able to provide was probably unavailable to the Soviet Union from any other source. It is better for the Kremlin to get 70% of Ceauşescu's total than nothing at all. (Almond 1988: 25)

In 1981 bilateral ties were disturbed when David Funderburk, a protégé of the conservative US senator Jesse Helms was appointed US ambassador to Bucharest. Funderburk knew the country, its people, and the language which set him apart from most other appointees who usually were career diplomats from within the State Department who had no special qualifications for the assignment (Funderburk 1994: 30). He challenged the policy of differentiation from which Romania benefited and which still continued during much of the period George Schulz was President Ronald Reagan's Secretary of State. Funderburk drew attention to Romania's voting record at the UN to argue his case that it did not deserve special treatment. Romania voted alongside the USA hardly more often than other Soviet bloc countries including the USSR itself (Funderburk 1994: 74). He argued that much greater vigilance towards Romania needed to be exercised and that the USA should not be afraid of intervening diplomatically to promote policies that benefited the Romanian people materially and improved their human rights (Funderburk 1994: 22). In his memoir of his Bucharest years, he struck a raw nerve in the State Department when he claimed that there was sometimes a convergence of interests between US career diplomats in Communist countries and their political hosts, US envoys preferring not to rock the boat by drawing undue attention to unsavoury aspects of state behaviour (Funderburk 1994: 222). He argued that concessions made by Bucharest, such as allowing Romanian Jews to emigrate to Israel and occasional gestures of independence towards Moscow, were not worth the approval successive administrations had lavished on the Romanian regime. He criticised the readiness of US Congressmen to visit Romania and be used by the regime which told its people it was proof of how respected communist Romania was in the world. In 1986 Vernon Walters, US ambassador to the UN, visited Romania despite the poor reputation of the Ceauşescu regime for no other apparent reason than to fulfil his desire, as an enthusiast for subways, to see the newly opened Bucharest metro and take the controls of one of the trains (Kirk and Raceanu 1994: 89). Unsurprisingly, Ambassador Funderburk was frozen out of the policy-making arena because of his unorthodox approach to Romania. He claims in his memoir that 'practically every group, official or unofficial, which visited Romania was instructed by the Department [of State] that "the ambassador was dangerous"' (Funderburk 1994: 142). But the criticisms he vented publicly upon his resignation in 1985 became, according to Bennett Kovrig, 'conventional wisdom' three years later (Kovrig 1991: 141). Kovrig has written that: 'The State Department displayed remarkable bureaucratic rigidity in clinging against all evidence to a positive image of Ceauşescu as a Warsaw Pact maverick' (Kovrig 1991: 186).

After 1985 Romania was reduced to being a closed society as the arbitrary and increasingly grotesque character of Ceauşescu's personal dictatorship became increasingly apparent. Plans to bulldoze many thousands of villages and relocate their inhabitants in agro-industrial complexes leaked out in 1987; they were part of an Orwellian process to industrialize the countryside in order to create the perfect socialist man and woman: a process Ceauşescu dubbed 'systematisation'. In 1988 a campaign of solidarity got underway in Western Europe. The Belgian-inspired *Opérations Villages Roumains* promoted the adoption of many of these villages and lobbying efforts to save them from destruction; in April 1989, the heir to the British throne, Prince Charles publicly condemned systematisation and threw his weight behind the British campaign to adopt Romanian villages launched in June of that year (Deletant 1995: 313–14).

Earlier in the 1980s Ceauşescu had sought to demonstrate his independence by swiftly paying off the large hard currency debt, accumulated in the 1970s to finance a crash programme of industrialization. Energy-gulping factories had been built which often ruined the surrounding countryside, producing low grade heavy industrial products for which it was increasingly hard to find markets. Perhaps the worst of these mammoths was the aluminium plant erected in Slatina, the capital of the county in which he was born. The smelter was unable to refine aluminium economically and on a visit in 1986, the US ambassador noticed much of its produce lay unsold nearby (Kirk and Raceanu 1994: 99). However, its high energy consumption (as high as 10% of Romania's total energy use) frequently caused power-cuts in Bucharest and the whole sorry episode was a telling example of how ideological goals surpassed normal developmental ones.

Paying off the debt by the end of the 1980s was achieved at enormous cost to the economy and the Romanian people. Ceauşescu slashed imports from the West for food, medicines, and spare parts and resolved to export anything that could be sold abroad. Food exports to the Soviet Union were boosted (Romania becoming its chief foreign provider) while strict rationing was introduced at home. A 1982 study by the US Department of Agriculture showed that citizens of East Germany, Hungary and Czechoslovakia consumed three times more meat per head than Romanians (Funderburk 1994: 98). Romania's trade with other communist states, which had fallen from 65% in 1965 to 33.8% in the early 1980s rose sharply to the point of reaching 60% by 1988; trade with the USSR alone represented 33% of Romania's total by that year (Levesque 1997: 193). In 1988 Romania unilaterally cancelled its MFN agreement with the USA, Ceauşescu being well aware that the US Congress was unlikely to renew it for a communist regime with the most atrocious human rights regime of all the Warsaw Pact states.

INTELLECTUALS AND NATIONALISM

Because of the challenging nature of converting Balkan peasant societies into urban industrial states, the various Balkan communist regimes needed intellectuals who would act as apologists for the regime more than was the case in East-Central Europe.

Dissonant intellectual voices only became really prominent in Yugoslavia. This largely occurred after Tito's death in 1980 and it was as champions of unsatisfied nationalism that these intellectuals took the public stage. The colourless nature of the rotating leadership grappling with mounting problems in the first half of the 1980s meant that the audience prepared to heed intellectuals denouncing the shortcomings of the system was a substantial one.

This was especially so in the pivotal Yugoslav republic of Serbia. The decapitation of the liberal party leadership in the early 1970s and its replacement by uninspiring apparatchiks had pushed dissident intellectuals further into the limelight. The Serbian academic Nenad Dimitrijević has argued that an informal alliance grew up between the party and intellectuals with a strong socialist orientation who were known as 'loyal nationalists'. He has written that '[T]he latter were allowed to organize themselves (primarily through the Serbian Academy of Science and Arts, and the Serbian Writers' Association), and to articulate their positions on social issues in the form of scholarly or aesthetic elaboration of the Serbian nationals question (again on the understanding that the regime would not be challenged). Feathers were ruffled occasionally, but the regime managed to remain remarkably tolerant: and only open messages of hatred were subject to censure' (Dimitrijevic quoted by Conversi 2000: 341).

The central figure in the Serbian nationalist revival was Dobrica Ćosić, Serbia's foremost writer. His novels focus on 'the terrible Serb struggle in the two Balkan wars and World War I', the underlying theme being 'one of an enormous sacrifice in blood that bore little fruit' (Doder and Branson 1999: 41–2). Until 1968 he had been close to Tito and even talked him out of imposing the communist bloc's favourite literary style, that of socialist realism, on Yugoslav writers. But in 1968 he was expelled from the central committee for warning that Kosovo's Albanian leaders were separatists along with Voivodina's Hungarian politicians (Judah 2000: 47).

With increasing boldness, Ćosić depicted the Serbs, in the words of Dennison Rusinow, 'as a victimized and diminishing nation, whose sacrifices and victories on the battlefield and on behalf of others as well as themselves were perennially betrayed by the egoism and deviousness of ... others' (Rusinow 1995: 403). He gathered around him young dissidents who would later be prominent in post-1991 Serbian politics such as Vojislav Šešelj and Vuk Drasković, himself a novelist specialising in romantic nationalist themes. Complaints about the post-1945 internal republican frontiers of Yugoslavia began to be heard, especially after the 1974 constitution further decentralized the federation. The earlier division of Serbia into one large republic and two autonomous provinces, Kosovo and Voivodina, was seen as proof of anti-Serb discrimination. The argument that such powers had to be given to Serbia's provinces otherwise Serbia, as by far the most populous republic, would dominate the rest of Yugoslavia, was regarded as specious (Judah 2000: 49). The decision not to divide Croatia, by giving autonomy to Dalmatia and parts comprising the old Hapsburg military frontier with local Serb majorities, deepened the sense of persecution felt by nationalist members of the Serbian cultural elite. Their ranks were swelled by leading members of the Praxis group of dissident Marxist philosophers. Mihailo Marković, their principal ideologist, had been purged from Belgrade university as early as 1968 (Meier 1999: 19, Magaš 1993: 4). Victimisation at the hands of Tito perhaps made it easier for Marković and colleagues to reconfigure their dissent along nationalist lines. In 1988 Marković was lauding the new Serbian party head, Milošević, as 'the best leader we Serbs have had since Rancović' (Magaš 1993: 123).

The issue which disgruntled Serb intellectuals were able to make common cause over was Kosovo, for long depicted as the cradle of

Serbian culture, faith and statehood—the Serb Jerusalem (Rusinow 1995: 403). Alarm was expressed that the quasi-confederal 1974 constitution gave Kosovo most of the attributes of a separate republic. More resentment was generated as Albanians agitated for full *de jure* republican status in the early 1980s which Serb intellectuals saw as a prelude to separation. The first sign that concern about Kosovo extended beyond their ranks came at the funeral of Alexander Ranković in 1983. Tens of thousands attended the funeral of the implacable functionary who had ruled Kosovo with an iron hand till the mid-1960s (Judah 2000: 47).

The proportion of Serbs and Montenegrins in the Kosovo population had fallen from 20.8 to 14.9% between 1971 and 1981. This gave rise to claims in Belgrade that Albanians had resorted to methods ranging from intimidation to what amounted to genocide in order to create an ethnically pure Albanian Kosovo (Rusinow 1995: 402). This anti-Slav offensive was supposedly going on exactly at the time when the jails were being filled with thousands of Albanians whom the nervous Belgrade authorities suspected of being dissidents of one sort or another (Meier 1999: 21). The most emotive charge made by Serb nationalists (and taken up by the Serbian media in the late 1980s) was that Slav women were subjected to widespread rape. Noel Malcolm has written that:

> The only serious study of this issue was carried out by an independent committee of Serbian lawyers and human rights experts in 1990. Analysing all the statistics for rape and attempted rape in the 1980s, they found first of all that the frequency of this crime was significantly lower in Kosovo than in other parts of Yugoslavia: while inner Serbia, on average, had 2.43 cases per year for every 10,000 men in the population, the figure in Kosovo was 0.96. They also found that in the great majority of cases in Kosovo (71%) the assailant and the victim were of the same nationality. Altogether, the number of cases where an Albanian committed or attempted the rape of a Serbian woman was just thirty-one in the whole period from 1982 to 1989: an average of fewer than five per year. (Malcolm 1998: 339)

The arguments about the sharply changing demographic picture in Kosovo at this period will probably rage long into the future. While not denying that Serbs were leaving because they felt increasingly unwelcome or had been threatened, Malcolm prefers to emphasise economic factors: during the later Tito years there had been large-scale internal migration from under-developed to more prosperous areas. Bosnia-Herzegovina, the second poorest part of Yugoslavia after Kosovo witnessed a proportionately larger outflow of its population by 1981 (Malcolm 1998: 33). Marina Blagojević, in a book by Serbian academics charting the Serbian path to war, rejects the sensational accusations, but argues that Serbs faced subtle and escalating forms of discrimination, especially within state structures and that fear for the future of their children was a primary impulse to move (Blagojević 2000: 226–31).

The case of disaffected Serbian intellectuals against Tito's experiment was emphasised in a Memorandum of the Serbian Academy of Sciences and Arts drafted in the spring of 1986. The Memorandum mixed legitimate complaints about the way Yugoslavia was misgoverned with accusations expressed in highly-emotive language that the creation of a Federal Yugoslavia had been a Comintern conspiracy directed against the Serbian people. The claim is backed up with the argument that the Comintern had supported the idea of a Balkan federation in the 1930s (Meier 1999: 48).

In one of its most emotive passages, the Memorandum asserted that '[T]he physical, political, legal and cultural genocide of the Serbian population in Kosovo ... is the worst defeat in the Serbian-led battles of liberation from Orasac in 1804 to the 1941 uprising' (Rusinow 1995: 338).

It warned that:

Unless things change radically, in less than ten years' time there will no longer be any Serbs left in Kosovo, and an 'ethnically pure' Kosovo, that unambiguously stated goal of the Greater Albanian racists ... will be achieved ... Kosovo's fate remains a vital question for the entire Serbian nation. If it is not resolved ... if genuine security and unambiguous equality for all peoples living in Kosovo ... are not established; if objective and permanent conditions for the return of the expelled nation are not created, then this part of the Republic of Serbia and Yugoslavia will become a European issue, with the gravest possible unforeseeable consequences. (Judah 2000: 50)

The Memorandum demanded the removal of the 1974 Constitution and the creation of a state which would assure 'the equality' of Serbs and the 'cultural and spiritual unity of the Serbian people' (Meier 1999: 50).

What became a charter of Serbian nationalism was initially condemned by the Belgrade authorities but, soon enough, became a programme of action for Slobodan Milošević and conservative apparatchiks as they captured institutions at Serbian, provincial and Yugoslav levels. Milošević realised what national Stalinists had already grasped elsewhere in the region, that appeals to nationalism could give communists weighed down by policy failures a new lease of life and a clean identity. Tapping into this powerful emotional resource meant that not only could they prevail over their inner party rivals but they stood a chance of becoming permanent players in politics if the shift towards multi-party politics became an irreversible one as a result of the reforms being promoted by the Soviet Union.

Tito had occasionally sought to foster all-Yugoslav solidarity by adopting a hostile stance to neighbours like Albania and Bulgaria who were thought to have designs on Yugoslav territory owing to the presence of national communities, the Albanian Kosovars and the Slavic Macedonians, which previously had been identified with Greater Albanian and Greater Bulgarian state-building projects. But Milošević gave a new twist to this strategy of appealing to solidarity by identifying a national threat *from within*, from disloyal minorities like the Albanians, or treacherous fellow South Slavs like the Croats.

His debut as a communist nationalist began while on a visit to Kosovo Polje on 24 April 1987. Newly installed as head of the communist party in Serbia and with only five years' experience in the party leadership, the 46-year-old Milošević went on the suggestion of his mentor Ivan Stambolić, President of Serbia and an upholder of Tito's political legacy. Local Serbs up in arms about their subordinate status in Kosovo had attracted the attention of Belgrade through their vociferous protests. Instead of distancing himself from bigoted calls for the expulsion of the Albanians, Milošević told a large Serbian crowd that 'no one should dare to beat you' (Silber and Little 1995: 27–8). From then on he used the nationalist agenda as his path to power. First of all he needed to dispose of his superior, Stambolić, who steadfastly refused to flirt with nationalism. Milošević exploited an incident on 8 September 1987 when an Albanian conscript in the JNA opened fire on other soldiers, killing or wounding ten of them. Despite the fact that only one casualty was Serbian, the state media in Belgrade unleashed an atmosphere of nationalist hysteria (Pesić 2000: 47 n. 51). This was possible because Milošević had been inserting supporters of his nationalist line into editorial offices, including those of *Politika*, the venerable Belgrade daily newspaper which had always sought to maintain a professional and even liberal approach during different eras of authoritarian politics. The media was cleverly used to deliver the coup de grâce to his rival. At a meeting of the Serbian central committee at the end of September 1987, the first ever to be televised, Stambolić was hounded out of office in front of millions of viewers. Milošević's readiness to speak clearly after years of colourless leaders using the incomprehensible babble associated with Yugoslavia's complex political arrangements made him appear a leader of real substance (Gordy 1999: 26). Many Serbs must have been thrilled at the way that the political system was opening up to allow them to observe and even judge the deeds of the powerful. But Milošević's televised central committee execution was an inner party coup possessing few elements of democratic legitimacy. Yugoslavia was about to obtain its first strongman after Tito.

A regime whose counterparts would soon be sidelined everywhere else in Eastern Europe underwent a relaunch in Serbia after 1986 through relegitimising nationalist symbols and goals. Milošević in fact acquired many of the ideas which would reinforce his nationalist strategy from intellectuals whose place was on the right of politics. Their provocative outbursts lowered inhibitions about destroying Tito's careful system of balances. Milan Komnenić, a stalwart of the Orthodox Church, and Vice-President of the Serbian Renewal Party (SPO), soon to be the main opposition force to Milošević, virtually declared war on the Albanian population at a meeting between Serb intellectuals and Albanian representatives in April 1988. On that occasion he said:

> Hand on my heart, I have nothing to discuss with you. You have already said clearly enough and done what you intended. For that I offer you bitter thanks. … Sir, we are at war. As we already know this, why do we hide it. A segment of the Albanian people—I don't know how many—has brought war against the Serbian people, without notice. If they haven't declared war with weapons, they have done so with their consciences'. (Stojanović 2000: 458)

Vuk Drasković, the future leader of the SPO and better known in the 1980s as a novelist specialising in historic works where Serbs are victimised by other nationalities, recommended drastic action to reduce the high Albanian birth rate. He recommended new legislation to limit child benefits to a maximum of four children: 'If you want to have five children, you will lose all benefits on the first four, and you will be taxed on the fifth. You will pay double tax for the sixth, a quadruple tax for the seventh, and so on. If Allah orders Albanians to have twenty children each so that they can take over the Serbian state, then Allah must find money for them' (quoted in Doder and Branson 1999: 40).

Drasković used inflammatory language to contend that the Serbs had the right to fix the boundaries of their own state. Speaking at the beginning of 1989, he claimed that 'the western borders of Serbia … are where Serbian pits and graves lie'. He warned that in the event of the dissolution of Yugoslavia, the federal borders would cease to count 'and a free vote would be made by both Jasenovac and Jadovno [Croatian concentration camps during the Second World War], and by all our burial places, and by all Serbs who were driven or relocated from Croatia, Slavonia, Bosnia, Dalmatia, Hercegovina, Kordub, Lika and Banija' (Stojanović 2000: 462–3). In regular news broadcasts, state television in Serbia television was already relaying pictures of the exhumation of graves containing Serbian victims of the fratricidal conflict in wartime Yugoslavia. Zarana Papić, a prominent Serbian feminist and member of the Belgrade circle 'Women in Black', has recalled that 'we were given a continuous visual presentation—between 30 and 60 minutes of TV every day—of the exhumation of mass graves in Herzegovina' (Papić 2000).

Drasković was adopting the dangerous course of ascribing collective and hereditary guilt to an ethnic foe and insisting that retribution needed to be paid by a whole people for deeds committed in their name during a previous generation. Ivica Račan, the communist leader of Croatia, was habitually branded as Ustaša in the official Serbian press despite the fact that his family had been murdered in the First World War by them (Magaš 1993: 241). Azem Vllasi, the moderate head of the Kosovo communist party for much of the 1980s, was arrested in 1989 on charges of 'counter-revolutionary activity' after having been similarly demonised in the media.

The Serbian national opposition's intellectual authority was a key asset for Milošević in his power-conserving strategy: they 'first prepared the ground for him, and then, having the ideological initiative, they continued to open new and complicated questions which he would take over as required' (Stojanović 2000: 466). As well as these intellectuals, Milošević rehabilitated other groups which had been banished to the shadows in Tito's Yugoslavia. Russophile communists who had instinctively sided with Stalin in the Yugoslav–Soviet schism of 1948 were removed from obscurity and disgrace. They were known as the Goli Otaki on account of the prison island in the northern Adriatic on which they were incarcerated in the 1950s. Television programmes devoted many hours to chronicling their suffering and, with fewer and fewer inhibitions, questioning the whole edifice of inter-ethnic peace on which Tito's Yugoslavia had been based (Veljanovski 2000: 578).

Milošević sought to take advantage of the revitalisation of the Orthodox Church which was evident by the mid-1980s. Beforehand, religion had enjoyed scant appeal among Serbs and the church revival would certainly not permeate the urban working-class majority to any degree: opinion polls published in 1982 'revealed that in traditionally

Catholic regions one-third of the youth are religious, one-third atheists, and one-third either passive believers or uncertain. In traditionally Serbian Orthodox regions, by contrast, only 3% of the youth felt religious, while 90% claimed to feel positive aversion towards religion' (Ramet 1985: 301).

Since many of Serbia's most precious religious monuments were located in Kosovo, it is not surprising that there was an enthusiastic church welcome for Milošević's militant line. One important contribution to the regime's nationalist offensive was the solemn procession of the remains, allegedly of Prince Lazar, the Serbian ruler killed at the Battle of Kosovo Polje in 1389, through Serbian-populated areas of Yugoslavia before arriving at the monastery of Gračnica in Kosovo where they would rest during the celebration of the 600th anniversary of the Battle of Kosovo Polje on 28 June 1989. At a rally which lasted for more than 24 hours, Milošević warned that 'today we are again in battle and facing battle. These battles do not involve weapons, although such battles are not yet excluded' (Milosavljević 2000: 69).

It was Serbian nationalists from a Četnik background who were most comfortable with this increasingly menacing chauvinist message and best able to articulate it. Milošević brought them out of obscurity and they were found places in the Belgrade-controlled media. He probably felt that by being reliant on his goodwill and patronage, right-wing nationalists would be easy to control. By 1990, Serbia's most prominent weekly, *NIN*, once known for its liberalism, was carrying articles sympathetic to Spain's General Franco, praising Oswald Spengler's *Decline of The West* and hailing the 'iconoclasm' of Gabriele D'Annunzio, the poet who had seized the Croatian port of Rijeka on the eve of Mussolini's coming to power (Magaš 1993: 263). Milošević's intention to rip up the national compromise which had been the basis of federal communism had been made clear in 1988 by several symbolic acts. In November the 19th-century Pan-Slav song *Hej Slaveni!* ('Come Slavs!') was adopted as the country's official anthem— a rebuff to the founding values of the state and its non-Slav inhabitants. Weeks later, the country officially commemorated—for the first time— the 70th anniversary of the creation of royalist Yugoslavia. It was none other than the aged Vasa Čubrilović who presided over the occasion, notorious for his long-standing advocacy of removing the Albanians from Kosovo (Magaš 1993: 160). Thus Yugoslavia witnessed the public emergence of a 'red-brown' alliance, sponsored from above and uniting the extremes of left and right behind a common defence of collectivist nationalism, a trend which would acquire emulators elsewhere in the region.

In communist Romania intellectuals displayed little of the boldness of their Serbian counterparts in seeking to shape the state's political agenda. The communist leadership had regrouped around national values as early as the 1960s. It was a survival strategy on the part of Gheorghiu-Dej who feared that he might be removed at Khruschev's instigation. It was then taken much further by Ceaușescu as Marxism-Leninism alone was seen to be ineffectual in mobilising and controlling the masses.

The regime's shrewd manipulation of nationalism attracted and misled many intellectuals who flocked to join the party when Ceaușescu appeared to stand firm against the Soviets in 1968. The percentage of intellectuals who were party members rose from 10% in 1965 to over 20% in the mid-1980s (Shafir 1985: 87). The Romanian state offered a social contract to intellectuals prepared to sing from its nationalist hymn-sheet. Resources were allocated to publishing houses for the publication of large print-runs of books and a wider range of periodicals in the humanities were published than in many other eastern bloc states (Petrescu 1998: 50). The condition was that indigenous values were to be promoted and later a new one was added: adherence to the personality cults of Ceaușescu and his wife. The price intellectuals were to pay was to disavow freedom of speech and condemn western influences as cosmopolitan and therefore unsuitable for Romania. The trend was obvious in the realm of popular music. Western rock was out, but the 1980s saw the emergence of the 'Song of Romania' phenomenon, festivals of patriotic singing in which groups competed with one another to produce music that represented the essence of the Romanian soul. The spontaneity and irreverence of western musical events was mimicked in gatherings which provided one of the few outlets for young people to indulge their high spirits in such a rule-bound and oppressive society.

But the signing of the Helsinki Accords in July 1975, the culmination of the East–West détente process, loosened the controls which totalitarian states exercised over their citizens. It soon became clear that the outcome of the 1975 Conference on Security and Co-operation in Europe (CSCE) opened up new possibilities for challenging repressive regimes. The Soviet Union and its allies signed the Helsinki Final Act, Principle 7 of which committed its signatories to 'endeavour jointly and separately ... to promote universal and effective respect' for human rights. According to Bennett Kovrig, the message was clear: 'the rights of individual citizens were no longer a purely domestic political matter but also a valid issue of international relations linked to security' (Kovrig 1991: 169).

The Kremlin was prepared to make what it thought were purely rhetorical concessions in order to obtain multilateral confirmation of the territorial status quo in Europe (especially the permanent division of Germany), as well as easier access to West European markets and technology. But the CSCE became an ongoing process which offered a framework for the scrutiny of human rights. The diplomatic wall behind which the Soviet-bloc states freely violated political and civil rights had been breached (Kovrig 1991: 170). In several communist states, including the Soviet Union itself, human rights activists were soon testing the extent to which their regimes would honour the Helsinki accords.

The Charter 77 movement in Czechoslovakia was the best-known of the dissident movements inspired by the 1975 Helsinki agreement. It in turn inspired the Romanian Charter 77 which would be the largest dissident challenge ever mounted against the Ceauşescu regime. The two movements were comparable in size. But the objectives of the Romanian chartists were more limited. The great majority of the over 200 signatories of the letter drafted by the writer Paul Goma were moved to join because of problems related to their personal and professional lives: in particular, many wished to emigrate. Unlike the Chartists in Czechoslovakia, they 'were not interested in creating a human rights movement that would aspire to restrict the abuses of the regime, improving the general situation in Romania', which was Paul Goma's own aim (Petrescu 1998: 24). Only two well-known intellectuals were prepared to identify with Goma. The psychiatrist, Dr Ion Vianu, concerned at the way that opponents of the regime 'were annihilated by hospitalisation in clinics for mental diseases' was one (Petrescu 1998: 26). The writer Ion Negoitescu was the other, but he was forced to retract after the regime blackmailed him because of his homosexuality. Vianu was dismissed from his university position and granted an emigration passport as were many other signatories, including Goma.

Privileges and carefully modulated intimidation encouraged intellectuals to stay quiet and sometimes even police their professions on behalf of the regime. Cristina Petrescu (paraphrasing the Hungarian Miklos Haraszti) has claimed that 'if Solzhenitsyn had lived in Romania, he would have been appointed the president of the Writers' Union in time so that he would not have written *The Gulag Archipelago* or, if someone else had, Solzhenitsyn would have voted for his expulsion from the Union' (Petrescu 1998: 27).

In Romania the tradition of intellectuals enjoying few organic ties with society and instead being linked with a state whose resources they wished to enjoy and whose cultural agenda they wished to influence, was already a strong one in pre-communist times. The opportunist inclinations of a large segment of Romanian intellectuals made it much easier for the communist state to control the realm of ideas even as its policies grew increasingly irrational. At least one source is convinced that consent rather than coercion was the crucial ingredient, the fabled *Securitate* not being as ruthless or as efficient as the legend that grew up around it suggested (Petrescu 1998: 47–9). The compliant role of most intellectuals in the Ceauşescu era (with honourable exceptions such as Ana Blandiana, Doina Cornea and Mircea Dinescu) prevented them playing an important role in the post-communist era except as promoters of ethnocentrism.

In Bulgaria, nationalism was invoked by the regime in order to distance the population from unwelcome realities and enable the party to claim to be the living embodiment of the continuing independence struggle. Polemics with Yugoslavia rumbled on over Macedonia which have been described as 'the most extensive and bitter of any of the nationality debates between communist parties' (R.R. King 1973: 218). But compared with Romania, the Zhivkov regime behaved with restraint at least in its internal policies. It counterbalanced its promotion of indigenous values with continuous demonstrations of adherence to the Soviet Union (Gigova 1998: 53). The Agrarians enjoyed a separate existence from the BCP (though without having freedom of action), and pre-war military reformers like Colonel Kimon Georgiev were able to hold top political posts right until the end of the 1950s. Also the overt rejection of Western values was not as apparent as in Romania.

It was the Bulgarian leader's daughter, Liudmila Zhivkov who shaped cultural policy from 1975 when she was appointed head of the committee of arts and culture until 1981, when she was in charge of the Politburo committee on science and culture (Crampton 1997: 204). She was not an uneducated parvenu like Elena Ceauşescu, 'a chemist' weighed down by honours who was unlikely to know the chemical properties of water (Pacepa 1999: 21). Zhivkova was a woman with sophisticated tastes who spent a year studying at Oxford University. A cautious process of cultural opening with the West occurred. American journals such as *New Republic*, *Commentary* and the *National Interest* were freely available in Sofia's National Library by the start of the 1980s. A newspaper like *The Times* was occasionally seen on sale in Bulgaria's second city, Plovdiv. In private, Liudmila Zhivkov showed an interest in mysticism: in

Romania harsh sanctions were employed over intellectuals drawn to the transcendental meditation movement. Presumably an absorption with eastern mysticism denoted a lack of commitment to the socialist reality that Ceauşescu was seeking to construct.

In 1981 huge celebrations were ordered to mark the 1300th anniversary of the founding of the Bulgarian state, but Zhivkova died in July of that year, aged 39, giving rise to rumours that her cultural nationalism had caused her to fall foul of Moscow. It is hard to see how the Soviets would have relished her unabashed cultural nationalism, especially since it carried the risk of having awkward political side-effects (Brown 1992: 117).

Intellectuals may not have been regimented to the degree they were in Romania but the price of dissent could be high, as shown by the fate of Georgi Markov, an émigré writer who broadcast for the BBC and West German external broadcasting services. His revelations about the lifestyle of the Bulgarian elite and criticism of Todor Zhivkov brought him a large listening audience (Crampton 1997: 202). In 1977 Zhivkov apparently told a Politburo meeting that he wished Markov silenced and, in June 1978, he was murdered in London, poisoned by a pellet shot from an umbrella (Cummings 1996). The Bulgarian secret service was also implicated in the attempt on the life of Pope John Paul II in 1981. Even though two trials failed to prove the Italian prosecution's allegation that Bulgarian secret servicemen, acting on behalf of Moscow, had hired the would-be killer of the Pope, Bulgaria's reputation was badly tarnished. In July 1982 the USA branded Bulgaria as a country engaged in 'state-sponsored terrorism'.

LIGHT FROM THE EAST

In the 1980s the political and economic controls on Eastern Europe imposed by Stalin and maintained by his successors were demolished through unforeseen changes emanating from the Soviet Union itself. Mikhail Gorbachev became the Soviet party chief in 1985 as the growing burden of the arms race on the Soviet economy was allowing new thought to permeate the higher reaches of the party. Leaders like Brezhnev and Constantin Chernenko had exemplified the atrophy of the system and their failures enabled energetic reformers with an agenda not unlike that of the 1968 Czech reformers to come to the fore. Gorbachev wanted to humanise the communist system and make it more efficient. He believed the problem was 'a crisis of performance' rather than 'a crisis of the system' (Gati 1990: 65). But his commitment to glasnost (openness) would set in train a wave of change that would topple the communist system from within.

Romania openly questioned the ideological soundness of the new Soviet thinking. Stefan Andrei, the former foreign minister, representing Romania at the July 1988 Comecon summit in Prague, expressed his leader's contempt for the idea of glasnost when he said he did not understand the word and needed a translator (Almond 1988: 25). There was consternation in Bucharest in case Gorbachev received a warm welcome from the people on two visits he made in 1987 and 1989.

Having paid off Romania's foreign debt, Ceauşescu was in a position to mimic the Soviet reforms by stressing economic flexibility and trying to satisfy some of the consumer needs of the population. But he refused to take this path. The unwritten contract between the communist party and the working class, under which the state ensured a decent standard of living for the workers in return for their political compliance, was trampled underfoot by Ceauşescu (Brucan 1993: 126–7). He was undoubtedly unaware of the scale of the economic crisis and the tensions it was producing even within the regime's own ranks. Officials concealed bad news from their boss and his wife, Elena, made sure that frank dispatches revealing the scale of Romania's economic plight never landed on the desk of her co-ruler (Deletant 1995: 339). The November 1989 party congress was the apotheosis of the regime: the cult of personality was reaffirmed along with senseless economic policies which had despoiled the country.

Romania was in fact back almost at square one after attempting for three decades to build an indigenous brand of socialism based on self-sufficiency. Instead of having competitive industries fulfilling consumer needs and securing reliable overseas markets, Romania was saddled with industrial dinosaurs which sold low-grade products mainly to slow-paying Third World states. In the 1980s the Soviet Union's demand for Romanian agricultural produce had been the only secure economic lifeline for the regime: thus Romania had reverted back to being an agricultural supplier to the Soviet market, a humiliating status which Ceauşescu's industrial strategy was designed to end forever.

Ceauşescu also effectively repudiated communist Romania's belief in the sovereign independence of Warsaw Pact states. On 4 December 1989, in Moscow for the last time, Ceauşescu refused to sign a Warsaw Pact resolution which condemned the 1968 invasion of Czechoslovakia. This declaration also repudiated the Brezhnev doctrine which had introduced the concept of limited sovereignty for the satellite states (Zidaru 1999). Romania's lame excuse for refusing to sign was that it had never supported it in the first place. In August 1989, however, Ceauşescu had shown himself to be a late convert to Brezhnevism when he demanded that collective action be taken to end the 'counter-revolutionary' process taking place in Poland (Levesque 1997: 119).

Bulgaria, at least on the surface, still appeared an oasis of stability capable of keeping in step with the new music emanating from Moscow. One unwary American commentator writing in 1987 claimed that after 'forty years of generally shared progress ... it seems that the BCP will be the forum for settling any foreseeable social-political conflicts' (McIntyre 1988: 174). But the Soviet changes also posed a fundamental challenge to the Bulgarian regime of Todor Zhivkov. The Bulgarian language, being very similar to Russian, enabled much of the population to follow what was happening in the Soviet Union. With one channel of Bulgarian television relaying Soviet programmes, Bulgarians were tuned into the latest developments. Instead of challenging glasnost and perestroika, Zhivkov adopted the slogans and policies flowing from it. This was in keeping with the long-standing Bulgarian approach of staying in step with the latest policy pronouncements from Moscow. Zhivkov even tried to show that he was ahead of Moscow as an innovator by announcing the introduction of a new model of socialism and fundamentally revising the party's role in society (Levesque 1997: 167). Ministries were eliminated, 30,000 officials removed, and the 28 administrative districts reduced to 8, the number of ancient Bulgarian provinces (Levesque 1997: 167). But the Soviets were unimpressed by changes imposed by decree without heed to the practical consequences. They warned that the rapidity and improvised character of such measures could lead to difficulties resulting in the discrediting of perestroika itself (Levesque 1997: 167–8).

Zhivkov was already borrowing massively from the West in the face of declining Soviet subsidies and a worsening economic climate. Living standards had stopped rising in the mid-1980s and dissent began to spread beyond narrow circles of intellectuals. In 1988–9 Zhivkov resorted to the well-worn tactic of diverting attention from domestic policy failures by stepping up efforts to assimilate an unpopular minority. In the summer of 1989, 300,000 ethnic Turks and some Muslim Slavs left for Turkey as state policies requiring them to adopt Bulgarian names, discouraging the public use of Turkish, and restricting the practice of their religion, intensified (Crampton 1994:

383, 395). The regime may also have acted in this way because of the faster Turkish birth-rate: despite previous waves of induced emigration, Turks comprised 10% of the population. One noted specialist on Bulgaria has suggested that the Zhivkov regime might have feared demands for autonomy from Turks in areas where they were in a majority: thus there may have seemed good reasons for promoting the assimilation of a potentially troublesome minority (Crampton 1997: 210). However, the operation did not go smoothly and protests against oppression by this embattled minority were the first signs of public dissent in over 30 years.

Zhivkov was removed by senior colleagues on 10 November 1989, a week after a demonstration of 5,000 people protesting over pollution and economic problems had been staged in Sofia (Brogan 1990: 203). Contrary to rumours which have persisted to this day, the Soviets played a peripheral role in the events leading to this palace coup. When Zhivkov's successor, Petur Mladenov had managed to exchange a few words with Gorbachev at a Warsaw Pact summit in July 1989 and told him, 'We are determined to carry out change in Bulgaria', the Soviet leader responded, 'We sympathise with you, but it's your business' (Levesque 1997: 171–2).

Claims that the Kremlin and the KGB had played a leading role in the tangled events which led to the violent overthrow of Ceauşescu in December 1989 have enjoyed even stronger currency. Ion Iliescu, the second-ranking communist who replaced him when the communist party transmuted into the National Salvation Front, had been involved in a plot to topple Ceauşescu in 1984, but the Soviets had refused to give direct assistance to the coup, and were reluctant to get involved (Ratesh 1991: 93–8). In November 1988 Silviu Brucan, a Romanian top official in the Dej era who was able to travel relatively freely and had access to the Kremlin, was received by Gorbachev who stated to him that he was in favour of Ceauşescu's overthrow on condition that it should be carried out in such a way as to leave the Communist Party as the leading force in the country; he evinced no enthusiasm for intervening in Romania (Deletant 1995: 257).

On 17 December 1989, the day after riots in the city of Timşoara had brought the challenge to his regime into the open, Ceauşescu told his Politburo that the events were the result of actions 'by foreign espionage groups' (Ratesh 1991: 26). Many Romanians remain convinced that the putsch, mounted by political insiders following the outbreak of popular unrest, was orchestrated from Moscow and that Iliescu was acting out a plan to install a Gorbachev-style regime in Bucharest to prevent much greater upheavals.

However, the Soviet Union had shown disinterest towards its Balkan communist satellites, its economic links with them were not of crucial importance, and they were not central to Soviet security. To engage in such a high-risk strategy would have been at variance with its previous disposition. Events in Poland, East Germany, and Czechoslovakia were far more important to the Kremlin, especially because there might be ramifications in the West if bloodshed occurred, as so nearly happened in East Germany during the final days of the communist regime.

Iliescu made a request to Moscow for military assistance on 23 December when Bucharest was wracked by serious violence following Ceauşescu's flight from the capital (Levesque 1997: 204). Such a scenario did not trouble the United States. On 24 December, US Secretary of State, James Baker, declared on American television that the USA would not make any objections 'if the Warsaw Pact judges it necessary to intervene' in Romania. However, Eduard Shevardnadze, the Soviet foreign minister, told the US ambassador that the USSR was 'categorically opposed to any foreign intervention in Romania' (Levesque 1997: 204).

An incident during the fighting accompanying Ceausescu's overthrow suggests that European diplomats stationed in Bucharest did not necessarily see Romania's rightful place as even belonging to Europe or the Romanians as fully European. Veronica Atkinson, wife of a British ambassador who had a very honourable record in defending Romanian dissidents, had taken shelter in the cellar of their official residence during the worst of the fighting. She recounted that:

> We knew the shooting had to finish because it was so intense ... We were terrified, of course. I had been thinking that they are going to rape my daughter... Then came silence, you see, and there was a lull in the fighting. And suddenly we heard 'Hello, hello'. But the 'hello' sounded European, *and not Romanian* (my emphasis). (Hickman 1996: 266)

Among Romanians Secretary Baker's comments revived memories of 1944–5 when the Western allies had given the USSR a free hand in Romania. The finger of suspicion was pointed at the Malta summit (2–4 December 1989) between Presidents George Bush and Gorbachev, during which many Romanians believe that the details of Ceauşescu's removal, and his substitution by men who would not disturb the balance of power in the area, were worked out. In 1990 one of the most common chants of protestors, angry at Western inaction as the political vacuum was filled by men with roots in the communist regime, was 'Malta, Yalta', indicating their belief that the democracies were ready to abandon Romania to Russian captivity for a second time.

YUGOSLAVIA: COUNTDOWN TO TRAGEDY

Ceauşescu and his wife were executed by firing squad on 25 December 1989 on the orders of second-ranking communists as well as army officers who had served the dictatorship faithfully for years and were seeking to cover their tracks by removing someone who had now become a liability to them. As one tyrannical duo met a bloody end, another was starting to scale the heights of power next door in Yugoslavia. No one was closer to Slobodan Milošević than his wife Mirjana (Mira) Marković. They were childhood sweethearts in the town of Požarevac near Belgrade where they both grew up. Mira, a doctrinaire communist whose job was that of lecturer on the sociology of Marxism at Belgrade university, became his guide and helpmate. Her political lineage was far more impressive than that of her husband: he was the son of Montenegrin immigrants to Serbia who, despite his undoubted ability, would probably not have reached the very top without a wife possessing enormous ambition and a burning sense of personal grievance.

Mira's mother had been a prominent Partisan who had been executed during the war for allegedly revealing the names of other Partisans under torture (Judah 2000: 51). Her adopted father Moma Marković was a senior figure of the Tito era who opposed Milošević's nationalist course (Doder and Branson 1999: 51). Many in Serbia believe that Mira is the natural child of Tito himself and that her espousal of a dogmatic form of Marxism and support for vengeful policies, that have resulted in the collapse of Tito's federal state, stem from her traumatic family history.

In 1988–9 Milošević was the only communist leader in the world with steadily rising popularity thanks to his readiness to licence and spread divisive nationalist feelings, once previously at a manageable level. His immediate aim was to merge the nearly two million Serbs, 24% of Yugoslavia's total (according to the 1981 census), with those found in the Republic of Serbia proper. His most fervent supporters came from among the provincial party officialdom and the rural population (Thomas 1999: 48). Peasants and small-town residents were mobilised in 'spontaneous' demonstrations to drive from office local bureaucrats in these provinces loyal to Tito's decentralist precepts. People's power was being manipulated to forestall genuine democratic change and channel discontent along nationalist lines. Milošević championed non-party 'pluralism' which was designed not to dismantle the old regime but to reconstruct it in a new guise (Thomas 1999: 49). Thus Milošević anticipated post-communist nationalists elsewhere in the region who, in the 1990s, would also pursue top-down populist campaigns to preserve their own power.

The first decisive step along this road was the abolition of the autonomy of the province of Voivodina. A crowd organized by militant Serbs from Kosovo laid siege to the government headquarters in Novi Sad, capital of a province where Serbs made up little more than 50% of the population. An unprepared leadership, in a region where inter-ethnic relations were generally good, crumbled before the unexpected challenge and was ousted on 5 October 1988.

Three months of pressure by pro-Milošević supporters led to a similar denouement in Montenegro. As the 'anti-bureaucratic revolution' swept into the mountainous republic, there were even calls in the crowd for the Russians to intervene. Montenegro preserved strong Russophile traditions. In 1920, during Yugoslavia's first elections, the nascent communist party won 38% of the vote (Thompson 1992: 177). This was hardly due to the strength of proletarian consciousness in an overwhelmingly rural country and stemmed more from a willingness to identify with the revolutionary cause in a country long regarded as Montenegro's only protector from the Ottoman Turks. Later, in 1948, 5,000 people, 1.32% of the population in Montenegro, faced official sanctions because of their hostility to the break with Stalin's Russia, many ending up on the prison island of Goli Otok (Thompson 1992: 176).

It was a more difficult undertaking to establish Serbian control over the party and government of Kosovo which were still in Albanian hands. In late February 1989, 2,500 miners staged a hunger strike in the important Trepča zinc and lead mines in support of the 1974 constitution and the autonomy of Kosovo. An unrestricted state of emergency was declared in Kosovo on 27 February by the state presidency in Belgrade. Large numbers of JNA troops were stationed in Kosovo in the run-up to a vote in the Kosovo parliament on whether to accept a new constitution for Serbia, turning it into a unitary state. Tanks were stationed on all main street corners in Pristina, the capital, and deputies were warned that if they voted no, they would be treated as 'counter-revolutionaries' (Meier 1999: 92–3). Only ten deputies out of 187 decided to vote against the proposal which would have resulted in the abolition of their parliament, some of whom were later arrested. Large demonstrations in Pristina, in the days after the vote, were put down 'by special units of police with unusual brutality', 22 demonstrators and 2 police being killed (Judah 2000: 98). On 5 July 1990, the provincial parliament in Kosovo was finally declared dissolved. This was a prelude to the suppression of the Albanian electronic and print media and the removal of thousands of Albanians from state employment, most Albanian managers having been dismissed earlier (Meier 1999: 98).

The international community generally ignored an escalating campaign of repression in Kosovo which made Soviet actions in the Baltic States during the late 1980s, ones that evoked worldwide indignation, minuscule by comparison. But in the western republics of Slovenia and Croatia, there was mounting apprehension about what seemed to be a deliberate strategy to restore the inter-war hegemony of Serbia within an undemocratic Yugoslavia. After the events of 1988–9, Serbia controlled four of the eight regional leaderships represented in the collective state presidency, Yugoslavia's most authoritative political body (Burg 1993: 360). Slovenia, the only Yugoslav republic that could be described as largely homogeneous, was best placed to defy Milošević.

Slovenia had done enormously well out of communist Yugoslavia. The bias against raw material producers and high import duties on manufacturing, had helped subsidise the Slovenian economy for four decades (Denitch 1994: 111). Proximity to western markets, cheap labour and raw materials in Yugoslavia, along with its virtually captive market, enabled the Slovenian economy to flourish (Silber and Little 1995: 73). The subsidy in favour of the state's pro-industrial policies was invisible while Slovenia's contribution to the federal fund for underdeveloped regions (since its inception in 1965 meant to narrow the gap between richer and poorer regions) was highly visible. Slovenia, with 8% of the population, contributed 15.7% of Federal Yugoslavia's contribution to this fund (Milosavljević 2000: 60). In West European countries with similar regional economic imbalances, (such as Britain and Italy), not dissimilar state initiatives to narrow these disparities have rewarded success, largely because of the unimaginative top-down approach of the centre. In Yugoslavia, the wastage incurred in channelling funds to Kosovo was of a grander scale because of the nature of the political system. Much of the investment went into the state administration or into capital-intensive industries with low employment opportunities (Blagojević 2000: 238). Understandably, there was a growing lack of enthusiasm in Slovenia about the income transfer from north to south. It spilled over into outright resistance after the crackdown in Kosovo in the late 1980s which many Slovenians felt they were subsidising. By now Slovenia was in the vanguard of efforts to democratise Yugoslavia. In 1988 the JNA was being openly challenged through the widespread opposition in Slovenia to the military draft. The media was much freer than in the rest of the country. The communist party, under Milan Kučan, was committed to promoting a Slovenian national programme—one that, unlike its Serbian counterpart, rested on genuine multi-partyism and a confederal Yugoslavia.

Throughout 1989 the Slovene leadership sought to block further efforts to recentralise Yugoslavia around Serbia. In June 1989, a new Slovenian constitution was voted upon by the parliament in Ljubljana which affirmed Slovenian sovereignty and omitted reference to the leading role of the communist party. The law of the republic now took precedence over federal law, but it did not mean Slovenia's departure from Yugoslavia, at least for the time being.

Yugoslav centralists reacted with fury towards Slovenian developments. On 1 December 1989 plans to bring 'people's power' to Ljubljana by holding a rally where Slovenians would be shown that the policy of their leaders was 'false', were foiled when Kučan banned the demonstration and blocked the borders. Serbia then imposed a blockade on Slovenia, a huge headline in *Politika* announcing on 4 December that 'Serbia Breaks Relations with the Slovenian Regime' (Meier 1999: 121). A climactic battle of wills between the two regions then occurred at the 14th Congress of the League of Communists from 20 to 22 January 1990. Motions mostly presented by Slovenes affirming the principle of federalism and promoting human rights and democracy were voted down. The Slovenian party then walked out, accompanied by the Croatian party. A central pillar of Yugoslavia had disappeared overnight (Magaš 1993: 241).

The decision of the Croatian communists to defy Serbian centralism came as a surprise. Serbs were prominent in the party and its leader Ivica Račan was new and untested. Croatia had been known as 'the Silent Republic' on account of its quiescence since Tito's suppression of its national reform movement. No Croatian action had provoked the Serbian radicals who instead dwelt on Croatian Ustaša brutality towards Serbs in the Second World War. But in the Croatian party there was mounting nervousness when the Belgrade regime started to organize the Serbian minority in Croatia to pressurise the Croatian party and government to support its policies in Kosovo (Denitch 1994: 100). An aggressive Serbian nationalist upsurge was fomented before the electoral victory of Croatian nationalists in the spring of 1990; indeed it contributed to its success.

If Milošević had started out with the aim of becoming the new Tito in a Yugoslavia with the centralized system found in other communist states, he was learning that this was a complicated goal, perhaps ultimately beyond his power. In the face of mounting concern and resistance in the republics outside his immediate reach, he increasingly used conspiracy, deception and force to try and enforce his will. He found that his most ardent supporters were those whose commitment was to Yugoslavia on Serbian terms (conservative forces drawn from the party and the army) or else to a pan-Serbian state in which all Serbs would gather (the nationalist intelligentsia and emerging paramilitary formations). As usual, it was the opposition which expressed the radical alternative most succinctly. Drasković, at the foundation of his Serbian Renewal Party (SPO) on 7 January 1990 ignored the need to maintain Yugoslavia and supported 'the creation of a democratic, multi-party Serbian state within her historical and ethnic borders' (Obradović 2000: 463).

Soon, in preparation for multi-party elections which (thanks to Slovene pressure) were permitted in 1989 and would be held in all the Yugoslav republics during 1990, the Serbian Communists, renamed the Serbian Socialist Party, were stressing that peoples, not republics or minorities, had the right to self-determination. According to Marija Obradović, '[T]his practically meant that republics were denied the right to secession while peoples were acknowledged this right' (Obradović 2000: 440). The rationale thus existed in the minds of Milošević and his supporters for a Greater Serbia to be carved out of Yugoslavia. The belligerent statements of his supporters suggested that it would consist not just of Serbia proper and parts of other republics where Serbs had a local majority, but even areas which may have been Serbian in the distant past or where the Serbs felt themselves to have been the victims of the aggression of others.

As the Yugoslav crisis deepened in the early 1990s, Milošević's Serbia emerged as the key secessionist force (Silber and Little 1995: xxiv). Central secessionism under which the country was broken up from within and rearranged to suit its most powerful ethnic player became 'the key principle in the overall strategy of Yugoslavia's unravelling' (Conversi 2000: 348). But a unitary semblance was maintained in order to gain international as well as internal acceptance. Pressure from the army to maintain a unitary state, albeit one centralized on Belgrade, was still strong. Moreover, the international community continued to view a united Yugoslavia as vital for European stability, even after the end of the Cold War and with Russia preoccupied with its own problems. Until Yugoslavia was well on course for war, everything else—democracy, minority rights, the distribution of power within the federation—was secondary in Washington, London, and Paris.[1] Milošević cleverly positioned himself as the champion of international legality and the watchdog of the old geopolitical order by setting his face against attempts by several of the other republics to break away from a Serbian-dominated Yugoslavia (Conversi 2000: 351). It won him support among those Western policy-makers for whom a single Yugoslavia was the alpha and omega of stability in the Balkans. The fact that Belgrade centralisers were busy, for years before a shot was fired in the war, destroying the basis for ethnic coexistence first in Kosovo, then in Croatia and finally in Bosnia, was ignored, or else it failed to be noticed by Western diplomats, many of whom rarely moved outside Belgrade.

Milošević was unable to prevent the republics holding multi-party elections in 1990 and in December Serbia would follow suit, in a bid to obtain the legitimacy resulting from testing the popular will in a competitive ballot.

The first elections were held in Slovenia on 8 April 1990. A centre-right coalition won an absolute majority but so did the reform communist, Milan Kučan, in the presidential election held on 22 April, winning 58.6% of the vote in the second round. Soon after, the first non-communist government in post-1945 Yugoslavia was sworn in.

Elections in Croatia were held in two stages on 22 April and 6 May 1990. Reform communists under Ivica Račan decided on a quick poll before the opposition had a chance to effectively organize itself. The two- round majority electoral system which favoured the largest party was chosen, perhaps in expectation that it would benefit Račan's Social Democrats. But this is not how events turned out. Although launched only in June 1989 and hardly visible until early 1990, the Croatian Democratic Union (HDZ) made a considerable impact. It was a broad nationalist front which included right-wing Croatian émigrés, veterans of the Croatian Spring, and even members of the communist establishment. It was led by Franjo Tudjman, a veteran of the Partisans and Yugoslav army general who preferred a career promoting cultural nationalism in Croatia to one in the service of Tito's Yugoslavia. He suffered two periods of imprisonment in the 1970s and 1980s for his views, but the conditions were not onerous and he was able to travel freely during the rest of the 1980s (Silber and Little 1995: 84). He cemented links with Croatian émigrés, often militant nationalists with a romantic image of Croatia and visceral hatred of Serbs. They bankrolled his 1990 election campaign and became the most decisive element in his political alliance, with fateful consequences for Bosnia, many coming from the Herzegovina region which they considered as belonging to Croatia. The HDZ, with its greater funds, fought a better campaign than the Social Democrats and benefited from the long-stifled desire for change in Croatia. But on paper, the result was fairly close: the HDZ got 42% of the vote compared to the left's 36%. Nevertheless, the majority voting system gave the left's 68% of the seats and Tudjman 100% of the power (Emerson 2000: 36).

Milošević in the 1990s was described as being 'at once a Chetnik and a Partisan', seeking to embody the communist and nationalist wings of the Serbian cause in his person (Cohen 1998: 145). Tudjman also strove to act as a reconciler of the intolerant nationalism of the wartime Ustaša and the communist heritage that he and most of his supporters shared. At a rally on 24 February 1990 Tudjman insisted that the Ustaša state deserved to be remembered not because of the fascist outlook of its creators but because it affirmed the historic aspirations of the Croatian people for statehood (Silber and Little 1995: 86). On 17 March he declared: 'Thank God my wife is not a Jew or a Serb' (Tanner 1997: 228). In June a new draft constitution was unveiled which granted enormous powers to the President and deleted references to Yugoslavia. Under the former constitution, Croatia had been 'the national state of the Croatian nation and the state of the Serbian nation in Croatia', and the official scripts were Latin and Cyrillic. But Tudjman's document relegated the Serbs to the ranks of a national minority along with Hungarians and Italians and the only official script was to be Latin (Tanner 1997: 230).

Alarmed Serbs in rural areas where they comprised a majority, regarded this, and other moves by Tudjman to 'Croatianise' the state, as a provocation. An autonomous province of the Serbian Krajina was proclaimed on 25 August 1990 after a referendum among Serbs in an area which had suffered badly from Ustaša atrocities in the Second World War produced overwhelming endorsement for cutting links with Zagreb (Ramet 1996: 43). Most of Croatia's Serbian inhabitants in fact lived in the cities and were uninvolved in this upsurge of defensive Serbian nationalism, though they would soon feel the impact of Tudjman's

'Croatia First' policies in the employment field. The revolt, centred on the town of Knin, severed road and rail communications between northern Croatia and Dalmatia. There was nothing Tudjman could do about it. Prior to the election, the JNA had removed the weaponry of the territorial defence units in Croatia (Tanner 1997: 225). Later in 1990, military supplies were distributed in Serbian strongholds in Croatia at the behest of Milošević and the JNA head, General Velijko Kadijević (Tanner 1997: 225).

Tudjman and Milošević 'combined the worst features of communism and nationalism. They took the management skills that are part of standard communist training, plus the instruments of communist power ... and put them at the service of the demagogic advancement of narrow national interest' (Zimmerman 1999: 40). Two Yugoslav academics, a Serb and a Macedonian, have concluded that 'Tudjman's ultra-nationalism served as the single most important ideological resource in sustaining Milošević ...' (Udovicki and Torov 1997: 94). It is not hard to see why. Tudjman's rhetoric made Milošević's task of winning the JNA round to his strategy of using force to create a Serbian-dominated state from the shell of Yugoslavia much easier to accomplish. The presence of a nationalist demagogue in charge of Croatia, who was far less inhibited about using incendiary language than Milošević, also distracted the international community from Belgrade's actions. This in turn made it easier to argue that Yugoslavia, in its entirety, was succumbing to a collective fit of nationalist hysteria, that it was a disorder natural to the country and its people rather than a carefully contrived campaign to sow ethnic hatred which had one primary source and, finally, that little or nothing could be done by the rest of the world to hold its consequences in check.

Despite being in dispute over territory coveted by Croats and Serbs, Milošević and Tudjman had much in common and remained in contact, either directly or indirectly, far more often than any other two leaders in Yugoslavia both before and during the conflict that blew the state apart. Both sustained programmes of homogenising nationalisms which had little or no place for ethnic minorities, people of mixed race, or indeed liberals from the dominant nationalities who questioned the strategy of building ethnically pure states. Both found that they possessed considerable common ground over the future of Bosnia and Herzegovina, the republic in the centre of Yugoslavia with a Muslim majority of 41% (according to the 1991 census), but with significant Serbian (30%) and Croatian (17%) minorities as well as a sizeable ethnically mixed population. Bosnia, because of its ethnic mix, was seen as Yugoslavia in miniature, a place that would find it difficult to peacefully adjust to the break-up of the federation that had provided it with a sense of equilibrium.

Tudjman insisted that Bosnia was a natural part of the Croatian nation and (in the teeth of historical evidence) that 'Bosnia was a creation of the Ottoman invasion of Europe' (Tanner 1997: 242). He and Milošević shared the view that the Muslims were not a nation in their own right. Milošević repeated the Serbian nationalist nostrum that they were Serbs who had got separated from their true national allegiance, whereas for Tudjman they were Islamicised Croats (Doder and Branson 1999: 88–9). But both men, at a secret meeting held at Tito's hunting lodge at Karadjordjevo on 25 March 1991 agreed to the partition of Bosnia between Serbia and Croatia (Silber and Little 1995: 131–2). Nine months later, by which time Serbia and Croatia were at war, with Milošević's forces in occupation of nearly one-third of Croatian territory, Tudjman admitted to the US ambassador, Warren Zimmerman that he had discussed a carve-up of Bosnia with Milošević and that he trusted him to honour a deal to divide it up in a way that served the interests of both states (Zimmerman 1999: 182–3).

On 30 July 1990, the old Partisan stronghold of Koroza in north-west Bosnia was the launching-pad of a movement designed to rally pro-Yugoslav opinion and save the federation from destruction. Thousands of Serbs had been massacred there by the Ustaše in the early 1940s and in 1992 Serb militia would carry out atrocities against Muslim civilians (Silber and Little 1995: 210; Tanner 1997: 236). But in July 1990 tens of thousands turned out to cheer Ante Marković, Prime Minister of Federal Yugoslavia, who had chosen the spot to launch 'an alliance of reformist forces to build a new and prosperous Yugoslavia'. Marković, a Croat, had been a compromise choice for Federal Premier at the end of 1989 when the different republican leaderships were still interacting via the institutions at federal level. He enjoyed popularity because of his success in eliminating runaway inflation in a very short time and, by the early 1990s, making the Yugoslav dinar fully convertible. Trade was liberalized and he was planning to remove the limits on private ownership. Marković hoped to consolidate the unity of the country through such reforms. He had a champion in the US ambassador, Warren Zimmerman, who engineered an official visit to Washington by Marković. But it coincided with Operation Desert Storm in the Persian Gulf and the Yugoslav President was unable to see anyone of importance. It has been written that 'Marković was probably the only head of government who had to pay for all his meals in Washington; nobody was willing to offer a dinner or lunch in his honour' (Doder and Branson 1999: 108).

Marković's attempt to rally the forces of co-existence in Yugoslavia could only have succeeded with important international assistance. Washington was unaware in 1990 that Yugoslavia would in fact be the first extended test of US authority in the post-Cold War era. The fact that in years to come the USA and its allies offered far more hospitality to unsavoury ethnic politicians, in a bid to persuade them to retreat from extreme positions, would show how the administration of President George Bush misread the situation there.

Bosnia with its multi-faith traditions and apparently strong commitment to the continuation of Yugoslavia was to be the key test for Marković's movement. But in elections here in September 1990, it won only 13 out of 240 seats in a bicameral parliament. Most of the Bosnian electorate had voted along communitarian lines, not necessarily because of ethnic tensions but perhaps owing to the strength of ethnic identities which the communist state had itself licensed and also the low standing of the Bosnian communist party because of its recent involvement in financial scandals. Communitarian ideology had remained the chief organizing principle since before communism and it would have taken another generation of intermarriage in the cities before another one could have been expected to take hold (Bougarel 1996: 87). Marković's party had probably arrived too late on the Yugoslav scene to make an impact. Its results were equally disappointing in Macedonia, Yugoslavia's other main multi-ethnic republic. In December 1990 elections, parties with a Macedonian orientation won a majority, but the Presidency went to Kiro Gligorov, a reform communist sympathetic to Marković's ideas who would manage to shield his vulnerable republic from the inferno raging through much of the rest of Yugoslavia in the 1990s.

In Serbia, Milošević successfully managed to preserve the one-party system by modernising it and giving it multi-party trimmings which imposed no check on his power (Zimmerman 1999: 78). On 1 and 2 June 1990 he organized a referendum in which the electorate was persuaded to pass a new constitution first and have elections afterwards—the opposite pattern to all other countries of the region (Teokarević 1996: 183). On 28 September 1990, the old (still one-party) Serbian Assembly passed a new constitution. It created a strong

Presidency and was thus a legal device to confirm the huge personal power Milošević already enjoyed as chairman of the Presidency under the former constitution. In the Serbian elections of 9 December 1990, Milošević obtained 64% of the vote in the presidential race. His ex-communist Serbian Socialist Party (SPS) got 46.1% of the vote, but the majority voting system (similar to that which had been so helpful to Tudjman) gave the SPS 77.6% of all seats (Gordy 1999: 35). Milošević was helped by the decision of the Albanians in Kosovo to boycott the poll en masse. The Serbian opposition, centred on Draskovic's SPO, was unsure on what ground to oppose Milošević. The nationalist consensus about 'all Serbs in one country' still transcended government-opposition lines (Stojanović 2000: 476). By its statements, the SPO would soon make it clear that it saw Milošević's primary objective as the consolidation of his personal power and the preservation of his natural environment, the communist system. But in 1990 no Serbian party offered the electorate an effective alternative to Milošević's hyper-nationalism dressed up in left-wing garb, one that stressed the need to avoid war, reach a consensus with other regions, and begin the process of integrating with mainstream Europe.

The gulf between Serbia and the other republics widened after the Serbian elections when it emerged that Milošević had succeeded in secretly diverting over 1.5 billion dollars from the Yugoslav national bank to meet its budgetary requirements (Judah 1997: 260). On discovering this larceny, Slovenia and Croatia decided, on 28 December 1990, not to recognise any new financial obligations of the federation (Meier 1999: 162). Slovenia now embarked on preparing for full independence and showed itself uninterested in remaining efforts to salvage Yugoslavia (Silber and Little 1995: 148).

On 9 January 1991 Borislav Jović, the Serbian member of the eight-person Yugoslav presidency, and a close ally of Milošević, sought a majority in favour of authorising the JNA to use force against Slovenia and Croatia (Zimmerman 1999: 98). But he was foiled by the refusal of the Bosnian representative, Bogić Bogičević, to support him. Bogičević was a Bosnian Serb who was, nevertheless, unwilling to vote for an intolerant Serbian position (Zimmermann 1999: 99). According to Jović, who published his diaries after falling out with Milošević, by the start of 1991:

> We thought, Milošević and I, that there was no reason to keep Croatia by force and we thought the Army should have withdrawn to the Serb territories. But the Army could not understand this because they still believed they should defend Yugoslavia. (Silber and Little 1995: 114)

Indeed, on 10 January 1991, Milošević gave the clearest indication to date of his position: 'If Yugoslavia were to become a confederation of independent states, Serbia would demand territory from neighbouring republics so that all eight-and-a-half-million Serbs would be in the same state' (Cohen 1998: 191).

But Milošević faced unexpected trouble in his own backyard when, on 9 March, students poured on to the streets of Belgrade demanding his resignation. So large were the protests that Milošević called on the army to suppress them. By doing so, the JNA lost what remaining reputation it had as an independent force (Gordy 1999: 37). Resistance to conscription was already spreading across much of Yugoslavia and soon, in the central Serbian region of Sumadija alone, only one in four young people were responding to the call-up (Doder and Branson 1999: 98). In years to come, a huge exodus of liberal-minded young Serbs would occur which would make Milošević's task of controlling the state far easier. Excluding those of his own people who resisted his personal despotism could sometimes appear to be as much a priority for him as detaching parts of the state unlikely ever to want to succumb to his rule.

During the student crisis, Milošević outlined a tough new response to the wider Yugoslav crisis which was leaked (against his will) to the public: 'If we have to, we'll fight. I hope they won't be so crazy as to fight against us. Because if we don't know how to work and to do business, at least we know how to fight' (Silber and Little 1995: 129).

On 12 March 1991, General Kadijević of the JNA was sent to Moscow where he met with conservative army chiefs. It was one of several trips by JNA officers to assess how the international community would respond to a crackdown in Yugoslavia. According to Admiral Branko Mamula, 'we were interested in their [Russian] assessment as to whether the West would intervene to try to disarm the paramilitary units by force', a reference to forces under the authority of the Slovene and Croatian governments (Silber and Little 1995: 126–7). Conversi believes the message that the JNA obtained from its foreign soundings was that '[T]here was no credible threat to Serbian nationalism from the West' (Conversi 2000: 345).

On 15 May 1991, Serbia rendered the Yugoslav state presidency incapable of functioning by refusing to recognise the accession of the Croatian representative, Stipe Mesić, as the new chairman. Four days later, a referendum saw Croatia vote overwhelmingly in favour of independence. Last minute efforts by the leaders of the Bosnian and Macedonian republics to promote a compromise based on a loose federation got nowhere (Cohen 1998: 1888). Slovenia was by now set on independence. Tudjman naively felt that such a route could be taken by Croatia even though fighting had already erupted in areas disputed by Croatian and Serbian forces, with the Croats being heavily outgunned. Serbia would only accept a loose federation if it was accompanied by a change in the internal republican boundaries.

On 21 June 1991, four days before Slovenia's independence declaration was due, US Secretary of State James Baker paid a whirlwind visit to Yugoslavia. He held eleven meetings with the republic's presidents. His message, according to Jim Swigert, a US diplomat present, was quixotic: 'America opposed the breaking up of Yugoslavia but also opposed the use of force to hold it together' (Cohen 1998: 144). Brent Scrowcroft, Bush's National Security adviser, relates that Baker's stock comment to the escalating crisis was that 'we don't have a dog in this fight'. As for Bush himself, 'The President would say to me once a week, "Tell me what this is all about"' (Doder and Branson 1999: 105). The craven attitude of the world's undisputed superpower played into the hands of Milošević, who felt he faced few external restraints on his conduct as a compliant army and paramilitary forces started to remake Yugoslavia on their terms when fighting erupted first in Slovenia and then in Croatia during the summer of 1991.

CONCLUSION

The Balkan communist states were in a poor position to benefit from the end of the Cold War and the gradual introduction of open politics and competitive economics to the communist bloc.

The communist era had strengthened aspects of political culture in Southeast Europe inimical to democracy-building. Economic decisions had largely been made on crude political grounds at the expense of economic rationality. Ruthless social engineering policies had created dependent groups, largely made up of former peasants, who were trained solely for unskilled industrial tasks and who had little immediate future outside the heavy industry sector. The social constituency for minimal change was thus much larger in the Balkan communist states than in other satellites.

The strength of interests hostile to pluralist reform within the Yugoslav communist system was shown in the 1980s. After Tito's death, they were able to fight a successful rearguard action. The contract between the federal state and its multi-ethnic citizens was torn up by

Slobodan Milošević. Perhaps this should not occasion much surprise: the post-1917 experience has shown that communism is more suited to ethnic homogenisation than to promoting ethnic balance and pluralism. Nationalism was used to strengthen the threatened power of the party apparatus. This had already happened in Romania and Bulgaria where national communist elites targeted the Hungarian and Turkish minorities who were both treated as 'the enemy within'. But appeals to crude nationalism were only temporary palliatives for cornered despots whose economic policies were failing: Ceauşescu and his wife faced the firing squad in 1989 and long years in custody stretched ahead for Zhivkov.

Perhaps if Yugoslavia had not followed profoundly impractical economic policies, the balance of power would have shifted to moderate communists who could have contemplated playing successful roles in genuinely multi-party systems. But this was not to be. 'Brotherhood and Unity, the watchword of the Tito era, was to be on Serbian terms. Serbian hegemony was to result in 'a kind of dual Yugoslavia consisting of an inner core under direct Serbian control and a periphery under direct Serbian influence' (Meier 1999: 115). There was a reversal to sultanistic rule in Yugoslavia after 1986; Milošević, virtually Europe's last communist head, would end up doing more harm to his fellow Serbs than Ustaša, Nazis, Austrians, or even perhaps Ottoman Turks had inflicted in bygone centuries.

The revival of ethnically-rooted values is not just a feature of communist Europe. It was also happening in some western states. The north Italian separatists of Umberto Bossi used the contemptuous language about southern Italians that parts of the Belgrade elite reserved for Albanians and then Croats. The invective of the French neo-fascist Jean-Marie Le Pen towards immigrants was also cruder and more overt than that of national communist leaders towards their minorities. But democratic Europe was able usually to contain these nationalist shock-waves, unlike communist systems usually lacking strong popular legitimacy.

Interest groups and the forces of civil society committed to a decisive break with the communist past were weak in Southeast Europe. Balkan Communist dictatorships had regulated society and interfered in the private lives of their citizens far more systematically than in Poland or Hungary. But rigid controls on free speech and personal liberties underestimated the extent to which specific social groups, who could be said to comprise the nascent middle classes, desired democratic change.

Politics had remained conspiratorial in the communist era as Balkan despots manipulated party and government statutes to sideline rivals and maximise their personal power. The politics of conspiracy was much in evidence in Yugoslavia during the 1980s and would be used elsewhere to subvert or slow down the shift from dictatorial rule.

The Balkans continued to be seen as peripheral to the interests of the Atlantic democracies. The USA in the 1980s, under its own nationalist President, Ronald W. Reagan, found Western Europe with its kaleidoscopic politics difficult enough to track without taking into account the Balkans. The European Union was absorbed with its plans for economic and monetary union and scarcely perceived that it was worth paying attention to the implosion occurring in a communist federation a few hours' drive to the east. In 1934, Robert Schuman, a French deputy who later would become a co-architect of the European Union, had carried out an in-depth investigation into the failure of royal centralism in Yugoslavia which he believed might threaten the peace of Europe (Price 2000: 5–7). But in the 1980s the EU had few statesmen with both the vision and prudence to empathise with the problems of Europe's Southeast. With Tito gone, the country, and indeed the region which it belonged to, lacked the influential advocates in the EU and major member-states which had enabled time and resources to be set aside for integrating the former Iberian dictatorships into the Union. Despite being handicapped by its Balkan location, Greece had been allowed to join in 1981 because of its image as the cradle of western civilization. The Southeast European states under communist rule enjoyed no such pedigree. Indeed, the belief of D.S. Laskey, a lowly Foreign Office official, writing in 1943, who later became ambassador to Bucharest in the 1970s, that Communist regimes might be an improvement on a return to the traditional hatreds of the peoples of the Balkans, was one probably shared by a great many other diplomats even when the behaviour of some of these regimes cast grave doubt on such optimism (Rothwell 1982: 199).

Western indifference played a major indirect role in strengthening the position of nationalist hardliners in Yugoslavia in the 1980s. The nature of Balkan politics continued to be little understood in the West during the final years of the Cold War. The view that regimes like Ceauşescu's and Milošević's were primarily nationalist was hard to dislodge. Such a view was popularised by commentators like Paul Lendvai and distinguished diplomats like George Kennan who may have had the Balkans very much in mind when he wrote in the 1960s:

There is today no such thing as 'communism' in the sense that there was in 1947; there are only a number of national regimes which cloak themselves in the verbal trappings of radical Marxism and follow domestic policies influenced to one degree or another by Marxist concepts. (Quoted in Lendvai 1969: 358)

The information blockade allowed such flimsily-based attitudes to persist. The growth of corporatism and the managerial ethos in many Western countries during the later Cold War period even enabled some officials in contact with Eastern Europe to empathise with the bureaucratic managers of the communist system. According to Victor Meier, based in the Balkans for longer than any other Western journalist, Milošević was seen as a technocrat and a genuine moderniser by many western diplomats in the 1980s (Meier 1999: 40–41).

Such a defective approach should not be seen as surprising if placed in the context of Western perceptions of Balkan political processes over a long historical period. It is one that would give rise to blunders and delusions that would dwarf those seen in earlier periods and eventually lead to a new cycle of Western engagement with the minutiae of Balkan politics which, at the time of writing, shows no sign of coming to an end.[2]

NOTES

1. I am grateful to Kyril Drezov for this information.
2. The role of the international community from 1991 onwards will be explored in detail in a second volume in preparation.

Conclusion

This survey of the origins of contemporary Balkan politics shows that the negative image of the region is based on some solid foundations but that it is one needing to be qualified.

During the last millennium the region has enjoyed a lengthier period of political unification than the rest of Europe. Under the Ottoman Empire, it was a single territorial unit for 400 years (with the exception of small territories such as Transylvania and Montenegro and the city-state of Dubrovnik). But the Ottoman system failed to lay the basis for a common identity which could have enabled a unified Balkan state to emerge in its aftermath. It never consciously set out to create an integrated society. Instead it permitted self-contained religious groups that held aloof from each other. The Islamic faith was the predominant one but other religions enjoyed significant autonomy, which in Western Europe was usually simply not permitted to religions different from, or at variance with, that of the ruling dynasty.

Turkish historians today contrast the tolerance of diversity in Ottoman lands with the insistence on religious conformity in the West. It has even been claimed that 'there would be no Serbs, no Bulgarians, Romanians, and Greeks, had not the Ottoman Turks conquered the Balkans. If the ever-present and intimidating Catholic appetite had not been able to devour them, it has been so because of the Turkish invasion and conquest' (Bora 1994: 106).

But national histories after statehood was achieved for Balkan peoples usually depicted the Ottoman era as Southeast Europe's equivalent of the Western Dark Ages, an extended period of captivity and backwardness. Certainly, the second half of the Ottoman era was one characterised for long periods by a power vacuum at the centre. Breakdowns of law and order in the provinces and heavy taxation blighted commerce and saw the region fall far behind Western and Central Europe.

By the 1800s, the powerful states of Western Europe held out a strong attraction for literate and mobile groups on the European margins of the empire. They fashioned a political project out of their sense of religious distinctiveness, hoping to create national political units along Western lines.

But the state-building process in Western Europe had usually been an extended one in which national identity emerged gradually. Under the influence of the French revolutionary model, as well as the racial ideas associated with German idealistic philosophy, Balkan radicals hoped to speed up the process and create compact nation-states on ethnically mixed territories. National movements took shape based around linguistic and religious identities. The promotion of a common language was seen as essential in order to guarantee the success of the nation-building project. The mobilisation of a religious identity was often necessary in order to draw a line between the national group and co-inhabitants of its territory, especially if they were Muslim.

The ethnic heterogeneity permitted by the multicultural imperial policy of the Ottomans meant that the creation of compact nation-states was bound to be a violent process. The emphasis on language as the primary nation-building element precluded the integration of other linguistic groups, except through assimilation (Todorova 1997: 177). The topography of Southeast Europe furnished fewer 'natural' frontiers than in Western Europe within which nation-states could establish solid foundations.

The Ottoman Empire has frequently been blamed for unprovoked and indiscriminate cruelty, a charge that has validity for its final phases. But perhaps its biggest fault was that it did not provide sufficient outlets for internal reform that could have allowed gradualistic political change rather than the revolutionary break provided by homogenising national-isms. Perhaps giving religious autonomy a political dimension might have been a way forward. It might have been appealing to the Albanians and perhaps even the Bulgarians up to the 1860s. Stambulov, the Bulgarian Premier, was prepared to entertain a Bulgarian–Turkish partnership in the 1880s when relations between Sofia and St Petersburg grew sour. But by now the influence of Western-style nationalism in Turkey itself was too strong for multinational arrangements to be refined in this way.

The West, most particularly Great Britain, chose as its Eastern policy the maintenance of the integrity of the Ottoman Empire, without pressing for reforms, other than financial ones. Backing for a despotic empire was at variance with enlightened policies at home. The contradiction only burst to the surface occasionally, as during the 1876 Bulgarian crisis which galvanised British politics. The double standards underlying Western policies towards the region meant that there was a disinclination for policy-makers to familiarise themselves with its problems. They usually discouraged original thought, which increased the likelihood that policies devised in foreign ministries to deal with earlier Balkan crises survived remarkably unaltered.

The performance of the Balkan national states did not encourage the West to revise its attitudes. The new states remained centralist and remote from their subjects. Balkan elites had a tendency to use the ideology of nationalism to advance their own group or family interests rather than to concentrate on policies of economic development (Stokes 1997: 3). There were West European states, such as pre-1914 Italy, which behaved little differently. Many years would elapse before the major democracies would concern themselves with the political conduct of other states in a disinterested way. Usually, there had to be a sense of empathy for a people suffering under bad leadership or exploitation and it was largely lacking for the Balkan lands. The idea that bad rulers were largely representative of the people they ruled over originated not in the era of inter-war dictatorships or in the communist era, but probably rather earlier. Only Greece in the 1820s and Bulgaria in the 1870s were seen as deserving of active support in order to shake off unwanted tyranny, and these gestures of solidarity in Western countries were shortlived ones which did not alter broader perceptions of the region.

But it was the Western powers and Russia that established the boundaries in which nationalism would function as a dominant political paradigm. In 1878 their representatives gathered in Berlin to divide the Balkans in ways meant to satisfy their appetites and feelings of insecurity. The Congress of Berlin created a series of contested territories—Macedonia, Bosnia-Herzegovina, and Bessarabia—that envenomed relations between the new Balkan states, and between several of them and the chief local powers: Austria-Hungary and Russia. Thus the term 'Balkanization' entered the dictionary as a result of actions by the great powers who, later on, would blame the unforeseen consequences on the immaturity and allegedly uncivilized nature of local peoples and their leaders.

It is not surprising that nationalism played a preponderant role in the politics of the region. The role of intellectuals in the independence struggle and the importance accorded to cultural assimilation and unity during the formative years when both nation- and state-building were being attempted, gave the intellectuals a particular influence. Often they emphasised national themes for career reasons and to increase their access to the resources of the state at a time of scarcity. But the tempo and importance of identity politics varied from country to country and within countries fluctuated within specific time periods. It should not be forgotten that the spirit of the age in which Balkan states first emerged was an overwhelmingly nationalistic one. In giving nationalism a transcendent value, new states were, in many ways, simply emulating Russia and the West. France, with its emphasis on using the centralized state to create a uniform national society, was a particularly potent influence. Germany, where a 1913 nationality law (only effectively repealed in 1999) made ancestry, rather than place of birth, the criterion for citizenship, exercised a strong and underestimated influence on the collective values of the Balkan states. In the academic circles of Atlantic democracies, arguments about the hierarchy of nations enjoyed full respectability. Imperialism was one of the outcomes of the belief that the hierarchy which existed in the animal kingdom was replicated among nations.

So the emphasis in the new Balkan states of competition in order to establish which of them was fittest to dominate their neighbourhood and fulfil their historic mission was scarcely aberrant as the First World War approached. The domination of the powers was increasingly resented, especially by a state like Serbia where national ideology enjoyed its greatest attraction among the educated classes. The powers determined whether a Balkan people deserved to have a state and what its size should be. Their criteria were usually informal if not capricious: the patronage of France's Napoleon III in no small measure made possible the emergence of Romania in the 1860s. But in the 1870s the objections of Britain and Austria-Hungary prevented a strong South Slav state forming around Bulgaria; with the exception of Serbia, the crowned heads of the new Balkan states were farmed out by the leading royal houses of Europe. Given the fortuitous way that peoples had monarchs foisted upon them, it is hardly surprising that their record was a very mixed one.

National rivalries culminated in the two Balkan wars of 1912–13, which defined the negative image of the region. The Sarajevo assassinations in June 1914, which soon resulted in the First World War, saddled the region with a violent and anarchic image that it has never lost. Writing in 1940, the influential John Gunther, whose books on the politics of different continents and regions shaped the perceptions of a middlebrow English-speaking readership during the middle years of the last century, had no doubt that the Balkans had a lot to answer for:

> It is an intolerable affront to human and political nature that these wretched and unhappy little countries in the Balkan peninsula can, and do, have quarrels that cause world wars. Some hundred and fifty thousand young Americans died because of an event in 1914 in a mud-caked primitive village, Sarajevo. Loathsome and almost obscure snarls in Balkan politics, hardly intelligible to a

Western reader, are still vital to the peace of Europe, and perhaps the world. (Gunther 1940: 437)

These words appeared in 1940 when Europe was once again sliding into a civil war, one that this time the Balkan states were determined not to be drawn into. For most of the 1930s they had been promoting mutual security measures which had succeeded in drawing in former enemies on the battlefield such as Greece, Bulgaria and Turkey. It looked as if states with incompatible claims that had led to war in the past were prepared to interact peacefully and explore ways of reducing the enmity between them.

This was no small achievement: the Treaty of Versailles at the end of the First World War had promoted large states in Eastern Europe in the hope that this would check the revival of Germany and act as a buffer against Soviet Russian expansion. The amount of territorial grievances had accelerated, particularly in East-Central Europe, and one-quarter of the population in the states carved out of defeated empires were minorities.

The Great Depression then starkly revealed the dependence of the Balkan economies on global terms of trade over which they exercised little control. Economic collapse is a breeding ground for political extremism but, with the exception of Romania, internal politics in the Balkans during the 1930s were hardly more unstable than in other parts of Europe, excepting the countries of the northwest. The rise of Nazism and Fascism in Germany and Italy, the Spanish Civil War, and the internal polarisation of France along left–right lines, had surprisingly few echoes in Southeast Europe. The overwhelmingly peasant character of Southeast European society may have been a firebreak which insulated the region from the new radical ideologies.

But communism was imposed on all of the Balkans north of Greece in the mid-1940s. Probably the greatest legacy of the communist system was to transform the agrarian peasant economy into an increasingly urban one based on heavy industry. It solved the question of rural overpopulation but left many new ones in its wake. If Southeast Europe had stayed out of the communist orbit and experienced the economic changes seen in analogous societies such as Portugal and Spain, urbanisation would have occurred, but at a more measured rate and without many of the lasting sociological ill effects. The booming economies of Western Europe could have absorbed much of the surplus population. Growth rates would have been more convincing and enduring than the ones proclaimed by communist statistics.

There is surprisingly little debate about what the future might have been for the Balkans if it had avoided the sovietisation of its politics and economics. Many scholars are predisposed to believe that younger members of the Balkan inter-war elites would have been hard-pressed to rise above ethnic enmity and orientate their countries in more constructive directions if given the chance. But equally gloomy prognoses were made about the prospects of Italy breaking free from its fascist and weak democratic legacy in the mid-1940s and Spain doing the same thirty years later and both were proven wrong, Spain spectacularly so.

It was in the vital closing years of the Second World War that the negative image of Southeast Europe generally held by Western leaders had the most momentous effect on the region's future. It was unfortunate that the USA, the stronger of the Western allies, largely left the key negotiations with Stalin over the Balkans in the hands of Britain. Churchill's inestimable services to the cause of democratic freedom at a perilous moment for the world cannot disguise the fact that it was British national interests, rather than any wider considerations, which shaped his policy towards Greece, Bulgaria and Romania.

Western policy towards Yugoslavia after 1941 was more far-seeing. But it was Yugoslavia's communist leader Josip Broz Tito who checked Stalin's advance more effectively than the West. The Soviet–Yugoslav quarrel revealed how conflicting national objectives could bring communist states to the point of confrontation more quickly than democratic ones. Initially, at Stalin's bidding, and later independently of Moscow, various Balkan communist regimes were prepared to revive territorial disputes which had previously been dismissed as bourgeois tools designed to deepen the false consciousness of the masses.

Nationalism was appealing to communist chieftains shackled to a failed economic model because it lacked social content. It was a useful anaesthetic which enabled them to divert citizens from protesting against an imposed political system which was failing society. The countries where nationalism was taken furthest in a bid to acquire synthetic legitimacy were nearly all in the Balkans and it was here that internal challenges to the communist system were least apparent.

Of course Yugoslavia was a major exception to this rule during nearly all of its period as a communist state. The ability of the Tito regime to acquire genuine support at least among the federation's South Slav inhabitants, after the terrible bloodletting of 1941–45, shows the limitations of nationalism. If nationalist hatreds had remained raw, then it would have probably been beyond the power of Tito's police state to easily contain them. Yugoslavia possessed powerful integrative as well as centrifugal tendencies and it was the latter which slowly gained ascendancy owing to Tito's flawed approach to managing his multi-ethnic state. The regime failed to pursue realistic development policies that would capture the solidarity of the people and enable a common Yugoslav identity gradually to acquire precedence over ethnic ones. The growing obsolescence of a once-dynamic regime as its dependence on its ageing founder became increasingly obvious, enabled nationalism to be revived as a power-conserving project by conservative communists with results that have created a living hell for millions of its inhabitants.

After the 1960s the Kremlin was relatively uninterested in Yugoslavia and in its Southeast satellites. But the West failed to monitor Balkan developments closely and devise contingency plans to intervene at the diplomatic level to defuse crises of governance. It made some crass errors in its policy towards Stalinist Romania, which may have encouraged would-be emulators of Ceauşescu's red monarchy, such as Slobodan and Mira Milošević in Serbia, to assume that they could similarly hoodwink distant Western leaders.

For too long Western leaders were content to support the Tito regime as the primary guarantor of stability in a turbulent region. The West has had a long-standing tendency to promote a pet Balkan country or an admired leader in an uncritical fashion. It is not just leaders and diplomats but advocates on the left and right of politics who have backed a 'virtuous' country or a personality, as the internationalisation of the Yugoslav conflict has shown during its various stages.

Low-grade Western diplomacy and statecraft in the 1940s enabled Stalin to extend more control over Eastern Europe than the Soviets in the end knew what to do with. In the 1980s, Western inattention to the Balkans contributed to the survival of authoritarianism beyond the communist era. Policy failures in Greece and Cyprus probably discouraged the Atlantic democracies from involving themselves much further with the affairs of the region. The dogmatic nature of communism in Romania and Bulgaria was ascribed to local character-istics, rather than the need for an ideology to assume a ruthless form in areas where the natural economic and social conditions to sustain it were so obviously lacking.

Milošević, who knew the West through his closeness to Lawrence Eagleburger when the latter was American ambassador in Belgrade from 1977 to 1981, and also his own regular visits to New York on government business, assumed that he could hoodwink Western officials about his intentions for Yugoslavia. He pandered to their desire to view the Balkans in stereotypical terms, as he would do when he was at the centre of negotiations for a diplomatic peace to the wars he had started in the 1990s.

The confidence trick he performed on his own people was on a much grander scale. The failure of Tito's unwieldy self-management system in Yugoslavia resulted in a rejection of the Yugoslav ideal among well-placed groups. In the 1980s, many Serbs wished to recentralise the country, ensuring that their co-ethnics inside and outside Serbia belonged to one secure entity. Slovenes and Croats responded by promoting national strategies which would insulate them from Serb expansionism. People's power was invoked as the need for nations to re-establish their integrity. But across Europe for nearly two hundred years, calculating and obsessive figures had manipulated the collective emotions unleashed by appeals to nationalist values to maximise their own urge for power. Napoleon was the first to see the political advantages an appeal to nationalism provided for an individual whose ego was fulfilled by controlling the lands and destinies of millions of others.

Just like Napoleon in France, Milošević built up a mighty alliance of Serbs held together by nationalist appeals only to betray each segment in a fifteen-year spree of conquest and chicanery. He promised to uphold the national rights of Serbs disgruntled by the performance of Federal Yugoslavia, he promised to uphold their social rights and prevent them being trampled upon by capitalist economics, finally he offered security to Serb minorities outside Serbia proper by promising that the internal republican frontiers would be no obstacle in Belgrade coming to their defence. But gradually it became clear to nationalists of various hues, to workers, almost certainly to most Serb minorities in territories Milošević wanted to absorb into Serbia, and finally to most of his political allies in the Socialist party that emerged in 1990, that his own personal interests were the only ones he was really prepared to advance and defend.

If the Balkans were prone to see the rise of such leaders, then the explanation lies less in the inadequacies of their inhabitants and more in the imposition of ideologies and colonising projects that have their origins outside the peninsula. An unfavourable geopolitical position has made it difficult for the region to easily withstand such pressures. Where external occupation has, to some degree, respected local religious and cultural traditions, then the region has enjoyed long periods of internal peace, most notably during the first half of the Ottoman era. But external invasions that trample the values and aspirations of Balkan inhabitants invite a furious reaction, as various stronger European powers have found in the last one hundred years. Inevitably, the sense of insecurity instilled by such violent disruptions strengthens the position of politicians who wish to shape politics around defiant nationalism rather than an agenda for development. If Britain or the United States, instead of being located in regions of the world which meant that violations of their sovereignty were difficult to accomplish by an aggressor, had witnessed land grabs and invasions every few generations, then the problems of the Balkans would not seen so unfathomable to most Americans and Britons. Indeed, parts of the USA and Britain, notably the Deep South and Northern Ireland, have witnessed identity conflicts which have assumed a character arguably even more intransigent than anything seen in the Balkans outside Kosovo. It could be argued that reconciliation was slower to emerge in the southern states of the USA in the century after the 1861–65 American Civil War than it was in parts of Southeast Europe where the politics of ethnicity turned violent.

The 1945–89 communist era was the most disastrous foreign intervention the region has witnessed. It resulted in the imposition of a defective economic model which greatly increased the marginality of the region *vis-à-vis* the rest of Europe. Yugoslavia and then other countries may have broken out of the Soviet straitjacket, but they maintained many of the classic features of the Soviet command economy which placed them on the path to underdevelopment. The rigidity of communist rule prevented dissident movements with a human rights, ecology, peace or religious freedom agenda from emerging to challenge the regime. Different forms of nationalism became the currency of political activism when a second transformation shook that part of Eastern Europe forty years after the Yalta agreement.

This book has argued that external mishandling of the territories making up the Balkan peninsula, particularly during the 20th century, has contributed in no small measure to the crisis of governance and economic sustainability which grips much of Southeast Europe at the start of a new century. The impact of faulty external policies is now starting to be recognised in the Atlantic democracies. Time will soon tell whether the response of powerful and prosperous free states in the rest of Europe and across the Atlantic is imaginative and generous enough to prevent the Balkans becoming the permanent slum of Europe.

Bibliography

Achim, Viorel (1998), *Ţiganii în istoria României*, Bucharest: Editura Enciclopedica.

Alexandrescu, Sorin (1998), *Paradoxul Român*, Bucharest: Univers.

Almond, Mark (1988), *Decline Without Fall: Romania Under Ceauşescu*, London: Institute for European Defence and Strategic Studies.

Almond, Mark (1992), *The Rise and Fall of Nicolae and Elena Ceauşescu*, London: Chapmans.

Anderson, M.S. (1966), *The Eastern Question, 1774–1923: A Study in International Relations*, London: Macmillan.

Anzulovic, Branimir (1999), *Heavenly Serbia: From Myth to Genocide*, London: Hurst.

Arnakis, George G., (1963), 'The Role of Religion in the Development of Balkan Nationalism', in Jelavich, Charles and Jelavich, Barbara (eds) *The Balkans in Transition*, Berkeley: University of California Press.

Ashdown, Paddy (1999), 'How to win the peace when the conflict is over', *Independent on Sunday*, London: 18 April.

Ball, George (1982), *The Past Has Another Pattern: Memoirs*, New York: Norton.

Barker, Elisabeth (1948), *Truce in the Balkans*, London: Percival Marshall.

Barker, Elisabeth (1976), *British Policy in South-East Europe in the Second World War*, London: Macmillan.

Barnes, Hugh (1999), 'A dictator's secret', *Financial Times*, London: 10–11 July.

Bebler, Anton (1993), 'Yugoslavia's Variety of Communist Federalism and Her Demise', *Communist and Post-Communist Politics*, vol. 26, no. 1, March.

Bell, John D. (1977), *Peasants in Power: Alexander Stamboliski and the Bulgarian Agrarian National Union, 1899–1923*, Princeton: Princeton University Press.

Beloff, Nora (1985), *Tito's Flawed Legacy, Yugoslavia and the West: 1939–84*, London: Gollancz.

Berend, Ivan T. (1987), 'The Cultural Identity of Central and Eastern Europe', *New Hungarian Quarterly*, vol. 28, no. 107.

Berindei, Mihnea (1998a), 'Romania lui Ceauşescu—un naufragiu planifiat I', *22*, vol. 9, no. 46, Bucharest: November.

Berindei, Mihnea (1998b), 'Romania lui Ceauşescu—un naufragiu planifiat II', *22*, vol. 9, no. 47, Bucharest: November.

Bethell, Nicholas (1995), *Spies and Other Secrets: Memoirs From the Second Cold War*, London: Penguin.

Bideleux, Robert and Jeffries, Ian (1998), *Eastern Europe: Crisis and Change*, London: Routledge.

Black, Cyril E. (1982), 'The View From Bulgaria', in Hammond, Thomas T., *Witnesses to the Origins of the Cold War*, Seattle and London: University of Washington Press.

Blagojević, Marina (2000), 'The Migration of Serb from Kosovo during the 1970s and 1980s', in Popov, Nebojša (ed.), *The Road To War in Serbia: Trauma and Catharsis*, Budapest: Central European University Press.

Bookman, Milica Zarković (1994), *Economic Decline and Nationalism in the Balkans*, New York: St Martin's Press.

Bora, Tanil (1994 estimate) 'Turkish National Identity, Turkish Nationalism, and the Balkan Question', in Özdoğan, Gunay Göksu and Saybasili, Kemali (eds), *Balkans: Mirror of the New International Order*, Istanbul: Eren.

Borsody, Stephen (1993), *The New Central Europe, Triumphs and Tragedies*, Boulder, Colorado: East European Monographs.

Bougarel, Xavier (1996), 'Bosnia and Hercegovina—State and Communitarianism', in Dyker, David and Vejvoda, Ivan, *Yugoslavia and After: A Study in Fragmentation, Despair and Rebirth*, London: Longman.

Brailsford, H.N. (1971), *Macedonia: Its Races and their Future*, New York: Arno Press.

Brezianu, Andrei *et al.* (1989), *Romania: A Case of Dynastic Communism*, New York: Freedom House.

Bringe, Tone (1995), *Being Muslim The Bosnian Way: Identity and Community in a Central Bosnian Village*, Princeton: Princeton University Press.

Brogan, Patrick (1990), *Eastern Europe 1939–1989: The Fifty Years War*, London: Bloomsbury.

Brown, J.F. (1970), *Bulgaria Under Communist Rule*, London: Pall Mall Press.

Brown, J.F. (1992), *Nationalism, Democracy and Security in the Balkans*, Aldershot: Dartmouth Publishing.

Brown, L. Carl (1984), *International Politics and the Middle East: Old Rules, Dangerous Games*, Princeton: Princeton University Press.

Brown, L. Carl (1996), *Imperial Legacy: The Ottoman Imprint on the Balkans and the Middle East*, New York: Columbia University Press.

Brucan, Silviu (1993), *The Wasted Generation: Memoirs of the Romanian Journey from Capitalism to Socialism and Back*, Boulder and London: Westview.

Bruce Lockhart, R.H. (1938), *Guns and Butter: War Countries and Peace Countries of Europe Revisited*, London: Putnam.

Burg, Steven (1993), 'Why Yugoslavia Fell Apart', *Current History*, November.

Burks, R.V. (1961), *The Dynamics of Communism In Eastern Europe*, Princeton: Princeton University Press.

Cadogan, Sir Alexander (1971), *The Diaries of Sir Alexander Cadogan, O.M., 1938–1945*, ed. David Dilkes, London: Cassell.

Calinescu, Matei (1995), 'Ionesco and *Rhinoceros*: Personal and Political Backgrounds', *East European Politics and Societies*, vol. 9, no. 3, fall.

Campbell, John (1967), *Tito's Separate Road: America and Yugoslavia In World Politics*, New York: 1969.

Campbell, John (1970), *French Influence and the Rise of Roumanian Nationalism*, New York: Arno Press [Ph.D. originally submittted to the History Department of Harvard University in 1940].

Carabott, Philip (ed.) (1995), *Greece and Europe in the Modern Period: Aspects of a Troubled Relationship*, London: Centre for Hellenic Studies, King's College London.

Carlton, David (1981), *Anthony Eden: A Biography*, London: Allen Lane.

Carnegie Endowment for International Peace (1st ed. 1914, re-issued 1993), *Report of the International Commission to Inquire into the Causes and Conduct of the Balkan Wars*, New York: Carnegie Trust.

Carver, Robert (1998), *The Accursed Mountains: Journey in Albania*, London: John Murray.

Castellan, Georges (1992), *History of the Balkans: From Mohammed the Conqueror to Stalin*, New York: Columbia University Press.

Chace, James (1998), *Acheson: The Secretary of State who Created the American World*, London: Simon & Schuster.

Charlton, Michael (1983a), 'The Eagle & the Small Birds: 1. The Spectre of Yalta', *Encounter*, London: June.

Charlton, Michael (1983b), 'The Eagle & the Small Birds: 3. The Eclipse of Ideology', *Encounter*, London: September–October.

Charmley, John (1993), *Churchill: The End of Glory, A Political Biography*, London: Hodder & Stoughton.

Chirot, Daniel (1976), *Social Change in a Peripheral Society, The Creation of a Balkan Colony*, New York: Academic Press.

Churchill, Sir Winston S. (1954), *The Second World War, Volume 6: Triumph and Tragedy*, London: Cassell.

Ciobanu, Mircea (1997), *Convorbiri cu Mihai I al României*, Bucharest: Humanitas.

Clinton, William Jefferson (1999), 'On Track in Kosovo Towards Balkan Renaissance', *International Herald Tribune*, Paris: 24 May.

Clogg, Richard (1992), *A Concise History of Greece*, Cambridge: Cambridge University Press.

Close, David H. (1995), 'The Changing Structure of the Right, 1945–50', in Iatrides, John and Wrigley, Linda (eds), *Greece at the Crossroads: The Civil War and its Legacy*, Pennsylvania: Pennsylvania State University Press.

Cohen, Roger (1998), *Sagas of Sarajevo: Hearts Grown Brutal*, New York: Random House.

Colville, Sir John (1981), *The Fringe of Power: Downing Street Diaries*, London: Hodder & Stoughton.

Colville, Sir John (1986a), 'How the West Lost the Peace in 1945: Part 1', *Contemporary Review*, London: January, vol. 248, no. 1440.

Colville, Sir John (1986b), 'How the West Lost the Peace in 1945: Part 2', *Contemporary Review*, London: February, vol. 248, no. 1441.

Connor, Walker (1993), 'Beyond reason: the nature of the ethnonatinal bond', *Ethnic and Racial Studies*, vol. 16, no. 3.

Connor, Walker (1994), *Ethnonationalism: The Quest for Understanding*, Princeton: Princeton University Press.

Constantiniu, Florin (1997), *O Istorie Sincera A Poporului Român*, Bucharest: univers enciclopedic.

Conversi, Daniele (2000), 'Central secession: towards a new analytical concept? The case of former Yugoslavia', *Journal of Ethnic and Migration Studies*, vol. 26, no. 2.

Crampton, R.J. (1994), *Eastern Europe in the Twentieth Century*, London: Routledge.

Crampton, R.J. (1997), *A Concise History of Bulgaria*, Cambridge: Cambridge University Press.

Cretzianu, Alexandre (1957), *The Lost Opportunity*, London: Jonathan Cape.

Crossman, Richard (1976), *The Diaries Of A Cabinet Minister, Volume 2*, London: Hamish Hamilton & Jonathan Cape.

Cummings, Richard (1996), 'Bulgaria: Georgi Markov, Victim of an Unknown Cold War Assassin', *Radio Free Europe/Radio Liberty*.

Davies, Norman (1996), *Europe: A History*, Oxford: Oxford University Press.

Dedijer, Vladimir (1967), *The Road To Sarajevo*, London: MacGibbon and Kee.

Deletant, Dennis (1995), *Ceauşescu and the Securitate: Coercion and Dissent in Romania 1965–1989*, London: Hurst.

Deletant, Dennis (1999), *Communist Terror in Romania: Gheorghiu Dej and the Police State 1948–1965*, London: Hurst.

Denitch, Bogdan (1994), *Ethnic Nationalism: The Tragic Death of Yugoslavia*, Minneapolis and London: University of Minnesota Press.

Deringil, Selim (1989), *Turkish Foreign Policy During the Second World War: An 'Active' Neutrality*, Cambridge: Cambridge University Press.

Detez, Raymond (1998), *Historical Dictionary of Bulgaria*, Lanham, MD, and London: Scarecrow Press.

Dilkes, David (ed.) (1971), *The Diaries of Sir Alexander Cadogan O.M., 1938–1945*, London: Cassell.

Dimitrijević, Vojin (2000), 'The 1974 Constitution as a Factor in the Collapse of Yugoslavia or as a Sign of Decaying Totalitarianism', in Popov, Nebojša (ed.), (2000), *The Road To War in Serbia: Trauma and Catharsis*, Budapest: Central European University Press.

Djilas, Aleksa (1991), *The Contested Country: Yugoslav Unity and Communist Revolution, 1919–53*, Cambridge, MA: Harvard University Press.

Djilas, Aleksa (1995), 'Fear Thy Neighbour: The Break-Up of Yugoslavia', in Kupchan, Charles (ed.), *Nationalism and Nationalities in the New Europe*, Ithaca: Cornell University Press.

Djilas, Milovan (1962), *Conversations With Stalin*, New York: Harcourt Brace & Co.

Djilas, Milovan (1983), *Rise and Fall*, London: Macmillan.

Djuvara, Neagu (1995), *Între Orient și Occident, Târile române la inceputul epocii moderne*, Bucharest: Humanitas.

Doder, Dusko (1979), *The Yugoslavs*, London: Allen & Unwin.

Doder, Dusko and Branson, Louise (1999), *Milošević: Portrait of A Tyrant*, New York: Free Press.

Drezov, Kyril (2000), 'Bulgaria: transition comes full circle, 1989–1997', in Pridham, Geoffrey and Gallagher, Tom (eds), *Experimenting With Democracy: Regime Change in the Balkans*, London: Routledge.

Durandin, Catherine (1995), *Histoire des Roumains*, Paris: Fayarad.

Ekmecić, Milorad (1994), 'Beyond Yugoslavia's Disintegration', *Planet*, Aberystwyth, Wales: February–March.

Emerson, P.J. (2000), *From Belfast to the Balkans: Was Democracy Part of the Problem?*, Belfast: The De Borda Institute.

Fejtö, François (1974), *A History of the Peoples' Democracies*, Harmondsworth: Penguin.

Ferguson, Niall (1999), 'The truce that lied', *Financial Times*, 17–18 July.

Finney, Patrick B. (1995), '"An Evil For All Concerned": Great Britain and Minority Protection After 1919', *Journal of Contemporary History*, vol. 30, no. 4.

Fischer, Bernd J. (1995), 'Albanian Nationalism in the Twentieth Century', in Peter Sugar (ed.), *Eastern European Nationalism in the Twentieth Century*, Washington, DC: The American University Press.

Fischer, Bernd J. (1999), *Albania at War, 1939–1945*, London: Hurst.

Fischer, Ernst (1974), *An Opposing Man*, London: Allen Lane.

Fleming, K.E. (1999), *The Muslim Bonaparte: Diplomacy and Orientalism in Ali Pasha's Greece*, Princeton: Princeton University Press.

Friedman, Francine (1996), *The Bosnian Muslims: Denial of A Nation*, Oxford: Westview Press.

Fromkin, David (1991), *A Peace To End All Peace: Creating The Modern Middle East 1914–1922*, London: Penguin.

Funderburk, David B. (1994), *Un Ambassador American: Între Departmentul de Stat și Dictatura Comunista din România*, Constanta, Romania: Editura Dacon.

Gallagher, Tom (1995), *Romania After Ceaușescu: The Politics of Intolerance*, Edinburgh: Edinburgh University Press.

Gallagher, Tom (1997), 'To Be or Not to Be Balkan?: Romania's Quest For Self-Definition', *Daedalus*, vol. 126, no. 3, summer.

Gallagher, Tom (1998), 'Building Democracy in Romania: International Shortcomings and External Neglect', paper presented at conference on International Security Issues in Eastern Europe, European University Institute, Florence: May.

Gallagher, Tom (1999), 'Folly and Failure in the Balkans', *History Today*, London: vol. 49, no. 9, September.

Gard, Paul (2000), 'Les Balkans vus de France au xx siècle, *Esprit* no. 270, December.

Gati, Charles (ed.) (1976), *The International Politics of Eastern Europe*, New York: Praeger.

Gati, Charles (1990), *The Bloc That Failed: Soviet–East European Relations in Transition*, London: IB Tauris.

Gati, Charles (1992), 'From Sarajevo To Sarajevo', *Foreign Affairs*, vol. 71, no. 3.

Georgescu, Vlad (1992), *Istoria românilor: De la origini pina in zilele noastre*, Bucharest: Humanitas.

Gigova, Irina (1998), *Political Usage of Culture: Cultural Policies of the Bulgarian Communist Party in the Sixties and Seventies*, M.A. dissertation, Central European University, Budapest: History Department.

Goldstein, Erik (1991), *Winning The Peace in British Diplomatic Strategy: Peace Planning and the Paris Peace Conference, 1916–1920*, Oxford: Clarendon Press.

Goldsworthy, Vesna (1998), *Inventing Ruritania: The Imperialism of the Imagination*, New Haven and London: Yale University Press.

Goodwin, Jason (1999), 'The Balkans Could Do Worse Than Re-Visit The Far-Flung Empire', *International Herald Tribune*, Paris: 17 June.

Gordy, Eric D. (1999), *The Culture of Power in Serbia: Nationalism and the Destruction of Alternatives*, Pennsylvania: The Pennsylvania State University Press.

Gow, James (1994), 'Serbian Nationalism and the Hisssing Sssnake in the International Order: Whose Sovereignty? Whose Nation?', *SEER*, 72, 3, July.

Gunther, John (1940), *Inside Europe*, London: Hamish Hamilton.

Hagen, William V. (1999), 'The Balkans' Lethal Nationalism', *Foreign Affairs*, vol. 78, no. 4.

Halliday, Jon (1986), *The Artful Albanian: Memoirs of Enver Hoxha*, London: Chatto & Windus.

Hammond, Thomas T. (ed.) (1982), *Witnesses to the Origins of the Cold War*, Seattle and London: University of Washington Press.

Harriman, Averell and Abel, Elie (1975), *Special Envoy to Churchill and Stalin, 1941–1946*, New York: Random House.

Harrington, Joseph F. and Courtney, Bruce J. (1991), *Tweaking The Nose of the Russians: Fifty Years of American–Romanian Relations, 1940–1990*, Boulder, CO: East European Monographs.

Haslam, Jonathan (1999), *The Vices of Integrity: E.H. Carr, 1892–1982*, London: Verso.

Hessell Tiltman, H. (1936), *Peasant Europe*, London: Jarrolds.

Hibbert, Reginald (1991), *Albania's National Liberation Struggle*, London: Pinter.

Hickman, Kathie (1996), *Daughters of the Empire*, London: Flamingo.

Hitchens, Christopher (1997), *Hostage To History: Cyprus, From the Ottomans to Kissinger*, London: Verso.

Hitchins Keith (1994), *Rumania 1866–1947*, Oxford: Oxford University Press.

Hitchins, Keith (1998), 'Desavarsirea natiunii române', in Mihai Barbulescu *et al.*, *Istoria României*, Bucharest: Editura Enciclopedica.

Hoare, Attila (1999), 'Review of Michael Barratt Brown's "The Yugoslav Tragedy: Lessons For Socialists"', in Hoare, Quintin and Malcolm, Noel (eds), *Books on Bosnia: a critical bibliography of works relating to Bosnia-Herzegovina published since 1990 in west European languages*, London: The Bosnian Institute.

Hodos, George H. (1987), *Show Trials: Stalinist Purges in Eastern Europe, 1948–1954*, New York: Praeger.

Hoesch, Edgar (1972), *The Balkans*, London: Faber.

Hopken, Wolfgang (1994 estimate), 'Political Culture in the Balkan States during the Inter-War Period', in Özdoğan, Gunay Göksu and Saybasili, Kemali (eds), *Balkans: A Mirror of the New International Order*, Istanbul: Eren.

Hosking, Geoffrey (1997), *Russia: People and Empire 1552–1917*, London: Harper Collins, 1997.

Hupchick, Dennis P. (1994), *Culture and History in Eastern Europe*, New York: St Martin's Press.

Hyland, William G. (1999), 'The Solution: A Pan-European Peace Conference for the Balkans', *International Herald Tribune*, Paris: 1 April.

Iatrides, John O. (1980), *Ambassador MacVeagh Reports: Greece 1933–1947*, Princeton: Princeton University Press.

Iatrides, John O. (1981), *Greece in the 1940s: A Nation in Crisis*, Hanover: New England University Press.

Illyes, E. (1982), *National Minorities in Romania: Change in Transylvania*, Boulder, Colorado: East European Monographs.

Jászi, Ozskár (ed.) (1964), *The Dissolution of the Hapsburg Empire*, Chicago: University of Chicago Press.

Jelavich, Barbara (1983a), *History of the Balkans: Eighteenth and Nineteenth Centuries*, Cambridge: Cambridge University Press.

Jelavich, Barbara (1983b), *History of the Balkans: Twentieth Century*, Cambridge: Cambridge University Press.

Jelavich, Charles (1962), 'Serbian Nationalism and the Question of the Union with Croatia in the 19th Century', *Balkan Studies*, vol. 3.

Jelavich, Charles and Jelavich, Barbara (eds) (1963), *The Balkans in Transition*, Berkeley: University of Califiornia Press.

Job, Cvijeto (1993), 'Yugoslavia's Ethnic Furies', *Foreign Policy*, no. 92, fall.

Judah, Tim (1997), *The Serbs: History, Myth and the Destruction of Yugoslavia*, New Haven: Yale University Press.

Judah, Tim (2000), *Kosovo: War and Revenge*, New Haven: Yale University Press.

Kadare, Ismail (1995), *Albanian Spring: the Anatomy of Tyranny*, London: Saqi.

Kaplan, Robert D. (1993), *Balkan Ghosts: A Journey Through History*, New York: St Martin's Press.

Karakasidou, Anastasia (1997), *Fields of Wheat, Hills of Blood: Passages to Nationhood in Greek Macedonia 1870–1990*, Chicago and London: University of Chicago Press.

Kareeva, Elena (1998), *The Image of the Balkan Neighbour As Seen Through Bulgarian Political Caricature (1912–1948)*, M.A. dissertation, Central European University, Budapest: Southeast European Studies Department.

Kellogg, Frederick (1995), *The Road to Romanian Independence*, West Lafayette, Indiana: Purdue University Press.

Kennan, George, (1993), *The Other Balkan Wars, Report of the International Commission to Enquire into the Causes and Conduct of the Balkan Wars*, [first published 1914], Washington: Brookings Institute.

Khan, Mujeeb R. (1995), 'Bosnia-Herzegovina and the Crisis of the Post-Cold War International System', *East European Politics and Societies*, vol. 9, no. 3, 1995.

King, F.P. (1973), *The New Internationalism: Allied Policy and the European Peace 1939–1945*, Newton Abbot, David & Charles.

King, Robert R. (1973), *Minorities Under Communism*, Cambridge, MA: Harvard University Press.

Kirk, Roger and Raceanu, Mircea (1994), *Romania versus The United States: Diplomacy of the Absurd, 1985–89*, New York: St Martin's Press.

Kitromilides, P.M. (1994), *Enlightenment, Nationalism, Orthodoxy: Studies in the culture and political thought of south-eastern Europe*, London: Variorum.

Kitromilides, P.M. (1995), 'Europe and the Dilemmas of Greek Conscience', in Philip Carabott (ed.), *Greece and Europe in the Modern Period: Aspects of a Troubled Relationship*, London: Centre for Hellenic Studies, King's College London.

Korné, Mihai (1999), 'Nato's Contradictions', *Lupta*, no. 302, May.

Kostanick, Huey Louis, 'The Geopolitics of the Balkans', in Jelavich, Charles and Jelavich, Barbara (eds) (1963), *The Balkans in Transition*, Berkeley: University of California Press.

Kovrig, Bennett (1991), *Of Walls and Bridges: The United States and Eastern Europe*, New York: New York University Press.

Krizan, Mojmar (1994), 'New Serbian Nationalism and the Third Balkan War', in *Studies in European Thought*, Dordrecht, The Netherlands: vol. 46, nos 1–2, June 1994.

Kuniholm, Bruce R. (1980), *The Origins of the Cold War in the Near East: Great Power Conflict and Diplomacy in Iran, Turkey, and Greece*, Princeton: Princeton University Press.

Kyle, Keith (1984), *Cyprus*, London: Minority Rights Group.

Lamb, Richard (1997), *Mussolini and the British*, London: John Murray.

Lampe, John (1996), *Yugoslavia as History: Twice There Was a Country*, Cambridge: Cambridge University Press.

Lees, Lorraine (1996), *Keeping Tito Afloat: the United States, Yugoslavia and the Cold War*, Pennsylvania: The Pennsylvania State University Press.

Lendvai, Paul (1969), *Eagles In Cobwebs: Nationalism and Communism in the Balkans*, London: Macdonald.

Levesque, Jacques (1997), *The Enigma of 1989: The USSR and the Liberation of Eastern Europe*, Berkeley and London: University of California Press.

Linscott Ricketts, Mac (1988), *Mircea Eliade, The Romanian Roots, 1907–1945*, Boulder, Colorado: East European Monographs.

Livezeanu Irina (1995), *Cultural Politics in Greater Romania*, Ithaca: Cornell University Press.

Lukacs, John (1953), *The Great Powers and Eastern Europe*, New York: American Book Company.

Lukacs, John (1982), 'In Darkest Transylvania', *New Republic*, 3 February.

McCarthy, Justin (1996), 'Ottoman Bosnia 1800–1878', in Mark Pinson (ed.), *The Muslims of Bosnia-Herzegovina*, Cambridge, MA: Harvard University Press, 1996.

Macartney, C.A. (1965), *Hungary and Her Successors, The Treaty of Trianon and Its Consequences, 1919–1937*, Oxford: Oxford University Press.

Macartney, C.A. and Palmer, R.W. (1962), *Independent Eastern Europe: A History*, London: Macmillan.

McIntyre, Robert J. (1988), *Bulgaria: Politics, Economics and Society*, London: Pinter.

Mack Smith, Denis (1994), *Mazzini*, New Haven: Yale University Press.

Maclean, Fitzroy (1949), *Eastern Approaches*, London: Jonathan Cape.

McLynn, Frank (1994), *Fitzroy Maclean*, London: John Murray.

McNeill, William H. (1978), *The Metamorphosis of Greece Since World War II*, Oxford: Blackwell.

Magaš, Branka (1993), *The Destruction of Yugoslavia: Tracking The Break-Up 1980–92*, London: Verso.

Malcolm, Noel (1994), *Bosnia: A Short History*, London: Macmillan.

Malcolm, Noel (1998), *Kosovo: A Short History*, London: Macmillan.

Markham, Reuben H. (1996), *Romania sub jugul sovietic*, Bucharest: Fundatia Academica Civica.

Marriott, J.A.R. (ed.) (1958), *The Eastern Question: A Study in European Diplomacy*, Oxford: Oxford University Press.

Mayes, Stanley (1981), *Makarios: A Biography*, London: Macmillan.

Mazower, Mark (1998), *Dark Continent: Europe's Twentieth Century*, London: Allen Lane.

Meier, Victor (1999), *Yugoslavia: A History of its Demise*, London: Routledge.

Michener, James (1975), *The Bridge At Andau*, London: Corgi.

Miller, David (1978), *Queen's Rebels: Ulster Unionism in Historical Perspective*, Dublin: Gill & Macmillan.

Milosavljević, Olivera (2000), 'Yugoslavia as a Mistake', in Popov, Nebojša (ed.), *The Road To War in Serbia: Trauma and Catharsis*, Budapest: Central European University Press.

Mitrany, D. (1951), *Marx Against the Peasant: A Study in Social Dogmatism*, Chapel Hill, NC: University of North Carolina Press.

Mount, Ferdinand (1999), 'The public is right, so is the war', *Sunday Times*, London: 30 May.

Mouzelis, Nicos P. (1986), *Politics in the Semi-Periphery: Early Parliamentarism and Late Industrialisation in the Balkans and Latin America*, London: Macmillan.

Moynihan, Daniel Patrick (1993), *Pandaemonium: Ethnicity in International Politics*, Oxford: Oxford University Press.

Murtagh, Peter (1994), *The Rape of Greece: the King, the Colonels and the Resistance*, London: Simon & Schuster.

Nadeau, Remi (1990), *Stalin, Churchill and Roosevelt Divide Europe*, New York: Praeger.

Nagy-Talavera, Nicholas (1999), *N. Iorga – O Biografie*, Iasi: Institutul European.

Nicolson, Harold (1964), *Peacemaking 1919*, London: Methuen.

Nunez, Xosé M. (1994), 'National Minorities in East-Central Europe and the Internalisation of their Rights', in Beramendi, J.G., *et al.*, *Nationalism in Europe Past and Present*, Santiago de Compostela: Universidade de Santiago de Compostela.

O'Malley, Brendan and Craig, Ian (1999), *The Cyprus Conspiracy: America, Espionage and the Turkish Invasion*, London: I.B. Tauris.

Obradović, Marija (2000), 'The Ruling Party', in Popov, Nebojša, (ed.), *The Road To War in Serbia: Trauma and Catharsis*, Budapest: Central European University Press.

Oren, Nissan (1973), *Revolution Administered: Agrarianism and Communism in Bulgaria*, Baltimore and London: Johns Hopkins University Press.

Owen, David (1996), *Balkan Odysssey*, London: Gollancz.

Pacepa, Ion (1999), *Cartea Neagră A Securitătea*, Volume 3, Bucharest: Editura Omega.

Papić, Zarana (2000), 'The Forging of Schizophrenia', *Bosnia Report*, 8 June, http://www.bosnia.org.uk

Pavlowitch, Stevan (1999), *The Balkans 1802–1945*, (London: Longman).

Percival, Mark (1994), 'Britain's "Political Romance" with Romania in the 1970s', *Contemporary European History*, 4:1.

Percival, Mark (1997), *British–Romanian Relations 1944–65*, Ph.D. thesis, University of London: School of Slavonic and East European Studies.

Perry, Duncan M. (1995), *Stefan Stambulov and the Emergence of Modern Bulgaria 1870–1895*, Durham, North Carolina: Duke University Press.

Pešić, Vesna (2000), 'The War For Ethnic States', in Popov, Nebojša (ed.), *The Road To War in Serbia: Trauma and Catharsis*, Budapest: Central European University Press.

Petrescu, Cristina (1998), *Intellectual Dissent in Romania (1977–1989)*, M.A. dissertation, Central European University, Budapest: History Department.

Petrovich, Michael B. (1982), 'The View From Yugoslavia', in Thomas T. Hammond (ed.), *Witnesses to the Origins of the Cold War*, Seattle and London: University of Washington Press.

Pfaff, William (1995), 'Pan-Slavism Isn't Serious If The West Takes Itself Seriously', *International Herald Tribune*, Paris: 24 July.

Pippidi, Andrei (1993), 'Nation, Nationalisme et Démocratie en Roumanie', *L'Autre Europe*, parts 26–27.

Pollis, Adamantia (1992), 'Greek National Identity: Religious Minorities, Rights and European Norms', *Journal of Modern Greek Studies*, vol. 10.

Ponting, Clive (1994), *Churchill*, London: Sinclair–Stevenson.

Popov, Nebojša (2000a), 'The Traumatology of the Party State' in *The Road To War in Serbia: Trauma and Catharsis*, Budapest: Central European University Press.

Popov, Nebojša (ed.) (2000b), *The Road To War in Serbia: Trauma and Catharsis*, Budapest: Central European University Press.

Porter, Ivor (1990), *Operatiunea 'Autonomous'*, Bucharest: Humanitas.

Poulton, Hugh (1995), *Who Are The Macedonians?*, London: Hurst.

Price, David Heilbron (2000), *Schuman and the Yugoslav Crisis*, Bron Communications.

Prpa-Jovanović, Branka (1997), 'The Making of Yugoslavia 1830–1945', in Udovicki, Jasminka and Ridgeway, James (eds), *Burn This House: The Making And Unmaking of Yugoslavia*, Durham and London: Duke University Press.

Pundeff, Marin V. (1971), 'Bulgarian Nationalism', in Sugar, P. and Lederer, Ivo (eds), *Nationalism in Eastern Europe*, Seattle: Seattle University Press.

Ramet, Pedro (1985), 'Factionalism in Church–State Interactions', *Slavic Review*, summer 1985.

Ramet, Sabrina Petra (1996), *Balkan Babel: The Disintegration of Yugoslavia From the Death of Tito to Ethnic War*, Boulder, CO: Westview Press.

Ramet Sabrina P. (1998), *Nihil Obstat: Religion, Politics and Social Change In East-Central Europe and Russia*, Durham and London: Duke University Press.

Ratesh, Nestor (1991), *Romania: The Entangled Revolution*, New York: Praeger.

Ridley, Jasper (1972), *Lord Palmerston*, London: Panther.

Ridley, Jasper (1997), *Mussolini*, London: Constable.

Rinvolvori, Mario (1966), *Anatomy of a Church: Greek Orthodoxy Today*, New York: Fordham University Press.

Ristovic, Milan (1998), 'The Birth of Southeastern Europe and the "Death of the Balkans"', http://www.udi.org.yu/Founders/Ristovic/Birth.htm

Roberts, Frank (1991), *Dealing With Dictators: The Destruction and Revival of Europe 1930–70*, London: Weidenfeld and Nicholson.

Roberts, Henry L. (1951), *Rumania: Political Problems of an Agrarian State*, New Haven: Yale University Press.

Roberts, Henry L. (1963), 'Politics in a Small State: The Balkan Example', in Jelavich, Charles and Jelavich, Barbara (eds), *The Balkans in Transition*, Berkeley: University of California Press.

Rossos, Andrew (2000), 'Great Britain and Macedonian Statehood and Unification 1940–49', *East European Politics and Societies*, vol. 14, no. 1.

Rothschild, Joseph (1958), *The Communist Party of Bulgaria 1883–1936: Origins and Development*, New York: Columbia University Press.

Rothschild, Joseph (1974), *East-Central Europe Between The Two World Wars*, Seattle: University of Washington Press.

Rothschild, Joseph (1989), *Return To Diversity: A Political History of East-Central Europe Since World War II*, Oxford: Oxford University Press.

Rothwell, Victor (1982), *Britain and the Cold War, 1941–1947*, London: Jonathan Cape.

Runciman Steven (1971), *The Orthodox Churches and the Secular State*, Oxford: Oxford University Press.

Rupnik, Jacques (1994), 'Europe's New Frontiers: Remapping Europe', *Daedalus*, vol. 123, no. 3.

Rusinow, Dennison (1995), 'The Yugoslav Peoples' in Sugar, P. (ed.), *Eastern European Nationalism in the Twentieth Century*, Washington, DC: The American University Press.

Saiu, Liliana (1992), *The Great Powers and Rumania, 1944–1946: A Study of the Early Cold War Era*, Boulder, CO: East European Monographs.

Schopflin, George (1974), Rumanian Nationalism', *Survey*, vol. 20, Spring–Summer.

Schuyler, Courtland V.R. (1982), 'The View From Romania', in Hammond, Thomas T., (ed.), *Witnesses to the Origins of the Cold War*, Seattle and London: University of Washington Press.

Scurtu Ioan and Buzatu, Gheorghe (1999), *Istoria Românilor In Secolul XX*, Bucharest: Paideia.

Sells, Michael A. (1996), *The Bridge Betrayed: Religion and Genocide in Bosnia*, Berkeley: University of California Press.

Seton-Watson, Hugh (1945), *Eastern Europe, 1918–41*, Cambridge: Cambridge University Press.

Seton-Watson, Hugh (1960), *Neither War Nor Peace: the Struggle for Power in the Post-War World*, London: Methuen.

Seton-Watson, Hugh *et al.* (eds), (1976), *R.W. Seton-Watson and the Yugoslavs: Correspondence 1906–1941, vol. 1*, London and Zagreb: Graficki Savod Hrvatske.

Seton-Watson, Hugh and Christopher (1981), *The Making of a New Europe*, London: Methuen.

Seton-Watson, R.W. (1934), *A History of the Roumanians, From Roman Times To The Completion of Unity*, Cambridge: Cambridge University Press

Seton-Watson, R.W. (1943), *Transylvania, A Key Problem*, Oxford: The Classic Press.

Shafir, Michael (1985), *Romania: Politics, Economics, Society*, London: Pinter.

Shotwell, James (1949), *A Balkan Mission*, New York: Columbia University Press.

Sikavica, Stipe (1997), 'The Army's Collapse', in Udovicki, Jasminka and Ridgeway, James (eds), *Burn This House: The Making And Unmaking of Yugoslavia*, Durham and London: Duke University Press.

Silber, Laura and Little, Alan (1995), *The Death of Yugoslavia*, London: Penguin.

Souter, David (1984), 'An Island Apart: a review of the Cyprus problem', *Third World Quarterly*, vol. 6, no. 3, July 1984.

Sowell, Thomas (1998), *Conquests and Cultures: A World View*, New York: Basic Books.

Stavrianos, Leften (1958), *The Balkans Since 1453*, New York: Holt, Rinehart & Winston.

Steele, Ronald (1980), *Walter Lippmann and the American Century*, Boston: Little Brown.

Stillmann, Edmund (1966), *The Balkans*, Netherlands: Time-Life.

Stojanović, Dubravka (2000), 'The Traumatic Circle of the Serbian Opposition', in Popov, Nebojša, (ed.), *The Road To War in Serbia: Trauma and Catharsis*, Budapest: Central European University Press.

Stokes, Gale (1994), 'Nationalism, Responsibility, And The People-As-One', in *Studies In European Thought*, vol. 46, Nos. 1–2, June 1994.

Stokes, Gale (1997), *Three Eras of Political Change in Eastern Europe*, New York and Oxford: Oxford University Press.

Sulzberger, C.L. (1969), *A Long Row of Candles: Memoirs and Diaries 1934–1954*, London: Macdonald.

Sulzberger, C.L. (1987), *The World and Richard Nixon*, New York: Prentice Hall Press.

Sweeney, John (1991), *The Life and Evil Times of Nicolae Ceauşescu*, London: Hutchinson.

Tanner, Marcus, (1997), *Croatia: A Nation Forged in War*, New Haven and London: Yale University Press.

Tarau, Virgiliu and Bucur, Ioan Marius (1998), *Strategii şi polítici electorale in alegerile parlamentare din 19 noiembrie 1946*, Cluj: Centrul de Studii Transilvane/Fundatia Culturale Romana.

Teokarević, Jovan (1996), 'Neither War nor Peace: Serbia and Montenegro in the First Half of the 1990s', in Dyker, David and Vejvoda, Ivan (eds), *Yugoslavia and After: A Study in Fragmentation, Despair and Rebirth*, London: Longman.

Tepavać, Mirko (1997), 'Tito: 1945–80', in Udovicki, Jasminka and Ridgeway, James (eds), *Burn This House: The Making And Unmaking of Yugoslavia*, Durham and London: Duke University Press.

Thiesse, Anne Marie, (1999), 'La lente invention des identités nationales', *Le Monde Diplomatique*, Paris: June.

Thomas, Hugh (1986), *Armed Truce: The Beginnings of the Cold War, 1945–1946*, London: Hamish Hamilton.

Thomas, Robert (1999), *Serbia Under Milošević: Politics in the 1990s*, London: Hurst.

Thompson, Mark (1992), *A Paper House: The Ending of Yugoslavia*, London: Hutchinson-Radius.

Tinu, Dumitru (1998), 'August 1968–marea pacaleala', *Adevârul*, Bucharest: 21 August.

Todorava, Maria (1997), *Imagining The Balkans*, Oxford: Oxford University Press.

Todorova, Maria (1994) 'The Ottoman Legacy in the Balkans', in Özdoğan, Gunay Göksu and Saybasili, Kemali (eds), *Balkans: Mirror of the New International Order*, Istanbul: Eren.

Torode, John (1993), 'Ancestor Worship: Greek is the Word', *The Independent*, London: 31 March.

Toynbee, Arnold J. (1923), *The Western Question in Greece and Turkey*, London: Constable.

Trevel, Albert A. (1936), *History of Ancient Civilizations*, New York: Harcourt, Brace & Co.

Trevor-Roper, Hugh (1993), 'Aftermaths of Empire', in Urban, G.R. (ed.), *End of Empire: The Demise of the Soviet Union*, Washington, DC: American University Press.

Udovicki, Jasminka (1997a) 'Introduction' in Udovicki, Jasminka and Ridgeway, James (eds), *Burn This House: The Making And Unmaking of Yugoslavia*, Durham and London: Duke University Press.

Udovicki, Jasminka (1997b), 'The Bonds and the Fault-Lines' in Udovicki, Jasminka and Ridgeway, James (eds), *Burn This House: The Making And Unmaking of Yugoslavia*, Durham and London: Duke University Press.

Udovicki, Jasminka and Torov, Ivan (1997), 'The Interlude: 1980–1990', in Udovicki, Jasminka and Ridgeway, James (eds), *Burn This House: The Making And Unmaking of Yugoslavia*, Durham and London: Duke University Press.

Ulam, Adam (1995), 'Have We Won The Cold War?' in Conquest, Robert and Djordevich, Dusan J., *Political and Ideological Confrontations In Twentieth-*

Century Europe, Essays in Honor of Milorad M. Drachkovitch, New York: St Martin's Press.

Urban, George (1976), 'A Conversation with George F. Kennan', *Encounter*, September 1976.

Urban, George (1979), 'A Conversation with Milovan Djilas', *Encounter*, December 1979.

Urban, George R. (1997), *Radio Free Europe and the Pursuit of Democracy: My War Within The Cold War*, New Haven and London: Yale University Press.

Veljanovski, Rade (2000), 'Turning the Electronic Media Around', in Popov, Nebojša, (ed.), *The Road To War in Serbia: Trauma and Catharsis*, Budapest: Central European University Press.

Vickers Miranda (1995), *The Albanians: A Modern History*, London: I.B. Tauris.

Vickers, Miranda (1998), *Between Serb and Albanian: A History of Kosovo*, London: Hurst.

Volovici, Leon (1991), *Nationalist Ideology and Anti-Semitism: The Case of Romanian Intellectuals in the 1930s*, Oxford: Pergamon Press.

Vukadinović, Radovan (1994), 'Balkan Cooperation: Realities and Prospects' in Larrabee, Stephen (ed.), *The Volatile Powder Keg: Balkan Security After the Cold War*, Washington, DC: The American University Press.

Vulliamy, Ed (1994), *Seasons In Hell: Understanding Bosnia's War*, London: Simon & Schuster.

Wachtel, Andrew Baruch (1998), *Making A Nation, Breaking A Nation: Literature and Cultural Politics in Yugoslavia*, Stanford: Stanford University Press.

Waldeck, R.G. (1998), *Athene Palace*, Portland, Oregon and Iasi, Romania: The Centre for Romanian Studies.

Weber, Eugen (1974), 'Romania', in Rogger, H. and Weber, E. (eds), *The European Right, A Historical Profile*, Berkeley: University of California Press.

Weisman, Steven R. (1999), 'In Kosovo Another Setback For the Multi-Ethnic Ideal', *International Herald Tribune*, Paris: 18 June.

West, Rebecca, (1941), *Black Lamb and Grey Falcon*, London: Macmillan.

Wheeler, Mark (1980), *Britain and the War For Yugoslavia 1940–43*, Boulder, CO: East European Monographs.

Wheeler, Mark (1995) 'Not so black as it's painted: the Balkan political heritage', in Carter, F.W. and Norris, H.T. (eds), *The Changing Shape of the Balkans*, London: University College London Press.

Wilson, Sir Duncan (1970), *The Life and Times of Vuk Stefanović Karadzić 1787–1864*, Oxford: Clarendon Press.

Wilson, Harold (1979), *Final Term*, London: Weidenfeld & Nicholson/Michael Joseph

Wolff, Robert Lee (ed.) (1974), *The Balkans In Our Time*, Cambridge, MA: Harvard University Press.

Woodhouse, C.M. (1969), *The Philhellenes*, London: Hodder & Stoughton.

Woodhouse, C.M. (1982), *Karamanlis: The Restorer of Greek Democracy*, Oxford: Clarendon Press.

Woodhouse, C.M. (ed.) (1998), *Modern Greece: A Short History*, London: Faber.

Woodward, Sir Llewellyn (1970), *British Foreign Policy In The Second World War*, London: HMSO.

Woodward, Susan (1995), *Balkan Tragedy: Chaos and Dissolution After the Cold War*, Washington, DC: Brookings Institute.

Zidaru, Irina (1999), 'Tovarase Ceauşescu, cine stie daca ne vom reveadea', *Monitorul*, Iasi, Romania. http://www.monitorul.ro

Zimmermann, Warren (ed.) (1999), *Origins Of A Catastrophe*, New York: Times Books.

Zulfikarpasić, Adil (1998), *The Bosniak*, London: Hurst.

Index

Abukumov, V. 44
Abdul Hamid II 38, 50, 63
Acheson, D. 178, 212
Agnew, S. 216
Agriculture: Albania 51; Bulgaria 51–2, 66, 95, 207; collectivisation 207; competition for resources 7; land reform 94; Romania 55, 94–5; Serbia 53–4; state neglect of 94–6; tax burden on 94–5
Albania: between the wars, 93, 108; Hoxha rule 189, 204–5, 227; independence 63–5; isolationist policy 108, 204–5; Kosovo neglected 205; mass unrest 1; overtures to Greek Colonels 205; Second World War role 118, 120, 129–30, 139, 140–1; split with Moscow 204; Tito-Stalin split and 180–1, 183, 188–9; *see also* Kosovo
Albanians: ancestors of 19; backward according to King 93; extended family 51; nationalism emerges 49, 63–5; religious pragmatism 27; Serbs and in Ottoman Empire 27, 49, 63–4; service in Ottoman Empire
Alexander Cuza, Prince 42, 53
Alexander I, Tsar 37
Alexander, King of Yugoslavia 92, 96, 100–1, 111
Alexander of Battenberg 61
Alexander The Great 19
Ali Pasha (of Ioannina) 29, 32, 36, 205
Almond, Mark 241–2
Ambitelos, Betty 214
Andrei, Stefan 256

Angell, Sir Norman 103
Anghelescu, C. 88
Anti-Semitism 24, 26, 56, 59, 60, 96, 128
Antonescu, I. 119, 128, 153
Apis, Colonel (Dimitrijević, Dragutin) 69
Arafat, Y. 240
Armenians 50
Arsenije IV, Patriarch of Pecs 28
Ashdown, P. 8, 15, 46
Asquith, H. 75
Atatürk, K. 83–4, 104
Athos, Mount 23, 33, 60
Atkinson, V. 259
Atlantic Charter 130, 136
Attlee, C. 162
Austro-Hungarian Empire: assassination of Franz Ferdinand 69–70; Bosnia-Herzegovina 48, 63, 67–8; challenged in the Balkans 62–3, 65, 67–70; Congress of Berlin 47–8; dominating role in the Balkans 48–9, 61–2; failure of Balkan policy 61–2, 68–71; Hungary's role 54–5; partition of (1919) 77–9; pre-First World War crises and 64–5, 69–71; revolutionary challenge (1848) 42; rivalry with Russia 45–7, 63, 67–8, 71; Serbia and 48–9, 61–2, 68–71; unimaginative policies 67, 69–70

Baker, James 200, 259
Baldwin, S. 83–4
'Balkanization' 2, 10, 16, 279

Tito, J.B. *(continued)*:
222, 229; authoritarianism of
regime 220, 221–2; background
105; Balkan Pact (1954) 192;
Ceauşescu and 238; communist
monarch 22, 223, 230; criticism of
231; debts grow under 235; defies
Stalin 174–5, 179–81, 183, 187,
282; economic policy 193–4, 234–
5; excuse for purges 186; failure of
ambitious plans 194, 220–2, 230–1;
federal system 220–22, 228, 229–
31; hardline communist (1945–8)
162–3; intellectuals and 244–5;
legacy assessed 283; manoeuvres
between East and West 192–5;
plans for Albania 188; promotes
mediocrities 232–3; restored to
Russian favour 191, 192–3, 219;
Serb mood under 229, 244–5;
uninterested in EU 234; USA and
193; wartime controversies
suppressed 221–2; weakness of
regime 194, 219–20, 220–2
Titulescu, N. 112
Todorova, Maria 2
Todorov-Gorunya, I. 209
Tolstoy, Leo 43
Tolstoy, Nikolai 163
Toynbee, Arnold 25, 50, 84
Transylvania 8–9, 54–5, 88–9, 90, 99,
114, 119, 173
Trieste 147, 163
Truman, Harry S. 160–1, 165, 177–8,
185
Trumbić, Ante 91
Tsaldaris, P. 111–2
Tsvetkovich, D. 122
Tucević, D. 66
Tudjman, Franjo: background 11,
265; covets Bosnia 267–8;
imprisoned 232, 265–6; marked by
communist background 267;
nationalism of 232, 266, 267;
similarities with Milošević 267–8;

Ustaša rehabilitated by 266
Turks: Armenian massacre 50; growth
of nationalism 49–50; Young Turk
revolution 63–4
Turkey: Britain and 83–4, 197–8,
218; Cold War and 178–9, 183,
197–8, 211, 217–9; Cyprus
Question and 197–8, 211–2,
217–9; exchange of populations 84,
116; Greece and 84, 195–6, 198,
211; invades Cyprus (1974) 217–9;
modern state emerges 83–4; Second
World War role 138–40; USA and
212, 218; Yugoslavia and 116, 122
Turnovo constitution 57

Ulster: Balkan parallels 38–9, 71, 81,
224, 285
Uniate Church 33, 55
United States: admiration for Russian
sacrifice 141; Allied Control
Commission and 166, 171;
American Civil War 285; American
ignorance of Soviet Russia 131,
135, 136, 137, 157, 158, 181–2;
blocks Soviets in the Balkans
175–8; calibre of State Department
158; clumsiness in Balkans 178–9,
195, 198–201, 213–16, 224; CIA in
S.E. Europe 185–6, 199–200,
214–15, 216–19; Cold War plans
185–6, 199–200; complacency
towards Milošević 200, 240,
259–60, 268–9, 272; Cyprus and
196, 211–3, 224; Deep South and
the Balkans 285; disinterested in
European unity 142, 156; First
World War role 75–6; Greece and
177–9, 183, 213–19, 224;
importance of eastern
Mediterranean recognised 177–8;
interference in Greek politics 39,
178, 212, 213; Kennan's 'Long
Telegram' 176; military opposes
Balkan operation 138; offers Stalin